Economic Analysis of Law in European Legal Scholarship

Volume 9

The purpose of this book series is to publish high quality volumes in the growing field of law and economics research in Europe, from a comprehensive theoretical and practical vantage point. In particular, the series will place great emphasis on foundational and theoretical aspects of economic analysis of law and on interdisciplinary approaches in European Legal Scholarship. Following Nobel laureate Ronald Coase's famous essay "The Problem of Social Cost" (1960) fifty years ago law and economics has become the lingua franca of American jurisprudence. In recent decades, law and economics has also gained widespread popularity in Europe and its influence on Legal Scholarship is growing significantly.

Therefore, the economic analysis of law in European Legal Scholarship academic book series illustrates how law and economics is developing in Europe and what opportunities and problems – both in general and in specific legal fields – are associated with this approach within the legal traditions of European countries. Rather than further exploring economic analysis as such, the main focus of this series lies on the implementation of economic methods in legislation and legal adjudication from a European perspective. It takes into account the particular challenges the European legal systems face. Volumes will address law and economics research in Europe from a critical and comparative viewpoint. The studies in this series are strong and bold narratives of the development of economic analysis of law in European Legal Scholarship. Some are suitable for a very broad readership.

Contributions in this series primarily come from scholars in Europe. The purpose is to provide the next generation of European lawyers with the models and skills needed to understand and improve the economic analysis of law in their own legal field. The series includes monographs focusing on specific topics as well as collections of essays covering specific themes.

More information about this series at http://www.springer.com/series/11927

Klaus Mathis • Avishalom Tor
Editors

Consumer Law and Economics

Springer

Editors
Klaus Mathis
Faculty of Law
University of Lucerne
Lucerne, Switzerland

Avishalom Tor
The School of Law
University of Notre Dame
Notre Dame, IN, USA

Faculty of Law
University of Haifa
Haifa, Israel

Economic Analysis of Law in European Legal Scholarship
ISBN 978-3-030-49027-0　ISBN 978-3-030-49028-7 (eBook)
https://doi.org/10.1007/978-3-030-49028-7

This Springer imprint is published by the registered company Springer Nature Switzerland AG.
The registered company address is: Gewerbestrasse 11, 6330 Cham, Switzerland

Preface

This volume, Consumer Law and Economics, is the result of the 8th Law and Economics Conference held at the University of Lucerne on the 29th and 30th March 2019. The conference was organized in partnership with the Notre Dame Program on Law and Market Behavior (ND LAMB). The main focus of the conference was on European legal questions as presented by European legal scholars. These were complemented by insights from distinguished scholars from the USA, Asia, and New Zealand, to foster the dialogue between the different legal cultures. Thematically this volume spans both theoretical and practical developments in Consumer Law.

We take this opportunity to thank all those who have contributed to the organization of the conference and to the successful completion of this volume. First of all, we would like to thank Moritz Pachmann, MLaw, for his flawless coordination and organization of the conference. Furthermore, we wish to thank Laura Garbani, Blaw, Lynn Gummow, MLaw, and Roger Moser, Blaw for their reviewing and diligent proofreading. A special thanks goes to the Swiss National Science Foundation (SNSF), the Research Commission (FoKo) of the University of Lucerne, and the Institute Lucernaiuris, for supporting the conference. Finally, we are grateful to Kay Stoll and Anja Trautmann at Springer Publishers for overseeing the publishing process.

Lucerne, Switzerland — Klaus Mathis
Notre Dame, IN, USA — Avishalom Tor
Haifa, Israel
March 2020

Introduction

This edited volume "Consumer Law and Economics" is the result of the 8th Law and Economics Conference held in Lucerne on the 29th–30th of March 2019. The volume covers many challenges consumer law faces in both Europe and the United States of America. From fundamental theoretical questions, such as what goals consumer law should pursue, to practical questions raised by disclosure requirements, the GDPR, and technology advancements.

Part I, Behavioural Insights to Consumer Law, begins with Avishalom Tor's discussion of the opportunity costs of successful behavioural change resulting from the implementation of nudges. He shows that these opportunity costs are often neglected in the analysis of behavioural policies. This means the full welfare effects of nudges are not accounted for, so at times they are mistakenly employed when it would have been more efficient to use traditional policy tools instead or avoiding intervening altogether.

The chapter "Complex Mortgage Loans as a Case Study for Consumer Law and Economics" by Mariusz Golecki and Piotr Tereskiewicz analyses the challenges the foreign currency mortgage loans present to courts. These types of mortgage loans were heavily marketed in Central and Eastern Europe, particularly in Poland and Hungary. With interest rates being much lower in Switzerland than in Poland, the Swiss franc became an attractive currency for mortgage loans. By 2010, 64% of mortgage loans were indexed in foreign currency and mostly in Swiss francs. The rise of litigation in this area resulted in CJEU applying the Unfair Contract Terms Directive. The authors use behavioural economic analyses to explain why consumers may have opted for such high-risk mortgage products.

Rainer Baisch, in his chapter "The PRIIPs Regulation in View of Behavioural Research: an Example of Hyperbolized Mandated Disclosure", illuminates the traditional disclosure-paradigm based on the assumption that mandated disclosures will lead to well-founded investment decisions. Using the European PRIIPs regulations, along with other systems aimed at improving investor decisions, the author describes how these attempts to provide smarter information to the investors should improve decision-making and yet may still lead to poor investment choices.

Furthermore, developments in technology such as "robo-advice" are described to highlight the potential pitfalls in decision-making these systems will present.

Part II, Mandated Disclosure begins with the chapter "From Disclosure to Transparency in Consumer Law" by Rolf H. Weber. In his chapter, the author describes the failings of the current regulations requiring mandated disclosures in favour of consumers. However, he argues that the core idea of transparency based on the right holders' approach should not be discounted, simply because of the flaws mandated disclosures present. Using this as a basis, the author argues that consumer law should move away from the detailed rulemaking and the use of mandated disclosure and instead shift the focus to transparency. By transparency, the author does not mean to flood the consumer with all possible information, but to provide tailor-made and appropriate information to allow the consumer to make a reflected decision.

"No Need to Read 'Self-enforcing' Pre-contractual Consumer Information in European and German Law", by Sören Segger-Piening, take a detailed look at the regulations in Germany and the EU regarding pre-contractual consumer information in light of the criticism levelled at mandated disclosures by Ben-Shahar, Schneider, Bar-Gill et al. In particular, he discusses the ex post effect of pre-contractual information. While he agrees that the disclosures therein are often not fully understood or applied prior to signing a contract by the consumer, he argues that they provide the consumer with contractual remedies by informing the consumer of these remedies, as well as providing a tool to apply pressure on traders to offer the actually desired products.

The next chapter by Ann-Sophie Vandenberghe investigates unfair terms in standard contract forms by means of a comparative law and economics approach to understand whether or not the use of them is efficient. In particular, the four legal solutions to the "signing-without-reading" problem are described. Subsequently, the developments in Dutch law regarding unfair terms are discussed to see whether or not these developments are moving towards an efficient solution.

Fernando Gómez and Mireia Artigot describe the wave of litigation in Spanish Courts that resulted due to the ex post unfairness controls of the EU Directive 93/13. Spanish Courts and the Court of Justice of the European Union (CJEU) have held many standard terms regarding the allocation of risk, the division of mandatory taxes, and fees associated with mortgages as unfair and hence, non-binding on consumers. Against this background, the authors illuminate the impacts the court rulings have had on the contract design of Spanish mortgage loans.

The chapter "Correcting Information Asymmetry via Deep Consumer Information; Compelling Companies to Let the Sunshine In" by Danny Friedmann, builds on the challenges described by Ben-Shahar and Schneider regarding the mandated disclosure system and explores the idea of a disclosure system not based on mandates but on companies being compelled to disclose information pertaining to the ethicality of their products based solely on market forces. This system, Deep Consumer Information, attempts to correct the asymmetry between company and consumer, on the one hand, the company and government on the other.

Part III Data Protection Regulation begins with the chapter by Shmuel I. Becher and Uri Benoliel discussing the EU General Data Protection Regulation (GDPR) and its impacts six months after its implementation. The GDPR requirement that privacy terms must be communicated using "clear and plain language". Based on this requirement, the authors conduct an empirical study examining the readability of the privacy policies of 300 popular websites. Their results indicate that most of the privacy policies analysed are largely unreadable and therefore not in compliance with the GDPR's requirement. While the authors agree with the principle of improving readability in order for consumers to be better equipped in their decision-making process regarding privacy, simply having a legal requirement to do so does not necessarily lead to the desired result.

Miriam C. Buiten further illuminates the GDPR's failings by means of the example of Direct-to-Consumer Genetic Testing. In "Your DNA is One Click Away: The GDPR and Direct-to-Consumer Genetic Testing" she delves into the problems presented by the readily sacrificed privacy that consumers are willing to hand-over regarding their own genetic fingerprint. In the last decade, direct-to-consumer genetic testing has become readily available allowing consumers to find out about their ancestry, genetic traits, and propensity to genetic diseases. Testing companies operate a two-sided model by generating revenue through selling genetic data to pharmaceutical and research industries. In her chapter, she describes the market-failings associated with this two-sided market and discusses to what extent the GDPR is able to mitigate these failures. The author concludes that the broad research exemption in the GDPR leaves a regulatory vacuum for DTC genetic testing companies and biobanks alike leaving consumers insufficiently protected.

This volume closes with Part IV, Further Applications. In their chapter "The Poisonous Fruit of Foreign Currency Loans for Consumers in Selected Central European States—the Dilemma for Macroeconomic Policy", Jarosław Bełdowski and Wiktor Wojciechowski describe the impact of the determinants that shape public intervention in three CEE countries (Hungary, Croatia, and Poland) regarding the foreign currency loan market. The public authorities in these countries were faced with the dilemma of whether or not to raise requirements of private contracts regarding foreign currency loans to reduce the consumers' burden or to act in order to stabilise the domestic banking sector. Their chapter illuminates the different types of public interventions implemented and showed that the choice of which type of intervention was guided greatly, whether or not the intervention was targeting the financial sector or the macroeconomic stability of the country. They conclude that there was less need for intervention after the crisis in countries which had focused on macroeconomic stability.

Fabrizio Esposito and Anne-Lise Sibony delve into the EU Consumer Law "Fitness Check" or REFIT to see if explicit goals of EU Consumer Law are defined. They concluded that a stronger conceptualisation of what harms the law seeks to protect consumers against, is required. Against this background, they establish a theory of harm, which is mostly missing within the REFIT documentation. Instead, they found that the REFIT has adopted a rather circular approach by defining consumer harm as instances of under-enforcement of the law. This presupposes that all possible harms are already accounted for in the law and only occur when the law is not properly enforced. What the REFIT does delineate is a normative space in which to develop a theory of harm for the future. It consists of a virtuous triangle of empowerment, trust, and a well-functioning internal market. The REFIT also suggests that an economic-based theory of harm would need to interact with several legal elements. Consumer weakness, empowerment, and legitimate expectations constitute ingredients for an economically grounded, behaviourally sensible, and legally workable theory of harm.

The final chapter by Felix Ekardt and Jutta Wieding turns its attention on whether or not consumer law could be a policy instrument for the pursuit of ecological goals. The discussion on environmental protection through consumer law is part of a broader discussion on whether private law can serve for environmental protection purposes. To discuss the environmental protection potential of consumer law, the type of environmental problems that could be covered need to be defined. For this, the authors propose that immediate health hazards could be more readily accessed by consumer law. To help illustrate this, the authors use two projects conducted by the German Federal Government and a study by the German Federal Parliament on environmental protection through civil law.

Contents

Contributors

Mireia Artigot Faculty of Law, Universitat Pompeu Fabra, Barcelona, Spain

Rainer Baisch University Research Priority Program Financial Market Regulation, University of Zurich, Zurich, Switzerland

Samuel I. Becher School of Accounting and Commercial Law, Victoria University of Wellington, Kelburn, New Zealand

Jarosław Bełdowski Department of International Comparative Studies, Warsaw School of Economics, Warsaw, Poland

Uri Benoliel School of Law, College of Law and Business, Tel Aviv, Israel

Miriam C. Buiten Law School, University of St. Gallen, St. Gallen, Switzerland

Felix Ekardt Research Unit Sustainability and Climate Policy, Leipzig, Germany

Fabrizio Esposito Faculty of Law, University of Louvain, Louvain-La-Neuve, Belgium

Danny Friedmann School of Transnational Law, Peking University Shenzhen, Shenzhen, Hong Kong

Mariusz J. Golecki Department of Legal Theory and Philosophy of Law, Faculty of Law and Administration, University of Łódź, Łódź, Poland

Fernando Gómez Faculty of Law, Universitat Pompeu Fabra, Barcelona, Spain

Kai Purnhagen Faculty of Law, Wageningen University & Research, Wageningen, The Netherlands

Hannah Schebesta Faculty of Law, Wageningen University and Research, Wageningen, The Netherlands

Sören Segger-Piening Faculty of Law University of Würzburg, Würzburg, Germany

Anne-Lise Sibony Faculty of Law, University of Louvain, Louvain-La-Neuve, Belgium

Piotr Tereszkiewicz Faculty of Law and Administration, Jagiellonian University of Cracow, Cracow, Poland

Avishalom Tor The School of Law, University of Notre Dame, Notre Dame, IN, USA
Faculty of Law, University of Haifa, Haifa, Israel

Ann-Sophie Vandenberghe Rotterdam Institute of Law and Economics (RILE), Erasmus School of Law, Rotterdam, The Netherlands

Rolf H. Weber Faculty of Law, University of Zurich, Zurich, Switzerland

Jutta Wieding Research Unit Sustainability and Climate Policy, Leipzig, Germany

Wiktor Wojciechowski Department of International Comparative Studies, Warsaw School of Economics, Warsaw, Poland

Part I
Behavioural Insights to Consumer Law

The Target Opportunity Costs of Successful Nudges

Avishalom Tor

Abstract Nudges are increasingly popular, in large part due to the typically low costs required to implement them. Yet most often the main cost of nudging is due not to their implementation, but rather to the opportunity costs of its successful change of the behavior of its targets. Accounting for these target opportunity costs is essential for the appropriate assessment of the welfare effects of nudges. Nonetheless, the extant literature on behavioral policies largely ignores these costs or underestimates their magnitude and, consequently, overestimates the net benefits of nudges. At times, nudges remain the most attractive policy alternative even after their opportunity costs are accounted for. On other occasions, however, traditional instruments or a no-intervention approach turn out to make more efficient policy alternatives.

1 Introduction

Nudging—shorthand for behavioral policy making—is increasingly popular around the globe.[1] Recently, for instance, the U.K.-based Behavioral Insights Team (BIT) reported having run more than 780 projects in dozens of countries since 2010.[2] Behavioral policy making focuses on the novel policy prescriptions suggested by evidence regarding the behavioral patterns exhibited by real, boundedly rational individuals.[3]

---

[1]European Commission (2016) and OECD (2017).

[2]BIT (2018).

[3]Sibony and Alemanno (2016), Thaler and Sunstein (2008) and Tor (2019).

A. Tor (✉)
The School of Law, University of Notre Dame, Notre Dame, IN, USA

Faculty of Law, University of Haifa, Haifa, Israel
e-mail: Avishalom.Tor.3@nd.edu

K. Mathis, A. Tor (eds.), *Consumer Law and Economics*, Economic Analysis of Law in European Legal Scholarship 9, https://doi.org/10.1007/978-3-030-49028-7_1

Nudges employ various formats of information presentation, frame alternatives, select desirable default options, shape or convey social norms, and more.[4] Unlike many traditional instruments, these non-coercive policies only encourage people to engage in desired behaviors, while leaving them free to go their own contrary way. For this reason, nudges usually require no costly investment in enforcement on the part of the government. By preserving freedom of choice, moreover, nudges also appear less costly for the people they target than hard policies that require their compliance regardless of personal costs. Some scholars even argue that individuals who submit to non-coercive interventions reveal through their conduct that they benefit from these policies, even while their nudge-resisting peers remain unharmed thanks to their freedom to pursue the alternative choices they find more personally beneficial.[5]

The perception that nudges are low-cost policies, both for the government and for the individuals they target, is a major source of their appeal as regulatory instruments.[6] This becomes apparent once we consider nudges through the lens of cost-benefit analysis (CBA)—the dominant framework for evaluating U.S. regulation[7] and an increasingly important factor in policy assessment in Europe.[8] CBA supports the adoption of interventions that generate "net benefits" and calls for selecting from the available options the most efficient policy, which is the one that offers the greatest net benefits.[9] Hence, an intervention that promises modest benefits but entails low costs may offer greater net benefits than—and is consequently preferable to—a competing policy whose high benefits are accompanied by high costs.

Although the low implementation costs of nudges make them appealing under CBA, a closer look reveals that they entail pervasive, often substantial, target opportunity costs (OCs), because of the forgone benefits that the successfully nudged previously enjoyed from their former course of action. Nudges entail opportunity costs even when they improve the welfare of the individuals whose behavior they modify, but they can generate even greater, enhanced opportunity costs when they diminish their targets' welfare by encouraging them to change their conduct to their personal detriment.

Contrary to the view of many behavioral policy making scholars, moreover, non-coercive policies are capable of generating enhanced OCs.[10] This is a typical result, for instance, of nudges that shape behavior by using social norms, which can impose psychological, social, and even economic costs on their targets if they are seen to violate these norms.[11] On other occasions, behavioral policies that distort

[4]Sunstein (2016).

[5]Sunstein (2018a).

[6]European Commission (2016).

[7]Sunstein (2018b).

[8]European Commission (2017).

[9]Boardman et al. (2018).

[10]Tor (2019).

[11]cf. Aviram and Tor (2004).

their targets' beliefs may lead people to make costly changes in their behavior that make them worse off.

Through these and similar processes, nudges can generate enhanced opportunity costs that further diminish their net benefits. Such policies may still be efficient and superior to alternative interventions, but when a nudge leads a significant portion of its targets to make personally costly changes in their behavior, the outcome may be inefficient as compared to alternatives.

In general, opportunity costs tend to diminish the net benefits of most nudges compared to the conclusions of analyses that ignore or underestimate these costs. Accounting for OCs might reveal certain nudges to be less attractive than traditional instruments, while on other occasions it could show that both nudges and traditional policies generate net costs that render them inferior to a no-intervention approach.

2 The Seemingly Low Costs of Nudges

Cost-benefit analysis is the dominant approach to policy assessment in most regulatory areas. Its use is mandated for U.S. federal regulation and is increasingly considered in legislative reforms and regulation at the state level.[12] CBA also plays an important role in the regulatory impact assessment process in numerous jurisdictions globally, including the European Union[13] and many OECD member countries.[14]

As its name indicates, cost-benefit analysis is a method for quantifying in monetary terms the social consequences of any given intervention. The conceptual framework is straightforward: From the perspective of efficiency, the value of a policy to society is measured by its net benefits—that is, its aggregate social benefits minus its aggregate social costs.[15]

The assessment of policies based on their net benefits has clear implications. Most obviously, a policy that fails to offer any net benefits vis-à-vis status quo is clearly inefficient and thus undesirable. When comparing alternative interventions, moreover, CBA directs policy makers to select the option that offers the highest net benefits. Consequently, this approach can mandate the selection of a nudge that offers lower absolute benefits than its alternative, if these lower benefits are accompanied by even lower costs that render the former the higher net-benefit option of the two. The net-benefits metric therefore directs attention to the costs of policies,[16]

---

[12]Sunstein (2018b).

[13]European Commission (2017).

[14]OECD (2014).

[15]Boardman et al. (2018).

[16]Sunstein (2018b).

rendering low-cost interventions particularly attractive candidates for policy selection.[17]

Nudge proponents thus point to the typically low costs required for their implementation by the government as an important advantage they possess over most interventions that aim to change people's behavior through traditional tools, such as mandates or bans with their associated sanctions, taxes, subsidies, or other economic incentives.[18]

Mandates and bans entail substantial government implementation costs because they seek compliance by all of their targets. Some of these costs—particularly those pertaining to legal enforcement—are avoided when policy makers instead encourage their targets to modify their behavior through non-coercive means. However, the implementation of traditional taxes or subsidies can also be quite costly for the government despite being non-coercive (with respect to the targeted behavior), because the financial incentives they employ can carry a significant budgetary price tag.

In contrast, a government that nudges its targets successfully bears dramatically lower implementation costs, as demonstrated by recent research that compared the costs of behavioral policies to those of traditional, mostly financial, interventions.[19] These authors reviewed empirical studies in major areas of behavioral policy making, such as retirement savings and energy consumption. In each area, Benartzi and his colleagues assessed the effectiveness and cost of different interventions (by dividing a measure of policy effectiveness by implementation cost), to determine the relative efficacy of behavioral vs. traditional interventions.

Most importantly for present purposes, Benartzi et al.'s comparisons showed the most effective of the nudges they examined in each policy area held a substantial advantage over the most effective of the interventions that used traditional tools to advance the same goal.[20] A closer look reveals, moreover, that nudges outperformed traditional financial incentive policies due to their dramatically lower implementation costs rather than because they were more effective.

This research demonstrates how the low implementation costs of nudging render it attractive to policy makers. Yet this seeming comparative advantage of nudges over traditional policy instruments could be illusory if the assessment of competing policies ignores or understates important cost categories. If this were the case, accounting more fully for these additional costs might change policy makers' view of the relative attractiveness of nudges as policy tools.

---

[17]Of course, policy makers who face budgetary constraints are likely to be concerned with their government implementation costs irrespective of the policy assessment method they employ (cf. Levin and Belfield 2015).

[18]Sibony and Alemanno (2016).

[19]Benartzi et al. (2017).

[20]Benartzi et al. (2017).

3 Target Opportunity Costs

The literature on nudging emphasizes the low implementation costs directly borne by the government implementing such policies. A fuller assessment, however, cannot ignore another, particularly significant cost category—namely, the opportunity costs that all successful policies entail for the individuals they target.

Policies that change the behavior of individuals necessarily entail opportunity costs for them. This is obviously the case for coercive policies. People who modify their conduct to comply with a mandate or a ban forgo the benefits they previously obtained from their pre-mandate course of action. Yet non-coercive traditional instruments, such as subsidies or taxes, also entail OCs. In the case of either approach, these costs are borne only by those who change their behavior due to the policy, but not by their counterparts who would have acted as envisioned by the intervention even in its absence or who do not follow the policy.

Hence, the forgone benefits of past behaviors that were changed by an intervention are an unavoidable, pervasive source of opportunity costs. All successful policies, even those that impose no other costs on their targets, entail them. Moreover, OCs are usually of a substantial magnitude compared to policy benefits. Consider, for instance, a program that offers low- to middle-income individuals full matching of all annual retirement savings increases up to $1000.[21] Assume that the program successfully increases its targets' savings by $500 annually, which amounts to a 20% increase from their pre-intervention baseline contribution rate. This savings increase may be impressive, but it is inevitably associated with substantial opportunity costs—namely, the benefits of consuming an additional $250 of income that the policy's targets now divert annually to their retirement savings. The socio-economic status of the targeted individuals also suggests that they sacrifice substantial consumer surplus at present as they increase their retirement savings. Hence, while the program is efficient if it offers net benefits, it likely involves substantial opportunity costs.

Moreover, successful policies can generate even greater ("enhanced") opportunity costs for some, occasionally all, of their targets, thus decreasing their individual welfare instead of increasing it. Some policies intentionally impose enhanced OCs on individuals when they cause them to abandon behaviors that are personally more beneficial in favor of conduct that is less beneficial to them. This is frequently the case with interventions whose primary goal is to advance social goals—such as internalizing negative externalities—that intentionally impose costs on some individuals to generate net social benefits.

Importantly, however, even paternalistic policies that seek to advance the welfare of the individuals they target—rather than only that of society as a whole—can entail enhanced opportunity costs for at least three familiar reasons: Honest error, intentional manipulation, and target heterogeneity.

---

[21] cf. Duflo et al. (2006).

The problem of honest error by government decision makers who do not possess all relevant information about complex economic processes—also known as the "knowledge problem"[22]—is of particular concern for interventions that aim to improve individual welfare. To name just some of the information policy makers require to make their targets better off, they must identify when, how, and to what extent individual judgments and decisions fall short; determine how different deviations from rationality interact both within individuals and in their interpersonal behaviors; and find the most effective means to address these failings.[23] Hence, the complex nature and scope of the necessary information increases the likelihood of error in the choice and implementation of nudges that aim to advance the individual welfare of their targets.

In addition, the limits of human rationality revealed by behavioral research apply to policy makers as well and exacerbate the knowledge problem.[24] Some scholars even argue that such factors militate for opposing all policy making that aims to advance individuals' welfare.[25] At the same time, however, despite their undeniable limitations, policy makers who are removed from the choices they seek to impact and enjoy the benefits of expert advice and deliberation also possess certain advantages over the individuals whose behavior they target.[26]

Intentional manipulations of target behaviors to benefit policy makers or powerful interests they support offers another possible reason for which some interventions may diminish their targets' welfare contrary to their stated purpose.[27] In particular, policy makers could be "captured" by interest groups, such as regulated firms, who have the incentives and the means to invest in promoting regulatory actions that favor them at the expense of the diffuse public.[28] Unlike in the case of the direct industry regulation that public choice scholars usually study, however, those who stand to benefit from paternalistic interventions are often only indirect beneficiaries of the behavioral changes the policies bring about and therefore face somewhat more limited opportunities to benefit from regulatory capture.

Finally, paternalistic policies face a challenge of heterogeneity, because most regulatory tools apply to all of the individuals targeted by them despite their significant differences in circumstances, beliefs, preferences, and more. Yet, due to these differences, the same change in behavior brought about by an successful intervention will make some targets worse off—generating enhanced opportunity costs for them—even while benefiting others.

To illustrate, policy makers may seek to increase the rate at which employees save for retirement because they find that current average savings are too low for

---

[22]Coase (1960) and Hayek (1945).

[23]cf. Rizzo and Whitman (2009).

[24]Glaeser (2006).

[25]Mannix and Dudley (2015a, b).

[26]Jolls et al. (1998) and Tor (2008).

[27]Mueller (2003).

[28]Peltzman (1976) and Stigler (1971).

projected retirement needs. Because employees are heterogeneous, their optimal contribution level will vary, but if regulators mandate a minimum contribution rate of 6% of salary, all employees will have to make at least that minimum contribution. Those who previously contributed at lower rates will now contribute at least 6% of their salary, which will make many of them of better off on balance despite the opportunity costs they bear. Nonetheless, the same increase will make those employees who would have been better off with a lower contribution (e.g. 4%), such as those who have more pressing and valuable uses for the same income at present, worse off on balance. The latter, in other words, will bear enhanced OCs because the policy mandates a change in behavior to their personal detriment.

All in all, due to these three causes of welfare-diminishing interventions—namely, error, manipulation, and heterogeneity—even paternalistic policies may impose substantial enhanced opportunity costs on some or all of the targets they seek to make better off. Nevertheless, a common view in the literature is that policy makers can avoid such undesirable outcomes by employing nudges instead of traditional policy instruments.

4 The Opportunity Costs of Nudges

Like traditional interventions, successful nudges routinely entail substantial opportunity costs even when they increase the well-being of the individuals whose behavior they modify. But scholars who recognize that opportunity costs inevitably accompany successful interventions still tend to assume that the non-coercive nature of nudges guarantees that these policies will not lead their targets to change their behavior to their personal detriment.[29] This assumption is critical for the assessment of nudges as policy tools, since policies that entail very low implementation costs, never impose enhanced OCs, and produce some benefits are likely to make net-benefit interventions on balance.

The argument that nudges cannot make their targets worse off when changing their behavior seems straightforward: The heavy-handed approach of most traditional regulation can lead its targets to engage in conduct that is personally harmful. In contrast, those who change their behavior in response to a nudge that they were free to ignore reveal by their choice that they have not been harmed.[30]

While intuitively appealing, however, further scrutiny shows this argument is mistaken, since nudges can lead their targets to change their behavior in personally costly ways. Most obviously, social welfare policies successfully employ nudges to change behavior, at the expense of their targets. For example, policy makers seeking to reduce environmental externalities may nudge residential consumers to conserve electricity by sending them reports that compare their consumption to that of their

[29] Thaler and Sunstein (2008).

[30] Sunstein (2014, 2018a).

neighbors and imply the presence of a social norm favoring energy conservation.[31] Naturally, households that are successfully nudged by this intervention bear the opportunity costs of the forgone benefits of their previous, higher electricity usage. Moreover, at least some of these consumers, such as those who reduce their usage only because they wish to avoid violating what they were led to believe is the prevailing social norm, likely bear enhanced OCs that exceed their personal benefits from lower energy consumption.

These and similar findings on the effects of social welfare nudges (e.g., the use of default contribution levels to increase charitable donations)[32] make clear that non-coercive nudges are capable of encouraging behavior changes that make individuals worse off and already have been employed to that end. But perhaps the same nudges cannot exert the same harmful effect when employed paternalistically?

Alas, a closer look at both the circumstances that provide regulators with the opportunity for beneficial paternalistic interventions in the first place and the policy tools commonly used for nudging reveals that paternalistic nudges are capable of leading individuals to change their behavior to their own detriment.

Policies meant to promote individual welfare are needed only when people act in ways that fail to advance their well-being.[33] A paternalistic nudge may modify such conduct, bringing it closer to what policy makers judge is best for their targets. Yet the same failure of individuals' behavior to increase their well-being that motivated the intervention in the first place also means that whether a nudge has in fact increased individual welfare is a question that regulators must answer based on something beyond their mere success in changing behavior.[34]

The situation might be different if nudges were limited to interventions that help their targets correct their deviations from rationality so that individual choices would better align with what people (rationally) judge to be in their own best interests. But most nudges do not even attempt to promote rationality, only to shape behavior through "choice architecture,"[35] designing the environment in which people make their decisions, as well as various features of the choices they face, to activate a variety of psychological processes.[36] These processes, in turn, increase individuals' propensity to act in ways that policy makers consider desirable.[37] The outcome-oriented nature of most nudges thus prevents us from relying on a successful change of behavior as stand-alone proof that their targets are better off following the intervention.

Paternalistic policies that employ nudges are therefore capable of imposing enhanced opportunity costs on their targets. In fact, common choice architecture

[31] cf. Allcott (2011).

[32] Altman et al. (2018).

[33] Thaler and Sunstein (2008) and Tor (2016).

[34] Tor (2019).

[35] Thaler and Sunstein (2008).

[36] Thaler et al. (2013).

[37] Loewenstein et al. (2013) and Munscher et al. (2016).

tools raise the specter of troubling variants of the three familiar challenges of error, manipulation, and heterogeneity that further increase the risk that paternalistic interventions will turn out to diminish individual well-being.

For one, the problem of honest error is amplified when policy makers employ nudges because these behavioral tools are particularly difficult to calibrate. Nudges that seek to change behavior may exert too weak or, which is of greater concern here, too strong an effect on their targets. Consequently, they may lead people to excessively engage in the behavior policy makers try to encourage, to their personal detriment (e.g., increase their retirement savings at the expense of more valuable present consumption).

The challenge of properly calibrating nudges is further reinforced by the propensity of some of the tools of nudging to distort the judgement and decision processes of the individuals they target. For example, nudges may also distort the beliefs of their targets when they trigger their emotions. Behavioral research shows that people often make heuristic judgments based on affective "tags" they associate with the subject of their judgment.[38] In such cases, emotional reactions—rather than cognitive assessments—may drive behavior.[39] Consider the possibility of exposing new employees to vivid images of retirees living in penury because of inadequate savings, to encourage them to choose a higher rate of savings for retirement. Such an intervention could succeed in leading its targets to increase their savings rate, but its success would not be guarantee that the employees' welfare has improved so long as they changed their conduct primarily due to an emotional response to the nudge rather than, say, a more careful and attentive consideration of their retirement needs.

The problem of distortion also applies to nudges that aim to shape their targets' ultimate behavior, but nevertheless impact their judgments incidentally. For instance, researchers have identified a number of distinct psychological processes that underlie the efficacy of setting default arrangements, one of the most common and effective tools of nudging.[40] One of these processes concerns the implicit recommendation embedded in some policy defaults.[41] Some who follow the default may do so to their own detriment because they erroneously view it as a recommendation that applies to their situation (rather than a suggested minimal choice or the optimal behavior for the average person rather than for them individually).

The specific challenges of calibration and distortion that exacerbate policy makers' knowledge problem also create unique opportunities for inconspicuous manipulation through nudging. For instance, the difficulty of properly calibrating behavioral interventions could permit policy makers intentionally to nudge their targets more strongly than a truly paternalistic approach calls for, in a direction they or powerful interests desire (e.g., excessive retirement savings), without appearing to engage in heavy-handed interventions. When nudges distort judgments or decisions,

[38]Slovic et al. (2006).

[39]Loewenstein et al. (2001).

[40]Dinner et al. (2011).

[41]Jachimowicz et al. (2018) and McKenzie et al. (2006).

moreover, they also diminish individuals' ability to determine whether the behaviors they encourage are likely in fact to increase their personal well-being.

Finally, paternalistic nudges can generate enhanced opportunity costs because of individuals' heterogeneity in rationality.[42] Different people exhibit different levels of susceptibility to different nudges. Some are more likely than others to follow default arrangements, for example, while other individuals respond more strongly to interventions that elicit emotions. As a result, some of those who are more strongly affect by a particular nudge may change their behavior to their own detriment and bear enhanced OCs. In fact, certain nudges may be most efficacious in changing the behavior of those whose welfare is more likely to be diminished by a successful nudge (e.g., encouraging those who already save enough to save even more at the expense of present consumption).[43]

5 Nudges' Opportunity Costs Largely Ignored

All successful nudges entail opportunity costs and many nudges are capable of generating further, enhanced opportunity costs, but that is not the impression given by the behavioral policy making literature. Until the last few years, the literature in the field was almost exclusively concerned with the potential benefits and efficacy of behavioral policies rather than with their target costs. More recent scholarship occasionally takes the opportunity costs of nudging into account, but these exceptions both prove that the rule is OC neglect and still tend to underestimate the scope of target opportunity costs.

One recent review of 72 empirical studies of nudging towards pro-environmental behavior notes, for instance, that only a few of the reviewed studies even addressed the costs of the tested interventions.[44] A similar pattern emerges in another review that limited itself to 44 high-quality papers on energy conservation nudges, which finds that only a handful sought to assess any of the costs of their policies.[45]

Moreover, on the occasions that the literature considers some of the costs of nudging, it usually reflects the notion that nudges are low-cost policies, which is cited as one of their key virtues. As Thaler and Sunstein stated: "we believe that .... many of those [behavioral] policies cost little or nothing; they impose no burden on taxpayers at all."[46] This early assertion, much like the large body of scholarship and commentary that followed it, emphasizes the low implementation costs of nudges for the government that render them attractive to policy makers.[47]

---

[42] Tor (2014, 2016).

[43] Thunstrom et al. (2018).

[44] Byerly et al. (2018).

[45] Andor and Fels (2018).

[46] Thaler and Sunstein (2008), p. 13.

[47] European Commission (2017) and Sibony and Alemanno (2016).

The scholarly emphasis on behavioral policies' implementation cost advantage is vividly demonstrated by Benartzi et al. recent publication calling on governments to invest more in nudging.[48] As already noted, these researchers argue that nudges are more cost-effective than traditional interventions (primarily those based on financial incentives). Yet all of the comparisons Benartzi et al. make among the respective costs of traditional and behavioral policies are based exclusively on government implementation costs, thus ignoring the opportunity costs of these interventions.[49]

Furthermore, the prominence of the Benartzi et al. study has already led more recent scholarship to embrace their conclusions without scrutiny. Consequently, the claim that nudges are more cost-effective than traditional policy instruments is now routinely repeated.[50] On occasion, moreover, commentators even make the further erroneous assertion that Benartzi et al. show nudges are sometimes more efficient than traditional policies,[51] despite the fact that the former scholars explicitly acknowledge that their analyses do not address questions of efficiency (which require a cost-benefit analysis).

Only limited scholarly attention has been given, on the other hand, to the target costs of nudges, and the few scholars who explicitly address these costs largely ignore opportunity costs. For instance, Camerer et al., who were among the early advocates of behaviorally-informed policy making, favored policies of "asymmetric paternalism" that substantially benefit the boundedly rational whose behavior they successfully modify while imposing much smaller costs on those who neither require these policies nor are influenced by them.[52] Notably, however, though they explicitly account for some target costs, Camerer et al. did not consider opportunity costs (implicitly assuming the policies they advocate, on balance, must benefit the boundedly rational whose behavior they successfully modify).

Similarly, while Thaler and Sunstein noted in passing that behavioral policies entail some target costs, they identified only two such costs—namely, taxpayers' fractional burden of funding the government's policies and the direct costs borne by those who wish to resist the nudge.[53] However, neither of these costs, which Thaler and Sunstein correctly characterize as "minimal,"[54] concern the opportunity costs borne only by individuals that policy makers successfully nudge.

There are a few exceptions to the common pattern of opportunity cost neglect, instances in which scholars who consider certain target costs of behavioral

[48]Benartzi et al. (2017).

[49]Benartzi et al. (2017).

[50]Brandon et al. (2019) and Tannenbaum et al. (2017).

[51]De Jong et al. (2018).

[52]Camerer et al. (2003).

[53]Thaler and Sunstein (2008).

[54]Thaler and Sunstein (2008), p. 242.

interventions do not completely neglect OCs. *The Cost-Benefit Revolution*,[55] a recent book by Sunstein, who is not only a leading advocate of nudging but also a long-standing champion of cost-benefit analysis, provides such an example. In this book, Sunstein illustrates some challenges facing CBA in the context of mandatory labeling laws, including in assessments of these policies' costs. During his discussion of various target costs, Sunstein notes how mandatory labeling that successfully changes behavior leads its targets to forego some consumer surplus—that is, to bear opportunity costs.[56]

Yet this uncommon acknowledgement of the potential significance of OCs for policy analysis is not only an exception that proves the rule, but also concerns policies that primarily function as traditional, disclosure-based interventions rather than nudges. Sunstein also repeatedly asserts that mandatory labeling probably makes those targets whose behavior it changes better off on balance, though our earlier analysis revealed that the case is far less clear cut.[57] At any rate, the pertinent point is that even scholarship that highlights the role of OCs in the cost-benefit analysis of a (somewhat) behavioral policy understates the likely presence and potential significance of enhanced opportunity costs.

Finally, Allcott evaluates a series of programs run by a company that employs social-information nudges to promote energy conservation on the part of consumers.[58] These popular programs send consumers reports that encourage them to reduce energy usage by providing social comparison information regarding households' energy usage, social norm information that categorizes the households' usage verbally and pictorially vis-à-vis "efficiency standards," as well as various energy conservation tips.

One of the ways in which Allcott assesses the programs is by their cost-effectiveness, with the calculated costs being limited solely to their implementation costs—that is, to the costs of producing and delivering the programs' reports to consumers.[59] However, Allcott notes that while this common measure of costs, which focuses on the costs that are most readily measured and matter most to program administrators, is useful for comparison with existing work, it provides "a highly incomplete account of welfare effects."[60] He then identifies private costs to energy consumers as one important source of welfare effects that are difficult to quantify. In other words, Allcott recognizes that consumers who reduce their energy consumption necessarily lose the benefits they previously obtained from using the forgone energy—namely, that they bear standard opportunity costs.[61]

[55]Sunstein (2018b).

[56]Sunstein (2018b).

[57]Sunstein (2018b).

[58]Allcott (2011).

[59]Allcott (2011).

[60]Allcott (2011), p. 1089.

[61]Allcott (2011).

Allcott further observes that the welfare outcomes of the programs for consumers depend on the specific mechanisms through which they exert their effects.[62] But even this careful analysis understates the prevalence of enhanced OCs, which can accompany the provision of social (and other) information. Some consumers, for instance, may pay too much attention to certain aspects of the information or weigh it too heavily, make biased judgments or decisions due to their emotional reactions to the information, and so on. More generally, the behavioral effects of information provision go well beyond transmitting its content and vary from one person to the next. The information provided by this policy may thus benefit some of those successfully nudged consumers but harm others.

6 Conclusion

The immediate and obvious implication of accounting for opportunity costs is to diminish the net benefits of nudges—and therefore their attractiveness compared to other policy alternatives—under cost-benefit analysis. After all, according to CBA, alternative policies can be ranked in order of their efficiency, such that interventions that are expected to generate higher net benefits are superior to those that generate lower net benefits.[63]

The effects of a full accounting for the opportunity costs of nudges can be significant even when only standard OCs are involved. Thus, a nudge that appears attractive when opportunity costs are neglected will usually turn out to be less appealing when they are considered, and could even prove altogether unattractive if OCs amount to a sufficiently large fraction of its benefits. Of course, further accounting for the full opportunity costs of nudges, including their enhanced OCs, will sometimes have an even more dramatic effect on their attractiveness.

Hence, the analysis in this chapter calls for a more thorough assessment of nudges. Such further scrutiny could still show many nudges to be attractive policy instruments that offer higher net benefits than those generated by traditional policy instruments. On other occasions, however, traditional policies—either coercive or non-coercive—may prove more efficient. And finally, there will be circumstances in which neither nudges nor traditional policies would offer net benefits, once their opportunity costs are fully considered. In the latter cases, even policy makers pursuing desirable goals should avoid intervention altogether.

[62] Allcott (2011).

[63] Boardman et al. (2018).

References

Allcott H (2011) Social norms and energy conservation. J Public Econ 95:1082–1095

Altman S, Falk A, Heidhues P, Jayaraman R, Teirlinck M (2018) Defaults and donations: evidence from a field experiment. Rev Econ Stat

Andor MA, Fels KM (2018) Behavioral economics and energy conservation—a systematic review of non-price interventions and their causal effects. Ecol Econ 148:178–210

Aviram A, Tor A (2004) Information sharing in critical infrastructure industries: understanding the behavioral and economic impediments. Alabama Law Rev 55(2):231–279

Behavioral Insights Team (2018) Annual Report 2017–2018

Benartzi S, Beshears J, Milkman KL, Sunstein CR, Thaler RH, Shankar M, Tucker-Ray W, Congdon WJ, Galing S (2017) Should governments invest more in nudging? Psychol Sci 28 (8):1041–1055

Boardman AE, Greenberg DH, Vining AR, Weimer DL (2018) Cost-benefit analysis: concepts and practice, 5th edn. Cambridge University Press, Cambridge

Brandon A, List JA, Metcalfe RD, Price MK, Rundhammer F (2019) Testing for crowd out in social nudges: evidence from a natural field experiment in the market for electricity. PNAS 116 (12):5293–5298

Byerly H, Balmford A, Ferraro PJ, Wagner CH, Palchak E, Polasky S, Ricketts TH, Schwartz AJ, Fisher B (2018) Nudging pro- environmental behavior: evidence and opportunities. Front Ecol Environ 16(3):159–168

Camerer C, Issacharoff S, Loewenstein G, O'donoghue T, Rabin M (2003) Regulation for conservatives: Behavioral economics and the case for "asymmetric paternalism". Univ Pa Law Rev 151(3):1211–1254

Coase RH (1960) The problem of social cost. J Law Econ 3:1–44

De Jong P, Zeelenberg M, Verlegh PWJ (2018) Putting the public Back in behavioural public policy. Behav Public Policy 2(2):218–226

Dinner I, Johnson EJ, Goldstein DG, Lui K (2011) Partitioning default effects: why people choose not to. J Exp Psychol Appl 17(4):332–341

Duflo E, Gale W, Liebman J, Orszag P, Saez E (2006) Savings incentives for low- and middle-class families: evidence from a field experiment with H&R Block. Q J Econ 121:1311–1346

European Commission (2016) Behavioral Insights Applied to Policy. European Report 2016. Available on https://ec.europa.eu/jrc/en/publication/eur-scientific-and-technical-research-reports/behavioural-insights-applied-policy-european-report-2016

European Commission (2017) Better Regulation Guidelines. Available on https://ec.europa.eu/info/sites/info/files/better-regulation-guidelines.pdf

Glaeser E (2006) Paternalism and psychology. Univ Chicago Law Rev 73(1):133–156

Hayek FA (1945) The use of knowledge in society. Am Econ Rev 35(4):519–530

Jachimowicz JM, Duncan S, Weber EU, Johnson EJ (2018) When and why defaults influence decisions: a meta-analysis of default effects. Behav Public Policy. Available on https://doi.org/10.1017/bpp.2018.43

Jolls C, Sunstein CR, Thaler R (1998) A behavioral approach to law and economics. Stanford Law Rev 50:1471–1550

Levin HM, Belfield C (2015) Guiding the development and use of cost-effectiveness analysis in education. J Res Educ Effect 8:400–418

Loewenstein G, John LK, Volpp K (2013) Using decision errors to help people help themselves. In: Shafir E (ed) The behavioral foundations of public policy. Princeton University Press, Princeton

Loewenstein GF, Weber EU, Hsee CK, Welch N (2001) Risk as feelings. Psychol Bull 127 (2):267–286

Mannix BF, Dudley SE (2015a) The limits of irrationality as a rationale for regulation. J Policy Anal Manage 34(3):705–712

Mannix BF, Dudley SE (2015b) Please don't regulate my internalities. J Policy Anal Manage 34 (3):715–718

McKenzie CRM, Liersch MJ, Finkelstein SR (2006) Recommendations implicit in policy defaults. Psychol Sci 17(5):414–420
Mueller DC (2003) Public choice III. Cambridge University Press, Cambridge
Munscher R, Vetter M, Scheuerle T (2016) A review and taxonomy of choice architecture techniques. J Behav Decis Mak 29:511–524
Organisation for Economic Co-operation and Development (2014) OECD framework for regulatory policy evaluation. OECD Publishing
Organisation for Economic Co-operation and Development (2017) Behavioral insights and public policy: lessons from around the world. OECD Publishing, Paris
Peltzman S (1976) Toward a more general theory of regulation. J Law Econ 19(2):211–240
Rizzo M, Whitman D (2009) The knowledge problem of new paternalism. Brigham Young Univ Law Rev 2009:905–968
Sibony AL, Alemanno A (2016) The emergence of behavioural policy-making. In: Alemanno A, Sibony AL (eds) Nudge and the law: a European perspective. Hart, Oxford, pp 1–25
Slovic P, Finucane ML, Peters E, MacGregor DG (2006) The affect heuristic. In: Lichtenstein S, Slovic P (eds) The construction of preference. Cambridge University Press, Cambridge, pp 434–453
Stigler GJ (1971) The theory of economic regulation. Bell J Econ Manag Sci 2(1):3–21
Sunstein CR (2014) Nudges.gov: Behaviorally informed regulation. In: Zamir E, Teichman D (eds) The Oxford handbook of behavioral economics and the law. Oxford University Press, New York, pp 719–747
Sunstein CR (2016) The council of psychological advisors. Annu Rev Psychol 67:713–737
Sunstein CR (2018a) "Better off, as judged by themselves": a comment on evaluating nudges. Int Rev Econ 65(1):1–8
Sunstein CR (2018b) The cost-benefit revolution. MIT Press, Cambridge
Tannenbaum D, Fox CR, Rodgers T (2017) On the misplaced politics of behavioural policy interventions. Nat Hum Behav 1(7):130
Thaler RH, Sunstein CR (2008) Nudge: improving decisions about health, wealth, and happiness. Penguin Books, New York
Thaler RH, Sunstein CR, Balz JP (2013) Choice architecture. In: Shafir E (ed) The behavioral foundations of public policy. Princeton University Press, Princeton, pp 428–439
Thunstrom L, Gilbert B, Ritten CJ (2018) Nudges that hurt those already hurting–distributional and unintended effects of salience nudges. J Econ Behav Organ 153:267–282
Tor A (2008) The methodology of the behavioral analysis of law. Haifa Law Rev 4:237–327
Tor A (2014) Understanding behavioral antitrust. Tex Law Rev 92(3):573–667
Tor A (2016) The critical and problematic role of bounded rationality in nudging. In: Mathis K, Tor A (eds) Nudging–possibilities, limitations and applications in European law and economics. Springer, Switzerland, pp 3–10
Tor A (2019) Nudges that should fail?. Behavioral Public Policy. Available on https://doi.org/10.1017/bpp.2019.5

Complex Mortgage Loans as a Case Study for Consumer Law and Economics

Mariusz J. Golecki and Piotr Tereszkiewicz

Abstract This contribution analyses the challenge to courts posed by foreign currency mortgage loans, risky type of mortgages that were broadly marketed in the Central and Eastern Europe in the last 15 years. There is considerable evidence that foreign currency mortgage loans constitute a "dark chapter" in the history of European mortgage financing. We attempt to show that behavioural analysis can be used as a helpful tool in explaining at least some of the reasons why consumer borrowers opted to choose this type of risky mortgage products.

1 Foreign Currency Mortgage Loans in Europe

A recent example of risky mortgage contracts are foreign currency indexed mortgage loans, broadly marketed in a number of Central and Eastern European countries, in particular in Poland and Hungary in the last two decades. After 2004, as interest rates were much lower in Switzerland than in Poland and other central and Eastern European countries, the Swiss franc emerged as an attractive currency for mortgage loans. In 2010 around 64% mortgage loans were indexed in foreign currency (mostly CHF) with the total value of 40 billion Euro.[1] Other Central and Eastern European

[1]Rzeczpospolita from 26 January 2015, http://www.ekonomia.rp.pl/artykul/710047,1174464-Kim-jestes-frankowcu-.html?referer=redpol; Rzeczpospolita from 5 February 2015, http://www.ekonomia.rp.pl/artykul/710047,1177051-Gdzie-mieszkaja-frankowicze.html?referer=redpol; The Economist from 15 November 2014, Forint exchange, http://www.economist.com/news/finance-and-economics/21632651-hungarys-government-gives-struggling-borrowers-break-forint-exchange.

M. J. Golecki
Department of Legal Theory and Philosophy of Law, Faculty of Law and Administration, University of Łódź, Łódź, Poland

P. Tereszkiewicz (✉)
Faculty of Law and Administration, Jagiellonian University of Cracow, Cracow, Poland
e-mail: piotr.tereszkiewicz@uj.edu.pl

K. Mathis, A. Tor (eds.), *Consumer Law and Economics*, Economic Analysis of Law in European Legal Scholarship 9, https://doi.org/10.1007/978-3-030-49028-7_2

countries, including Austria, Hungary, Croatia and Romania, witnessed similar developments. In Austria, 25% of mortgage loans in 2010 were indexed in foreign currency, with the total value of 30 billion Euro.[2] In Hungary, by the second half of 2008, the household debt was close to 40% of the country's GDP, and two thirds of that debt was denominated in foreign currency, where over 90% of the household's foreign currency debt was denominated in Swiss francs.[3] In 2014 the total value of foreign currency indexed mortgage loans was 10 billion Euro.[4] The sharpest marketing of foreign currency mortgage loans in Poland took place around 2006 and 2007. In order to promote foreign currency indexed mortgage loans, the financial industry framed the options for a mortgage loan of 300.000 PLN for the duration of 30 years as follows: On the one hand, a monthly instalment payable if a mortgage loan was in Polish currency would be 2.130 PLN. On the other hand, a monthly instalment payable if a loan was indexed in Swiss francs would be 1.409 PLN, given the currency exchange rate between the Polish and Swiss currencies at that time. Apparently, a monthly instalment of a CHI-indexed mortgage loan was around 30% lower compared to a mortgage loan in Polish currency.[5] It is claimed that 75% of examined clients considered the foreign-currency indexed mortgage loan to be cheaper.[6] The first 2 or 3 years of the mortgage loan contract's duration may have justified the decision to choose it, as the currency exchange rates remained beneficial for borrowers. From 2010 on, the situation began to change abruptly. The value of Swiss franc began to rise, from around 2.1–2.3 francs per zloty in 2006–2007, toward 3.5 or close to 4 francs per zloty in 2014 and subsequent years.[7] This dramatic rise of currency exchange rates had a huge impact on the extent of the monthly credit instalments in foreign currency indexed loans which increased automatically. The increase of debt value around 30% means that borrowers have to repay amounts which clearly exceed the value of the property financed with the foreign currency indexed mortgage loan. This also means that selling property will not generate enough funds to repay the foreign currency indexed loan. In general, unexpectedly higher instalments weaken debtors' ability to pay and significantly increase the probability of default.

[2]See the official position of the Austrian Financial Market Supervision Authority (Österreichische Finanzmarktaufsicht, FMA) on foreign currency loans: Position der Finanzmarktaufischt zu Fremdwährungskrediten und Informationen zur derzeitigen Lage, https://www.fma.gv.at/de/sonderthemen/fremdwaehrungskredite.html.

[3]Balogh and others (2011), p. 1.

[4]The Economist from 15 November 2014, Forint exchange, http://www.economist.com/news/finance-and-economics/21632651-hungarys-government-gives-struggling-borrowers-break-forint-exchange.

[5]Rzeczpospolita from 2 March 2015, http://www.ekonomia.rp.pl/artykul/1183012.html.

[6]Rzeczpospolita from 2 March 2015, http://www.ekonomia.rp.pl/artykul/1183012.html.

[7]The development of exchange rate of franc versus PLN is accessible at the website of the Polish central bank (Narodowy Bank Polski), http://www.nbp.pl/homen.aspx?f=/kursy/kursyen.htm.

2 The Jurisprudence of the Court of Justice of the European Union

Litigation regarding foreign currency mortgage loans in several Members States of the European Union, in particular in Hungary, Romania and Croatia, led to a sequence of judgments by the Court of Justice of the European Union (subsequently referred to as CJUE) on this matter.[8] In these judgments, the CJUE examined central questions regarding the content of foreign currency mortgage loan contracts in light of European consumer contract law. Most importantly, the CJUE applied the Unfair Contract Terms Directive 93/13[9] and two major tests that this Directive provides, that is the unfairness test (Article 3 and 4 Directive), and the transparency requirement (Article 5 Directive).

It is useful to provide an example of a clause that was used in one of foreign currency indexed mortgage loan contracts, examined by the CJUE in the case OTP. This clause poses questions similar to those encountered in other cases decided by the CJUE.

The loan contract at issue was denominated in Swiss franc on the basis of the exchange rate of the day. The loan contract contained terms stipulating, first, a difference between the exchange rate applicable to the disbursement of the loan and that applicable to the repayment of the loan, respectively the buying and the selling rate used by OTP Bank ("the difference in exchange rates") and a power to make unilateral amendments in favour of the lender, allowing it to increase the interest rate, costs or commissions.[10] In particular, paragraph 4.7.1 of the loan contract stated that

> the debtor is required to fulfill the payment obligations to which he is subject, denominated in the currency of the loan, by transfer of the exchange value in Hungarian forints to the "credit" account… opened with [OTP Bank] for the purposes of this loan. The debtor is required to fulfill the applicable payment obligations at the latest on the day the debt become due, in accordance with the selling rates of the currency concerned, published under the provisions of the internal regulations, ensuring to replenish the account referred to above, at the latest on the due date, up to the exchange value in Hungarian forints. The creditor shall convert into Hungarian forints the debtor's payment obligations denominated in a foreign currency in accordance with the rates referred to in this paragraph on the due date and it shall debit that sum from the 'credit' account in Hungarian forints.[11]

[8] C-26/13, Árpád Kásler, ECLI:EU:C:2014:282; C-110/14, Horațiu Ovidiu Costea v. SC Volksbank România, ECLI:EU:C:2015:538; C-186/16, Ruxandra Paula Andriciuc v. Banca Românească SA, ECLI:EU:C:2017:703; C-51/17, OTP Bank Nyrt., OTP Faktoring Követeléskezelő Zrt. v. Teréz Ilyés, Emil Kiss, ECLI: EU:C:2018:750; C-118/17, Zsuzsanna Dunai v. ERSTE Bank Hungary Zrt., ECLI:EU:C:2019:207; C-38/17, GT v HS, ECLI:EU:C:2019:461.

[9] Council Directive 93/13/EEC of 5 April 1993 on unfair terms in consumer contracts, OJ EC No L 95/29.

[10] OTP Bank Nyrt, para. 17.

[11] OTP Bank Nyrt, para. 18.

3 Assessing the Unfairness

The CJUE holds that a national court is required to assess of its own motion whether a contractual term falling within the scope of Directive 93/13 is unfair, compensating in this way for the imbalance which exists between the consumer and the lender as seller, provided that it has available to it the legal and factual elements necessary for that task. The obligation of the court is then to identify, in the place of the consumer as an applicant, any unfairness of the terms in a contract concluded between a lender as seller and that consumer. Fundamentally, the CJEU has adopted a narrow understanding of the terms that "lay down the essential obligations of the contract and, as such, characterize it," which means that they are excluded from the assessment of the unfairness under Article 4 (2) Directive, as the exclusion concerns only the adequacy of the price or remuneration as against the services or goods supplied in exchange.[12] In the *Kásle*r case, the CJUE held that the exclusion of the assessment of the unfairness of a term does not apply to terms that merely determine the conversion rate of the foreign currency in which the loan is denominated, in order to calculate the repayment instalments.[13] In the *Matei* case, the CJUE extended this position to contract terms relating to "risk charges" applied by the lender and the lender's right to unilaterally alter the interest rate.[14] The pro-active stance of national courts in examining the contract terms on their own volition is justified, as the CJUE holds, by the necessity to ensure that the consumer enjoys effective protection, given the risk that he or she is unaware of his or her rights or encounters difficulties in enforcing them.[15]

4 Substituting Unfair Contract Terms with Provision of National Law

In the *Kásle*r judgment, the CJUE held that the national court may substitute an unfair term with a provision of national law in order to restore a balance between the parties to the contract and maintain the validity of the contract, when the contract concluded between the parties cannot continue in existence after an unfair term has been deleted as a result of the unfairness test. In practice, this may in particular concern indexation clauses in the foreign currency indexed mortgage loan contracts.[16] The position taken in *Kásle*r was subject to re-consideration in the most

[12] Kásler, para. 54; Matei, para. 55; Andriciuc, para. 34.

[13] Kásler, para. 54 and seq.

[14] Matei, para. 77 and seq.

[15] OTP Bank Nyrt, para. 88.

[16] Kásler, para. 85.

recent *Dziubak*[17] case. The *Dziubak* judgment constituted a response to a request for a preliminary ruling by a Polish court. Referring to the *Kásler* judgment, the Polish court asked the CJUE whether, after their removal, the unfair terms may be replaced by general provisions of Polish law which provide that the effects expressed in a contract are to be completed by the effects arising from the principles of equity or established customs.[18] Further, the Polish court also asked the CJUE whether the Unfair Terms Directive permits it to annul the contract where the maintenance of the contract without the unfair terms would result in altering the nature of its main subject matter since, even though the loan at issue would no longer be indexed to CHF, the interest would continue to be calculated on the basis of the rate applicable for that currency.[19] In the *Dziubak* judgment, the CJUE found that the possibility of substitution established by the *Kásler* judgment is restricted to supplementary provisions of national law or those applicable in the event of agreement by the parties and is based, inter alia, on the ground that those provisions are presumed not to contain unfair terms. Those provisions are presumed to reflect the balance that the national legislature wished to establish between the rights and obligations as a whole of parties to certain contracts in cases where the parties did not depart from a standard rule laid down by the national legislature for the contracts concerned or expressly selected the applicability of a rule established by the national legislature for that purpose.[20] However, as the CJUE emphasised, general provisions of Polish law, referred to by the claimant, do not appear to have been specifically assessed by the legislature in order to establish that balance, such that they do not benefit from the presumption that they are not unfair.[21] Consequently, the CJUE finds that those provisions cannot remedy the gaps in a contract caused by the removal of unfair terms that appeared in it.[22] Further, the CJUE considered that, since the possibility of substitution seeks to ensure the attainment of consumer protection by safeguarding consumers' real and actual interests against the possible detrimental consequences that could result from the annulment of the contract at issue as a whole, those consequences must be assessed in relation to the current or foreseeable circumstances at the time of the proceedings relating to the removal of the unfair terms concerned and not those existing at the time when the contract was concluded. The CJUE stated that under the Unfair Terms Directive a contract from which the unfair terms have been removed remains binding on the parties as regards the other terms that it contains, provided that it can continue in existence after the unfair terms are removed and that such continuity of the contract is legally possible under the rules of domestic law. In that regard, the CJUE noted that, according to the national court,

[17]C-260/18, Kamil Dziubak, Justyna Dziubak v. Raiffeisen Bank International AG, ECLI:EU:C:2019:819.

[18]Dziubak, para. 28.

[19]Dziubak, para. 28.

[20]Dziubak, para. 60.

[21]Dziubak, para. 61.

[22]Dziubak, para. 62.

after the removal of the terms on the difference in exchange rate, the nature of the main subject matter of the contract appears to be altered by the cumulative effect of abandoning the indexation to the CHF and the continued application of an interest rate based on the CHF rate. Since such an alteration appears to be legally impossible under Polish law, the Unfair Terms Directive does not preclude the annulment of contract in question by the Polish court.[23] On that point, the Court emphasized that the deletion of the terms at issue would lead not only to the removal of the indexing mechanism and the exchange difference but also, indirectly, the loss of the exchange risk, which is directly connected to the indexation of the loan to a currency. Finally, the CJUE held that, where the consumer prefers not to rely on the system of protection established by the Unfair Terms Directive, this Directive does not apply. In that regard the CJUE clarified that the consumer must also be able, in accordance with that system, to refuse to be protected against the detrimental consequences caused by the annulment of the contract as a whole where the consumer does not wish to benefit from that protection.[24]

The *Dziubak* judgment will undoubtedly have far-reaching implications for the future fate of foreign currency indexed mortgage loans in Poland. Yet, it is still too early to anticipate how Polish courts will implement that judgment in disputes between lender and borrowers.

5 The Notion of Transparency: Lender's Obligations Towards the Borrower

In addition to specifying the limits of unfairness assessment under Article 4 Directive, the CJUE has adopted a broad notion of "transparency" regarding the currency conversion clauses in foreign currency mortgage loans. Transparency of the conversion clause should be assessed having regard to all the relevant information, including the promotional material, but also the information provided by the lender in the negotiation of the loan agreement. This position of the CJUE was established in the *Kásler* judgment and upheld ever since. In the most recent judgment *GT v HS*, the CJUE explicitly acknowledges that the design of foreign currency indexed loans may make it impossible for the lender to provide all the information about the loan costs before the conclusion of contract. What are the consequences for pre-contractual obligations of the lender according to the CJUE? Fundamentally, the Court recognises that the lender cannot be expected to have specified all details at the time the agreement was concluded.[25] This position of the Court can be understood as a realistic act of judicial self-restraint. Were the Court to hold the opposite, that is, that lenders are expected to have specified all details at the time the agreement

[23]Dziubak, para. 45.
[24]Dziubak, para. 55.
[25]GT v HS, para. 36.

was concluded, its holding could open the possibility of challenging most of foreign-currency indexed loans subject to the EU legislation on unfair terms. This is why one should not too eagerly describe the Court's position as lender friendly. The assessment of all transactional details in specific cases is left to national courts and these courts may reach differing conclusions depending on factual settings.[26]

The CJUE position in *GT v HS* judgment is remarkable for referring to the lender's knowledge at the time the loan contract was concluded. Most fundamentally, the CJUE rules that the circumstances taken into account in the assessment as to whether a contractual term is unfair under Article 4 (1) of Unfair Terms Directive are those

> which could have been known to the seller [lender] at that time agreement was concluded and which were of such a nature that they could affect the future performance of the agreement.[27]

Undoubtedly, this is a very powerful statement when one considers that the knowledge of lenders about possible market and product risks of foreign currency indexed loans is relevant also for their liability towards borrowers. The Court clearly invites national courts—within respective procedural rules—to examine what lenders actually knew and could have known regarding the future performance of foreign currency mortgage loans before mortgage loan contracts were concluded. While the CJUE analyses the issue only in the context of the Unfair Terms Directive, findings regarding the lender's knowledge of circumstances which could affect future performance of foreign currency mortgage loans will be undoubtedly relevant from the perspective of liability for non-disclosure or misrepresentation.[28] It is submitted that the CJUE reference to hypothetical knowledge of lenders of circumstances which could affect the future performance of the mortgage loans should be read in connection with its above-quoted statement regarding the impossibility of specifying all relevant details at the time the agreement was concluded. These two statements can be reconciled in an abstract manner as follows: While in certain cases lenders cannot have been expected to specify all contract relevant details in advance, their hypothetical knowledge of any circumstances relevant to future performance of foreign currency indexed mortgage loans should be taken into account. Interpreted in this manner, the ruling of the CJUE may actually strengthen the position of borrowers in private lawsuits against lenders.

---

[26] Cf. the guidance provided by the CJUE in the judgments: GT vs. HS, para. 36; OTP Bank Nyrt, para. 77; Andrucic, para. 56.

[27] GT v HS, para. 40.

[28] Cf. Tereszkiewicz (2016).

6 The Concept of the Average Reasonable Consumer

The above sections were devoted to discussing relatively specific (rule-like) conduct requirements laid down by the CJUE in the process of interpreting the Unfair Terms Directive with regard to foreign currency indexed mortgage loans. In addition to mandating specific conduct requirements, the CJUE applies the concept of the average reasonable consumer as a further legal criterion of what can be justifiably expected of a consumer borrower. As is commonly known, the concept of the reasonable consumer plays a key role in the jurisprudence of the CJUE.[29] It has been extensively examined in the scholarship as regards its general content and function.[30]

From the perspective of this contribution, it is important to demonstrate how this concept was applied in the sequence of the CJUE judgments regarding foreign currency mortgage loans. The *Kásler* case was the first major judgment dealing with foreign currency mortgage loans in which the CJUE applied the *leitbild* of the "average consumer." It is worthwhile to quote the crucial paragraph of the judgment in full:

> it is for the referring court to determine whether, having regard to all the relevant information, including the promotional material and information provided by the lender in the negotiation of the loan agreement, the average consumer, who is reasonably well informed and reasonably observant and circumspect, would not only be aware of the existence of the difference, generally observed on the securities market, between the selling rate of exchange and the buying rate of exchange of a foreign currency, but also be able to assess the potentially significant economic consequences for him resulting from the application of the selling rate of exchange for the calculation of the repayments for which he would ultimately be liable and, therefore, the total cost of the sum borrowed.[31]

The *Kásler* formula of "reasonable average consumer" was further developed in the *Andriciuc and Others*, *OTP Bank Nyrt* and *GT v HS* judgments. In *Andriciuc and Others*, while determining the transparency requirement regarding a clause in a foreign currency mortgage loan contract, the Court held that

> a term under which the loan must be repaid in the same foreign currency as that in which it was contracted must be understood by the consumer both at the formal and grammatical level, and also in terms of its actual effects, so that the average consumer, who is reasonably well informed and reasonably observant and circumspect, would be aware both of the possibility of a rise or fall in the value of the foreign currency in which the loan was taken out.[32]

In *OTP Bank Nyrt* case, the Court ruled that

> a term relating to the foreign exchange risk must be understood by the consumer both at the formal and grammatical level and also in terms of its actual effects, so that the average

[29] Cf. Leczykiewicz and Weatherhill (2016), in particular Albors-Llorens and Jones (2016).

[30] Micklitz (2018), pp. 231 seqq.

[31] Kásler, para. 74.

[32] Andriciuc, para. 51.

> consumer, who is reasonably well informed and reasonably observant and circumspect, would not only be aware of the possibility of a depreciation of the national currency in relation to the foreign currency in which the loan was denominated, but would also be able to assess the potentially significant economic consequences of such a term with regard to his financial obligations.[33]

Finally, in the most recent case, *GT v HS*, the Court held that the transparency requirement applied to foreign currency mortgage loans means that

> the mechanism for calculating the amount lent, expressed in foreign currency, and the exchange rate applicable must be indicated transparently, so that a reasonably well-informed and reasonably observant and circumspect consumer may evaluate, on the basis of clear, intelligible criteria, the economic consequences for him of entering into the agreement, including, in particular, the total cost of the loan.[34]

The sequence of the above-mentioned judgments nicely illustrates how the *leitbild* of the "average consumer" was applied to different contract clauses or product risks in the mortgage loan contracts examined by the CJUE. Drawing on the CJUE jurisprudence, one may conclude that a "reasonably well informed and reasonably observant and circumspect consumer" is required to be aware of the following factors when faced with foreign currency mortgage loan offers:

First, the possibility of a depreciation of the national currency in relation to the foreign currency in which the loan was denominated.[35] Second, the existence of the difference, generally observed on the securities market, between the selling rate of exchange and the buying rate of exchange of a foreign currency. Third, the possibility that the selling rate of exchange for the calculation of the repayments for which the consumer would ultimately be liable will be less beneficial to the consumer than the buying rate. Fourth, the potentially negative economic consequences resulting from the application of the selling rate for the calculation of the due repayments.

Market risks resulting from the instability of currency exchange rates and the impossibility to exactly predict their development could be regarded as common knowledge expected of all legally capable adult people. This should not appear questionable. Things are far less certain when it comes to the manner in which the uncertainty regarding the currency exchange rate is built into the clauses of the mortgage loan contract and deployed in technical language to determine the extent of due repayments. Consumer borrowers can only be expected to understand contract clauses referring to currency exchange rates provided these clauses are drafted in "plain intelligible language," which means among others that a term must be understood by the consumer both at the formal and grammatical level, and also in terms of its actual effects.[36] It is apparent from the CJUE case law that Article 4 (2) Directive 93/13 must be interpreted as meaning that the requirement for a contractual term to be drafted in plain intelligible language cannot be reduced merely

[33] OTP Bank Nyrt, para. 78.

[34] GT v HS, para. 34.

[35] OTP Bank Nyrt, para. 78.

[36] Andriciuc, para. 44; OTP Bank Nyrt, para. 73.

to it being formally and grammatically intelligible.[37] There is no doubt that the CJUE considers clauses referring to currency exchange risk (or currency speculation) admissible as long as they fulfill a rigorous standard of transparency, set out with respect to several types of clauses examined.[38]

7 Assessment

What is remarkable is that the CJUE in the above quoted judgments does not provide any guidance to national courts as to how the "average consumer" should be defined and by whom: *ex post* by judges, *ex ante* by regulators? One may only assume that the Court refers to its well-established line of case-law applying the concept of "average consumer" to different products and services. This brings us to the crucial question, which we believe has not been yet meaningfully discussed. Should the concept of the "average consumer" be specified more closely, e.g. by referring to temporal (the year) or geographical (a Member State) criteria? The context of foreign currency mortgage loans appears to justify a more nuanced approach to the "average consumer" *leitbild*. To begin, the cases subject to the review of the CJUE come from Central and Eastern European countries (or, if one prefers, countries which joined the EU 2004 or later): Hungary, Rumania, Croatia or Poland. This geographical dimension of the question at hand is not incidental.[39] To our knowledge, comparable mortgage loan contracts were not offered on the domestic mortgage markets of Western European countries, with the notable exception of Austria.[40] This raises the question of how the public in those countries perceives the stability of their domestic currencies in relation to foreign currencies, such as Swiss franc. Most importantly, there may be significant differences among these countries, resulting from their general economic conditions, the level of financial consumer protection, the structure of the banking system, the rate of house-ownership and many other factors, which cannot all be referred to here. National mortgage markets in the European Union differ significantly, so that one should speak of *European mortgage markets* rather than of a European mortgage market.[41] This was even more true at the time foreign currency mortgage loans have entered the domestic markets of Member States on a mass-scale. Given this diversity in mortgage markets across Member

---

[37] Andriciuc, para. 44; OTP Bank Nyrt, para. 73.

[38] For an analysis of transparency see Golecki and Tereszkiewicz (2019).

[39] Micklitz and Reich (2014) note a similar pattern in consumer law cases referred to the CJUE between 2008 and 2012, which came mostly from new Member States and Spain. However, the cases discussed by Micklitz and Reich (2014) did not concern foreign currency mortgage loans.

[40] Cf. the study by H-J. Dübel and S. Walley Regulation of Foreign Currency Mortgage Loans: The Case of Transition Countries in Central and Eastern Europe, December 2010, available at http://documents.worldbank.org/curated/pt/383871468336712836/pdf/693820RSC0P1130tgage0loans0Jan02011.pdf.

[41] Aalbers (2012), p. 124.

States, the meaning of the "average consumer" concept will be different in relation to different Member States.

Moreover, there is a crucial temporal aspect to the "average consumer" *leitbild* that is not evident on the first reading of CJUE judgments. Foreign currency indexed mortgage loans entered the market generally after 2005 and their distribution reached its peak in the following few years. Around 2005 or so, foreign currency mortgage products were clearly unknown to the general public, so that an average consumer was much more susceptible to marketing strategies by the industry that might have underplayed the product risks.[42] After a decade or more, when CJUE judgments discussed above were rendered (2015–2019), foreign currency mortgage loans acquired a negative image in the public eye following well-documented and broadly-publicized struggles of many borrowers to repay outstanding debt. It follows that an average consumer of 2018 in Central and Eastern European countries would be much more cautions when offered to take out such a loan.[43] It is submitted that "average consumers" of 2005 differ dramatically from those of 2018 in their perception of foreign currency mortgage loans. How shall national courts apply the "average consumer" *leitbild* following the CJUE jurisprudence? From a formal perspective, Article 4 (1) Unfair Terms Directive provides guidance in this respect, as it mandates that "the unfairness of a contractual terms shall be assessed (. . .) by referring, at the time of conclusion of the contract, to all the circumstances attending the conclusion of the contract." This means that courts shall undertake efforts to reconstruct the perception of "average consumers" prevailing at the time mortgage loans contract were concluded. It must be emphasized that an assessment on the basis of "all the circumstances attending the conclusion of the contract" (objective criterion) undertaken "on the date of conclusion of the contract" (temporal criterion) appears almost a legal fiction. The broad basis for the assessment can be taken into account only in the process of a retrospective inquiry, performed by adjudicative bodies, such as courts. Courts (judges) deciding suits against lenders regarding foreign currency mortgage loans face a considerable challenge of dealing with the "hindsight bias," which clearly affects the perception of risk resulting from that type of mortgage loans at present.[44]

[42]Tereszkiewicz (2015, 2016).

[43]Another matter is that meanwhile such mortgage loans were not offered any more due to well-deserved bad publicity which they generated.

[44]We refer to our contribution Golecki and Tereszkiewicz (2019).

8 Mortgage Loans and Behavioural Law and Economics: How Low Instalment Rates Lured Individuals and Judges Alike

From a behavioural perspective, one may inquire as to why such risky products as foreign currency mortgage loans gained in popularity among borrowers. It seems that consumer's choice in case of mortgage loans focuses on the amount of monthly instalment and not the aggregated cost of the whole mortgage loan. It is possible to explain why people choose riskier financial products instead of carefully calculating the average cost of mortgage loan denominated in foreign currency. Given the fact that the majority of borrowers have not been hedged against any change of currency rate, the choice seems to be suboptimal from both *ex ante* and *ex post* perspectives. The psychological background of this phenomenon is well known. Borrowing from the literature on behavioural law and economics one can suggest that the consumers in case of risky mortgage loan contracts in Central and Eastern Europe have been altogether lured by two parallel illusions. To begin with, they probably believed that the currency exchange rate risk was negligible. That was based on miscalculation, since given the fact that the depreciation of Swiss franc was discernible, the borrowers believed that the process was linear or that Swiss Franc was at least neutral and in case of any dramatic changes on financial markets the rise of its value would have not been higher than at the moment when the loan contract had been signed. This expectation was over-optimistic; however, the careless behaviour had some other reason as well, namely the amount of monthly instalment. This assumption was based on a mistake resulting from the so-called anchoring effect. Anchoring and adjusting heuristics are visible within the process of non-reflexive acceptance of a given number and subsequent adjustment of the quantity according to the process of receiving of further, more detailed information.

As Daniel Kahneman explains:

> The main moral of priming research is that our thoughts and our behavior are influenced, much more than we know or want, by the environment of the moment. (...) Anchoring effects are threatening in a similar way. You are always aware of the anchor and even pay attention to it, but you do not know how it guides and constrains your thinking, because you cannot imagine how you would have thought if the anchor had been different (or absent). However, you should assume that any number that is on the table has had an anchoring effect on you, and if the stakes are high you should mobilize yourself (your System 2) to combat the effect.[45]

The priming effect has been explained as based on suggestion, when selective activation of compatible memories stored in long-term memory takes place. It is assumed that the exemplars are stored in long-term memory (LTM) and the computations are performed with the engagement of working memory (WM). The categorization decision is thus based on a process of retrieving of the most similar exemplars of numbers or amounts belonging to the category, where it is assumed that

[45] Kahneman (2011), p. 128.

the exemplars had been previously identified as belonging to the category. The whole process is thus based on the retrieval of memorized objects, the comparison of the objects and the identification of the most similar one. In case of mortgage loans indexed with foreign currency, the anchoring effect concentrated on the level of the amount of monthly instalments instead of weighted costs of the whole loan discounted with the currency risk parameter. Thus, lower instalments and lower interest rates offers deluded the whole category of borrowers. All these processes seriously influence judges and consumers alike. It is widely accepted in the psychological literature that judgments are based on rules of thumb leading to systematic departures from models of rational predictions, whereas actual decisions usually violate the assumptions of expected utility theory, as it has been described within the framework of the prospect theory. Both judgments and decisions demonstrate systematic departures from the rational choice model. This finding refers both to legal and non-legal contexts. It has been observed that agents are generally prone to both types of departures from the standard rational choice model. It has also been demonstrated that many cognitive operations are in general based on automatic and unconscious processes, which could in many cases be supervised by other, deliberative and conscious processes, controlling the output of the former intuition-based cognitive operations.[46] The two processes seem to be not only very closely connected, but in fact they seem to be integrated in one model, containing the operations of both intuition and deliberation. However, these automatic-intuitive processes can be supervised and modified by additional operations of the deliberate system. Crucially, the deliberate decision mode is not conceived as a completely distinct and separable system. Rather, processes of information search, information production or information change affect the basic automatic process that finally determines the decision. Generally speaking, the role of intuition seems to be twofold: it is a condition, if not a necessary condition, for initiating a decision-making process. The significance of intuition is increasing within the situation of information deficit, shortening of the time horizon and activities performed within uncertainty. Hence, one may accept, following Posner's argument, that intuition is increasing the effectiveness of decision-making processes (also within the meaning of economics, that is allocative effectiveness which is connected to the economic costs of decision making and law application).[47]

As regards mortgage loans indexed with foreign currency rate, the anchoring effect resulted from both the present currency exchange rate and the amount of monthly instalment. Since the borrowing capacity became a serious obstacle for many borrowers, the concept of the borrowing capacity has been expanded significantly under the condition that the monthly instalment and the whole cost of loan meet lower interest rates in Swiss Franc than it would have been possible in case of local currencies. Thus, borrowers took past contingences as constant and stable, if not perpetual and additionally focused on the amount of monthly instalment rather

---

[46]Kahneman (2011).

[47]Posner (1992), p. 19.

than on the amount of the whole loan multiplied by the risk of appreciation of the Swiss Franc. Moreover, the policy of the Swiss National Bank seemed to be based on the assumption that any appreciation had to be linked with the actions of the Bank, since appreciation was certainly devastating for the Swiss economy. The so-called central bank anchor also loomed large on the horizon, since the expectation that the Swiss Central Bank would not have allowed any drastic rise of Swiss franc was well justified at that time. Therefore, Swiss Franc became the most favourable currency used as the benchmark for currency exchange rate risk based mortgage loans. This assumption has been to some extent reflected by the jurisprudence of the CJUE. The Court focused on economic effects of selected contractual clauses, taking the behavioural dimension into account. Given the fact that consumers acted irrationally, the question was whether the average well informed person would have entered into such a contract. The court thus acted as an ex post regulator, and necessarily based many of its decisions on evaluations which were affected by certain heuristics.

How should courts operate under those circumstances? Which model of judicial governance would fit best? The question remains as to which of those models fit best the contemporary complex structure of multilevel legal systems.

It is commonly believed that courts should supplement the market in case of high transaction costs. According to Ronald Coase,

> when the market transactions are so costly as to make it difficult to change the arrangement of rights established by the law (. . .) the courts directly influence economic activity. It would therefore seem desirable that the courts should understand the economic consequence of their decisions and should (. . .) take these consequences into account when making their decisions.[48]

Courts typically intervene also in case of market failures such as fraud, duress or deceit. Certainly, the problem of judicial governance might be scrutinized on a much broader basis. In the nineteenth century courts in the US started to establish and implement the common law doctrine against speculation. Courts thus became forerunners of the antispeculative policy adopted later on by statutory law, when the whole bunch of statutes has been adopted, encapsulating the Future Trading Act of 1921, the Grain Futures Act of 1922, the Commodity Exchange Act of 1936, regulating commodity futures, and finally the Securities Exchange Act of 1934, being the core of anti-speculative financial law. Even in the UK, where statutory provisions seem to play an important role in regulating derivatives, the ultimate application of statutory provisions rested upon courts. The legal definition of a wagering has been proposed by Hawkins J. in *Carlill v. Carbolic Smoke Ball Co.* [1892] 2 Q.B. 484, 490–491:

> a wagering contract is one by which two persons, professing to hold opposite views touching the issue of a future uncertain event, mutually agree that, dependent upon the determination of that event, one shall win from the other, and the other shall pay or hand over to him, a sum of money or other stake; neither of the contracting parties having any other interest in that

[48] Coase (1960).

> contract than the sum or stake he will so win or lose, there being no other real consideration for the making of such contract by either of the parties.

In this way the famous English case *Universal Stock Exchange Ltd v. Strachan* [1896] AC 166 set out the English doctrine of gaming transactions, thus substituting sec. 18 of the Gaming Act 1845, which stated:

> All contracts or agreements, whether by parole or in writing, by way of gaming or wagering, shall be null and void; and no suit shall be brought or maintained in any court of law or equity for recovering any sum of money or valuable thing alleged to be won upon any wager.

The same could be said about some peculiar aspects of risky contracts, such as the binding force of broker's commercial custom and its force for the principal (*Nickalls v. Merry*, L.R. 7 H.L. 530, *Robinson v. Mollett*, L.R. 7 H.L. 802). The nature of the unenforceable wagering contract has been endorsed in *Earl of Ellesmere v. Wallace* [1929] 2 Ch. 1. Additionally, the function of derivative transaction has been analysed in cases such as *Metelmann v. N.B.R* (1984), where it has been stated that contracts for differences may also serve as an efficient tool to mitigate loss due to the change of price (Ch. Lloyd's Report 1/1984, p. 614). Thus, there is nothing exceptional in a situation where the court is forced to adjudicate about the acceptable level of risk in the relatively well-established regulatory framework. But what does the interplay between the statutory regulation and judicial intervention show us? It seems that courts are residual lawmakers in cases of market failure and state (legislation/administration) failure. Courts intervened as the "interstitial legislators" in these highly complex derivative cases. What is the background of their decisions, as even recently judicial interventions play an important role in the regulatory framework? The comparative institutional analysis suggests three potential types of remedies being deployed in case of the so-called market failure.[49]

First, parties may insure against unpredictable events on the market. This strategy is strictly connected with the general equilibrium theorem and the concept of the complete contract (contingent contract claim), concerning all possible states of affair. In the economics scholarship it has been suggested by Kenneth Arrow. The economic theory of complete contingency contract is however seriously weakened by the assumption about the existence of transaction costs. If transaction costs are high enough then, it is not profitable for a party to spend resources on filling gaps in a contract. How the gap is to be filled ex post is no longer a problem of market governance given that in majority of cases it is up to the court to fill gaps in incomplete contracts. Hence the market solution under the assumption of positive transaction costs is effectively being transformed into the question of judicial governance.

Second, since the existence of transaction costs leads to gaps in contracts, the state could effectively prevent the ex post construction of contracts. The typical instrument then is just a set of default rules which operate if not bargained out by the

[49] Komesar (1994).

parties. The stronger regulatory instrument is a set of mandatory rules set out in case of a typical market failure, e.g. information asymmetry.

Third, it is commonly believed that courts should supplement the market in case of high transaction costs. According to Ronald Coase,

> when the market transactions are so costly as to make it difficult to change the arrangement of rights established by the law (...) the courts directly influence economic activity. It would therefore seem desirable that the courts should understand the economic consequence of their decisions and should (...) take these consequences into account when making their decisions.

Courts typically intervene also in case of a market failure such as fraud, duress, or deceit. According to Richard Posner:

> Economic analysis reveals no grounds other than fraud, incapacity, and duress (the last narrowly defined) for allowing a party to repudiate the bargain that he made in entering into the contract.[50]

Consequently, even gross inequalities between parties resulting from the difference in bargaining skill are justified. Nevertheless, legal doctrines such as unconscionability, or unfair exploitation of the weaker party, may play an important role especially in European jurisdictions. The question arises as to whether judges are prepared to solve the problem of allocation and distribution of resources under the assumption about the presence of uncertainty, risk and bounded rationality. This part of judicial practice seems to be criticized.[51]

The question remains as to which of these models best fit the contemporary complex structure of multilevel legal systems? It seems that the model of multilevel international judicial governance based on the Coasian approach to judiciary could provide a feasible solution under the assumption that the political process cannot offer an adequate remedy to the market failure. This proposition could draw on Sen's concept of normative evaluation and legal analogues in a multi-level global system.[52] Amartya Sen has observed that social science is predominantly based on the legal contractual paradigm. Additionally, he proposed to concentrate on the competitive idea derived from the Smithian "Impartial Spectator" paradigm. Thus, the competitive paradigm is marked by the triadic relationship, which characterizes arbitration and adjudication. The idea is based on the concept of impartiality, objectivity and fairness. Those ideals are not attainable within the world shaped by normative frameworks based on the contractarian paradigm. However, it does not necessarily mean that there are not attainable at all and that the whole idea of impartiality is too idealistic to be useful in real life. It seems that impartiality,

---

[50]Posner (2007).

[51]Komesar (1994, 2001) and Vermeule (2006). For other studies pertaining to the cognitive limitations of courts cf. Guthrie et al. (2000), Guthrie et al. (2007), Hadfield (2008), Hadfield (2011), Jolls et al. (1998), Kunda (1990), Nosofsky (1992), Petersen (2013), Ponzetto & Fernandez (2008), Rachlinski (1998), Sloman (2002), Sunstein (2000), Sunstein (2001), Wróblewski (1988).

[52]Sen (2006).

objectivity and fairness are still basic normative presuppositions of any adjudicative process. The legal process should be at least to some extent imbued with those values, corresponding with the idea of Smithian impartial spectator.

9 Conclusion

This contribution presented the challenge to courts posed by foreign currency mortgage loans, risky type of mortgages that were broadly marketed in the Central and Eastern Europe in the last 15 years. Currently, the litigation before the Court of Justice of the European Union regarding foreign currency mortgage loans appears to be at its peak. Given that the implementation of the CJUE jurisprudence at the level of Member States may even take years, not all legal and economic consequences of mass-scale distribution of foreign currency mortgage loans can be determined. Yet, the assessment appears justified that foreign currency mortgage loans were a "dark chapter" in the history of European mortgage financing. We believe to have shown that behavioural analysis can be used as a helpful tool in explaining at least some of the reasons why consumer borrowers opted to choose this type of risky mortgage products, and how courts have to approach disuptes resulting from that type of mortgage loan contracts.

Acknowledgments The paper has been prepared within the framework of the research project 2015/17/B/HS5/00495 financed by the National Science Center, Poland.

References

Aalbers MB (2012) European mortgage markets before and after the financial crisis. In: Aalbers MB (ed) Subprime cities. The political economy of mortgage markets. Wiley-Blackwell

Albors-Llorens A, Jones A (2016) The images of the 'consumer' in EU competition law. In: Leczykiewicz D, Weatherill S (eds) The images of the consumer in EU law: legislation, free movement and competition law. Hart, Oxford, pp 43–92

Balogh C, Gereben Á, Karvalits F, Pulai G (2011) Foreign currency tenders in Hungary: a tailor - made instrument for a unique challenge. Bank for International Settlements Papers No 73. Available at: http://www.bis.org/publ/bppdf/bispap73k.pdf

Coase RH (1960) The problem of social cost. J Law Econ 3:1–44

Dübel H-J, Walley S (2010) Regulation of Foreign Currency Mortgage Loans: The Case of Transition Countries in Central and Eastern Europe, December 2010, available at http://documents.worldbank.org/curated/pt/383871468336712836/pdf/693820RSC0P1130tgage0loans0Jan02011.pdf

Golecki MJ, Tereszkiewicz P (2019) Taking the prohibition of unfair commercial practices seriously. In: Mathis K, Tor A (eds) New developments in competition law and economics. Springer, Cham, pp 91–106

Guthrie C, Rachlinski JJ, Wistrich AJ (2000) Inside the judicial mind. Cornell Law Rev 86:777–830

Guthrie C, Rachlinski JJ, Wistrich AJ (2007) Blinking on the bench: how judges decide cases. Cornell Law Rev 93:1–43

Hadfield GK (2008) The levers of legal design: institutional determinants of the quality of law. J Comp Econ 36(1):43–73
Hadfield GK (2011) The dynamic quality of law: the role of judicial incentives and legal human capital in the adaptation of law. J Econ Behav Organ 79(1):80–94
Jolls C, Sunstein CR, Thaler R (1998) A behavioral approach to law and economics. Stanford Law Rev 50:1471–1550
Kahneman D (2011) Thinking, fast and slow. Macmillan, London
Kahneman D, Tversky A (1979) Prospect theory: an analysis of decision under risk. Econometrica 47:263–291
Komesar N (1994) Imperfect alternatives: choosing institutions in law, economics, and public policy. University of Chicago Press, Chicago
Komesar N (2001) Law's Laws: The demand and supply of rights. In: Samford C, Round T (eds) Beyond the republic: meeting the global challenges to constitutionalism. The Federation Press, Sydney, pp 230–240
Kunda Z (1990) The case for motivated reasoning. Psychol Bull 108(3):480–498
Leczykiewicz D, Weatherhill S (2016) The images of consumer in EU law. Hart. Oxford
Micklitz H-W (2018) The politics of Justice in European private law. Social justice, access justice, societal justice. Cambridge University Press
Micklitz H-W, Reich N (2014) The court and sleeping beauty. The revival of the unfair contract terms directive (UCTD). Common Market Law Rev 51:771–808
Nosofsky RM (1992) Exemplars, prototypes, and similarity rules. In: Healy AF, Kosslyn SM, Shiffrin RM (eds) From learning theory to connectionist theory: essays in Honor of William K. Estes, vol 1. Lawrence Erlbaum Associates, Hillsdale, pp 149–167
Petersen N (2013) Avoiding the common-wisdom fallacy: the role of social sciences in constitutional adjudication. Int J Const Law 11(2):294–318
Ponzetto GA, Fernandez PA (2008) Case law versus statute law: an evolutionary comparison. J Leg Stud 37(2):379–430
Posner R (1992) Economic analysis of law, 4th edn. Little Brown and Co., New York
Posner RA (2007) Economic analysis of law, 7nd edn. Wolters Kluwer Law & Business
Rachlinski JJ (1998) A positive psychological theory of judging in hindsight. Univ Chic Law Rev 65(2):571–625
Sen AK (2006) Normative evaluation and legal analogues, In: Drobak JN (ed) Norms and the law. Cambridge University Press, Cambridge, pp 80–96
Sloman SA (2002) Two systems of reasoning. In: Gilovich T, Griffin D, Kahneman D (eds) Heuristics and biases: the psychology of intuitive judgment. Cambridge University Press, pp 379–396
Sunstein CR (ed) (2000) Behavioral law and economics. Cambridge series on judgment and decision making. Cambridge University Press, Cambridge
Sunstein CR (2001) One case at a time: Judicial minimalism on the Supreme Court. Harvard University Press, Cambridge
Tereszkiewicz P (2015) Obowiązki informacyjne w umowach o usługi finansowe. Wolters Kluwer Poland, Warszawa
Tereszkiewicz P (2016) Neutral third-party counselling as nudge toward safer financial products? The case of risky mortgage loan contracts. In: Mathis K, Tor A (eds) Nudging – possibilities, limitations, and applications in European law and economics. Springer, Heidelberg, 112–133
Vermeule A (2006) Judging under uncertainty: an institutional theory of legal interpretation. Harvard University Press
Wróblewski J (1988) Sądowe stosowanie prawa. Państwowe Wydawn. Nauk., Warszawa

Mariusz J. Golecki Warsaw and Łódź. Financial Ombudsman (Poland), Financial Ombudsman Office: m.golecki@rf.gov.pl, https://rf.gov.pl/english, Al. Jerozolimskie 87, 02-001 Warszawa, Poland

Professor at the University of Lodz, Department of Legal Theory and Philosophy of Law, Director of the Laboratory for Cognitive Research in Law, University of Lodz, Faculty of Law and Administration, ul. Kopcinskiego 8/12, 90-232 Łódź, Poland mjgolecki76@gmail.com. Fields of Interest: Economic Analysis of Law, Behavioural Law and Economics, Theory of EU law, Comparative Law, Law and Finance.

Piotr Tereszkiewicz Kraków. Professor of Private Law at the Jagiellonian University of Cracow. PL-31-007 Kraków, Olszewskiego 2, Tel. + 48 (0)12 663 13 85; Fax + 48 (0)12 422 98 12.

piotr.tereszkiewicz@uj.edu.pl. Fields of Interest: Private and Commercial Law (Law of Obligations, Consumer Law, Financial Services), Comparative Law, Economic Analysis of Law, Legal Philosophy and Legal Theory.

The PRIIPs Regulation in View of Behavioural Research: An Example of Hyperbolized Mandated Disclosure

Rainer Baisch

Abstract *Omri Ben-Shahar* and *Carl E. Schneider* criticise the convenient policy option to enact mandated disclosure provisions to adequately inform consumers. They argue that this insufficiently challenges an all too common practice to overcome market failures caused by information asymmetry, deters lawmakers from adopting better regulations, impairs people's decisions, and inappropriately burdens the legally obligated market participants. Their main argument is that consumers tend to make the "economically rational" decision to n o t read the information provided under the mandated disclosure requirements. This contribution describes not only the traditional disclosure-paradigm, which assumes that transparent and effectively processed information will enable the investor to make well-founded investment decisions, but also the human flaws regarding the way we process information. Based on the failures of mandated disclosure discussed by *Ben-Shahar* and *Schneider*, the European PRIIPs regulation, which tries to enhance consumer protection based on smarter information requirements to give consumers a better chance to avoid decision they later regret, is analysed. Then additional pillars capable of bolstering the investment decision process are discussed, i.e. organisational standards, code of conduct, suitability requirements, product governance in combination with the more paternalistic element of product intervention. Finally, an outlook to future challenges posed by the potential impact of FinTech developments like robo-advice and tokenised assets will be elucidated.

R. Baisch (✉)
University Research Priority Program Financial Market Regulation, University of Zurich, Zurich, Switzerland
e-mail: rainer.baisch@rwi.uzh.ch

K. Mathis, A. Tor (eds.), *Consumer Law and Economics*, Economic Analysis of Law in European Legal Scholarship 9, https://doi.org/10.1007/978-3-030-49028-7_3

1 Introduction

Disclosure requirements should be designed for homo sapiens, not homo economicus.[1]

1.1 The Point of Departure

Omri Ben-Shahar and *Carl E. Schneider* reject the convenient policy option to enact mandated disclosure provisions to adequately inform consumers.[2] They criticize that this convenient, insufficiently challenged and all too common practice to overcome market failures caused by information asymmetry deter lawmakers from adopting better regulations. In addition, overloaded disclosure obligations impair people's decisions, and inappropriately burdens the legally obligated market participants.[3] One of their main arguments is that consumers anyhow tend to make the "economically rational" decision to not read the information provided under the mandated disclosure requirements.

Having a "homo oeconomicus" in mind the traditional *disclosure-paradigm*, which dominates the financial market regulation, assumes that transparent and effectively processed information is sufficient to empower the investor to make well-founded investment decisions.[4] Therefore, financial market laws used to be designed for this idea of responsible and knowledgeable actors. However, behavioural research proves that the provision of written information alone is not sufficient, since the capacity and willingness to handle such input is limited.[5] Therefore, if the limitations of retail investors are to be accepted the regulator should recognise that the idea of rational decision-making based on mandated disclosure will not lead to optimal capital allocation.[6] In principle, one could argue that under such circumstances a failure of informed consent could put the validity of a contract in question. After the financial crises, market failures and, in consequence, capital misallocation made it glaringly obvious that even experienced investors are prone to irrational decisions.[7]

In an era of low interest rate leading to a scarcity of investment opportunities and under-funded pension schemes, combined with unsecure pay-as-you-go public

---

[1]Sunstein (2014), p. 729.

[2]Ben-Shahar and Schneider (2011, 2014).

[3]Ben-Shahar and Schneider (2014), p. 169. However, tangible proposals «better» tackling the information asymmetry problem are missing.

[4]Baisch (2016a), p. 225; Dalley (2007).

[5]Baisch and Weber (2015), p. 161.

[6]Baisch (2016a), p. 219; Ulen (2013) delivers a good overview of behaviourally informed investor protection regulation and also advocates augmented disclosure obligations.

[7]Schwarcz (2008), p. 1110.

pension system consumers have to plan for their retirement despite their cognitive failings and their lack of training for the task; therefore, regulators have to react to these respective mental shortcomings.[8] For many years behavioural research discussed many biases almost mantra-like that cannot be prevented through disclosure.

During the last decade regulators started to integrate those findings into their legislative work: "Disclosure has considerable attractions as a retail market tool, but the challenge for regulators is to resist the temptation to make disclosure the panacea for investor protection."[9] The European PRIIPs regulation[10] reacted with "optimised" mandated disclosure and introduced a Key Information Document which must be provided to the customer prior to the sale of certain investment products.[11] The provisions for this information leaflet will be discussed in this chapter. Of course even the most optimised dissemination of information will not help investors relying on the strategy to buy "the hot new thing"[12] that their peers are buying—mainly because they find their actual returns boring.[13] Omri Ben-Shahar and Carl E. Schneider research is focused on the U.S. markets, but also in Europe "disclosure is not the panacea that drafters of federal securities laws may have thought it to be".[14]

1.2 The Disclosure Paradigm

The US New Deal Statutes the Securities Act 1933[15] and Securities and Exchange Act 1934[16] established the disclosure paradigm mandating extensive disclosure requirements whenever securities are issued or distributed. While in those days the main driver was to combat fraud and market abuse disclosure it comes with no surprise that "*during the debate over the original enactment of the federal securities laws, Congress did not focus on the ability of investors to understand disclosure of complex transactions*".[17] However, "*(o)ne of the key pillars undergirding the federal*

---

[8]Baisch (2016a), p. 225.

[9]Opening statement of Steven Maijoor, Chair of ESMA, at the ESMA Investor Day, 12 December 2012, Paris; http://www.esma.europa.eu/system/files/2012-_818.pdf.

[10]Regulation (EU) No 1286/2014 of 26 November 2014 on key information documents for packaged retail and insurance-based investment products (PRIIPs), OJ L 352/1–23, 9.12.2014.

[11]See also Moloney (2014), p. 821.

[12]In the last 2 years this phenomenon, investor herd behavior, could be identified regarding Initial Coin Offerings; see Zetzsche et al. (2019), p. 30.

[13]Davidoff and Hill (2013), p. 603.

[14]Black (2013), p. 1507.

[15]Securities Act of 1933, 15 U.S.C. § 77a to 77 mm.

[16]Securities Exchange Act of 1934, 15 U.S.C. § 78a to 78 jj.

[17]Schwarcz (2004), p. 7.

securities laws — that investors effectively process information — is under pressure. An extensive literature shows that investors and other securities market participants are subject to cognitive biases and, because of bounded rationality, adopt heuristics in making investment decisions."[18] Despite that fact, from then onwards disclosure has been seen as "*the cornerstone of any investor protection regime in securities markets*".[19] In the EC and later also the EU, all security related directives and regulations incorporated the disclosure paradigm.[20]

Closely linked to the reliance on disclosure is the economic theory behind it. Liberalised financial market regulations incorporated the modern finance theory;[21] important for the functioning of this theory is that rational actors process all available information effectively which results in prices reflecting that; in consequence, also retail investors could benefit as free riders.

As already mentioned, the disclosure paradigm is critically scrutinized by authorities accepting behavioural insights. In principle, as "*complexity increases, the disclosure paradigm of securities law has been diminishing in effectiveness.*"[22] Therefore, "*the long-held disclosure paradigm, in which sophisticated investors and securities analysts bring market prices into line with disclosure*" is not reliable because the "*information asymmetry between companies and their investors will remain*".[23] The disclosure paradigm was also contributory to the last financial crisis: "*The old disclose and self-regulate paradigm in financial markets has been widely castigated as the main culprit of the current global financial catastrophe.*"[24]

Despite these conceptual failures and the resulting potential suboptimal allocation of capital regarding institutional investors the disclosure paradigm was not discarded; instead the favoured strategy was to improve the disclosure obligations. In the U.S., the *Consumer Financial Protection Bureau* (CFPB) has to ensure that

---

[18]Paredes (2003), p. 484.

[19]Avgouleas (2009), p. 442.

[20]Directive (EC) 2003/71 of 4 November 2003 on the prospectus to be published when securities are offered to the public or admitted to trading and amending Directive 2001/34/EC, *OJ L 345/64–89, 31.12.2003;* Directive (EC) 2004/109 of 15 December 2004 on the harmonisation of transparency requirements in relation to information about issuers whose securities are admitted to trading on a regulated market and amending Directive 2001/34/EC, *OJ L 390/38–57, 31.12.2004;* Directive (EC) 2003/6 Directive 2003/6/EC of 28 January 2003 on insider dealing and market manipulation (market abuse), *OJ L 96/16–25, 12.4.2003 (MAD); r*eplaced by Regulation (EU) No 596/2014 of 16 April 2014 on market abuse (market abuse regulation) and repealing Directive 2003/6/EC and Directives 2003/124/EC, 2003/125/EC and 2004/72/EC, *OJ L 173/1–61, 12.6.2014 (MAR);* Directive (EC) 2004/39 Directive 2004/39/EC of 21 April 2004 on markets in financial instruments amending Council Directives 85/611/EEC and 93/6/EEC and Directive 2000/12/EC and Directive 93/22/EEC, *OJ L 145/1–44, 30.4.2004, (MiFID I)*; replaced by Directive 2014/65/EU of 15 May 2014 on markets in financial instruments and amending Directive 2002/92/EC and Directive 2011/61/EU, *OJ L 173/349–496, 12.6.2014 (MiFID II).*

[21]*Markowitz* (1952), *Fama* (1970, 1991, 1998).

[22]Schwarcz (2008), p. 1121.

[23]Schwarcz (2004), p. 36.

[24]Avgouleas (2009), p. 474.

"*consumers are provided with timely and understandable information to make responsible decisions about financial transactions*".[25] The CFPB defines rules "*to ensure that the features of any consumer financial product or service, both initially and over the term of the product or service, are fully, accurately, and effectively disclosed to consumers in a manner that permits consumers to understand the costs, benefits, and risks associated with the product or service, in light of the facts and circumstances*".[26] And in the EU the PRIIPS regulation mandated basic leaflets not only to inform retail investors but also to allow a comparison of investment products.[27]

1.3 The Acceptance of Behavioural Research

Already two decades ago economists started "to abandon their assumption that humans behave rationally, and instead are finally coming to grips with the crazy, mixed up creatures we really are".[28] During this time many international organisations and standard setters accepted failures resulting from consumer biases and suboptimal information provisions, and have discussed the respective regulatory challenges:

- OECD: "A standard for intervention to protect those who are less informed or less sophisticated has been developed by the behavioural economist Colin Camerer and his colleagues. Known as "asymmetric paternalism," such intervention is relevant not only when failure results from behavioural biases but also more generally when failure results from information deficiencies."[29]
- IOSCO (International Organization of Securities Commissions): "... as explained in greater detail below, research indicates that retail investors exhibit

[25]Dodd-Frank Act, 2010, 12 U.S. Code § 5511—Purpose, objectives, and functions; Title X of the Dodd-Frank Act (aka Consumer Financial Protection Act of 2010) created the *Consumer Financial Protection Bureau* as an independent agency within the Board of Governors of the Federal Reserve System to regulate the offering and provision of consumer financial products and services under federal consumer financial laws.

[26]Dodd-Frank Act, 2010, 12 U.S. Code § 5532—Disclosures.

[27]Based on fundamental ideas in the EU strategy to form a single market for financial services laid-out in the *Financial Services Action Plan* (FSAP) from 1999 and stated in the *Commission Recommendation on disclosure of financial instruments* aiming at "*enhanced disclosure of the activities of banks and other financial institutions to allow investors to take informed decisions, and to foster market transparency and discipline as a complement to prudential supervision*". See Communication of the Commission, Financial Services: Implementing the Framework for Financial Markets: Action Plan, COM(1999) 232, 11.5.1999, 29.

[28]The Economist, Irrationality: Rethinking Thinking, 16.12.1999; http://www.economist.com/node/268946.

[29]The Organisation for Economic Co-operation and Development (OECD). Roundtable of Economics for Consumer Policy: Summary Report, 26 July 2007, p. 13; http://www.oecd.org/internet/consumer/39015963.pdf.

a range of behaviours and biases in the decision-making process, including acting on emotion, rather than on facts. These behaviours should be understood and considered to the greatest degree possible when developing a regulatory approach".[30]

- IOSCO: "Regardless of where they obtain the information, the research indicates that retail investors exhibit a range of behaviours and biases in the decision-making process. For instance, these might include the impact of: Emotion – Investors make decisions based on how they feel as opposed to what they know or think they know; Overconfidence and overestimation of investment knowledge and abilities – Retail investors may interpret past successes as due to their own expertise rather than market conditions; Representativeness biases – Investors are overly influenced by strong or poor recent past performance or false reference points; and Inertia, procrastination and status quo biases – Investors stick with a familiar, pre-existing or established position, for instance relating to the appropriateness of following a particular investment strategy.; also "The needs and abilities of the target investor should be considered to ensure that the content of the information is relevant, the organization of the information is logical and the language appropriate"[31]
- Joint Forum: "Recommendation 4: The POS disclosure document should be clear, fair, not misleading and written in a plain language designed to be understandable by the consumer."[32]
- G 20: "Where possible consumer research should be conducted to help determine and improve the effectiveness of disclosure requirements."[33]

The availability of information alone does not solve the problem, simply because many do not possess the ability to process it—partially due to a limited intellectual capacity,[34] numeracy and financial literacy;[35] additionally it lacks on the willingness

[30]International Organization of Securities Commissions (IOSCO). Principles on Point of Sale Disclosure, Consultation Report, November 2009, p. 2; http://www.iosco.org/library/pubdocs/pdf/IOSCOPD310.pdf.

[31]IOSCO, Principles on Point of Sale Disclosure, Final Report, February 2011, p. 11 and 31; http://www.iosco.org/library/pubdocs/pdf/IOSCOPD343.pdf.

[32]Joint Forum (Basel Committee on Banking Supervision—BCBS, IOSCO und International Association of Insurance Supervisors—IAIS), Point of Sale Disclosure in the Insurance, Banking and Securities Sectors, April 2014; www.iosco.org/library/pubdocs/pdf/IOSCOPD439.pdf.

[33]G 20, High-level Principles on Financial Consumer Protection, October 2011; http://www.oecd.org/daf/fin/financial-markets/48892010.pdf.

[34]Ben-Shahar and Schneider (2011), p. 712: "Most of the people in another study had at least some college education, but 40% 'could not solve a basic probability problem or convert a percentage to a proportion'." For details see Lipkus et al. (2001), p. 39.

[35]Ben-Shahar and Schneider (2011), p. 657: "Financial literacy education is an important component of the disclosure and informed consent paradigm, and much evidence now shows that this effort has largely failed." Willis (2008), pp. 208–209 finds that financial education programs have no effect or small paradoxical results. See also Lusardi and Mitchell (2014).

to do so and to invest time.[36] Behavioural research has described the most diverse human weaknesses in information processing, which are also widely present when acting on financial markets.[37]

However, behavioural research and the adaption of its results will not solve the problem: "As policymakers use it to devise programs, it's becoming clear that behavioral economics is being asked to solve problems it wasn't meant to address. Indeed, it seems in some cases that behavioral economics is being used as a political expedient, allowing policymakers to avoid painful but more effective solutions rooted in traditional economics."[38] Behavioural economics identifies a typical Ouroboros problem (the snake that eats its own tail): choice-preserving policies[39] are often unlikely to be sufficiently effective, ironically, for reasons based on behavioural research. "Fuller, simpler, and more effective disclosure [...] is often not a realistic way to adequately rectify individual incapacity to make accurate, informed judgments based on the appropriate time horizons. Instead, these widespread individual failings might well suggest regulatory tools beyond disclosure: policies that limit choices or mandate specific substantive outcomes in ways characteristic of earlier modes of government action".[40] In consequence, this confirms that sometimes more traditional regulation is preferable instead of optimized disclosure or sophisticated default rules.[41] Therefore, often "... an economic incentive or a mandate might be the best solution".[42]

2 The Failure of Mandated Disclosure: Analysis

2.1 Mandated Disclosure in Financial Market Law

Some thoughts and arguments developed and discussed by *Ben-Shahar* and *Schneider* (2011, 2014) already found resonance in the introduction. Their in-depth analysis of mandated disclosure (2011) starts with examples of the prevalent technique used to protect personal autonomy in modern society; after the

[36]Baisch (2016a), p. 226. In daily living nearly nobody reads boilerplate information, see Ben-Shahar and Schneider (2011), p. 671. In this context fits also the "accumulation problem" (described by Ben-Shahar and Schneider (2011), pp. 689–690): the vast amount of en masse disclosures in every day live is too overwhelming so discloses "*give up any inclination they may have had to devote their lives to disclosures*".

[37]Baisch and Weber (2015).

[38]Loewenstein G, Ubel P, Economics Behaving Badly, The New York Times, 14 July 2010, http://www.nytimes.com/2010/07/15/opinion/15loewenstein.html.

[39]Sunstein and Thaler 2003 and Camerer et al. (2003).

[40]Bubb and Pildes (2014), p. 1598.

[41]Sunstein (2013a), p. 56: Default rules "... identify the consequences if choosers do nothing. In part because of the power of inertia, default rules tend to stick."

[42]Sunstein (2013b), p. 1845.

summary of the use of mandated disclosures in part (1) and a literature review in part (2), part (3) analyses why mandated disclosures fail to focus on the involved protagonists and the systematic factors that impair lawmakers, disclosers, and disclosees;[43] part (4) lists some unintended consequences that might harm the disclosees. Based on this article the book "More Than You Wanted to Know" opens the critique to a wider audience; *Bar-Gill* summarises the book as follows: "*Ben-Shahar and Schneider argue that disclosure does not work and that it cannot be fixed. Lawmakers should, therefore, abandon this ineffective and, possibly, harmful regulatory approach and look elsewhere or . . . do nothing.*"[44]

While *Ben-Shahar* and *Schneider* discuss many examples from other areas like health, credit card overdrafts and *Miranda* warnings, this chapter is focused on investment decisions. Especially relevant for investment decisions is that when it comes to financial products consumers are placed at a significant informational disadvantage which cannot be solved by the "opportunity to read" principle.[45]

2.2 *Protagonists: Lawmakers, Disclosers and Disclosees*

2.2.1 Lawmakers: The Root of All Evil?

In principle, financial market lawmakers are aware of the central problem; the information asymmetry which makes investors vulnerable to be hoodwinked by their opponents. Mandated disclosure is at least part of the appropriate regulatory method to overcome this problem. However, it is challenging to decide what kind if disclosure is best suited and then articulate the standard of disclosure without getting pushed towards an excessive mandate.[46]

Disclosure resonates with two fundamental ideologies, the free-market principles and the autonomy principle.[47] However, neither caveat emptor as a disclaimer of warranties arising from the fact that disclosees have less information about the financial product they are purchasing, while the discloser has more information, is the right solution regarding financial products nor most of the people are sufficiently qualified to argue they would make better decisions for themselves than anyone can make for them. Therefore, lawmakers should resist the temptation to just introduce simple forms of mandated disclosure simply because this seems to be a cheap, easy

---

[43] Ben-Shahar and Schneider (2011), p. 665: "First, disclosers do not always provide, and disclosees do not always receive, information. Second, disclosees often do not read disclosed information, do not understand it when they read it, and do not use it even if they understand it. Third, mandated disclosure does not improve disclosees' decisions."

[44] Bar-Gill (2015), p. 75.

[45] Ben-Shahar and Schneider (2011), p. 657. At p. 659 it is truly stated that a "classic instance of mandated disclosure is the congeries of securities laws and regulations".

[46] See Ben-Shahar and Schneider (2011), p. 679, describing the situation of lawmakers.

[47] Ben-Shahar and Schneider (2011), p. 681.

and effective looking solution. Financial markets need a more sophisticated approach; by which overload effects can be avoided.[48]

2.2.2 Disclosers: Producers, Distributors and Advisors

Many of the failures related to the disclosures as described by *Ben-Shahar* and *Schneider* are absolutely relevant for the distribution of financial products:

- Data collection: the discloser must locate and assemble a lot of data which often are speculative and also monitor, update the disclosures and must hunt down changes; some information might even be too complex to assemble.[49]
- Data reception: ambiguity and confusion by discloses are hard to avoid, e.g. how to describe a risk when people's risk awareness varies a lot, numbers in general lead to similar puzzles and the way a fact is framed notoriously affects perceptions of it, because all information necessarily comes in some frame.[50]
- Problems rooted in the acceptance and resulting behavior of disclosers are easier to tackle, like over-disclosure in order to exacerbate the overload of disclosees. This can be identified when looking at the PRIIPs regulation: EU lawmakers distrusted disclosers and tried to dictate the way information is provided by specifying many details of disclosure forms and defining the precise data to be disclosed.[51]

2.2.3 Disclosee: Incapable, Innumerate and Biased

Undoubtly, "the success of mandated disclosures depends on how much better disclosees consequently make important, complex, and unfamiliar decisions."[52] Manyfold impediments impair the sufficient cognition even if information is provided in an optimised format. Some are routed in the way we retrieve and process information, others are just based on inertia and procrastination. Often the disclosees are unmotivated, affected by many biases and prone to unstable preferences. In today's world everyone is exposed to so many stimuli and impulses that a clear decision is needed to absorb selected information otherwise the informational content will not penetrate us efficiently.

If that task is mastered successfully the widespread illiteracy and innumeracy becomes the next sticking point.[53] In combination intelligence, experience, and at

48 Ben-Shahar and Schneider (2011), p. 687.
49 Ben-Shahar and Schneider (2011), pp. 695–696.
50 Ben-Shahar and Schneider (2011), pp. 696–698.
51 Ben-Shahar and Schneider (2011), pp. 698–702.
52 Ben-Shahar and Schneider (2011), pp. 704–705.
53 Ben-Shahar and Schneider (2011), pp. 711–716.

least a basic theoretical background (expertise) is required to come to the right conclusions, i.e. analyse and then decide in line with this analysis. In consequence, "*people avoid financial decisions, and when they do make a decision, they use less information than they need and could get*".[54] *Ben-Shahar* and *Schneider* conclude "*particularly when people are confused and need protection, knowledge is not intrinsically valued. People may want to know less, not more, and so they may find information a burden, not a privilege. They may begrudge the time and trouble it takes to learn and use the amount and kind of information disclosures provide. They may dislike reading contracts, manuals, warnings, notices, forms, charts, and instructions, or burrowing through endless data*".[55]

2.3 Interim Results

Before the European PRIIPs regulation is analysed the findings regarding disclosure are shortly summarized. Therein, criticism and opinions regarding *Ben-Shahar*'s and *Schneider*'s theory are also taken into consideration. Some arguments against mandated disclosure cannot stay undisputed, others are absolutely cogent; additionally, there are some possible improvements when implementing disclosure requirements.

One quite important defense is to argue that mandated disclosure is not a complete failure because it leads to certain positive outcomes; however, *Ben-Shahar* and *Schneider* name this a "*peripheral defense*".[56] Another important effect of disclosure is related to professional investors utilising, processing and trading on that information. From *Ben Shahar*'s and *Schneider*'s perspective this means to shift the goals of disclosure to indirectly achieved general benefits.[57]

It is important to reflect any of the detrimental effects that are conducive to the failure of mandated disclosure when designing "smarter" disclosure requirements. Major improvements are possible when the needs of the disclosee is the central focus when designing disclosure requirements; facilitated perception and reduced time demands are the main success factors. *Bar-Gill* argues that simplification using "cores" (one-dimensional summary of one or more product features) may be the key to effective disclosure.[58] Scores provide two main benefits, they facilitate comparison and minimise the overload problem. Smart (behaviourally informed) disclosure could be an ideal regulatory solution because it preserves consumer

[54]Ben-Shahar and Schneider (2011), p. 728.

[55]Ben-Shahar and Schneider (2011), p. 729.

[56]Ben-Shahar and Schneider (2015), p. 84.

[57]Ben-Shahar and Schneider (2015), p. 84.

[58]Bar-Gill (2015), p. 76.

choice, trusts in market mechanisms and is less invasive and cheaper than alternatives like mandatory terms or minimum standards.[59]

Due to the fact that cost and benefits of disclosure are hard to measure exactly, the contention[60] "*that mandated disclosure must overcome so many barriers that its benefits rarely justify its costs*" can be called into question. *Ben Shahar*'s and *Schneider*'s "*jeremiad occasionally paints with too broad a brush*" and ignores that some applications help consumers e.g. food labeling.[61] Therefore, it could be concluded that the regulation should combine smart disclosure with mandatory provisions standardizing the appearance of disclosure. Additionally, "big data" (technological innovations in the field of data collection and processing) not only creates some legitimate fears but could also have a valuable impact on the functioning of pre-contractual disclosures as a means of consumer protection. In general, disclosure can be positively affected from the trend towards more personalisation.[62] Similar to the methods used by the tech giants to present us with personalised advertisements the data gathered by financial intermediaries could be used to individualise disclosure.

3 PRIIP

3.1 Concept

One of the latest creations of Europe's financial markets policy makers is the PRIIP-KID[63] which intends to improve the quality and comparability of mandated disclosure provided to retail investors in the EU.[64] The key element is a mandatory disclosure document, named "Key Information Document". Since January 2018, the KID provides the nature of the product, the risks including performance scenarios, all initial, ongoing and exit costs and certain other information on no more than three pages; the KID has to be supplied to retail consumers before they decide to invest in a financial product.[65] Similar provisions are contained in other directives

---

[59]Marotta-Wurgler (2015), p. 63.

[60]Ben-Shahar and Schneider (2015), p. 84.

[61]Radin (2015), p. 53.

[62]Busch (2016), pp. 235–237.

[63]PRIIP: Packaged retail investment and insurance-based investment products; KID: Key Information Document. After a 1 year delay the PRIIPs regulation (Regulation (EU) 1286/2014 of 26 November 2014 on key information documents for packaged retail and insurance-based investment products [PRIIPs], OJ L 352/1-23, *9.12.2014*) is into force since January 2018.

[64]The regulation covers structured deposits, structured products, insurance products with an investment element (but not pension products) and funds.

[65]See also continuative (in German) Baisch (2016b) and Dittschar (2018).

(UCITS[66] and retail AIF[67]) as basis for national law provisions regarding the UCITS-KIID (Undertakings for Collective Investment in Transferable Securities, Key Investor Information Document). The intention was that the PRIIP-KID replaces the UCITS-KIID starting from 2020, however, due to the delayed start and the ongoing review of the PRIIP regulation this might be postponed.[68]

Rectical (1) of the PRIIPs regulation states:

> Existing disclosures to retail investors for such PRIIPs are uncoordinated and often do not help retail investors to compare different products, or understand their features. Consequently, retail investors have often made investments without understanding the associated risks and costs and have, on occasion, suffered unforeseen losses.

The idea was to establish uniform rules on transparency at Union level to prevent national divergences by specifying a common standard for key information documents in a uniform fashion based on a harmonised format and content. Given difficulties many retail investors have in understanding specialist financial terminology, information on PRIIPs must be accurate, fair, clear and not misleading while particular attention is paid to the vocabulary and style of writing used in the document. In Rectical 15 of the PRIIP regulation concerns are addressed that there is a risk that retail investors will not use the KID; therefore, to allow informed investment the information must be short and concise containing only key information regarding (i) the nature and features of the product, (ii) whether it is possible to lose capital, (iii) the costs (all costs/fees charged by the manufacturers and intermediaries in the investment chain) and risk profile of the product and (iv) relevant performance information. Additionally, "not simple" products must include a *comprehension alert* to the investor, which reads: "*You are about to purchase a product that is not simple and may be difficult to understand.*"[69]

---

[66] UCITS: Undertakings for Collective Investment in Transferable Securities; The original UCITS Directive 85/611/EEC was adopted in 1985 and is a regulatory framework of the European Commission that creates a harmonised regime throughout Europe for the management and sale of mutual funds. Directives 2001/107/EC and 2001/108/EC (UCITS III) broadened the investment spectrum of UCITS funds and relaxed restrictions for index funds. Now in force is UCITS IV (Directive 2009/65/EC, of 13 July 2009 on the coordination of laws, regulations and administrative provisions relating to undertakings for collective investment in transferable securities [UCITS] OJ L 302/32–96, 17.11.2009) amended by UCITS V (Directive 2014/91/EU, Directive 2014/91/EU of 23 July 2014 amending Directive 2009/65/EC as regards depositary functions, remuneration policies and sanctions, OJ L 257/186–213, 28.8.2014) which went into force in March 2016.

[67] AIFMD: The Alternative Investment Fund Managers Directive: Directive 2011/61/EU of 8 June 2011 on Alternative Investment Fund Managers and amending Directives 2003/41/EC and 2009/65/EC and Regulations (EC) No 1060/2009 and (EU) No 1095/2010, OJ L 174/1–73, 1.7.2011.

[68] Interestingly and confusingly enough, the calculation methodology as well as the presentation of risk, performance and cost is different; therefore, as of 1 January 2020, retail funds would have to provide simultaneously a UCITS-KIID and PRIIP-KID.

[69] PRIIPs regulation, rectical (18): "A product should be regarded as not being simple and as being difficult to understand in particular if it invests in underlying assets in which retail investors do not commonly invest, if it uses a number of different mechanisms to calculate the final return of the investment, creating a greater risk of misunderstanding on the part of the retail investor or if the

Since the adoption of the MiFID II/MiFIR-package[70] there is further regulation in place also addressing aspects of communication with clients.[71] While MiFID II at level 1 (accompanied by level 2 implementing directives and level 3 regulatory as well as implementing technical standards) focuses on suitability and conflicts of interests, the PRIIP regulation just addresses the KID.

3.2 *Consumer Testing Study*

The standardised format of the KID (allowing investors to directly compare different products), the presentation and the information content give due consideration to consumer behaviour and capabilities thereby maximizing the understanding and subsequent use of information in the decision-making process. In developing this standard, existing and ongoing research into consumer behaviour, including results from testing the effectiveness of different ways of presenting information to consumers, was taken into account.[72]

An extensive study tested various forms of presentation within a KID. The study identified some specific areas, which had caused confusion among participants. These were the:[73]

- understanding of capital guarantees: the concept of capital guarantees in combination with the possibility that the guarantees fails or is limited;
- understanding the likelihood of performance scenarios: grasping the likelihoods correctly when performance scenarios are shown, independently whether information on how probable they are is included or not;
- understanding that the cost figures were not exact: only a minority of participants understood that the costs shown might vary;
- understanding the cost figures in general: poor performance on the questions relating to cost (comparing overall costs and cost components between products, identifying the different cost components and how they apply, and estimating costs where there is an early exit).

investment's pay-off takes advantage of retail investor's behavioural biases, such as a teaser rate followed by a much higher floating conditional rate, or an iterative formula."

[70]MiFID: Markets in Financial Instruments Directive; MiFIR: Markets in Financial Instruments Regulation.

[71]According to Art. 24 (4) (b) MiFID II the information to be provided to client shall include guidance on and warnings of the risks associated with investments in financial instruments or in respect of particular investment strategies.

[72]London Economics, Consumer Testing Study of the Possible New Format and Content for Retail Disclosures of Packaged Retail and Insurance-based Investment Products, MARKT/2014/060/G for the Implementation of the Framework, Final Report, 2015; https://ec.europa.eu/info/sites/info/files/consumer-testing-study-2015_en.pdf.

[73]London Economics 2015, p. xiv.

3.3 Discussing the Details

The European Supervisory Authorities (ESAs)[74] were mandated by the PRIIPs Regulation to develop Regulatory Technical Standards (RTS) on the content and presentation of the KID to ensure consumer-friendly information about investment products.[75] The ESAs then consulted intensively on the details laid out in the RTS with regard to the presentation and the content of the KID, the standardised format of the KID, the methodology underpinning the presentation of risk and reward and the calculation of costs, as well as the conditions and the minimum frequency for reviewing the information contained in KID.

The process developing the technically standards not only exemplifies many of the discussed failures of mandated disclosure but also shows potential ways to solve them. With the ESA's Discussion Paper (ESA-DP)[76] the process was launched; the paper highlights many issues that need to be addressed in order to balance the desire for conciseness and simplicity while facing the complexity of investment product's risks and costs. An important task is to allow for comparability. Most of the document is dedicated to the especially tricky areas of risk and return disclosure and costs disclosure, which become even more difficult for products that offer multiple options and/or are linked to insurance contracts. For the presentation of risk and return the ESA-DP discusses general types or ways of presenting information, considered in abstract rather than specific terms. Various concrete examples from different European countries are shown to illustrate visual elements. A Technical Discussion Paper[77] followed to provide stakeholders with an opportunity to comment on certain specific technical areas related to risk, performance and cost information. Then at the end of 2015 the ESAs invited the stakeholders to comment on the draft RTS regulating the presentation and content of the KID, methodologies for calculating risks and rewards, rules around the review, revision and republication of the KID and conditions for providing the KID in good time.[78] In March 2016 the

[74]ESAs (European Supervisory Authorities): European Banking Authority (EBA), European Insurance and Occupational Pensions Authority (EIOPA), and European Securities and Markets Authority (ESMA).

[75]See for details https://eba.europa.eu/regulation-and-policy/consumer-protection-and-financial-innovation/regulatory-technical-standards-on-the-content-and-presentation-of-the-kids-for-priips/-/regulatory-activity/discussion-paper.

[76]Discussion Paper of the Joint Committee of European Supervisory Authorities (JC ESAs), Key Information Documents for Packaged Retail and Insurance-based Investment Products (PRIIPs), 17 November 2014 (JC/DP/2014/02); https://eba.europa.eu/documents/10180/899036/JC+DP+2014+02+-+PRIIPS+Discussion+Paper.pdf.

[77]JC-ESAs, Technical Discussion Paper, Risk, Performance Scenarios and Cost Disclosures in Key Information Documents for Packaged Retail and Insurance-based Investment Products (PRIIPs), 23 June 2015 (JC DP 2015 01); https://esas-joint-committee.europa.eu/Publications/Consultations/JC DP 2015 01.pdf.

[78]JC-ESAs, Joint Consultation Paper, PRIIPs Key Information Documents, Draft regulatory technical standards with regard to presentation, content, review and provision of the key information document, including the methodologies underpinning the risk, reward and costs information in

final draft was published.[79] The proposed Delegated Regulation was adopted by the Commission in June 2016; however, in September 2016, the European Parliament objected to it. The finally adopted Delegated Regulation contains some amendments by the Commission.[80]

The ESA's address "consumer behaviour" as one of the issues for retail investors and "in order for the KID to be easy to use by the retail investor", they envisage that "the KID should have a clear behavioral purpose for the retail investor":[81]

> Given this, a traditional approach to disclosures focused solely on information and with little regard to its presentation, is in being superseded in policy making by an approach that is more informed by insights into consumer behaviours. For instance, the framing of information can be considered, so as to counter cognitive biases which may distort perceptions and provide information in a way that is both simple to understand but also salient for the consumer (i.e. capable of drawing the consumers' attention and appearing important for the decision to be made). The PRIIPs Regulation reflects these considerations already at 'level one'.

The EU confirmed this approach in 2015:[82]

> Consumers need information that is easily understandable. Information should be clear and concentrate on the elements that allow the consumer fully to understand a product; it should also take consumer behaviour into account. Financial education can help, but when consumers purchase a product they need to know how much they are being charged, by whom and how they are benefiting from it. They need to be able to compare costs and benefits to make an effective choice.

From this it should be considered that the financial industry also uses behavioural insights to promote their products.[83] The potential manipulation must also be

accordance with Regulation (EU) 1286/2014 of the European Parliament and of the Council, 11 November 2015 (JC 2015 073); https://www.eba.europa.eu/documents/10180/1268855/JC+2015+073+CP+PRIIPs+Key+Information+Documents.pdf.

[79]Final draft regulatory technical standards with regard to presentation, content, review and provision of the key information document, including the methodologies underpinning the risk, reward and costs information in accordance with Regulation (EU) No 1286/2014 of the European Parliament and of the Council, 31 March 2016 (JC 2016 21); https://www.esma.europa.eu/sites/default/files/library/jc_2016_21_final_draft_rts_priips_kid_report.pdf.

[80]Commission Delegated Regulation 2017/653 of 8 March 2017 supplementing Regulation (EU) No 1286/2014 on key information documents for packaged retail and insurance-based investment products (PRIIPs) by laying down regulatory technical standards with regard to the presentation, content, review and revision of key information documents and the conditions for fulfilling the requirement to provide such documents (C/2017/1473), *OJ L 100/1-52, 12.4.2017.*

[81]ESA-DP (fn. 76), pp. 17–18; with reference to Sunstein (2011).

[82]European Commission, Green Paper on retail financial services: Better products, more choice, and greater opportunities for consumers and businesses, Brussels, 10.12.2015 COM(2015) 630 final; https://ec.europa.eu/transparency/regdoc/rep/1/2015/EN/1-2015-630-EN-F1-1.PDF.

[83]Sousa Lourenço et al. (2016), p. 12: in the field of financial services behavioural insights "had often been used by providers in their sales strategies (e.g. using framing to emphasise certain features of products), but are now also being used by regulators to improve financial consumer protection (e.g. simplification and standardisation of product information to reduce the negative impact of framing and decrease information overload)".

monitored by the regulatory authority.[84] This thread is not limited to unsophisticated investors, referring to *Kahnemans*'s two way of thinking and "*in line with the insights of the behavioural literature, (...) high financial 'literate' individuals are not necessarily free of inclination towards behavioural biases*".[85] And similar to *Ben Shahar*'s and *Schneider*'s perspective the EIOPA concluded:[86] "*Whereas it is assumed that information leads to understanding, to the willingness to act and subsequently to appropriate actions, this appears most often not the case.*"

3.4 Key Information Document

The RTS specify the presentation and content of a KID; all the different sections of a KID are addressed like the underlying methodologies required for obtaining and calculating the figures in relation to risks, rewards and costs. Next to the mandatory template with details of the layout that must be followed also certain texts are mandatory (Annex I). Of special interest are three features: (i) the summary risk indicator (SRI), the performance scenarios and (iii) the presentation of costs.

3.4.1 Summary Risk Indicator

The key element of the risk and reward section of a KID is the SRI that comprises of seven classes which are to be presented within a given format and calculated and presented according to Annex II and III (an example of this can be seen in Fig. 1 below). Next to the market risk also credit risk and liquidity risk must be included. The market risk calculation is based on the annualised volatility corresponding to the value-at-risk (VaR) at a confidence level of 97.5% over the stated recommended holding period;[87] therefore a mandated formula to calculate the level of risk must be applied.

After a short description of the product the consumer will see the question *"What are the risks and what could I get in return?"*. Subsequently, the SRI itself, the most eye-catching element on the front page of a KID, indicates the risks involved. However, the general problem of the calculations based on VaR (or similar statistical methods) lies in the fact that it is based on the measurement of past volatility. This

[84] Sunstein (2016), p. 243: "In the context of consumer financial products, various forms of manipulation are a widespread problem." See also Bar-Gill (2012) and Akerlof and Shiller (2015).

[85] Gentile et al. (2015), p. 10.

[86] EIOPA (2013) Good practices on information provision for DC schemes - Enabling occupational DC scheme members to plan for retirement, 24 January 2013 (EIOPA_BoS_13/010), p. 8.; https://eiopa.europa.eu/publications/reports/report_good_practices_info_for_dc_schemes.pdf.

[87] VaR measures the risk of loss for investments by estimating how much an investment might lose (e.g. at given probability level of 97.5%) under normal market conditions in a often relatively short time period.

PRIIP manufacturers shall use the format below for the presentation of the SRI in the key information document. The relevant number shall be highlighted as shown depending on the SRI for the PRIIP.

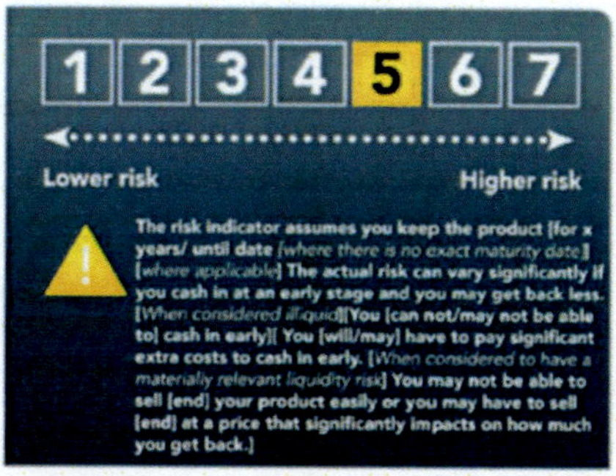

Fig. 1 Presentation of summary risk indicator (SRI). Source: ESMA, Final Draft Regulatory Standards, JC 2016 21, Annex III

Investment of 10,000 GBP				
Scenarios		1 year	4 years	30/08/2024
Stress scenario	What you might get back after costs	7,171	6,047	5,907
	Average return each year	-28.31%	-9.88%	-6.16%
Unfavourable scenario	What you might get back after costs	11,126	11,250	11,250
	Average return each year	11.26%	5.79%	5.79%
Moderate scenario	What you might get back after costs	11,126	11,250	11,250
	Average return each year	11.26%	5.79%	5.79%
Favourable scenario	What you might get back after costs	11,366	11,563	11,563
	Average return each year	13.67%	5.89%	5.89%

Fig. 2 Presentation of scenarios

means that this calculation only allows a comparison of the historic volatility which does not predict the future performance. Therefore, the SRI could be harmful to investors because it is not a summary of potential risks but a projection of past performance into the unknown future.

3.4.2 Performannce Scenarios

The future is predicted based on the historical volatility. Annex IV and V give a detailed outline on the calculation methodology and how the SRI is to be presented. Under this presentation requirement four performance scenarios are mandatory to show a range of possible returns: (a) a favourable scenario; (b) a moderate scenario; (c) an unfavourable scenario; (d) a stress scenario. The stress scenario includes further negative impacts not covered in the unfavourable scenario. The scenarios are derived from a model, which simulates possible outcomes based on the returns or prices, and fluctuations in those returns only over the previous 5 years. The results are to be presented in tables, showing the projected performance for different time periods based on the uncertain assumptions underlying the four scenarios (See Fig. 2).

It is a truism that the past performance of an investment is no guide to the future. Historical figures can provide some useful context, especially the volatility in comparison to other products; however, retail investors should not just rely on the past. The design approach of the KID tends attribute too much importance to this aspect by using a table of scenarios based on historical figures. Combined with the mandatory text *"What you might get back after costs"* a consumer might develop an overoptimistic expectation of what they might receive in the future. Especially, if the underlying date relies on periods of good market performance compared to the lows experienced due to the financial crisis the scenarios. Additionally, the fact that the future performance scenarios are based on historic performance data is not made sufficiently clear to the consumer in the KID.

3.4.3 Presentation of Costs

The requirements regarding the presentation of costs, the figures that must be calculated and the format to be used are described in Annex VI and VII. The cost figures present the accumulation of the costs in monetary and percentage terms in relation to a certain period as well as breakdown of these costs. By making costs comparable the compulsory methodology to disclose costs has some weaknesses. The determination of costs ex-ante combined with market movements which occur after the decision to deal has been made, can lead to a negative cost figure thereby hiding the actual trading costs.[88] By spreading the costs of entering, holding and exiting a product across the recommended holding period instead of showing the costs explicitly, fees can be disguised. The same might be true when transaction costs are mixed up with and distribution charges. Deposit charges by the bank are missing anyway on the KID.

3.5 Experiences with the KID

The good intentions of the regulator by setting technical standards tends to get lost due to the complexity of the addressed problem and finally leads to a very complicated practical application. Furthermore, the historical dimension can lead to a flawed presentation and may mislead consumers. Another problem is that for the different methodologies to calculate the SRI a product or at least its underlying need to have an adequate performance history—which is not possible for new products. Another restriction is the space provided to describe other main risks that are not included in the SRI, which is limited to 200 characters. In general, future performance information should not come without a prominent warning stating that such

[88]The calculated transaction costs include the bid-offer spread and commission costs, but the actual settlement may be closed at price on the advantageous end of the spread, resulting in negative costs.

forecasts are not reliable indicators of future performance. There is also the potential that consumers are misled by the so-called "moderate" scenario because the wording gives the impression that this one is the most probable, which it is absolutely not.

Regarding the uses of disclosure as a behaviourally informed regulatory tool *Sunstein*'s postulates: [89]

> It is important to distinguish between summary disclosure, often provided at the point of purchase, and full disclosure, typically provided on the Internet. A central point is that disclosure policies should be based on an understanding of how people process information.

Therefore, the criticism of some KID features comes as no surprise.

The KID as a means of summary disclosure concentrates on the important elements for the evaluation of financial products: the risk and the cost. Since the first introduction of MiFID the efforts in Europe foster a clear disclosure of any kind of administrative cost in connection with the purchase of an investment product.[90] The PRIIPs regulation together with the relevant RTS provide an answer on how risk and return should be presented. *Sunstein* stresses the importance of "*plain language, clarity, and simplicity*",[91] based on that idea a KID tries to make investment decision easier for the average household. However, when one critically scrutinises this form of mandated disclosure it might come partially true that "*accurate disclosure of information may be ineffective if the information is too abstract, vague, detailed, complex, poorly framed, or overwhelming to be useful*".[92]

First of all the three-page A4 standard format KID can only help a consumer who is willing to read and process the provided information to understand and compare investment products if they have a correct understanding of the total costs involved and are able to critically analyse the risk-reward profile.. Undoubtedly, the KID optimises the documentation for financial products sold to retail investors. However, its practical analysis reveals that there might be still a certain fraction of investors that is not capable of understanding the information presented in a KID.[93]

> Traditional failures are often addressed by information provision or disclosure: to mitigate asymmetric information, to reduce search costs and limit market power, (...). But mandated information provision may be an ineffective remedy if consumers either do not understand the information or believe that it is not relevant to their decision making. For example, if consumers mistakenly believe that they will pay their credit bill on time every month, clear and transparent disclosure of late fees and interest rates may not change behavior because consumers deem the information irrelevant at the time they make a purchase [94]

---

[89] Sunstein (2014), p. 727.

[90] See Article 33 of the level 2 MiFID-ID (MiFID Implementing Directive, Commission Directive 2006/73/EC of 10 August 2006 implementing Directive 2004/39/EC of the European Parliament and of the Council as regards organisational requirements and operating conditions for investment firms and defined terms for the purposes of that Directive, 2.9.2006, OJ L 241/26–58) regarding the obligation to inform clients about costs.

[91] Sunstein (2014), p. 728.

[92] Sunstein (2014), p. 729.

[93] Walther (2015), p. 145.

[94] Campbell et al. (2011), p. 95.

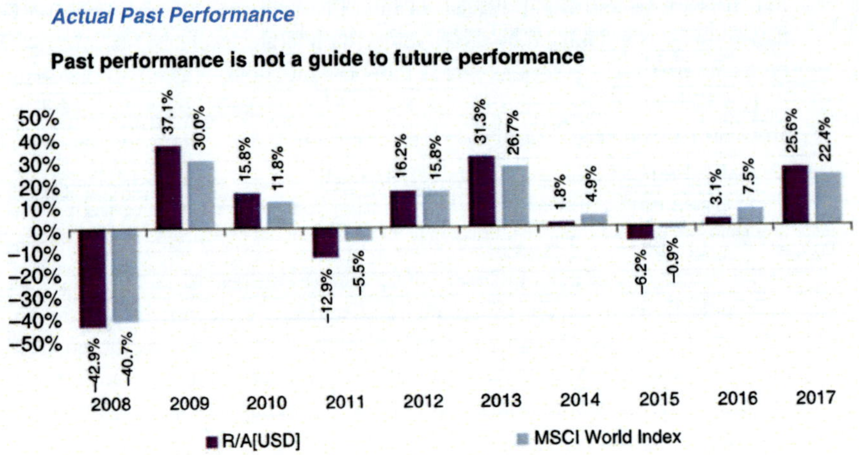

Fig. 3 Information about past Performance (R/A = anonymized UCICS share class). Source: ESMA, Joint Consultation Paper concerning amendments to the PRIIPs KID, JC 2018 60, p. 17

Therefore, scepticism remains from two sides: (i) will a retail investor really process that information? and (ii) is the provided information flawed by its historical context?

3.6 *Revision of the PRIIPs KID*

At the end of 2018 the ESAs consulted the industry by publishing a Joint Consultation Paper concerning amendments to the PRIIPs KID and seeking feedback also from consumers on improved cost and risk disclosures required within a KID.[95] Particularly the positive performance of many asset classes within the currently applicable 5 year period which is relevant for the mandatory calculations within the KID resulted in feedback. Concerns were raised that these performance scenarios lead to inappropriate expectations. To resolve this, it is proposed to increase the time frame to 10 years. However, this extension of the historical period will only reduce the overall positive performance rating if the data also includes the performance during the financial crisis. Therefore, in the near future the impact may again become invisible. Furthermore, as market cycles can last for more than 10 years this modification to the methodology will not lead to more reliable outcomes. Only the highlighting of the stress scenario may dampen exaggerated expectations (Fig. 3).

[95]European Supervisory Authorities (ESAs), Joint Consultation Paper concerning amendments to the PRIIPs KID, Draft amendments to Commission Delegated Regulation (EU) 2017/653 of 8 March 2017 on key information documents (KID) for packaged retail and insurance-based investment products (PRIIPs), 8 November 2018 (JC 2018 60); https://eiopa.europa.eu/Publications/Consultations/Joint%20Consultation%20Paper%20on%20targeted%20amendments.pdf.

The proposed amendments are aimed at enhancing the user-friendliness of the KID by including optimised visualisations, a simplification of the performance scenarios as well as new calculation methodologies for performance scenarios, market risk measures, and the holding period. One of the major changes is the implementation of clearly stated information on past performance in the KID whenever it is available and not just the adaption of past figures in the scenarios. Combined with a more prominent statement that the scenarios are based on simulations[96] the narrative explanations will be shortened and key messages highlighted in bold.

The planned measures could support a better understanding of the KID performance scenarios for retail investors. Additional narrative explaining that the scenarios are based on simulations and the explicitly stated fact that the potential future performance cannot be predicted accurately can only ensure a better understanding when the wording is actually read and understood. It is not unlikely that those words share the same fate as that of small print. The optimised illustration of the performance scenarios instead of a table of four is convincing;[97] however, the real picture might look less appealing when focusing on the stressed scenario. This measure in particular has the potential to improve the consumer's understanding of possible outcomes by avoiding the misleading term "moderate scenario". During 2019 the ESAs intended to submit the revised RTS to the European Commission for endorsement together with a final report on the received feedback. It was planned that the amendments would apply from 1 January 2020. However, based on the feedback received, the ESAs decided to not propose targeted amendments at this stage and to initiate a more comprehensive revision of the PRIIPs Delegated Regulation during 2019.[98] In addition, the ESAs issued a Supervisory Statement[99] according to Article 29(2) of the ESAs' Regulations as a convergence tool to promote common supervisory approaches and practices regarding the performance scenarios to promote consistency. Aiming to improve the protection of investors in view of the risk that performance scenarios may mislead the expectations of investors about the possible returns they might receive. The ESAs recommend PRIIP manufacturers include a warning in the KID to raise the awareness regarding the limitations of the figures provided in the performance scenarios (Fig. 4).

---

[96]Heading above the table: Simulated future performance, Market developments in the future cannot be accurately predicted. These scenarios are only an indication of the range of possible returns.

[97]See De Goeij et al. (2014) and Cox et al. (2018).

[98]*JC-ESAs*, Final Report following joint consultation paper concerning amendments to the PRIIPs KID, 8. Februar 2019; https://www.esma.europa.eu/press-news/esma-news/esas-publish-recommendations-changes-priips-key-information-document.

[99]JC-ESAs, Joint ESA supervisory statement concerning the performance scenarios in the PRIIPs KID, 8 February2019 (JC 2019 6.3); https://eiopa.europa.eu/Publications/Statements/2019-02-08%20PRIIPs_KID_Supervisory_Statement_Performance_Scenarios%20%28JC%202019%206.3%29.pdf.

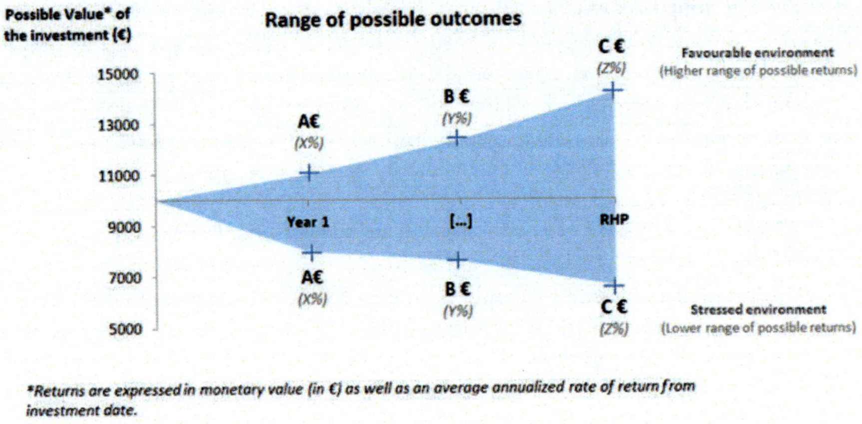

Fig. 4 Information about the range of possible outcome

4 Further Pillars of Investor Protection

4.1 POS Regulation

Disclosure regulation addresses just one feature within the process of investment decisions. The KID with all its weaknesses will only influence a decision when it becomes a part of the decision process. Thereby, the procedures at the point of sale (POS) have a major impact. This is in line with international political ideas where these issues also were picked up. In the *OECD G20 High-Level Principles on Financial Consumer Protection* the principle *Disclosure and Transparency* is stressed in section 4; the following formulation exemplifies that this principle is clearly understood in a comprehensive manner:[100]

> Financial services providers and authorised agents should provide consumers with key information that informs the consumer of the fundamental benefits, risks and terms of the product. They should also provide information on conflicts of interest associated with the authorised agent through which the product is sold.

Addressing risks it stated:

> The provision of advice should be as objective as possible and should in general be based on the consumer's profile considering the complexity of the product, the risks associated with it as well as the customer's financial objectives, knowledge, capabilities and experience. Consumers should be made aware of the importance of providing financial services providers with relevant, accurate and available information.

[100]OECD G20 High-Level Principles on Financial Consumer Protection, October 2011, http://www.oecd.org/regreform/liberalisationandcompetitioninterventioninregulatedsectors/48892010.pdf.

In addition to disclosure, rules to address conflicts of interest (e.g. incentives for the advisor), to treat the customer fairly (*Code of Conduct*) and the requirement to recommend only investments, which are suitable for the client, must be in place.[101] Advice is not independent as long as retrocessions and similar payments from product producers towards investment advisors or portfolio managers influence the process.[102] The problematic field of inducements, motivating bankers to create and sell products, which are not in the best interest of their clients, is addressed in the Europe Union by provisions within MiFID.[103]

The mandatory suitability or appropriateness tests[104] prior to any investment advice combined with an on-going assessment of the suitability of the recommended financial instruments especially foster investor protection.[105] These tests not only analyse the individual situation of the customer but also embrace loss-aversion and attitude towards risk features. Investors expect predictable returns while they hate losses. However, often the downside-potential of an investment is not sufficiently clarified to the customer. An average investor accepts to surrender part of the up-side potential in combination with a cap of potential losses. Thereby it is important to focus on the individual risk attitude, which really matters, and not just on the pure risk absorbing capacity.[106]

The MiFID I already provided for such tests. Assessing investment suitability addresses diverging consumer experience, heterogeneous personal investment objectives as well as individually varying risk-capabilities and risk-tolerances. The assessment of suitability determines on an individual basis, whether the customers have not only the necessary expertise to invest in a specific financial instrument, but also whether they understand it and are willing to take the associated risks; additionally, all of that has to accord with the individual financial status and investment objectives.[107] In consequence, the KID is in an advisory environment just a tool within a process.[108]

---

[101] See Schwarcz (2016), p. 1462 discussing "*supplemental protections*".

[102] Baisch and Weber (2015), p. 161 and pp. 171–172.

[103] Art. 24 MiFID II.

[104] While suitability contains a link to present as well as future aspects, appropriateness mainly reflects the past. These tests are realising the general obligation to act fairly, honestly and professionally and in accordance with the best interests of the client—previously known as fiduciary duty.

[105] IOSCO, Suitability Requirements With Respect To the Distribution of Complex Financial Products Final Report, January 2013, Principle 5.

[106] Baisch and Weber (2015), pp. 172–174 and pp. 182–187.

[107] According to Rapp (1998), p. 212, "*the most common characterization offered is that suitability is an amorphous concept, with no accepted definition, and bereft of case law guidance*".

[108] See Burn (2010), p. 167: "... it must be understood that short-form disclosure can never contain sufficient information to enable investors to take an investment decision. Such decisions require fulsome disclosure".

4.2 Product Governance

The MiFID II system (Art. 24 (4)-(5) MiFID II) of investor protection is primarily based on mandatory disclosure, however, the product governance regime (Arts. 16 (3) and 24 (2) MiFID II) reflects some limits of disclosure.[109] MiFID II not only respects the limits of disclosure and intends to make disclosed information more effective by simplifying, standardising and better visualising the provision of information,[110] but also there are additional requirements to improve the investor protection.

Product oversight and governance (POG) or "Product governance", for short, promotes a responsible and sustainable manufacturing and distribution process for financial products geared towards clients' interests. The POG rules cover the entire life cycle of a financial product and widen the regulatory scope. Regulatory activities used to address just the financial services and the distribution process, and with POG also the product itself and its entire life cycle, is affected. Now a product approval procedure accompanies the manufacturing process to ensure that a product is compatible with the interests and needs of the potential clients. Therefore, a target market has to be defined looking at the client's needs and characteristics.

5 New Challenges

5.1 Robo Advice

Robo advice—as part of the FinTech evolution—can be defined as the automated provision of financial advice without direct human intervention during the process of investing.[111] In principle, a fully automated investment platform offering internet-based advisory services provides cheap and convenient assistance for consumers. However, it all depends on the programmed features of the software, which uses algorithms to create investment recommendations.[112]

On some of these platforms the client on-boarding process is quite cumbersome in order to ensure compliance with the regulatory framework. Acquiring the necessary knowledge to assess the individual risk profile needs a lot of information, therefore, many questions and ticked boxes are required at the start of robo advice. Afterwards a portfolio mix consisting of various *Exchange Traded Funds* (ETF)[113] secure diversification and a low cost structure is presented/established/suggested.

---

[109] Brenncke (2018), p. 862.

[110] Brenncke (2018), p. 863.

[111] See regarding the FinTech regulatory challenges Weber and Baisch (2018).

[112] See OECD (2017).

[113] ETFs are funds which are similar to mutual funds but trade like stocks; an ETF tracks a stock index, commodities, bonds or a basket of assets.

The models and algorithms of a robo advisor are based on modern portfolio theory[114] and follow a passive investment approach. Therefore, a robo-advised portfolio is prone to market fluctuations.

The growing volumes of ETF investment, additionally boosted by robo advisors, is cause for concern as potential bubbles could get reinforced and the reduced volume of actively managed assets does not foster the processing of information.[115] An additional concern is based on the design of synthetic ETFs, which are common in Europe and Asia. Such ETFs also replicate the performance of an underlying index but are just using derivatives and swaps instead of the real physical securities. Tracking an index without owning any physical securities could create additional negative effects in a crisis due to counterparty risks.

Robo advice causes many of the typical regulatory challenges compared to traditional financial advice from human advisors. Generally, the existing legislation applies with regard to the application of the duty of care requirements, the prevention of conflicts of interest, safeguarding of transparency and disclosure and access to dispute resolution and redress. But there are additional challenges caused by the nature of investment platforms like the supervision of the algorithms instead of human behaviour.[116] The British FCA (Financial Conduct Authority) supervises theses development closely and insists on the fact that the rules on suitability of advice apply regardless of the medium through which a service is offered.[117]

5.2 *Tokenization of Assets*

Asset tokenisation combines real world assets with a token stored and administered on a distributed ledger (e.g. blockchain). Such a token can represent any type of a participation rights (from physical goods to traditional financial instruments) in form of decentralised protocol and is effectively a means to represent ownership of assets on a Distributed Ledger Technology application (DLT). The tokenisation of assets has the potential to become a long term trend because it could create beneficial outcomes for both market participants and investors.[118] Tokenisation is a method that converts rights to an asset into a digital token. Next to benefits, like reduced costs, some challenges have to be closely monitored. Especially, that new, often unregulated, service providers bear the risk of fraud and cyberattacks.

---

[114]Based on Fama (1970), Sharpe (1964), Tobin (1958) and Markowitz (1952).

[115]See for details Grill et al. (2018).

[116]For a good analysis see Betterfinance, Robo-Advice: European Individual Investors take a Look under the Hood, June 2018; https://betterfinance.eu/wp-content/uploads/Robo_Advice_Report_2018_-_for_website.pdf.

[117]FCA, Automated investment services - our expectations, May 2018; https://www.fca.org.uk/publications/multi-firm-reviews/automated-investment-services-our-expectations.

[118]See ESMA (2017).

There is the potential for a more efficient trading environment by reducing the limitations involved in the creation, buying, and selling of securities. However, the decentralized nature of a DLT application is not in line with the typical regulatory approach towards security trading and the supervision of market integrity.

As usual some of the potential shortcomings can be found in the details of the practical application. The proper functioning of tokenisation demands that the transfer of ownership via a DLT protocol guarantees that the asset itself changes ownership. Therefore, potential difficulties occur if the protocol is the not the only way to transfer ownership of an asset; e.g. an asset is destroyed in the real world but the connected token is still "alive". Trust in such a system is based on the guarantee that one receives the corresponding physical asset without high information and transaction costs to verify the authenticity of a token. However, a solution for this problem might be costly and inconvenient which can outweigh the potential savings promised by implementing a DLT solution.

6 Conclusion

The fundamental criticism challenging mandated disclosure being the "all-purpose weapon" of regulation is based on many justified arguments but securities regulation cannot live without regulation either. As discussed there are some good initiatives simplifying disclosure and additional elements complementing it, therefore, one should not throw the baby out with the bathwater. A lot has to do with the way we access the information and whether we value to invested time. Depending on the down-side potential of not reading the information the regulator is challenged to provide effective nudges to motivate the addressee.[119] Besides disclosure as a nudge itself, further nudges like default rules could work well in financial regulation.[120] By setting defaults or more paternalistic means of regulation—e.g. combining a warning plate with a barrier tape, or looking at financial products, adding sales restrictions[121] to warnings[122]—a certain level of investor protection can materialise.[123] When

[119]Baisch (2016a), p. 223; there are important challenges regarding the best way to implement nudges, they are part of the regulatory toolkit but not a panacea.

[120]Baisch (2016a), p. 223.

[121]The ESMA adopted product intervention measures on the provision of contracts for differences (CFDs) and binary options to retail investors; https://www.esma.europa.eu/press-news/esma-news/esma-adopts-final-product-intervention-measures-cfds-and-binary-options.

[122]The ESMA alerted investors of the high risk of losing all of their invested capital as ICOs are very risky and highly speculative investments; https://www.esma.europa.eu/press-news/esma-news/esma-highlights-ico-risks-investors-and-firms.

[123]Ulen (2014), 120: "Law – by taking due account of these predictable, routine deviations from rationality – can better influence behavior to realize both social goals and to help individuals better enhance their well-being."; see also Mitchell (2014), pp. 182–184, regarding the interaction of behavioural law and economics with legal norms.

setting defaults, the challenging question is to assess what would one do if fully informed and well advised.[124]

Whenever it is mandatory to provide information, the focus should not just lie on fairness and disclosure must not be seen as an end in itself; it is essential to incorporate efficiency aspects and evaluate its effectiveness. Therefore, it is important to keep an eye on the bigger picture and not just look at the consumer (not) reading the information.

> Providers of information may well overestimate the likely effect of the disclosure on consumers, partly because that disclosure seems so salient to providers. As a result of the telltale heart effect, information disclosure can have beneficial effects, even when it fails to change consumer behavior.[125]

Mandatory disclosure helps to promote the distribution of socially eligible and conducive information. Securities research and data verification would potentially be reduced in the absence of a mandatory disclosure system, because there is no incentive to procure or supply the information due to the involved costs while benefits might spread among free riders.[126] Mandatory disclosure systems reduce price dispersion and thereby enhance the allocative efficiency within the capital market.[127]

Regarding the necessary simplification of information behavioural research indicates the way:

> The results (...) show that consumers struggle with even the simplest of investment choices, and are likely to make errors by acting on misperceptions about risks and returns. We find that attempts to improve investment decision-making by explaining financial terms or attempting to de-bias consumers have little impact, but simplifying and standardising the way in which product information is disclosed leads to a significant increase in the optimality of consumers' investment decisions. In particular, reducing the amount of information presented, or standardising the information across products, appears to help with choices between similar products. Enabling product comparisons by providing pre-calculated and standardised information about the effective return of each product appears to somewhat mitigate potential biases.[128]

Therefore, the ingredients needed are transparency, comprehensibleness, and comparability; qualitative criteria are clarity and alignment with the needs of the addressee.[129] Typical patterns in decision making include the use of heuristics and

---

[124]Campbell et al. (2011), p. 95.

[125]See Loewenstein et al. (2014), p. 414; the industry response to disclosure laws may have additional effects: e.g. forcing a fast-food restaurant to post calorie information may have little effect on consumer purchases but it may nonetheless spur the chain to begin offering healthier alternatives because the issue becomes more salient to them. Forcing the financial industry to post risks and cost might have a similar resonance.

[126]Loewenstein et al. (2014), p. 396.

[127]Coffee (1984), p. 751.

[128]Chater et al. (2010), pp. 19–20.

[129]See Oehler and Wendt (2017).

various deviations in conflict with the rational choice assumption.[130] The regulator must be aware that consumers are often neither competent nor motivated to incorporate all available information in the decision making process.[131]

In addition and as always: better education can help. However, holding retail investors responsible, often called *empowerment*, in combination with the imposition of obligations as self-responsible financial citizens will not transform the majority. Therefore, an approach, which looks at retail investors as consumers is more realistic.[132]

Acknowledgement This contribution was written within the University Research Priority Program *Regulation of Financial Markets* from the University of Zurich.

References

Akerlof GA, Shiller RJ (2015) Phishing for phools the economics of manipulation and deception. Princeton University Press, Princeton

Avgouleas E (2009) The global financial crisis and the disclosure paradigm in European financial regulation: the case for reform. Eur Company Financ Law Rev 6:440–475

Baisch R (2016a) Nudging – information, choice architecture and beyond – theory and applications in financial markets law. In: Mathis K, Tor A (eds) Nudging – possibilities, limitations and applications in European law and economics. Springer, Dordrecht, pp 217–246

Baisch R (2016b) Basisinformationsblatt: Gute Produktinformation oder "Bett des Prokrustes"? In: Grosz M, Grünewald S (eds) Recht und Wandel - Festschrift für Rolf H. Weber. Schulthess, Zürich, pp 295–324

Baisch R, Weber RH (2015) Investment suitability requirements in the light of behavioural findings - challenges for a legal framework coping with ambiguous risk perception. In: Mathis K (ed) European perspectives on behavioural law and economics. Springer, Dordrecht, pp 159–192

Bar-Gill O (2012) Seduction by contract - law, economics, and psychology in consumer markets. Oxford University Press, Oxford

Bar-Gill O (2015) Defending (smart) disclosure: a comment on more than you wanted to know. Jerusalem Rev Legal Stud 11:75–82

Ben-Shahar O, Schneider CE (2011) The failure of mandated disclosure. Univ Pa Law Rev 159:647–749

Ben-Shahar O, Schneider CE (2014) More than you wanted to know. Princeton University Press, Princeton

Ben-Shahar O, Schneider CE (2015) Coping with the failure of mandated disclosure. Jerusalem Rev Legal Stud 11:83–93

---

[130]Sunstein (2014), p. 727, "A central point is that disclosure policies should be based on an understanding of how people actually process information. On this count, behavioral findings are essential."

[131]Gigerenzer (2014), proposes that with the teaching of critical thinking about statistical probability and heuristics individuals can get more *risk savvy*. See also Kahneman (2011, 2013).

[132]Moloney (2012), p. 177.

Black B (2013) Behavioral economics and investor protection: reasonable investors, efficient markets. Loyola Univ Chicago Law J 44:1493–1508

Brenncke M (2018) The legal framework for financial advertising: curbing behavioural exploitation. Eur Bus Organ Law Rev 19:853–882

Bubb R, Pildes RH (2014) How behavioral economics trims its sails and why. Harv Law Rev 127:1593–1678

Burn L (2010) KISS, but tell all: short-form disclosure for retail investors. Cap Mark Law J 5:141–168

Busch C (2016) The future of pre-contractual information duties: from behavioural insights to big data. In: Twigg-Flesner C (ed) Research handbook on EU consumer and contract law. Edward Elgar Publishing, Cheltenham, pp 221–240

Camerer CF, Issacharoff S, Loewenstein GF, O'Donoghue T, Rabin M (2003) Regulation for conservatives: behavioral economics and the case for 'asymmetric paternalism'. Univ Pa Law Rev 151:1211–1254

Campbell J, Jackson H, Madrian B, Tufano P (2011) Consumer financial protection. J Econ Perspect 25:91–114

Chater N, Steffen Huck S, Inderst R (2010) Consumer decision-making in retail investment services: a behavioural economics perspective. Final report, November 2010; https://ec.europa.eu/info/sites/info/files/retail_investment_services_2010_en.pdf

Coffee JC (1984) Market failure and the economic case for a mandatory disclosure system. Va Law Rev 70:717–753

Cox R, de Goeij P, van Campenhout G (2018) Are Pictures Worth a Thousand Words? Infographics and Investment Decision Making. https://ssrn.com/abstract=3277502

Dalley PJ (2007) The use and misuse of disclosure as a regulatory system. Florida State Univ Law Rev 34:1089–1131

Davidoff SM, Hill CA (2013) Limits of disclosure. Seattle Univ Law Rev 36:599–637

De Goeij P, Hogendoorn T, van Campenhout G (2014) Pictures are worth a thousand words: graphical information and investment decision making. https://www.aeaweb.org/conference/2015/retrieve.php?pdfid=384

Dittschar AK (2018) Kurzinformationsblätter als Mittel des informationsbasierten Privatanlegerschutzes. Kovac, Hamburg

ESMA (2017) The distributed ledger technology applied to securities markets. https://www.esma.europa.eu/system/files_force/library/dlt_report_-_esma50-1121423017-285.pdf

Fama EF (1970) Efficient capital markets, a review of theory and empirical work. J Finance 25:383–417

Fama EF (1991) Efficient capital markets II. J Finance 46:1575–1617

Fama EF (1998) Market efficiency, long-term returns, and behavioral finance. J Financ Econ 49:283–306

Gentile M, Linciano N, Lucarelli C, Soccorso P (2015) Financial Disclosure, Risk Perception and Investment Choices, Evidence from a Consumer Testing Exercise, Commissione Nazionale per le Società e la Borsa (CONSOB). http://www.consob.it/documents/11973/204072/qdf82.pdf/58dc22f8-504b-4bad-9679-610306359dfc

Gigerenzer G (2014 in German 2013) Risk savvy: how to make good decisions. Lane, London

Grill M, Lambert C, Marquardt P, Watfe G, Weistroffer C (2018) Counterparty and liquidity risks in exchange-traded funds. ECB Fin Stab Rev 2

Kahneman D (2011) Thinking, fast and slow. Farrar, Straus and Giroux, New York

Kahneman D (2013) Behavioral economics and investor protection: keynote address. Loyola Univ Chicago Law J 44:1333–1340

Lipkus IM, Samsa G, Rimer BK (2001) General performance on a numeracy scale among highly educated samples. Med Decis Making 21:37–44

Loewenstein G, Sunstein CR, Golman R (2014) Disclosure: psychology changes everything. Ann Rev Econ 6:391–419
Lusardi A, Mitchell O (2014) The economic importance of financial literacy: theory and evidence. J Econ Liter 52:5–44
Markowitz HM (1952) Portfolio selection. J Financ 7:77–91
Marotta-Wurgler F (2015) Even more than you wanted to know about the failures of disclosure. Jerusalem Rev Legal Stud 11:63–74
Mitchell G (2014) Alternative behavioral law and economics. In: Zamir E, Teichman D (eds) Oxford handbook of behavioral economics and the law. Oxford University Press, Oxford, pp 167–191
Moloney N (2012) The investor model underlying the EU's investor protection regime: consumers or investors? Eur Bus Organ Law Rev 13:169–193
Moloney N (2014) EC securities regulation and financial markets regulation, 3rd edn. Oxford University Press, Oxford
OECD (2017) Robo-Advice for Pensions. https://www.oecd.org/pensions/Robo-Advice-for-Pensions-2017.pdf
Oehler A, Wendt S (2017) Good consumer information: the information paradigm at its (dead) end? J Consum Policy 40:179–191
Paredes TA (2003) Blinded by the light: information overload and its consequences for securities regulation. Wash Univ Law Rev 81:417–485
Radin MJ (2015) Less than i wanted to know: the submerged issues in more than i wanted to know. Jerusalem Rev Legal Stud 11:51–62
Rapp RN (1998) Rethinking risky investments for that little old lady: A realistic role for modern portfolio theory in assessing suitability obligations of stockbrokers. Ohio NUL Rev 24:189–279
Schwarcz SL (2004) Rethinking the disclosure paradigm in a world of complexity. Univ Ill Law Rev: 1–37
Schwarcz SL (2008) Disclosure's failure in the subprime mortgage crisis. Utah Law Rev: 1109–1122
Schwarcz SL (2016) Regulating financial change: a functional approach. Minn Law Rev 206:1441–1494
Sharpe WF (1964) Capital asset prices: a theory of market equilibrium under conditions of risk. J Financ 19: 425–442
Sousa Lourenço J, Ciriolo E, Almeida SR, Troussard X (2016) Behavioural insights applied to policy: European Report 2016. publications.jrc.ec.europa.eu/repository/bitstream/JRC100146/kjna27726enn_new.pdf
Sunstein CR (2011) Empirically informed regulation. Univ Chicago Law Rev 78:1349–1429
Sunstein CR (2013a) Deciding by default. Univ Pa Law Rev 162:1–57
Sunstein CR (2013b) The Storrs Lectures: behavioral economics and paternalism. Yale Law J 122:1826–1899
Sunstein CR (2014) Nudges.gov: Behaviorally informed regulation. In: Zamir E, Teichman D (eds) The Oxford handbook of behavioral economics and the law. Oxford University Press, Oxford, pp 717–747
Sunstein CR (2016) Fifty shades of manipulation. J Behav Market 1:213–244
Sunstein CR, Thaler RH (2003) Libertarian paternalism is not an oxymoron. Univ Chicago Law Rev 70:1159–1202
Tobin J (1958) Liquidity preference as behavior towards risk. Rev Econ Stud 25:65–86
Ulen TS (2013) A behavioral view of investor protection. Loyola Univ Chicago Law J 44:1357–1376
Ulen TS (2014) The importance of behavioral law. In: Zamir E, Teichman D (eds) Oxford handbook of behavioral economics and the law. Oxford University Press, Oxford, pp 93–124
Walther T (2015) Key investor documents and their consequences on investor behaviour. J Bus Econ 2:129–156

Weber RH, Baisch R (2018) FinTech – eligible safeguards to foster the regulatory framework. J Int Bank Law Regul 33:335–350

Willis LE (2008) Against financial-literacy education. Iowa Law Rev 94:197–285

Zetzsche DA, Buckley RP, Arner DW, Föhr L (2019) The ICO Gold Rush: it's a scam, it's a Bubble, it's a super challenge for regulators. Harv Int Law J 60:267–315

Rainer Baisch, Zurich, Research Fellow at the University Research Priority Program Financial Market Regulation at the University of Zurich, CH-8001 Zurich, Rämistrasse 74/38, rainer.baisch@uzh.ch. Fields of interest: Private and Corporate Law, Financial (Capital) Market Law, FinTech regulation and Behavioural Economics & Law.

Part II
Mandated Disclosure

From Disclosure to Transparency in Consumer Law

Rolf H. Weber

Abstract Paternalistic detail-oriented rule-making as well as mandated disclosure in favor of consumers have become subject to criticism. Behavioral sciences and economics show that too much regulation might not be beneficial. Furthermore, over-information and overconfidence are jeopardizing the consumer protection objectives. Therefore, this contribution attempts to develop an approach relying on the consumer as right-holder and on an appropriate transparency concept. Clear and comprehensive information should empower the consumers to take reflected decisions.

1 Introduction

Consumer law has grown from its infancy some 20 years ago to a remarkable new legal discipline. Consumer law does not follow the traditional approach of vertical legal segments laid down in the Roman law normative framework (e.g. family law, property law, criminal law, etc.), but implements a horizontal model across the existing legal areas such as contract, financial market, health, or food law.

In substance, consumer law has developed into a rule-intense legal field since the regulatory objectives intend to fulfil the aim of protecting the so-called weaker members of civil society. However, materially the question remains to be answered to which degree a rules-oriented approach (instead of a principles-based model) really is inevitable. The respective challenges have been discussed by (partly extensive) interdisciplinary research during the last 20 years.

This contribution addresses the relevant issues as follows: Traditionally, consumer protection is based on specific rule-making. Detailed provisions should balance the weaker negotiation position of consumers and combat the information asymmetries. This regulatory model, even if still applied in new legislative activities,

R. H. Weber (✉)
Faculty of Law, University of Zurich, Zurich, Switzerland
e-mail: rolf.weber@rwi.uzh.ch

K. Mathis, A. Tor (eds.), *Consumer Law and Economics*, Economic Analysis of Law in European Legal Scholarship 9, https://doi.org/10.1007/978-3-030-49028-7_4

does not really meet the needs of consumers. The model has also been challenged by behavioral sciences and economics; the respective discussions will be reflected hereinafter. Nevertheless, a complete waiver of mandated disclosure does not appear to be convincing. Moreover, an alternative approach promoting a societal perspective with consumers as right-holders and with an appropriate concept of transparency must be developed.

2 Legal Tradition: Consumer Protection by Rule-Making

Consumer law usually contains mandatory rules, for example encompassing written form requirements for the contract conclusion, pre-contractual and ongoing information obligations, termination rights, restrictions related to the choice of applicable law and jurisdiction, etc. This type of (often paternalistic) rule-making is usually justified by the argument that:

- the consumer regularly is the weaker contract party than the supplier of goods and services[1] and
- the structural information asymmetries between the market participants in principle jeopardize the efficient allocation of economic resources.[2]

A particularly important part of consumer law concerns mandated disclosure of information, which has the objective of counterweighing the assumed information asymmetries. Even if mandated disclosure is not seen as a traditional paternalistic approach since the consumer does not become the beneficiary of specific behavioral requirements to be fulfilled in his/her favor, the respective provisions nevertheless lead to a detailed rule-making approach that imposes far-reaching obligations on the supplier.

The disclosure paradigm applies horizontally in all consumer businesses, as the EU Consumer Rights Directive of 2011 containing a long detailed list of information requirements shows.[3] Disclosure requirements are particularly prevalent in financial market law;[4] the most recent regulations in the EU (i.e. Prospectus Regulation for the primary markets or MiFiD II, MiFiR, PRIIP and the concrete Interpretation Guidelines thereto for the secondary [trading] markets) encompassing hundreds of pages contain widespread disclosure obligations.

Disclosure of information can also be mandatory in an inverse order, from the consumer to the financial services' provider: For example Article 35 of MiFiD II

[1] Shinar-Plato and Weber (2015), pp. 238 et seqq.

[2] This problem was already 50 years ago addressed by Akerlof (1970).

[3] See below Sect. 3.2.

[4] For more details see Baisch and Weber (2015), pp. 171 et seqq.

states the following information requirements in the context of a client suitability test:[5]

- *Investment objectives* (para 4): Information about investment period, risk preference, risk profile, investment purpose;
- *Risk absorbing capacity* (para 3): Information about source and extent of income, liquid assets and investments, real property, financial commitments;
- *Experience and knowledge* (para 1): Information about product experience, transaction experience, education, profession.

The far-reaching information requirements are subject to manifold critical assessments. The respective regulatory approach particularly contradicts the research results showing that mandated disclosure can have negative effects,[6] for example impair consumers' decisions, burden enterprises with "lost" costs, and exacerbate inequality.[7]

The appropriateness of specific tools in the hands of consumers that could help them to come to better decisions or to better transactional arrangements is more and more contested. Such regulations are at risk of not meeting the efficacy criterion and of leading to an undesirable expansion of governmental interventions into private relations; at least the question must be tackled as to which degree a certain paternalistic emphasis would be inevitable.[8] Or alternatively: Can human shortcomings be de-biased through law while avoiding paternalism?[9]

The recent proposal of the European Commission to implement a "New Deal for Consumers"[10] does not principally change the previous regulatory approach. This proposal intends to implement stronger consumer rights and additional tools to get redress in case of violation. Measures which are considered to reinforce consumer rights are the protection against unfair commercial practices, the improvement of transparency in online marketplaces and on online platforms, the protection against aggressive doorstep-selling, the application of consumer rights also in case of so-called "free" digital services, the improvement of the tools to obtain collective redress, the boosting of alternative and online dispute mechanisms and the introduction of effective penalties for violations of EU consumer law. However, all these (particularly the substantive) measures follow the traditional approach of tightening the regulatory regime.

The new ideas of behavioral sciences and economics are hardly taken into account in the "New Deal for Consumers" and an intention to re-direct the approach by including different perspectives cannot be seen. The same assessment holds true

[5]Directive 2014/65/EU of 15 May 2014 on markets in financial instruments and amending Directive 2002/92/EC and Directive 2011/61/EU, *OJ L 173/349-496, 12 June 2014 (MiFID II).*

[6]Ben-Shahar and Schneider (2014), passim.

[7]For a detailed discussion see below Sect. 3.2.

[8]Baisch and Weber (2015), p. 160.

[9]Baisch and Weber (2015), p. 162.

[10]European Commission, A New Deal for Consumers, 11 April 2018.

for recent national consumer laws. Therefore, this contribution attempts to look for more appropriate consumer protection approaches.

3 Challenges: Findings of Behavioral Sciences and Economics

3.1 Behavioral Sciences in General

The (detailed) rule-oriented approach has mainly been challenged since the early days of this century. However, the roots go much further back; the analyses in philosophical and economic theories addressing aspects of rational behavior already encompass Bernoulli's expected utility hypothesis, Bayes' theorem and Smith's invisible hand.[11] As mentioned, the basic challenge consists in the assessment of the possibility to de-bias detrimental human shortcomings through law while avoiding deterring paternalism.[12]

The rationality paradigm ("rational choice") of many economists[13] has proven to be shortsighted since decisions taken by individuals do not always maximize personal preferences and since uncertainties result in value changes.[14] In other words, individual predictions are not necessarily foreseeable, heuristics may lead to errors, preferences may change and personal harm can emerge due to a lack of self-control.[15]

In addition, biases as a further behavioral element can also play an important role and should not be underestimated.[16] Even if the results of behavioral economics' research are partly contested in the literature, its general findings should not be neglected; to the contrary, some insights are noteworthy and will be considered hereinafter.

This assessment can again be exemplified by way of a reference to the discussions lead in the context of financial market regulation:

The *efficient market hypothesis* proclaims that prices in financial markets reflect the fundamental values and are balancing any new information. In contrast, behavioral sciences describe anomalies that are inconsistent with this thesis and assume that the influence of arbitrage is limited for the following reasons:[17] Humans do not act only rational but also based on emotions; therefore, they tend to regret a former decision. Additionally, reference biases and the manner, how information is framed

[11]Baisch and Weber (2015), p. 163.

[12]For a further discussion of behavioral insights see Baisch (2016), pp. 225–230.

[13]See Camerer et al. (2003).

[14]See already Tversky and Kahneman (1973); later also Sunstein and Thaler (2003).

[15]Sunstein and Thaler (2003).

[16]Akerlof and Shiller (2010).

[17]Langevoort (1992) and Avgouleas (2012), pp. 57–58.

and anchored, do have a major impact on the way information is processed. Especially, innumeracy influences the assessment of probabilities and due to inertia and procrastination decisions are deferred or refused.

Therefore, behavioral sciences advocating for an extended inclusion of human elements in the rule-making processes merit being taken into account in the development and implementation of consumer protection rules.

3.2 *Mandated Disclosure in Particular*

As mentioned, mandated disclosure has become a major topic in the Law & Economics (L&E) discussions related to consumer protection. Critical voices gained weight as the extent of information requirements increased. Suppliers of goods and services are requested to disclose more and more information to (potential) consumers, generally according to the Consumer Rights Directive 2011/83[18] and specifically based on detailed regulations in certain business sectors such as the financial markets.

Proponents of mandated disclosure are of the opinion that information requirements would not interfere with the principle of consumer autonomy[19] and equally keep the (additional) costs for suppliers relatively low. The respective obligations are considered market-friendly since the key terms of contracts would remain outside of the scope of the regulatory intervention.[20]

In recent times, the most severe L&E objections against the "mandated disclosure paradigm" has been phrased by Omri Ben-Sharar and Carl E. Schneider under the heading "More Than You Wanted to Know: The Failure of Mandated Disclosure".[21] Apart from the hidden costs caused by such kind of disclosure, the two L&E scholars argue that mandated disclosure would exacerbate inequality, impair consumers' decisions and deter lawmakers from adopting better regulations. Furthermore, the question arises whether consumers indeed read and understand the mandatorily provided information.[22]

A partial solution could consist in the approach by the regulator to limit the information load by requiring from the suppliers of goods and services to provide more concise and precise information to the consumers in a manner being easily understandable by them.

[18] Information requirements encompass the main characteristics of the goods or services, the identity of the trader, the total price of the goods or services, the arrangements for payment, delivery and performance, the product guarantee, the duration of the contract, the functionality of digital goods, etc.

[19] For a description of this term see Weber (2013), pp. 6–7; for a discussion see below Sect. 4.2.

[20] See also Baisch and Weber (2015), p. 161.

[21] Ben-Shahar and Schneider (2014).

[22] To this aspect see also Baisch and Weber (2015), p. 166 and below Sect. 4.1.

This approach has recently been chosen by the EU financial markets regulator: The (over-)detailed prospectus which must be published by the financial intermediary if a new financial instrument is offered to the public needs to be complemented by a so-called "Key Information Document" (KID) that summarizes the most important data on 3 pages.[23] Whether this new concentrated document can really overcome the weaknesses of (overly) mandated disclosure is subject to discussions.[24] Experiences and empirical studies are not yet available.

Sometimes the provided information whether individually aggregated or based on advice "will not adequately help the naïves in their dealings with the sophisticated".[25] Therefore, a potential way to assist individuals in making better decisions is to direct choices through nudges without mandating a certain outcome. Based on preset defaults and smart incentives people are softly pushed to hopefully wise decisions, however, one is still allowed to skip the default and choose individually.[26] Often it is important to overcome procrastination and inertia by a default in order to ensure people engage in valuable activities such as saving for retirement.[27]

The European Supervisory Authorities in the financial markets tried to address and balance the desire for conciseness and simplicity facing the complexity of investment products' risks and costs. An important issue was to allow for comparability. Most of the KID documents are dedicated to the especially tricky areas like risk and return disclosure and cost information. The regulation addresses consumer behavior as key issue for retail investors and, therefore, the KID has a clear behavioral purpose for the retail investor. While the traditional approach to disclosure is focused on the content and the way information is presented, the framing of information within the KID tries to counter cognitive biases that can distort perceptions. Information is provided in a simple format with ratings and illustrations.

As discussed, the mandated disclosure is confronted with several challenges. Nevertheless, the proposal to completely waive mandated disclosure does not appear convincing. Therefore, as alternative approach promoting a societal perspective an individual rights-oriented concept of transparency will be outlined hereinafter.

[23]Regulation (EU) 1286/2014 of 26 November 2014 on key information documents for packaged retail and insurance-based investment products (PRIIPs), OJ L 352/1-23, *9.12.2014*.

[24]See the contribution of Rainer Baisch in this Volume.

[25]Ben-Shahar and Schneider (2011), p. 748.

[26]Thaler and Sunstein (2008).

[27]See also Baisch (2016), p. 223.

4 Societal Perspective: Right-Holders' Approach and Transparency Concept

Even if mandated disclosure did not reach the intended objectives and is confronted with inherent weaknesses, the transparency concept based on a right-holders' approach should not be condemned. Transparency is a valuable "asset" when informational misdirection can be avoided.

4.1 *Informational Misdirection*

4.1.1 Over-Information

Looking from a societal perspective, too much transparency could have two negative effects:[28]

- The sheer volume and intensity of information leads to a confusion effect since the recipients (consumers) are not (anymore) able to cope with all information details and lose the necessary overview of the data; in case of *confusion*, reasonable decisions by individuals are not to be expected; in addition, information can become deprived of a potential authoritative value.
- The permanent delivery of (similar) information causes a *Kassandra effect*; even if the consumers take note of the information, its contents is no longer taken as being serious and reliable, i.e. the information is not "converted" into actual behavior.

More than 20 years ago, reference was already made to expressions such as "don't info-pollute"[29] or "Data Smog – Surviving the Information Glut"[30] or "lost in the information jungle".[31] The general wisdom (coming from the food perspective) that overconsumption can be negative or even risky also applies with respect to information. Insofar, the following aspects (learned from L&E analyses) must be taken into account:

- Attention is a scarce resource; a person cannot dispose of this resource in an unlimited way.[32]
- As stated by the well-known legal sociologist Niklas Luhmann, over-information consumes working and leisure time on the supplier and the consumer side.[33]

---

[28]Weber (2002), p. 407.

[29]Weber (1999), p. 66.

[30]Shenk (1997).

[31]Weber (2002), p. 407.

[32]Rötzer (1998), pp. 83 et seqq.

[33]Luhmann (1997), pp. 1090, 1097.

- Over-information increases the risk that messages or data being spread out are considered to be redundant.[34]
- The utilization level of the (potential) informational supply is decreasing in case of data overload.[35]

The mentioned *Kassandra effect* is of particular relevance in the over-information context. The well-known (East-) German author Christa Wolf wrote in her novel "Kassandra" that Kassandra could say[36] "*ich war mit meinem Recht allein*" ("I was alone with my right"), but the question would remain unanswered whether humans should not believe an individual who proves her right.[37] The Greek tragedy "Oresteia" of Aeschylus has shown that indeed nobody did believe Kassandra, her words remained unheard; the same effect can happen in case of over-information in our time.

Consequently, the excessive information supply causes an unsuitable attempt to communicate a message to an individual, i.e. the information dissemination evanishes without any effect or the information dissemination occurs in vain.[38] In general, it can be said that the *Kassandra effect* will be the more substantial the more difficult it is for an individual to get access to the specifically relevant information being of personal interest.[39]

Ben-Shahar and Schneider also address this problem:

> "Lawmakers have no good solution to this problem. There is rarely a good solution in principle: incomplete disclosure leaves people ignorant, but complete disclosure creates crushing overload problems. Thus, a sophisticated lawmaker could recognize that «less is more» but still fear that «less is not enough». Furthermore, and crucially, the lawmaker's incentives generally push it toward ever more disclosure."[40]

Regulators need to incorporate the findings regarding the decision-making processes when designing disclosure regulations.[41] One option would be to reduce the volume of information, the other is to address the way information is delivered in order to optimize the outcome of the information process. In principle, the source of the problem described as information overload is not rooted in the disclosure requirements but in the way individuals filter information. Therefore, salience matters when certain information is essential for the individual or general welfare.[42]

---

[34] Luhmann (1997), pp. 1102 et seq.

[35] Luhmann (1997), p. 1090.

[36] Wolf (1983), p. 45.

[37] Wolf (1983), p. 29.

[38] Weber (2002), p. 407.

[39] Weber (2002), p. 407.

[40] Ben-Shahar and Schneider (2011), p. 647.

[41] For further sources see Roetzel (2018).

[42] Sunstein (2011), p. 1353; Baisch (2016), pp. 227–228.

4.1.2 Overconfidence

According to the 2002 Nobel Laureate Daniel Kahneman, "the illusion that we understand the past fosters overconfidence in our ability to predict the future".[43] Psychological studies have shown that "a vast majority of people say they are above average [assessing their capabilities], although, of course, only half can be".[44] Overconfidence is not always bad, for example if the expectation of a long life leads to higher savings. However, often the tendency to overestimate the benefits due to overwhelming information and to underestimate the costs leads to the assumption of too high risks. This assessment particularly applies in respect of people investing in financial instruments.[45]

According to Kahneman, illusions are generated by the pervasive optimistic bias: people assume that they have substantial control over the lives and/or over initiated projects.[46] Such kind of overconfidence tends to foster misdirected judgments since not all relevant elements are taken into account. The mind of overconfident persons mainly deals with "known knowns", rarely considers the "known unknowns" and obviously disregards the possibility of "unknown unknowns".[47] Alternatively in the words of Grubb:

> Overconfidence is just one of several biases that lead consumers to systematically misweight the various dimensions of product price or quality when computing the expected utility of a purchase.[48]

Overconfidence also tends to foster a misdirected judgment, since in such case humans have the illusion, that they are in control of a planned project or their lives. Actually, overconfidence refers not only to over-optimism but also to over-precision, i.e. misinterpretation of probabilities. While over-optimistic persons do not judge their individual skills or perhaps their performance correctly, an over-precise person is not valuing the potential variance of a certain chosen option, e.g. is not adequately expecting the likelihood of a potential loss. In consequence, a person can misweigh potential costs or benefits (i.e. undertake an insufficient probability analysis). The impact becomes particularly problematic in situations in which firms do exploit consumer overconfidence.[49]

---

[43] Kahneman (2011), p. 218.

[44] Camerer and Lovallo (2009), p. 306; see also Grubb (2015), p. 9.

[45] Baisch and Weber (2015), p. 170.

[46] Kahneman (2011), p. 255.

[47] In this context, Kahneman (2011), pp. 85 et seqq., has introduced the so-called WYSIATI concept: "What You See Is All There Is".

[48] Grubb (2015), p. 10.

[49] Grubb (2015), passim.

4.2 Right-Holders' Concept

Real-life experience shows that consumers are not (or should at least not be) only passive objects of protective regulations, but that they are to be generally accepted as holders of rights. Since consumers do have a right to make individual decisions, the perception should apply in the consumer law context that the respective human beings are vested with specific fundamental rights and values.

This general understanding can be condensed more concretely as follows:[50] (i) From a substantive point of view the kind of right or rights for promotion to qualify as a fundamental right in favor of consumers must be assessed and liaised with the aspect of regulatory protection. (ii) From a perceptual perspective the strategy necessary for enabling the appropriate access to data as well as the effective independent assertion of rights by individual consumers should become the predominant issues that merit more attention.

So far, consumers have too often not been considered as actors in the sense of expected beneficiaries of fundamental rights' protection. From a philosophical angle, if an interest is converted into a fundamental right it achieves a higher currency. In Dworkin's well-known argument, such a fundamental legal entitlement "trumps" any opposing, utilitarian interest or policy.[51] The impact of the fundamental rights argument must be realized at the meta-level as well as at the more specific level and context of individual cases, for example by evaluating whether the assessment is adequately balancing the technical measures against the (potential) interference with consumer rights.[52]

Since consumers are likely to be at a disadvantage in terms of resources and general awareness and since a lack of collective manifestation is a particular aspect of consumer vulnerability, the provision of better transparency and adequate access to information, but also the establishment of a possible direct participation in policy-making becomes imperative.[53] Because improved transparency can contribute to the empowerment of consumers, the development of such a concept is undertaken hereinafter.

---

[50] Weber (2013), p. 6.

[51] Dworkin (1977).

[52] Weber (2013), p. 24.

[53] Weber (2013), p. 24.

4.3 Transparency Concept

4.3.1 Yardsticks of Transparency

Transparency is usually defined as "easily seen through, [...] evident, obvious, clear".[54] Historically, with reference to Supreme Court Judge Louis Brandeis, the early promoter of privacy (in the form of a "right to be let alone", 1890) as well as of transparency ("sunlight is said to be the best of disinfectants", 1914), the term "transparency" can be understood as the prohibition of arbitrary and unforeseeable actions by the information controlling persons.[55]

Often, four different categories of transparency are distinguished, namely political, substantive, procedural and operational.[56]

(i) Whereas political and substantive transparency address aspects such as the access to decision-making mechanisms and the establishment of rules containing the desired substance of regulations, standards and provisions, (ii) procedural and operational transparency encompass rules in the structure of organizations and the processes of governance.

Not surprisingly, empirical evaluations and assessments of these categories lead to rather complex, partly even inconclusive results.[57]

Furthermore, four directions of transparency mirroring the flow of information are worth to be differentiated.[58]

(i) Transparency upwards reflects the hierarchical superior/principal direction of information disclosure, (ii) transparency downwards means that the addressee is in a position to observe the conduct and behavior of the information sender, (iii) transparency outwards shows whether the hierarchical subordinate or agent is in a position to judge what is happening "outside" the organization, and (iv) transparency inwards makes apparent whether those outside are in a position to see what is going on inside the organization.

Again, information flows can become quite complex depending on the multitude of directions.

4.3.2 Implementation of Transparency

In all circumstances, the basic objectives of transparency require robust and general rules, not necessarily more regulation. As shown in connection with the *Kassandra*

---

[54]Oxford English Dictionary Online, 2nd edn (1989).

[55]For more details see Kaufmann and Weber (2010), p. 782.

[56]Weber (2009), p. 122.

[57]Kaufmann and Weber (2018), p. 523.

[58]Weber (2009), pp. 122–123.

effect,[59] the improvement of transparency does not mean to have a quantitative increase of information, but "more" in terms of higher information quality.[60]

This aspect is also mirrored in the discussions mainly conducted with respect to financial markets. The question is debated whether a rules-oriented or principles-based regulation does have higher merits. In the meantime, the opinion prevails that a principles-based approach is to be favored. The legislator should nail down the basic regulatory objectives; their concretization can be left to a standards-setting by self-regulation organizations.[61]

As a consequence, regulators should strive at introducing legal obligations which promote (or request) the disclosure of *relevant* information on certain business activities in relation to consumers; obviously, the determination of the relevance leaves some room for discretion, but as long as the legislator limits its rule-making activity to basic principles of transparency, the disadvantages of mandated disclosure can be avoided. Transparency can also be seen as a comparative advantage in a competitive environment.

A possible analogy could be drawn to the General Data Protection Regulation 2016/679 (GDPR) of the European Union applicable since 25 May 2018. The transparency obligations are far-reaching, but the information must be given "in a concise, transparent, intelligible and easily accessible form, using clear and plain language" (Article 12 para. 1 GDPR).

In addition, access to that information must be assured and strengthened as individual right for all stakeholders with legitimate interests.[62] From a material perspective, the enhancing of transparency should also be linked to the prevailing strategies adopted to encourage transparency.[63]

Briefly, a future-oriented understanding regarding transparency must observe the following elements:[64]

- Definition of the information recipient as a right-holder and an essential component for the perception of both information and transparency;
- Provision of publically reliable information, i.e. substantive quality standards related to information, supported by an adequate legal framework which influences people's choices since a rational person would arguably organize his or her conduct in accordance with the law;
- Availability of disclosure procedures and observance of the time element, i.e. transparency implies constant visibility of information.

---

[59]See above Sect. 4.1.

[60]Weber (2002), pp. 406–407; Kaufmann and Weber (2010), p. 788; Kaufmann and Weber (2018), p. 520.

[61]To the problem that the complexity exceeds the reasonably expectable capacities of the addresses of rules see Kaufmann and Weber (2010), p. 789.

[62]Kaufmann and Weber (2018), p. 520.

[63]Mitchell (1998), pp. 109–110.

[64]Weber (2009), p. 131.

In order to complete the picture of a potential new transparency concept the following should be added: Transparency also relates to good governance and accountability as further fundamental pillars of the regulatory environment since it is essential for providing legal certainty and for maintaining trust in the concerned market.[65] With the aim of adequately shaping the transparency policies, appropriate objectives and principles that are understandable by all stakeholders must be implemented.[66] Transparency equally plays a role in connection with the development of corporate governance concepts in public institutions and private enterprises by requiring publicly assessable accounts as a pre-condition for a sustainable society.[67]

Finally, it must be reiterated that transparency does not equal mandated disclosure being expressed as details-oriented set of regulatory provisions. Moreover, transparency reflects the individual data access and information rights of human beings, i.e. the core is embedded in the Constitution.

5 Conclusion

The assessments of this contribution show that consumer law should strive for another regulatory path. Instead of detailed rule-making and of mandated disclosure, the notion of transparency must become key driver of consumer protection. Transparency means that the foundation is laid down for offering a clear and comprehensive set of information that is understandable and self-explicatory and empowers the consumers as right-holders to take reflected decisions. Transparency does not mean that an overwhelming disclosure is made, but that the available information is appropriate and tailor-made.

References

Akerlof GA (1970) The market for "lemons": quality uncertainty and the market mechanism. Q J Econ 84(3):488–500

Akerlof GA, Shiller RJ (2010) Animal spirits: how human psychology drives the economy, and why it matters for global capitalism. Princeton, Princeton University Press

Avgouleas E (2012) Governance of global financial markets. Cambridge University Press, Cambridge

Baisch R (2016) Nudging – information, choice architecture and beyond – theory and applications in financial markets law. In: Mathis K, Tor A (eds) Nudging – possibilities, limitations and applications in European law and economics. Springer, Berlin, pp 217–246

[65] See also Kaufmann and Weber (2018), p. 519.

[66] Kaufmann and Weber (2018), p. 519.

[67] Hood (2006), pp. 17 and 20.

Baisch R, Weber RH (2015) Investment suitability requirements in the light of behavioural findings. In: Mathis K (ed) European perspectives on behavioural law and economics. Springer, Berlin, pp 159–192
Ben-Shahar O, Schneider CE (2011) The failure of mandated disclosure. Univ Pa Law Rev 159:647–749
Ben-Shahar O, Schneider CE (2014) More than you wanted to know: the failure of mandated disclosure. Princeton University Press, Princeton
Camerer CF, Lovallo D (2009) Overconfidence and excess entry: an experimental approach. Am Econ Rev 89:306–318
Camerer CF, Issacharoff S, Loewenstein GF, O'Donoghue T, Rabin M (2003) Regulation for conservatives: behavioural economics and the case for 'asymmetric paternalism? Univ Pa Law Rev 151:1211–1254
Dworkin R (1977) Taking rights seriously. Harvard University Press, Cambridge
Grubb MD (2015) Overconfident consumers in the marketplace. J Econ Perspect 29:9–36
Hood C (2006) Transparency in historical perspective. In: Hood Ch, Heald D (eds) Transparency: the key to better governance? Oxford University Press, Oxford, pp 3–23
Kahneman D (2011) Thinking fast and slow. Straus Giroux, Farrar
Kaufmann C, Weber RH (2018) Transparency of central banks' policy. In: Conti-Brown P, Lastra RM (eds) Research handbook on central banking. Edward Elgar, Cheltenham, pp 518–534
Kaufmann C, Weber RH (2010) The role of transparency in financial regulation. J Int Econ Law 13 (3):779–797
Langevoort DC (1992) Theories, assumptions, and securities regulation: market efficiency revisited. Univ Pa Law Rev 140:851–920
Luhmann N (1997) Die Gesellschaft der Gesellschaft, vol 2, Suhrkamp, Frankfurt
Mitchell RB (1998) Sources of transparency: information systems in international regimes. Q J Econ 42:109–130
Roetzel PG (2018) Information overload in the information age: a review of the literature from business administration, business psychology, and related disciplines with a bibliometric approach and framework development. Business Research, pp 1–44
Rötzer F (1998) Aufmerksamkeit – der Rohstoff der Informationsgesellschaft. In: Brill A, de Vries M (eds) Virtuelle Wirtschaft. VS Verlag für Sozialwissenschaften, pp 174–191
Shenk D (1997) Data smog – surviving the information glut. Harper, San Francisco
Shinar-Plato R, Weber RH (2015) Consumer protection through soft law in an era of global financial crisis. In: Weiss F, Kammel AJ (eds) The changing landscape of global financial governance and the role of soft law. Brill Nijhoff, Leiden, pp 233–257
Sunstein CR (2011) Empirically informed regulation. Univ Chicago Law Rev 78:1349–1429
Sunstein CR, Thaler RH (2003) Libertarian paternalism is not an oxymoron. Univ Chicago Law Rev 70:1153–1215
Thaler RH, Sunstein CR (2008) Nudge: improving decisions about health, wealth and happiness. Yale University Press, New Haven
Tversky A, Kahneman D (1973) Availability: a heuristic for judging frequency and probability. Cogn Psychol 5:207–232
Weber RH (1999) Information und Schutz Privater. ZSR 118:1–86
Weber RH (2002) Kassandra oder Wissensbroker – Dilemma im Global Village. In: Becker J, Hilty RM, Stöckli J-F, Würtenberger T (eds) Festschrift für Manfred Rehbinder. Stämpfli and Beck, Bern and München, pp 405–421
Weber RH (2009) Shaping internet governance: regulatory challenges. Schulthess, Zurich
Weber RH (2013) Consumer autonomy – challenges from un unfair competition and human rights perspective. Int J Public Law Policy 3(1):1–32
Wolf C (1983) Kassandra, Erzählung. Luchterhand, Darmstadt

Rolf H. Weber Zurich. Professor emeritus of International Business Law at the University of Zurich and practicing attorney-at-law in Zurich. CH-8001 Zurich, Rämistr. 74/38, Tel. +41 (0)634 48 84. rolf.weber@rwi.uzh.ch. Fields of Interest: Information Technology and Internet Law, Competition Law, International Finance and Trade Law.

No Need to Read: 'Self-Enforcing' Pre-Contractual Consumer Information in European and German Law

Sören Segger-Piening

Abstract The focus of this paper will be (in part) an apology of pre-contractual information in European and German consumer contract law against the critique by Ben-Shahar, Schneider, Bar-Gill et al. However, the paper will not try to fight the central assumptions and behavioural insights pointed out by the above mentioned and others. Rather, it looks at statutory examples that turn the debate partly from the top to the bottom by shifting the protective dimension being analysed. Further, based upon those statutory examples it aims to develop a more general concept of an ex post consumer protection through ex ante information.

1 Introduction

Pre-contractual consumer information and disclosure in general are a widely discussed and disputed area. The European and thus the German consumer image relies mainly on the information model and therefore the neoliberal economic standard model with the homo oeconomicus as normative base (see infra 2.1). The traditional approach focuses on giving the consumer the needed pre-contractual information for making the 'right', well-informed choice ex ante in relation to the moment of the conclusion of the contract. This ex ante perspective is the core of pre-contractual information and disclosure. "[Mandated disclosure] aspires to improve decisions people make in their economic and social relationships [. . .]."[1] On the other side, it has been shown that consumers are often not reasonably well informed and observant. They rather tend to generally ignore pre-contractual information, underlie cognitive capacity boundaries, are subject to cognitive errors and

[1] Ben-Shahar and Schneider (2011), pp. 649, 730; see also i.a. Helleringer and Sibony (2017), p. 627 seq.; Gillis (2015), p. 46 seq.

S. Segger-Piening (✉)
Faculty of Law, University of Würzburg, Würzburg, Germany
e-mail: s.segger-piening@jura.uni-wuerzburg.de

K. Mathis, A. Tor (eds.), *Consumer Law and Economics*, Economic Analysis of Law in European Legal Scholarship 9, https://doi.org/10.1007/978-3-030-49028-7_5

much more (see infra 2.2). Even though the details of this inadequate information processing are not always clear, the doctrine of pre-contractual information is in demand for justification.

One excusatory cause is provided by the concept here named "self-enforcing" information and disclosure. It focuses on an ex post dimension of consumer protection. This shall be further developed hereafter. In the beginning, the theoretical framework and its two main elements shall be provided in Sect. 3. Afterwards, the first of the two main elements—the promoting of private law enforcement—shall be looked in Sect. 4. Subsequent (see infra 5) the second element regarding the shaping of remedies due to a detailed pre-contractual product description shall be scrutinized. Finally, the possibilities—de lege lata and de lege ferenda—of an indirect regulation through an obligatory and detailed product description will be discussed.

2 The Concept and Problems of Information Based Consumer Protection

In a first step, the doctrinal foundation of pre-contractual information and the development of the consumer image in Germany and Europe shall be looked at. Subsequently, this approach shall be confronted with behavioural insights and specific problems of pre-contractual information and disclosure. This first part serves as a short introduction into the current debate.

2.1 Doctrinal Foundation and Development of the Consumer Image

Interestingly, the German Federal Court of Justice (hereafter FCJ)[2]—in matters of unfair commercial practices—had been promoting a consumer image, which—retrospectively—seems to be much more in accordance with today's behavioural insights. The FCJ described consumers as cursory and immature.[3] Hence, a high level of protection was assured to consumers, critically observed by many commentators.[4]

On the European level, however, another approach was taken. The foundation can be found in the so called "information model".[5] It rests on the assumption that

---

[2]In German: Bundesgerichtshof or just BGH.

[3]FCJ, GRUR 1956, 187 (English-Lavender); GRUR 1970, 425 (Melitta-Kaffee); GRUR 1982, 564 (Elsässer Nudeln). For secondary sources see inter alia: Tamm (2011), p. 152; Weber (2019), p. 33 seq.

[4]Leible (1994), p. 178; Heiderhoff (2004), pp. 259 seqq.

[5]Dauner-Lieb (1983), pp. 62 seqq.; Howells and Wilhelmsson (2003), pp. 380 seqq.; Fleischer (2000), p. 780 seq.; Martinek (2000), pp. 518 seqq.; Heiderhoff (2004), pp. 266 seqq.

necessary information for concluding informed contracts is not available in today's economic setting. Information duties were seen as the prime tool for restoring a balance between the parties and also had the desirable effect of a minimal market intrusion. They were meant to enhance the choices consumers make before concluding the contract.[6]

The consumer image of the Court of Justice of the European Union[7] mainly[8] relies on the information model.[9] Therefore, consumers should be "reasonably well-informed and reasonably observant and circumspect".[10] This consumer image has been especially developed in conjunction with the free movement of goods.[11] Nowadays the above stated definition of the CJEU constitutes the standard approach towards the so-called average consumer.[12] In light of the primacy of European Union law towards law of the member states, the FCJ finally adopted the consumer image of the CJEU.[13]

This development has been analysed against the background of the standard approach towards a neoclassical model and thus rational and information-seeking actors.[14] It still seems to be the dominant approach in European consumer law, whereas in the U.S. consumer legislation a shift towards behavioural approaches[15] is more and more accepted.[16] On the other side, recent developments in EU consumer law and policy illustrate an increased awareness for and openness to behavioural challenges especially in matters of the consumer image. In May 2017, a study for the fitness check of EU consumer and marketing law was published.[17] One of the findings is that the concept of the average consumer as stipulated by the CJEU needs to be revaluated.[18] In particular, attention is drawn to the need to take behavioural insights into consideration. Furthermore, the blacklist of the Unfair Commercial Practices Directive shall be scrutinized and possibly extended in

[6]See already above at fn. 1; see further Dauner-Lieb (1983), p. 63; Whitford (1973), pp. 403 seqq., however, Whitford also shortly mentions the ex post dimension of pre-contractual disclosure at pp. 463 seqq.; his ideas share some of the policy intentions further elaborated infra at section 4.

[7]Hereafter CJEU.

[8]But see also towards a more social model i.a. Brownsword et al. (1994) and Lurger (1998).

[9]See Wilhelmsson (1996), p. 55 seq.; Busch (2016), pp. 222 seqq.; Tamm (2011), pp. 152 seqq.; and supra n. 5.

[10]CJEU, 16.07.1998, C-210/96 (Gut Springenheide), recital 31.

[11]See CJEU, 06.07.1995, C-470/93 (Mars), no. 24; CJEU, 13.01.2000, C-220/98 (Estée Lauder); see also supra n. 10.

[12]See i.a. Tamm, pp. 153 seqq.; Heiderhoff (2004), pp. 266 seqq.; Cartwright (2016), pp. 199 seqq.

[13]FCJ GRUR 2000, 619, 621 (Orient-Teppichmuster); for secondary sources see i.a.; Tamm (2011), p. 152.

[14]See i.a. Cartwright (2016), pp. 202 seqq.; Hacker (2016), Dauner-Lieb (2007), pp. 111 seqq.

[15]See further infra under 2.2.

[16]See for a comparison between the EU and the U.S. consumer legislation before this background Hacker (2016). See further for the shift in the U.S. legislation below at 2.2.

[17]European Commission (2017).

[18]See on this and subsequent European Commission (2017), pp. 291 seqq.

accordance with behavioural findings. The impact of this recent study has to be awaited, but it—and the New Deal for Consumers[19]—demonstrates a change of attitude by the EU institutions.

2.2 The Informed Consumer and False Assumptions: Behavioural Insights

This shift towards a more realistic view of human behaviour has been promoted for quite some time in economic writing. Herbert Simon already introduced the concept of bounded rationality in the 1950s[20] and illustrated that the utility maximizing function attributed to the homo oeconomicus often does not hold true.[21] In the 1980s Kahneman and Tversky demonstrated that the expected utility theory rested on false assumptions and instead introduced the prospect theory.[22]

In 1998 the work of Jolls, Sunstein and Thaler[23] made the concept of behavioural law and economics available to a widespread audience. From there on it did not take too long for several scholars to connect their findings to the consumer image of the CJEU and point out the incompatibility with behavioural findings.[24]

The latest milestone is the discussion about the failure of mandated disclosure and pre-contractual information. As early as 1973, Whitford demonstrated the problems with pre-contractual disclosure especially in the context of the Truth in Lending Act.[25] Nearly 40 years later Ben-Shahar and Schneider systematically proved that consumers are barely reasonably, well-informed and observant.[26] They rather tend to ignore pre-contractual information or are not able to process it sufficiently. The reasons are manifold. Besides the information overload problem[27] and issues regarding illiteracy and innumeracy,[28] the non-conformance of human nature with the standard model due to behavioural anomalies has been identified as a further cause.[29]

---

[19] See Com 2018(183), 11.04.2018.

[20] Simon (1955) and Simon (1972), p. 170.

[21] See i.a. Mathis and Steffen (2015), p. 36.

[22] Kahneman and Tversky (1979); for a reception see i.a. Jolls et al. (1998), p. 1476; Camerer et al. (2004); for a German introduction see i.a. Englerth and Towfigh (2017), pp. 237 seqq.; Hacker (2017), pp. 63 seqq., 96 seqq.

[23] Jolls et al. (1998).

[24] Ramsay (2012), pp. 56 seqq.; Cartwright (2016), pp. 202 seqq.; Ulen (2001), pp. 105 seqq.; Sibony (2015), pp. 71 seqq.; see further, infra n. 27, 39.

[25] See Whitford (1973); see also Howells and Wilhelmsson (2003), p. 380; Ramsay (2005), pp. 48 seqq.

[26] Ben-Shahar and Schneider (2011).

[27] Fleischer (2000), p. 788; Martinek (2000), pp. 518 seqq. Ben-Shahar and Schneider (2011), pp. 686 seqq.; Busch (2016), pp. 224 seqq.; Schürnbrand and Janal (2018), p. 7

[28] Ben-Shahar and Schneider (2011), pp. 711 seqq. with further references.

[29] For an (incomplete) list of documented cognitive errors see i.a Stark and Choplin (2010), pp. 89 seqq.

Pre-contractual information is or rather was often arranged in a format that makes it hard to understand; Stark and Choplin name this group as "inability to process user-unfriendly features of disclosure forms".[30] In recent years more and more scholars recognized the possibilities of framing information in a way that makes it easier or harder to understand.[31] Also a growing number of practical examples of i.a. structuring information pursuant to the demands of behavioural findings emerged.[32] This is (partly) the result of the framing discussion, which emerged in the 1980s and also based on behavioural insights particularly shaped by Kahneman and Tversky.[33] Another major distortion results from the use of availability heuristics.[34] Pre-contractual information or disclosures may point out certain risks that consumers are not familiar with; before the financial crises this held true inter alia for a high debt service ratio for loans. Since consumers "assess the risks associated with provisions by the ease with which they can imagine possible consequences of those provisions",[35] this leads to a wrong risk assumption and therefore an insufficient comparison between different products.[36] Another source of confusion can be the positive confirmation bias. It has been shown that people typically rather look for information that confirms rather than disconfirms their opinion.[37] Thus, certain messages or warnings in pre-contractual information might be ignored.

This analysis holds true for the European level as well. Ben-Shahar and Bar-Gill analysed the proposal of a Common European Sales Law (CESL) and found similar provisions and flaws.[38] The steadily growing body of pre-contractual information duties and disclosure laws has been analysed critically also by European scholars.[39] Even though the details of this inadequate information processing are not always clear,[40] the doctrine of pre-contractual information is in demand for justification.

---

[30] Stark and Choplin (2010), p. 97 seq.

[31] See further infra under 4.3.

[32] A prime example is the Social and Behavioral Sciences Team established by President Obama, which was meant to design laws according to behavioural insights, see for the last report: https://www.whitehouse.gov/sites/whitehouse.gov/files/images/2016%20Social%20and%20Behavioral%20Sciences%20Team%20Annual%20Report.pdf (visited on 18.06.2020).

[33] See i.a. Kahnemann and Tversky (1984); for a reception see i.a. Sunstein and Thaler (2003), Hacker (2017), pp. 445 seqq.

[34] See with further references also for the following Stark and Choplin (2010), p. 99 seq.

[35] Stark and Choplin (2010), p. 99 seq.

[36] The term "product" is used here in a very broad sense. Included are also services or contracts for work; for a similar approach see Willis (2015), p. 1309, n. 1.

[37] Englerth (2007), pp. 95 seqq.; Hacker (2017), pp. 87 seqq.

[38] Bar-Gill and Ben-Shahar (2013), p. 116 seq.

[39] See supra and Fleischer (2000), p. 788; Eidenmüller (2005), p. 221; Busch (2016), pp. 224 seqq.

[40] See i.a. Helleringer and Sibony (2017), pp. 621 seqq.

3 The Concept of 'Self-Enforcing' Information: Theoretical Framework

One excusatory cause is provided by the concept here named "self-enforcing" information and disclosure, which shall now be introduced. Starting point of this concept are rules according to which the pre-contractual information automatically becomes part of the contract. They shall be referred to as "inclusion rules" from now on. Art. 6 of the Directive on Consumer Rights[41] (DCR) in matters of distance and off-premises contracts provides a prime example.[42] Pursuant to art. 6 para. 5 DCR pre-contractual information as stipulated in art. 6 para. 1 DCR[43] shall form a part of the contract unless the parties explicitly agree otherwise.[44] Of course, the consumer does not have to read or process the information for it to become relevant and binding. But is this helpful for the consumer? What would be the effect?

One intention is to prevent the trader from changing the pre-contractual information to the disadvantage of the consumer due to the use of general terms and conditions.[45] This is a rather well known tool and accepted as efficient.[46] Bar-Gill and Ben-Shahar compare this kind of regulation with the "basis of the bargain" principle in warranty law, as stipulated for example in UCC (Uniform Commercial Code) paras. 2–313. Pursuant to this principle a pre-contractual product description normally becomes part of the contract, unless the seller can prove that it was not the "basis of the bargain";[47] details are disputed.[48]

However, this kind of regulation does more. Its effects become visible once the pre-contractual information duties it is combined with are further analysed. One group of information duties governed by art. 6 para. 1 DCR refers to product related information, namely littera a) regarding the main characteristics of the product and littera r) and s) regarding the functionality and interoperability of digital content. This product related information that must be disclosed ex ante, can shape the ex post remedies of the consumer, since it is a general principle in European law[49] that a remedy can be made use of if the product does not conform to the contractual description and part of this description is the pre-contractual information due to the inclusion rule. Besides situation oriented distance and off-premises contracts, this remedy shaping effect also occurs at different sectoral consumer contracts, namely: package travel, timesharing and consumer construction contracts. For each of those

[41]Directive 2011/83/EU of 25 October 2011 on consumer rights, hereafter DCR; this directive and all other directives mentioned hereafter can easily be found at https://eur-lex.europa.eu.

[42]For a (working) definition see infra 4.1.

[43]For an overview in matters of the pre-contractual information see 4.1.

[44]See for an analysis of this exemption infra 5.1, comparative analysis.

[45]In more detail infra 5.2.

[46]See Bar-Gill and Ben-Shahar (2013), p. 116 seq.

[47]U.C.C. § 2-313, Official Comment 3.

[48]See i.a. Murray (1982) and Holdych and Mann (1996).

[49]See infra 5.2.

product-related contracts a rule similar to art. 6 para. 5 DCR exists in European and/or German law. Furthermore, the trader has to disclose certain information about the product before concluding the contract and the amount of information to be disclosed beforehand is regulated closely. The specific pre-contractual information duties as well as the inclusion rules and their normative surroundings will be looked at under 5.1, whereas the remedy shaping and other effects will be elaborated more closely infra at 5.2.

A second group of information duties included in art. 6 para. 1 lit. l), m) DCR obliges the trader to inform the consumer about his legal rights. At the ex post level this information—that is part of the contract via the inclusion rule—can promote private law enforcement, since the consumer might use the information in case his product has a malfunction. This shall be further developed hereafter under Sect. 4. To be fair, in this example the information does need to be read, but not before concluding the contract, rather afterwards, when it is needed. Furthermore, the inclusion rule does not have a direct legal effect. Rather, it serves a practical purpose.[50]

In an abstract way this concept represents a shift from the ex ante perspective, where information shall help in making the 'right' decision, to an ex post perspective, where information is used inter alia to promote and shape the remedies one has in regard to the product. Therefore, the information duty becomes self-enforcing.

The concept thus depends on the proper fulfilment of the information duties by the trader. In case the trader does not fulfil his duties, the discussion about remedies for breach of information duties becomes relevant. However, this is not the focus of this chapter.[51]

4 Promoting Private Law Enforcement

The concept of promoting private law enforcement through pre-contractual information can be explained best by giving an example: A consumer who buys a product at a German or maybe French online shop is subject to the information requirements of the DCR and the implementing German or French legislation. Therefore, he receives information about his legal rights, although he will not process it at the point of purchase, as discussed above (supra 2.2). However, should there be a fault with the so purchased product the consumer will then begin the search for information regarding his rights of redress. At this point, the search is in accordance with the model of bounded rationality. Unlike in the ex ante situation—that is before concluding the contract—in this ex post situation a real demand for the information exists.[52] Can this demand be satisfied efficiently by the given information? The

[50]See further infra 4.

[51]But see Weber (2019), pp. 135 seqq.; and art. II.-3:109 DCFR.

[52]Comp. also Helleringer and Sibony (2017), p. 624; Whitford (1973), p. 466 seq.

answer to this question depends on two variables regarding the pre-contractual information about the legal rights of the consumer: the first being the subject matter of the information (infra 4.2) and the second the formal requirements for presenting the information (infra 4.3).

Before giving an overview about distance and off-premises contracts, it is important to note that in matters of the promoting of private law enforcement the inclusion rule pursuant to art. 6 para 5 DCR mainly serves to include the pre-contractual information into the contract. Unlike in matters of the remedy shaping function[53] it does not have a specific legal effect. However, in a practical sense it helps consumers since all necessary information is now stored in one document—the contract. Thus, regarding the prompting of private law enforcement, inclusion rules are helpful but not mandatory for the function of the concept. This does not hold true for the remedy shaping effect (see infra 5.2).

4.1 *Distance and Off-Premises Contracts: Overview*

To begin with, a short (normative) overview shall be given. The definitions of distance and off-premises contracts can be found in art. 2 para. 7, 8 DCR. They are rather lengthy and complicated. For the purpose of the following, it is sufficient to note that a distance contract requires an organized distance sales scheme or such like, a different physical presence of trader and consumer, and a conclusion of contract with the means of distance communication—a typical example is online shopping.[54] An off-premises contract is a contract concluded outside the premises of the trader, whether by means of doorstep selling or otherwise. Distance and off-premises contracts as legal categories are not content related, they could include services, goods, workmanship and so on; for the purpose of the following the term product will be used.[55]

The necessary pre-contractual information for those contracts is stipulated by art. 6 para. 1 DCR. It is divided into 15 different sections, marked with the letters a) to t). However, one can identify four main groups: First, there is product related information, especially pursuant to lit. a), r) and s).[56] The second group relates to legal information, inter alia according to lit. l) and m).[57] The third and fourth group can be identified as information about the trader (lit. b) – d), n)) and price related information (lit. e) – g), q)). The focus of this chapter will be directed towards the first (product related, see infra 5.1.4) and second (legal guarantees, remedies, see infra 4.2) group.

[53]See further infra 5.2 for the effects.

[54]See more closely i.a. Weatherill (2013), p. 133.

[55]See already supra at 2.2 note 36.

[56]See further infra 5.1.

[57]See further hereafter.

4.2 Legal Information: The Subject Matter

The concept of promoting private law enforcement relies on specific legal information in the first place. In the following section, the subject matter of this information will be more closely looked at by scrutinizing lit. l) and m) of art. 6 para. 1 DCR. It would certainly be interesting to further cover lit. t) regarding information about a recourse to an out-of-court complaint or lit. h) – k) regarding withdrawal rights. However, this is beyond the scope of this chapter.

4.2.1 Reminder of Legal Defect Liability

Pursuant to lit. l) a reminder of the existence of a legal guarantee for conformity of goods has to be provided.[58] In Germany, this information duty is implemented in art. 246a § 1 para. 1 s. 1 no. 8 EGBGB (*Einführungsgesetz zum Bürgerlichen Gesetzbuche*, i.e. Introductory Law to the German Civil Code).[59] It is disputed whether the trader simply has to give a reminder about the existence of legal remedies to the consumer or if he has to explain the basic principles of those legal rights. Most of the authors agree that it would be an undue burden for the trader if he had to explain to the consumer the principles of the legal rights.[60] Therefore, it is commonly accepted that a mere note is sufficient.[61] Only Koch demands more detailed information.[62]

However, when looking at the language of the provision it becomes clear that a mere hint is sufficient, since this resembles a "reminder". Also, an argumentum e contrario in relation to lit. m) can be drawn. In lit. m) it is explicitly stated that the existence *and conditions* of a guarantee have to be disclosed, whereas in lit. l) only the existence is mentioned. An exception to this narrow interpretation can be made with regards to the limitation period,[63] which lasts for 2 years pursuant to art. 5 para. 1 of the consumer sales directive.[64] Here an undue burden for the trader is rather unlikely, since it is easy to cope with. Furthermore, it may save the consumer unnecessary cost for seeking legal advice, even though his rights became time

[58]See generally Hall et al. (2012), pp. 146–148; Grundmann (2013), pp. 110–112.

[59]The EGBGB serves as introductory law to the German Civil Code (BGB).

[60]See explicitly Staudinger/Thüsing, § 312a BGB no. 29.

[61]Palandt/Grüneberg, art. 246 EGBGB no. 9; jurisPK/Junker, § 312d BGB no. 40; BeckOGK/Busch, art. 246 EGBGB no. 34; BeckOK/Martens, art. 246 EGBGB no. 20; Ehmann and Forster (2014), p. 166.

[62]Erman/Koch, § 312a BGB no. 14.

[63]See also MüKo/Wendehorst, § 312a no. 28.

[64]Directive 1999/44/EC on certain aspects of the sale of consumer goods and associated guarantees. The same holds true for the period of liability, see for the differentiation CJEU, 13.07.2017,C-133/16 (Ferenschild).

barred. This interpretation is also in conformance with the Guidance Document of the European Commission, which states that

> the seller should specify that, under EU law, he is liable for any lack of conformity that becomes apparent within a minimum of two years from delivery of the goods and that national laws may give the consumer additional rights.[65]

The interpretation of the European Commission goes further than most of the academic authors, since it demands a positive wording, i.e. "he is liable for any lack of conformity". Of course, the interpretation is not binding, nevertheless, it has a certain interpretative authority. In case the trader decides to modify the legal regime, he has to provide detailed information regarding the modifications and the remaining rights of the consumer.[66] Otherwise, the simple reference to the legal rights of the consumer would be misleading.

4.2.2 Conditions of After-Sale Services and Guarantees

In instances where the trader decides to offer the customer an after-sale customer assistance, after-sale services and/or a commercial guarantees—hereafter named additional service and guarantee—he is obliged to inform the consumer about the existence and conditions of these additional services and guarantees pursuant to lit. m). Unlike lit. l) this provision applies to all contracts and not only sale contracts. In Germany, the information duty is implemented in art. 246a § 1 para. 1 s. 1 no. 9 EGBGB. In contrast to lit. l) a mere reminder is not considered as sufficient. Rather, the trader is obliged to also inform about the conditions of the additional services or guarantees. Pursuant to the Guidance Document of the European Commission, the "information about the after-sales services should in particular explain where the service will be carried out and who bears the cost of transport (if applicable)."[67] Law academics[68] and courts agree: in a recent case the Higher Regional Court of Hamm qualified the mere declaration "5 years of warranty" as insufficient with regards to lit. m).[69] This is convincing. The argument of an undue burden does not apply here. After all, the trader himself decided to provide additional services and/or a guarantee. Thus, it is also his duty to explain those services thoroughly towards the consumer.

---

[65]DG Justice Guidance Document (June 2014), p. 27 seq.

[66]Palandt/Grüneberg, art. 246 EGBGB no. 9; Ehmann and Forster (2014), p. 166; Erman/Koch, § 312a BGB no. 14; jurisPK/Junker, § 312d BGB no. 41.

[67]DG Justice Guidance Document (June 2014), p. 28.

[68]Palandt/Grüneberg, art. 246 EGBGB no. 9; Ehmann and Forster (2014), p. 166; BeckOK/Martens, art. 246 EGBGB no. 21; MüKo/Wendehorst, § 312a no. 29; Erman/Koch, § 312a BGB no. 14.

[69]OLG Hamm, GRUR-RS 2016, 18361.

4.3 Formal Requirements and Behavioural Insights

Besides content related information duties the DCR also covers formal requirements regarding the presentation and language of the information that must be provided.[70] Pursuant to art. 6 para. 1 DCR the information for distance as well as off-premises contracts needs to be provided in a clear and comprehensible manner. For off-premises contracts art. 7 para. 1 DCR requires that the information shall be legible (presentation) and in plain, intelligible language (style of language). Regarding distance contracts, the information shall be made available in a way appropriate to the means of distance communication and be formulated again in plain and intelligible language (art. 8 para. 1 DCR). If the information is provided on a durable medium, it shall be legible. Hence, on the European level, one can find a differentiation between distance and off-premises contracts in matters of the question of the legibility of the information, whereas the language always has to be plain and intelligible and the information needs to be presented in a clear and comprehensible manner. The latter can be seen as a superordinate requirement.

In Germany, the formal requirements are implemented in a similar way in art 246a § 4 EGBGB. Law academics and courts interpret the requirement to provide the information in a clear and comprehensible manner broadly and derive requirements concerning the style of language on the one hand but also in matters of presentation on the other hand.[71] A differentiation between distance and off-premises contracts then occurs in art. 246a § 4 para. 2, 3 EGBGB regarding the medium of the information, the question of legibility and so on.

Therefore, a first look belongs to the style of language and afterwards the questions of presentation will be addressed. The interpretation of these formal requirements shall also take place before the background of behavioural insights. Especially in matters of pre-contractual information and disclosure a rich body of writing can be found.[72]

4.3.1 Style of Language

Plain language requires the information to be non-contradictory and precise.[73] Especially, when informing about a guarantee (art. 6 para. 1 lit. m) DCR)—besides giving a reminder about the legal rights (art. 6 para. 1 lit. l) DCR)—the trader has to point out the additional character of the guarantee. For example, a product guarantee

[70]See for the European level Hall et al. (2012), pp. 149–151; Grundmann (2013), pp. 111–112.

[71]MüKo/Wendehorst, § 312d no. 70; Staudinger/Thüsing, § 312d no. 77; BeckOGK/Busch, art. 246a § 4 EGBGB no. 7; BGH NJW 1988, 558; NJW 1989, 222; NJW 1999, 2279 (2280).

[72]See supra at 2.2 and further i.a.: Loewenstein et al. (2014), Ayres and Schwartz (2014), Schmolke (2014), pp. 840 seqq.; Hacker (2017), pp. 444 seqq., 875 seqq.; see also infra.

[73]See Staudinger/Wendland, § 307 no. 187 seqq.; BGH NJW-RR 2011, 1144; BAG (German Federal Labour Court) NJW 2008, 680.

could be limited to 1 year, however, this would not deprive the consumer of his legal rights in matters of the biennial defects liability after this 1 year guarantee has lapsed. This has to be formulated very clearly.

Intelligible language on the other hand requires the trader to use comprehensive and rather simple language.[74] Behavioural studies regarding consumer-aligned language have shown that technical terms should be avoided.[75] Irrespective of this, it has been shown, that the use of the term "legal guarantee of conformity of goods" regarding information pursuant to lit. l) can be used.[76] Nevertheless, consumers would be better off if traders were to explain this a bit further, which could be an option for a reform of the directive. Furthermore, short sentences can foster an intelligible language.[77] However, "shortening a whole subordinate clause into a single nominal usually increases the complexity of the deeper grammatical and semantic structure."[78] Finally, instead of using a nominal-style it is preferable to use verbs.[79]

4.3.2 Legibility: Layout, Composition, Extent

Questions regarding the legibility of a text or information refer to the sub-items layout and general presentation, composition and structure as well as extent. In matters of layout and general presentation, it has been shown that symbols, graphics and accentuations can help.[80] For certain special services—like an in-house service—a symbol of a merchant driving towards the client could be used. Accentuations can inter alia highlight important features of a special service or guarantee. They can also be used to separate different terms of a guarantee or special service in a clearly arranged manner. The trader should also ensure that information on the screen is legible. Nowadays bigger screens are more common and therefore it is central that enough line breaks are used to improve readability.

In matters of composition and structure it might be of value to inform the consumer right at the beginning that some information may be useful once the product has a malfunction. Questions regarding the extent of information do not play a central role when solely looking at special services and guarantees. A different question—beyond the scope of this paper—is the general extent of pre-contractual information in art. 6 DCR. Even without closer scrutinizing all 15 section (lit. a) – lit. t)) of para. 1, it seems legitimate to state that an information overload might be a problem.

---

74 See generally MüKo/Wendehorst, § 312d no. 70; Hacker (2017), pp. 461 seqq.

75 Charrow and Charrow (1979), p. 1336; Schendra (2004), p. 356; Hacker (2017), p. 462.

76 See supra 4.2.

77 Schendra (2004), p. 356; Hacker (2017), p. 462.

78 Charrow and Charrow (1979), p. 1321.

79 Charrow and Charrow (1979), p. 1321; Hacker (2017), p. 463.

80 See i.a. Bettman et al. (1986), p. 15; Hacker (2017), p. 464.

4.4 Interim Conclusion and Options for Reform

Even though the provision regarding the legal defects liability pursuant to lit. l) is interpreted rather narrowly it can still promote private law enforcement, since consumers will be informed that they enjoy different rights and remedies notwithstanding that the withdrawal period ended.[81] However, there is still space for improvement, especially when bearing in mind the problem posed by those who do not read at all. One point of possible reform might be a rule, asking the trader to remind the consumer one month before the end of his special guarantee and/or his biennial defects liability. This rule would have to be designed in a way to catch the elusive attention of the consumer. An idea might be an e-mail with the header "Your [guarantee] [legal defects liability] of [product name in a simple way, e.g. Samsung Faltscreen] ends in two month...". Inside the e-mail a closer and again easily comprehensible description of the guarantee or a reminder about the legal defects liability should be included. There also the differentiation between limitation period and period of liability could be explained.[82] This could be used as a strong incentive for the consumer to use the rights provided and thus further promote private law enforcement.

The obligation to reveal the conditions of additional services and guarantees pursuant to lit. m) can be regarded as a convincing provision. It can help consumers in a situation of need to get to know their special rights deriving from a guarantee or such like rather quickly.

Finally, the promoting of private law enforcement can be efficient, once the product has a malfunction and the consumer thus depends on his legal rights. In this situation of need it would be inefficient to encumber consumers with further information seeking costs. Furthermore, a promoting of private law enforcement could have the incentive for traders to design products that normally do not have malfunctions—during a certain legally determined period—since otherwise it is to be feared that consumers actually enforce their rights.

However, the central question whether or not consumers will really have a look at their pre-contractual information once the product has a malfunction can only be reliably estimated, once empirical testing is done. Such a test, however, is beyond the scope of this chapter. Therefore, only reasonable assumptions can be made. In the ex ante situation before concluding the contract it is in accordance with human behaviour to ignore at least some of the provided pre-contractual information. The information overload effect by itself is a valid cause. By shifting the protective dimension scrutinized towards the ex post level, however, it seems to be much more in accordance with behavioural insights to look for specific information once the product has a malfunction. The assumption that in case of a real problem information is going to be sought after seems rather legitimate, especially, if the current regime would further be strengthened by the above stated reform proposal.

[81]Emphasized by Ehmann and Forster (2014), p. 166.

[82]See further CJEU, 13.07.2017,C-133/16 (Ferenschild).

5 Pre-Contractual Product Information and Remedy Shaping

As already laid out above (supra 3), the second element of the concept of self-enforcing pre-contractual information is the shaping of remedies due to a pre-contractual product description combined with an inclusion rule. In a first step, the applicable law shall be examined (see infra 5.1). As already indicated above, specific sectoral consumer contracts—namely package travel, timesharing and consumer construction contracts—as well as situation orientated distance and off-premises contracts pursuant to the consumer rights directive will be looked at. Besides a short general introduction, the amount of information to be disclosed in the pre-contractual product description together with the inclusion rules and their normative surrounding will be reviewed. At the end of the section a comparative analysis will sum up and clarify similarities and differences between the different contracts in question. This examination serves as a basis for analysing the effects of inclusion rules and their interplay with the product description and thus enables one to clarify and elaborate the remedy shaping effect more thoroughly (infra. 5.2). Finally, an interim conclusion that also considers efficiency considerations shall be drawn (infra. 5.3).

5.1 The Law in Question

5.1.1 Package Travel Contracts

On the EU-level package travel has been regulated first by the directive 90/314/EEC[83] (DPT-1990). Nowadays, it is regulated by the directive on package travel and linked travel arrangements, 2015/2302/EU, hereafter: DPT-2015. In Germany it is implemented in §§ 651a–651y BGB (*Bürgerliches Gesetzbuch*, i.e. German Civil Code) as well as art. 250–253 EGBGB. The regulation in matters of package travel is regarded as part of the consumer acquis.[84] Nevertheless, since the reform, the subjective scope of application also includes traders,[85] even though regularly only consumers will book a package travel, as they "are normally limited on holiday travel".[86] Another result of the reform is the inclusion of retailers—i.e. traders that sell packages combined by an organiser[87]—into the scope of the directive.[88] Those

[83]Directive on package travel, package holidays and package tours, 90/314/EEC.

[84]See Serrat (2016), p. 361; Grundmann (1999), pp. 603 seqq.

[85]Pointed out inter alia by Führich (2016), p. 1205; but see art. 2 para. 2 lit. c) DPT-2015 for an exemption.

[86]Serrat (2016), p. 362.

[87]Traders that combine packages pursuant to art. 3 no. 8 DPT-2015.

[88]See art. 5 para. 1 DPT-2015; see also Bergmann (2018), p. 23.

retailers share the same information duties as an organiser. Concerning the objective scope of application, the dynamic packing of different travel services is now included[89] and thus an answer given to new forms of package travels distributed via the internet.[90] Travel services are defined in art. 3 no. 1 DPT-2015 and include inter alia carriage, accommodation and also rental of cars.

The amount of product related information to be disclosed is governed by art. 5 para. 1 lit. a) DPT-2015. A similar provision was already contained in art. 3 para. 2 s. 1 DPT-1990 and the annex of DPT-1990. Art. 5 para. 1 lit. b) to h) DPT-2015—in basic conformance with lit. g) to k) of the annex of DPT-1990—lay out further information requirements inter alia in matters of the trading name and geographical address of the organiser (lit. b)), the total price of the package (lit. c)), arrangements for payment (lit. d)) etc.

Regarding the product information art. 5 para. 1 lit. a) DPT-2015 contains eight different sections (i–viii), which are in basic accordance with the annex of DPT-1990. They shall be outlined hereafter: (i) travel destination, itinerary, and periods of stay, with dates as well as number of nights; (ii) means of transportation; interestingly, here also the duration and places of intermediate stops have to be included, this is new; (iii) information about the location and (iv) the meal plan; (v) visits and other services included in the agreed price; (vi) information what kind of services will be provided to the traveller as a group; (vii) language of tourist services, this is also new; (viii) suitability for persons with reduced mobility. In summary, it can easily be stated that package travel must be described in great detail.

The inclusion rule can be found in art. 6 DPT-2015, according to which the pre-contractual product description "shall form an integral part of the package travel contract and shall not be altered unless the contracting parties expressly agree otherwise."[91] In Germany it is implemented in § 651d para. 3 s. 1 BGB. A similar rule had been provided in art. 3 para. 2 s. 2 DPT-1990. Pursuant to it pre-contractual information in the brochure—if issued by the organizer—was declared binding.[92] This provision had become part of the directive due to an initiative of the European Parliament.[93]

5.1.2 Timeshare Contracts

Timeshare contracts have been regulated first by the Directive 94/47/EC "on the protection of purchasers in respect of certain aspects of contracts relating to the purchase of the right to use immovable properties on a timeshare basis" (hereafter:

[89]See art. 3 no. 2 DPT-2015 in detail.

[90]See recital 2 of DPT-2015.

[91]For an interpretation of the exemption ("unless the contracting parties expressly agree otherwise") see infra 5.1.5.

[92]See Weatherill (2013), p. 119.

[93]See OJ/C1989/69/97; Grundmann (1999), p. 605.

Directive 94/47/EC). However, in the year 2009 a new Directive 2008/122/EC "on the protection of consumers in respect of certain aspects of timeshare, long-term holiday product, resale and exchange contracts" was published (hereafter: DTS). This became necessary, since the original timeshare directive did not cover some products.[94] Furthermore, the concept of full harmonisation[95] was chosen. In Germany, the DTS is implemented in §§ 481–487 BGB.[96]

With regards to the scope of application, a comparison between the names of the original timeshare directive and the DTS already shows a greater scope of application. Firstly, pursuant to art. 2 para. 1 lit a) DTS timeshare contracts with a "duration of more than 1 year[97] under which a consumer, for consideration, acquires the right to use one or more overnight accommodation for more than one period of occupation" are contained. Furthermore, pursuant to art. 2 para. 1 lit b) – d) DTS several other forms—and this is new—like long-term holiday products—i.e. holiday clubs and such like—or exchange contracts are covered. Importantly, the legal design of providing the right—i.e. pure obligation or property right—is irrelevant.[98]

The necessary pre-contractual information is covered under art. 4 DTS. Art. 4 para. 1 DTS differentiates between timeshare, long-term holiday, re-sale and exchange contracts. For the following, a closer look will only be taken in matters of timeshare contracts, since they demand for the most detailed pre-contractual product related information. Art. 4 para. 1 lit. a) DTS refers to the Annex I of the DTS, which includes a standard information form. Besides references to the total price, the identity of the trader and the modalities of a withdrawal right, product related information is covered therein. It can be separated into three different groups: (1) information about the right, especially of any further provisions of the country where the immovable property is situated for exercising the right, also the time of use if restricted. (2) Information about the property, including a detailed description also about its location; services like electricity, water, maintenance to which the consumer has or will have access; information about common facilities like a swimming pool or a sauna. The detailed description also includes information about nearby shops, access to public transport and so on.[99] (3) In case the accommodation is still under construction when concluding the contract, detailed information about the state of completion, the deadline for completion, the number of the building permit and such like is required.

---

[94] See Weatherill (2013), pp. 122 seqq.

[95] Recital 3 of the DTS is very clear in that sense and states i.a.: "Member States should not be allowed to maintain or introduce in their national legislation provisions diverging from those laid down in this Directive."

[96] The necessary pre-contractual information duties are set out in art. 242 EGBGB.

[97] This used to be three years, see further Weatherill (2013), pp. 122 seqq.

[98] Comp. Downes (2008), p. 609; for a closer discussion of different legal designs see i.a. Mäsch (1997), pp. 182 seqq.

[99] Staudinger/Martinek, supp. to § 482 no. 6; MüKo/Frentzen, § 482 no. 27.

The inclusion rule is set out in art. 5 para. 2 DTS. Pursuant to this rule the information forms an integral part of the contract.[100] In Germany it is implemented in § 484 para. 2 s. 1 BGB. The original timeshare directive and the German implementation act provided a similar inclusion rule.[101]

5.1.3 Consumer Construction Contracts

The consumer construction contract does not have a background in European law. Rather, it is the product of a legislative reform in Germany regarding construction contracts and an adaption of the German law of sales to the case law of the CJEU in matters of the consumer sales directive.[102] Beforehand, construction contracts were not specifically addressed in the German Civil Code. Nowadays they can be found in §§ 650a seqq. BGB as a subchapter of the contract for work. §§ 650i seqq. BGB specifically address construction contracts between a trader and a consumer. However, the objective scope of application of a consumer construction contract is narrower than that of a construction contract. Pursuant to § 650i para. 1 BGB, only the building of a new structure or considerable replacement measures are encompassed, whereas a "normal" construction contract also includes i.a. the partly construction of a structure or even an outdoor facility.[103]

In matters of the product description § 650j BGB obliges the contractor to give a very detailed pre-contractual description of the structure to be built (hereafter: specifications for construction). The exact amount of information to be disclosed is treated under art. 249 § 2 para. 1 of the EGBGB.[104] Besides a general clause that asks for disclosing the essential characteristics of the structure to be built (art. 249 § 2 para. 1 s. 1 EGBGB) further specifications are to be found in a list of nine different clauses. Particular, they ask for disclosing the following: (1) a general description of the building, including inter alia the construction method; (2) the scope of work to be delivered by the contractor, i.e. the question if a turnkey completion is part of the contractual obligation; (3) plans, ground views and so on; (4) information about the energy, fire protection and sound control standard; (5) information about the structural design, including the question of the used building materials; (6) description of the interior work and the amount of work to be done by the contractor; (7 and 9) description of the building technology and the provided services as well as information about sanitary and outdoor facilities; (8) certain quality features like optical requirements or accessibility for people with disabilities. Furthermore, a mere functional description of the structure—like "common sound insulation"—is not

[100] For possible exemptions see the text of the norm and infra 5.1.5.

[101] See art. 3 no. 2 directive 94/47/EC.

[102] For the legislative background see i.a. jurisPK/Segger, § 650i no. 5 seqq.

[103] See further, jurisPK/Segger, § 650i no. 15 seqq.

[104] For the following see more closely i.a. jurisPK/Segger, § 650j no. 15 seqq., 28 seqq.

sufficient. Rather, technical details—pursuant to technical norms—have to be provided.

The inclusion rule[105] can be found in § 650k para. 1 BGB, according to which the pre-contractual information as stipulated in art. 249 § 2 para. 1 EGBGB becomes part of the contract.[106] Notably, § 650k para. 1 BGB is supplemented by § 650k para. 2 BGB, that provides two major instruments for interpreting the specification for construction:[107] In case those specifications are incomplete or unclear they shall be interpreted before the background of all accompanying circumstances of the contract, especially the further comfort and quality standards, § 650k para. 2 s. 1 BGB. For example, the specifications for construction could provide for a high standard in matters of energy, safety, fire protection, sound protection and so on, however, the resistance class of the windows—in matters of a burglary prevention—could not be specified. Here an interpretation of the specifications for construction pursuant to § 650k para. 2 s. 1 BGB would result in an obligation of the contractor to obstruct windows with a high resistance class. Pursuant to § 650k para. 2 s. 2 BGB in case of doubt the contract will be interpreted in favour of the consumer.[108]

5.1.4 Distance and Off-Premises Contracts

An overview including a working definition of those contracts has already been provided (see supra 4.1). The inclusion rule has also been set out above (see supra 3). In addition, some of the necessary pre-contractual information duties have already been analysed (see supra 4.1, 4.2). Regarding the pre-contractual product description, art. 6 para. 1 lit. a) DCR requires the main characteristics of the good or services to be disclosed. This is a rather unspecific provision and similar provisions are criticized inter alia for their unclear scope of application.[109] Pursuant to law academics, the trader has to provide information that is necessary for an informed conclusion of the contract.[110] The amount of information differs according to the subject matter of the contract. However, the consumer shall be able to compare different products. Thus, this requirement can go further than providing the *essentialia negotii* of the contract.[111] Pursuant to art. 6 para. 1 lit. r), s) DCR information regarding the functionality and interoperability of digital content have

---

[105] For a working translation see infra at the end of the contribution.

[106] For possible exemptions see the text of the norm and infra 5.1.5.

[107] For the effect see infra 5.2.

[108] See infra 5.2 for an analysis of this rule also in comparison to inclusion rules of the other consumer contracts discussed supra and infra.

[109] Baird (2013), pp. 297 seqq.

[110] BeckOK/Martens, art. 246 EGBGB no. 11; MüKo/Wendehorst, § 312a no. 18.

[111] See also Nordhausen Scholes (2009), p. 223; but compare Spindler/Schuster/Schirmbacher, § 312d no. 24 for a critical assessment.

to be disclosed. Unlike lit. a) this can have a notable effect i.a. for the remedy shaping.[112]

5.1.5 Comparative Analysis: Similarities and Differences

A comparative analysis of the different contracts in questions shows that a high amount of information has to be disclosed in the pre-contractual product description regarding the sectoral consumer contracts. The situation-related distance and off-premises contracts are less detailed. The obvious reason is the missing object-specific scope of application of the latter. This is accentuated by the rather specific provisions of art. 6 para. 1 lit. r), s), since they refer to an object-specific scope of application.

Regarding the inclusion rules, all contracts share a similar concept at the outset. They all state that the pre-contractual product description becomes part of the contract unless the parties explicitly agree otherwise. This exemption is an obvious consequence of the principle of party autonomy and thus justified. However, it has to be pointed out that an explicit agreement of the parties via general terms and conditions could easily be a violation of the transparency principle as laid out by art. 5 of the directive on unfair terms in consumers contracts[113] and national implementation norms as well as norm regarding the inclusion of terms like § 305c BGB.[114] Besides, some authors plainly neglect the possibility of an explicit agreement due to general terms and conditions.[115] This seems a bit too far-reaching, since a normative link is missing.

Furthermore, art. 5 para. 2 DTS regarding timeshare contracts and art. 6 para. 1 s. 2 DPT-2015 regarding package travel requires that consumers are specifically and clearly informed about the alterations in comparison to the pre-contractual phase. Therefore, it would not be possible for the trader to promise a certain aspect of the product in his pre-contractual product description and then change it without further notice.

5.2 *Effects and Purpose: Remedy Shaping and Others*

After analysing the law in question, the manifold effects and the purpose of the pre-contractual product description combined with an inclusion rule shall be further carved out hereafter. In the first place one has to differentiate between the ex ante and the ex post dimensions of consumer protection (see already supra at 3). This paper

[112]See infra 5.2.

[113]Directive 93/13/EEC on unfair terms in consumer contracts.

[114]See i.a. Kramme (2015), p. 280 seq.; jurisPK/Segger, § 650k no. 17 seq.

[115]MüKo/Wendehorst, § 312d no. 9; Stretz (2017), § 5 no. 105.

focuses on the latter. However, for the former it needs to be mentioned that in matters of consumer construction contracts the aim of the specifications for construction is not to enable the consumer to make a well-informed choice. Unlike the other contracts,[116] art. 249 § 2 para. 1 s. 1 EGBGB solely requires a clear but not a clear as well as comprehensible presentation and language. Background is the large part of sometimes very technical information that needs to be disclosed.[117] This information can hardly be put in an easy to understand manner. Thus, from an ex ante perspective, the information duties shall enable an (external) expert to compare different offers.[118]

5.2.1 Preserving the Pre-Contractual Product Description

Returning to the ex-post dimension a first important reason for inclusion rules in combination with a pre-contractual product description is to prevent the trader from changing the pre-contractual information to the disadvantage of the consumer (see supra 3). This reason applies to all the different contracts covered.[119] The impact of this function can clearly be seen when drawing a comparison between the status of package travels before and after implementing the package travel directive into the BGB. Before implementing the directive, a change of essential properties of the travel had been seen as a new offer, which was implicitly agreed on by the consumer, when starting the travel.[120] Those sometimes "hard" results are now prevented, since a change of the pre-contractual information in relation to the contract concluded requires an explicit approval of the consumer. Such an explicit approval is also required in matters of timeshare, consumer construction, off-premises and distance contracts.[121]

5.2.2 Reducing Conflicts About the Contractual Obligations Owed

Second, potential conflicts about the extent of the contractual obligations owed will be reduced. The consumer construction contract serves as a prime example. There, the inclusion rule ensures that the specifications for construction form an integral

[116]For package travel see art. 5 para. 3 DPT-2015; for timeshare contracts see art. 4 para. 1 DTS; for distance and off-premises contracts see supra 4.3.

[117]BT-Drs. 18/8486, p. 74; see also jurisPK/Segger, § 650j no. 26 seq.

[118]BT-Drs. 18/8486, p. 62; see also jurisPK/Segger, § 650j no. 5.

[119]For distance and off-premises contracts see: Grundmann (2013), p. 110 seq.; Kramme (2015), pp. 279 seqq.; BT-Drs. 17/12637, p. 54. For package travel contracts see: recital 26; see further BeckOGK/Alexander, § 651d no. 33; Staudinger/Staudinger, § 4 BGB-InfoV, no. 15. For timeshare contracts see: Downes (2008), p. 614; MüKo/Franzen, § 484 no. 10. For consumer construction contracts see: BT-Drs. 18/8486, p. 62; jurisPK/Segger, § 650j no. 5.

[120]Staudinger/Schwerdtner, 1991, § 651a no. 40 seq.; see also Grundmann (1999), p. 611.

[121]See supra 5.1; comparative analysis.

part of the contract and § 650k paragraph 2 BGB serves as a strong incentive for a complete and correct description as required by the specifications. Otherwise, the contract will be interpreted to the disadvantage of the contractor. This prevents contractors from using rather unspecific and "bloomy" specifications for construction and thus has a high practical value, since contractors often try to hide gaps in their specifications in order to generate a—necessarily inefficient[122]—supplement after the conclusion of the contract.[123] Many costly and lengthy disputes have been fought over such unclear specifications.[124] If the trader/contractor still decides to contest that a pre-contractual information became part of the contract and an inclusion rule applies, then the burden of proof for the exclusion of the pre-contractual description rests on the trader/contractor.[125]

However, rules comparable to § 650k para. 2 BGB cannot be found in matters of package travel, timeshare, off-premises and distance contracts. Still, comparable problems can occur there as well. Regarding distance and off-premises contracts, Kramme showed that the pre-contractual product description could differ from the contractual product description to the disadvantage of the consumer.[126] The same holds true for package travel and timeshare contracts. For the latter the problem is already intensively discussed. Some authors prefer to give the consumer a choice as to which information shall prevail.[127] Others prefer a result, whereupon the more favourable clause for the consumer—in relation to his goals—shall prevail.[128] The latter might be convincing, since this could help the consumer the most. Some of the functions of § 650k para. 2 BGB can thus be substituted by applying general principles of contractual interpretation. However, this approach seems to be barred regarding an interpretation like it is provided by § 650k para. 2 s. 1 BGB. This can be especially harmful if a certain formal requirement applies, as will be outlined hereafter.[129]

5.2.3 Remedy Shaping

Most importantly, the combination of a detailed product description and the outlined inclusion rules enables consumers to enforce the promises given to them. The contractual remedy is shaped due to the product information and there needs to be

[122]See i.a. Bickert (2014), pp. 199 seqq.

[123]See i.a. Jenkins (2014), pp. 29 seqq.; Eschenbruch (2015), p. 223.

[124]See i.a. Jenkins (2014), pp. 31 seqq.; jurisPK/Segger, § 650j no. 4 n. 11, with already six examples taken from decisions of the German Federal Court of Justice.

[125]See i.a. BeckOGK/Alexander, § 651d no. 40; Stretz (2017), § 5 no. 101 seq.

[126]Kramme (2015), pp. 280 seqq.; see also MüKo/Wendehorst, § 312d no. 11.

[127]MüKo/Franzen, § 484 no. 13.

[128]Mäsch (1997), p. 196; BeckOGK/Meier, 484 no. 16.

[129]See infra 5.2.4.

no vague interpretation in order to assess whether or not the pre-contractual product description became part of the contract.

It is a general principle in (European) contract law that a contractual remedy can be sought after if the product does not conform to the contractual description, e.g.: art. IV.A. – 2:301 lit. a) DCFR; art. 99 para. 1 lit. a) CESL; art. 35 CISG; § 434 para. 1 BGB.[130] By including the pre-contractual product description into the contract, the basis for contractual remedies is shaped. Several authors have already pointed out this remedy shaping effect: in matters of the proposal for a CESL Baird intensively discussed similar provisions like art. 6 para. 5, 1 DCR of the CESL before the background of the remedy shaping effect.[131] For distance and off-premises contracts Nordhausen Scholes and Weber pointed out the potential effects of inclusion rules and remedy shaping.[132] Schirmbacher illustrated the relation of informing about matters of interoperability and contractual remedies.[133] The same holds true for timeshare,[134] package travel[135] and consumer construction contracts.[136]

5.2.4 Apology Against Criticism

Of course, the concept of remedy shaping through obligatory pre-contractual product information is sometimes also criticized. Especially Baird pointed out that it could be an incentive for the trader to reveal less or less accurate information about the product.[137] This might hold true if the amount of product related information is not determined further. However, in case of the consumer construction contract as well as timeshare and package travel contracts a very detailed product description is combined with an inclusion rule. This combination is the central aspect and it makes the instrument efficient and powerful. On the one side, the mandated pre-contractual product description obliges traders to reveal certain characteristics about the product. On the other side, the inclusion rule ensures that the consumer can enforce these promises beyond all doubt via contractual remedies.

However, it is also contested whether or not such inclusion rules are really necessary. Several authors argue that similar results could be achieved with the regular instruments for interpreting the content of a contract.[138] Regarding package

[130]For a contextual anaylsis to the alternative regime of caveat emptor see Baird (2013), pp. 299 seqq.

[131]Baird (2013), p. 309 seq.

[132]Nordhausen Scholes (2009), p. 232; Weber (2019), p. 280 seq.

[133]Spindler/Schuster/Schirmbacher, § 312d no. 25; see also Grundmann (2013), p. 110 seq.

[134]BeckOK/Eckert, § 484 no. 8; BeckOGK/Meier, § 482 no. 15.

[135]BeckOK/Baumgärtner, § 651d no. 39; Bergmann (2018), p. 24; Staudinger/Staudinger, § 4 BGB-InfoV, no. 15.

[136]jurisPK/Segger, § 650j no. 5; Leinemann/Kues/Abu Saris, § 650k no. 4.

[137]Baird (2013), p. 309 seq.

[138]Kramme (2015), p. 297; Spindler/Schuster/Schirmbacher, § 312d no. 20; compare also BT-Drs. 17/12637, p. 97.

travel contracts—even before enacting the first package travel directive—it was agreed that information in a brochure or such like was crucial for interpreting the extent of the contractual performance duties and therefore possible contractual remedies.[139] On the other hand, it may remain unclear whether pre-contractual information does become part of the contract or whether it is to be qualified merely as some sort of advertisement.[140] In matters of art. 6 para. 5 DCR Grundmann states that "information can no longer be given without legal consequences."[141]

Especially regarding real estate sales contracts pursuant to German law it is contested whether or not pre-contractual information by a real estate agent can be qualified as a contractual description of the object in question.[142] This is further complicated due to the requirements in questions of form.[143] Furthermore, it is generally agreed upon that necessary information in matters of the energy standard of a building—pursuant to the implementation norm § 16 EnEV of the European directives on energy performance of buildings[144]—only constitutes a mere non-binding "knowledge statement" and cannot be qualified as a promised characteristic of the building.[145] An inclusion rule, however, can provide clear and certain results. Besides, rules regarding the contractual interpretation like § 650k para. 2 BGB become relevant if a pre-contractual product description does not become part of the contract due to reasons of formal requirements not met,[146] since the pre-contractual information could still be relevant for interpreting the contract.[147]

5.3 *Interim Conclusion and Possible Options for Reform*

Regulating the level of product information can be a very efficient tool, especially when combined with inclusion rules. Three different reasons have been carved out: First, the inclusion rules have an effect like the basis of the bargain principle, and this is—as stated supra at 3—considered as efficient. Furthermore, such a combination can help to reduce conflicts about the contractual obligations owed. Finally, the remedy shaping effect enables to enforce consumers the promises given to them.

---

139 Staudinger/Schwerdtner, 1991, § 651c no. 23 seq.; see also Grundmann (1999), p. 610 seq. with further references.

140 Compare supra n. 129–132.

141 Grundmann (2013), p. 110 seq.; see also Nordhausen Scholes (2009), p. 232.

142 Negated by law academics, see i.a. Lüttringhaus (2018), p. 1030; Gräf (2017), pp. 300 seqq. Affirmed by the case law, see BGH NJW 2018, 1954, no. 21; BGH NJW-RR 2018, 752, no. 10.

143 For this aspects see the sources supra at n. 142 as well.

144 Directive 2010/31/EU on the energy performance of buildings and Directive 2012/27/EU of on energy efficiency, amending Directives 2009/125/EC and 2010/30/EU and repealing Directives 2004/8/EC and 2006/32/EC.

145 Higher Regional Court Schleswig, NJW 2015, 2668; Cziupka and Hübner (2016), p. 335.

146 See i.a BeckOGK/Meier, § 484 no. 16.1.

147 Comp. MüKo/Busche, § 650u no. 7.

Regarding possible options for reform, it might be valuable to strengthen the existing inclusion rules of the other contracts via surrounding rules on interpretation like § 650k para. 2 BGB regarding the consumer construction contract. Such rules might serve as a further incentive for traders to formulate clear and non-contradictory product descriptions.

6 Regulation Through Product Description: An Emerging Concept?

This last section will take a look ahead and introduce or rather outline the concept of an indirect regulation through pre-contractual information and inclusion rules. The underlying idea is that traders would not be obliged to sell products that conform to a certain characteristic or standard. Rather those traders would "only" be obliged to inform if their product is in accordance with a certain characteristic or standard. A nonconforming product could then easily be identified as the "black sheep"—for example by a consumer association—and thus not be consumed.[148] In combination with inclusion rules consumers would also be able to individually enforce the promises given to them by the traders and thus put further pressure on those.

Before further explaining this idea, it has to be clarified that the underlying idea refers to the ex ante dimension of pre-contractual information, since it aims at changing the purchase decisions of consumers due to the bad reputation of a product or producer. However, a systematic difference occurs in so far as nowadays everybody can be a sender as well as a receiver on the internet, especially due to social media, twitter, etc. Thus a systematic change of communication occurred. Before this background, a bad product reputation has become a more demanding problem and producers seem to be very sensitive in order to prevent a so-called "shitstorm".

For a possible reform it could first be scrutinized whether already existing information duties that currently are not regarded as contractually binding, should be made a basis of the bargain and thus be enforced via contractual remedies. For example, this could apply to information in a Corporate Social Responsibility-report of a specific business.[149] A manufacturer of cloth for example might guarantee certain working conditions in his factories. These promises could form a part of the contract via an inclusion rule. Another example is the duty to reveal the energy performance of a building due to a European directive. This information is currently regarded as a mere non-binding knowledge statement. However, one would have to study further whether such statements are not already included by rules describing

[148] Compare also Ramsay (2012), p. 102 seq.

[149] For the legislative background see Directive 2014/95/EU amending Directive 2013/34/EU as regards disclosure of non-financial and diversity information by certain large undertakings and groups and further Segger (2018); compare also Lüttringhaus (2019).

the conformity with the contract in the European consumer sales directive[150] or implementation rules like § 434 para 1 s. 3 BGB. Furthermore, rules on unfair competition would have to be looked at much closer, since some contractually non-binding pre-contractual information like energy standards is covered by those rules.[151] Thus, measures of collective redress are already available. Nevertheless, it could at least be worthwhile to think about further strengthening the individual sphere.

A next step could be the introduction of further product related information duties combined with inclusion rules. The subject-matter of those disclosure duties would of course be a policy question. However, aspects of a sustainable manufacturing are nowadays more and more discussed and their importance is pointed out. For example, traders could be obliged to clarify whether their products were produced with green energy. This could lead to an indirect pressure towards a greater use of such energy.

7 Conclusion

The aim of this paper was to demonstrate the ex-post dimension of pre-contractual information. It is true that disclosures are often not processed thoroughly before concluding a contract. Nevertheless, they still can serve a meaningful purpose. On the one hand they can promote private enforcement by informing consumers about their contractual remedies. On the other hand—and this I believe to be the central point—they can shape remedies and put pressure on traders to offer products that are wanted. Rather than trying to find the "right" product before concluding the contract, pre-contractual information can be used to give consumers the product they want or rather shall want.

Acknowledgements For helpful comments I would like to thank Professor Oliver Remien, Professor Omri Ben-Shahar, Selina Schätzlein, Hannah Piening and Lynn Gummow.

Annex: Working Translation of § 650k BGB

§ 650k BGB—Content of the contract [Working translation by author]

[150]Since the Consumer Sales Directive does not apply to immovable property, this could only hold true for information in a corporate social Responsibility-report; see further Lüttringhaus (2019).

[151]See i.a. Götting/Hetman, in Fezer/Büscher/Obergfell, UWG, § 3a no. 158.

Para. 1
The information enclosed in the pre-contractually provided specifications for construction becomes part of the contract, unless the contracting parties expressly agree otherwise.

Para. 2
In case those specifications are incomplete or unclear, the contract shall be interpreted before the background of all accompanying circumstances of the contract, especially the further comfort and quality standards pursuant to the specifications. A case of doubt [ambiguity] when interpreting the obligations of the contractor is at his expense.

References

Monographies and Articles

Ayres I, Schwartz A (2014) The no-reading problem in consumer contract law. Stanford Law Rev 66:545–609

Baird D (2013) Precontractual disclosure duties under the common European sales law. Common Mark Law Rev 50:297–310

Bar-Gill O, Ben-Shahar O (2013) Regulatory techniques in consumer protection: a critique of European consumer contract law. Common Mark Law Rev 50:109–125

Ben-Shahar O, Schneider CE (2011) The failure of mandated disclosure. Univ Pa Law Rev 159:646–749

Bergmann S (2018) Das neue Reiserecht. Beck, München

Bettman JR, Payne JW, Staelin R (1986) Cognitive considerations in designing effective labels for presenting risk information source. J Public Policy Market 5:1–28

Bickert E (2014) Der Bauvertrag als symbiotischer Interessenwahrungsvertrag. Duncker & Humblot, Berlin

Brownsword R, Howells G, Wilhelmsson T (1994) Welfarism in contract law. Darthmouth, Aldershot

Busch C (2016) The future of pre-contractual information duties: from behavioural insights to big data. In: Twigg-Flesner C (ed) Research handbook on EU consumer and contract law. Edward, Cheltenham, pp 221–240

Camerer C, Loewenstein G, Rabin M (2004) Advances in behavioral economics. University Press, Princeton

Cartwright P (2016) The consumer image within EU law. In: Twigg-Flesner C (ed) Research handbook on EU consumer and contract law. Edward Elgar, Cheltenham, pp 199–220

Charrow RP, Charrow VR (1979) Making legal language understandable: a psycholinguistic study of jury instructions. Columbia Law Rev 79:1306–1374

Cziupka J, Hübner L (2016) Beschaffenheitsinformationen und Beschaffenheitsvereinbarungen beim Grundstückskaufvertrag. Deutsche Notar-Zeitschrift, 323–343

Dauner-Lieb B (1983) Verbraucherschutz durch Ausbildung eines Sonderprivatrechts für Verbraucher. Duncker & Humblot, Berlin

Dauner-Lieb B (2007) A special private law for B2C? Silver Bullet or Blind Alley? In: Schulze R (ed) New features in contract law. Sellier, München, pp 107–118

Downes N (2008) More about timeshare: a revised directive or a regulation? Incidence of other instruments of consumer protection. Eur Rev Priv Law 16:607–625

Ehmann T, Forster J (2014) Umsetzung der Verbraucherrechterichtlinie – Teil 1: Der neue "allgemeine Teil" des Verbraucherschutzrechts. Gesellschafts- und Wirtschaftsrecht (GWR):163–167
Eidenmüller H (2005) Der homo oeconomicus und das Schuldrecht: Herausforderungen durch behavioural law and economics. Juristenzeitung:216–224
Englerth M (2007) Behavioral law and economics – eine kritische Einführung. In: Engel C (ed) Recht und Verhalten. Mohr, Tübingen, pp 60–132
Englerth M, Towfigh E (2017) Verhaltensökonomik. In: Tofigh E, Petersen N (eds) Ökonomische Methoden im Recht. Mohr, Tübingen, pp 237–276
Eschenbruch K (2015) Projektmanagement und Projektsteuerung für die Immobilien- und Bauwirtschaft, 4th edn. Werner Verlag, Köln
European Commission (2017) Study for the Fitness Check of EU consumer and marketing law, May 2017, Final report, Part 1 – Main report. Available at: https://publications.europa.eu/portal2012-portlet/html/downloadHandler.jsp?identifier=f7b3958b-772b-11e7-b2f2-01aa75ed71a1&format=pdf&language=en&productionSystem=cellar&part= (visited on 18.06.2020)
Fleischer H (2000) Vertragsschlußbezogene Informationspflichten im Gemeischaftsprivatrecht. Zeitschrift für Europäisches Privatrecht:772–798
Führich E (2016) Die neue Pauschalreiserichtlinie. Neue Juristische Wochenschrift:1204–1209
Gillis TB (2015) Putting disclosure to the test: toward better evidence-based policy. Loyola Consum Law Rev 28:31–105
Gräf S (2017) Die Verkäuferhaftung aufgrund öffentlicher Äußerungen im richtlinienüberschießenden Anwendungsbereich des § BGB § 434 Abs. BGB § 434 Abs. 1 S. 3 BGB. Zeitschrift für Privatrechtswissenschaft 286–324
Grundmann S (1999) Europäisches Schuldvertragsrecht. Walter de Gruyter, Berlin
Grundmann S (2013) The EU consumer rights Directive: optimizing, creating alternatives, or a dead end. Uniform Law Rev 18:98–127
Hacker P (2016) More behavioral vs. more economic approach: explaining the behavioral divide between the United States and the European Union. Hast Int Comp Law Rev 39:355–388
Hacker P (2017) Verhaltensökonomik und Normativität. Mohr, Tübingen
Hall E, Howells G, Watson J (2012) The Consumer Rights Directive – an assessment of its contribution to the development of European consumer contract law. Eur Rev Contract Law 8:146–114
Heiderhoff B (2004) Grundstrukturen des nationalen und Europäischen Verbrauchervertragsrechts. Sellier, München
Helleringer G, Sibony A-L (2017) European consumer protection through the bavioral lense. Columbia J Eur Law 23:607–646
Holdych TJ, Mann BD (1996) The basis of the bargain requirement: a market and economic based analysis of express warranties - getting what you pay for and paying for what you get. DePaul Law Rev 45:781–857
Howells G, Wilhelmsson T (2003) EC consumer law: has it come of age? Eur Law Rev 23:370–388
Jenkins J (2014) International construction arbitration law. Wolters Kluwer, Alphen aan den Rijn
Jolls C, Sunstein CR, Thaler RH (1998) A behavioral approach to law and economics. Stanford Law Rev 50:1471–1550
Kahneman D, Tversky A (1979) Prospect theory: an analysis of decision under risk. Econometrica 47:263–291
Kahneman D, Tversky A (1984) Choices, values, and frames. Am Psychol 39:341–350
Kramme M (2015) Die Einbeziehung von Pflichtinformationen in Fernabsatz- und Außergeschäftsraumverträge. Neue Juristische Wochenschrift, 279–284
Leible S (1994) Abschied vom "flüchtigen Verbraucher"?. Deutsche Zeitschrift für Wirtschaftsrecht, 177–181
Loewenstein G, Sunstein C, Goldman R (2014) Disclosure: psychology changes everything. Ann Rev Econ 6:391–419

Lurger B (1998) Vertragliche Solidarität. Nomos, Baden-Baden
Lüttringhaus JD (2018) Vorvertragliche Beschaffenheitsangaben beim Immobilienkauf. Juristenzeitung, 1029–1034
Lüttringhaus JD (2019) Kaufrechtliche Gewährleistungsansprüche bei "ethischen" Produkten und öffentlichen Aussagen zur Corporate Social Responsibility. Archiv für Civilistische Praxis 219:29–62
Martinek M (2000) Unsystematische Überregulierung und kontraintentionale Effekte im Europäischen Verbraucherschutzrecht oder: Weniger wäre mehr. In: Grundmann S (ed) Systembildung und Systemlücken in Kerngebieten des Europäischen Privatrechts. Mohr, Tübingen, pp 511–558
Mäsch G (1997) Das deutsche Time-Sharing-Recht nach dem neuen Teilzeit-Wohnrechte-Gesetz. Deutsche Notar-Zeitschrift 180–213
Mathis K, Steffen AD (2015) From rational choice to behavioural economics. In: Mathis K (ed) European perspectives on behavioural law and economics. Springer, New York, pp 31–50
Murray JE Jr (1982) Basis of the bargain: transcending classical concepts. Minn Law Rev 66:283–325
Nordhausen Scholes A (2009) Information requirements. In: Howells G, Schulze R (eds) Modernising and harmonising consumer contract law. Sellier, München, pp 213–236
Ramsay I (2005) From truth in lending to responsible lending. In: Howells G, Janssen A, Schulze R (eds) Information rights and obligations. Ashgate, Dartmouth, pp 47–65
Ramsay I (2012) Consumer law and policy, 3rd edn. Hart, Oxford
Schendra CFG (2004) Die Vollständigkeit von Rechtstexten. Eine kritische Darstellung der Forschungslage. In: Lerch KD (ed) Die Sprache des Rechts, vol 1, Berlin, pp 321–374
Schmolke KU (2014) Grenzen der Selbstbindung im Privatrecht. In: Rechtspaternalismus und Verhaltensökonomik im Familien-, Gesellschafts- und Verbraucherrecht. Mohr, Tübingen
Schürnbrand J, Janal R (2018) Examens-Repetitorium Verbraucherschutzrecht, 3rd edn. C.F. Müller, Heidelberg
Segger S (2018) Europäisches Haftungsregime für Menschenrechtsverletzungen von Unternehmen?. In: Krajewski M, Saage-Maß M (eds) Die Durchsetzung menschenrechtlicher Sorgfaltspflichten von Unternehmen. Nomos, Baden-Baden, pp 19–60
Serrat JMB (2016) Consumer travel law. In: Twigg-Flesner C (ed) EU consumer and contract law. Edward Elgar, Cheltenham, pp 360–387
Sibony A-L (2015) Can EU consumer law benefit from behavioural insights? In: Mathis K (ed) European perspectives on behavioural law and economics. Springer, New York, pp 71–106
Simon HA (1955) A behavioral model of rational choice. Q J Econ 69:99–118
Simon HA (1972) Theories of bounded rationality. In: McGuire C, Roy R (eds) Decision and organization. North Holland, Amsterdam, pp 161–176
Stark DP, Choplin JM (2010) A cognitive and social psychological analysis of disclosure laws and call for mortgage counseling to prevent predatory lending. Psychol Public Policy Law 16:85–131
Stretz A (2017) Verbraucherbauvertrag. In: Dammert B, Lenkeit O, Oberhauser I, Pause H-E, Anna S (eds) Das neue Bauvertragsrecht. Beck, München, pp 117–200
Sunstein CR, Thaler RH (2003) Libertarian paternalism is not an oxymoron. Univ Chicago Law Rev 70:1159–1202
Tamm M (2011) Verbraucherschutzrecht. Mohr, Tübingen
Ulen T (2001) Information in the market economy - cognitive errors and legal correctives. In: Grundmann S, Kerber W, Weatherill S (eds) Party autonomy and the role of information. Walter der Gruyter, Berlin, pp 98–130
Weatherill S (2013) EU consumer law and policy, 2nd edn. Elgar, Cheltenham
Weber K (2019) Sanktionen bei vorvertraglicher Informationspflichtverletzung. Mohr, Tübingen
Whitford WC (1973) The functions of disclosure regulation in consumer transactions. Wis Law Rev:400–470

Wilhelmsson T (1996) Consumer images in East and West. In: Micklitz H-W (ed) Rechtseinheit oder Rechtsvielfalt in Europa. Nomos, Baden-Baden, pp 53–65

Willis L (2015) Performance based consumer law. Univ Chicago Law Rev 82:1309–1410

German Commentaries

Bamberger, Heinz Georg; Roth, Herbert; Hau, Wolfgang; Poseck, Roman (eds.). 2019. BeckOnline Kommentar BGB (cited: BeckOK/author). München: Beck

Fezer, Karl-Heinz; Büscher, Wolfgang and Obergfell, Eva Inés (eds.). 2016. *Lauterkeitsrecht Kommentar zum Gesetz gegen den unlauteren Wettbewerb (UWG)*, 3rd ed. München: Beck (cited: author, in: Fezer/Büscher/Obergfell, UWG)

Gsell, Beate; Krüger, Wolfgang; Lorenz, Stephan and Reymann, Christoph (eds.). 2019. *beck-online. Großkommentar*. München: Beck. (cited: BeckOGK/author)

Herberger, Maximilian / Martinek, Michael / Rüßmann, Helmut / Weth, Stephan / Würdinger, Markus (eds). *juris PraxisKommentar-BGB*, Band 2 (Recht der Schuldverhältnisse), § 312d BGB, 2017, 8th Ed.; §§ 650i-650o, 2020, 9th ed. Saarbrücken: juris GmbH (cited: jurisPK/author)

Leinemann, Ralf and Kues, Jan.-Hendrik (eds.). 2018. *BGB-Bauvertragsrecht*. München: Beck. (cited: Leinemann/Kues/author)

Palandt, Otto (org.). 2020. *Bürgerliches Gesetzbuch*, 79. ed., München: Beck (cited: Palandt/author)

Säcker, Franz Jürgen; Rixecker, Roland; Oetker, Harmut and Limperg, Bettina (eds.). *Münchener Kommentar zum Bürgerlichen Gesetzbuch*. §§ 311-432, 2019; §§ 433-534, 2019; 631-704, 2020, 8th ed. München: Beck (cited: MüKo/author)

Spindler, Gerald and Schuster, Fabian (eds.). 2019. *Recht der elektronischen Medien*. 4th. ed. München: Beck. (cited: Spindler/Schuster/author)

von Staudinger, Julius (org.): Kommentar zum Bürgerlichen Gesetzbuch mit Einführungsgesetzen. §§ 305-310; UKlaG, 2019. §§ 312, 312a-k, 2019. §§ 433-487, 2004; §§ 651a-651m, BGB InfoV, 2016; §§ 620-651k, 1991 (cited: Staudinger/author)

Grundewald, Barbara; Maier-Reimer, Georg; Westermann, Harm Peter (ed.). 2017. Erman BGB, Kommentar. 15th edition. Köln: Dr. Otto Schmidt

Sören Segger-Piening Würzburg. Akademischer Rat a.Z. (post-doc) at the Chair of Civil Law, European Economic Law, Private International Law and Litigation as well as Comparative Law (Prof. Dr. Oliver Remien), University of Würzburg, Domerschulstr. 16, 97070 Würzburg, Tel. +49 (0)931 31 85035, s.segger-piening@jura.uni-wuerzburg.de. Fields of Interest: Civil Law, Civil Procedure, Private International Law and Litigation, Comparative Law, Economic Analysis of Law, European Private Law.

The Law on Unfair Terms in Standard Form Contracts in Europe

A Comparative Law and Economics Approach

Ann-Sophie Vandenberghe

Abstract The research tests the efficiency hypothesis of law by using the method of comparative law & economics applied to unfair terms law. There are four theoretical legal solutions to the signing-without-reading problem and from an economic point of view a 'duty to draft efficient terms' imposed upon the drafter of the standard form contract is the best solution. The research has looked at the development of real-life Dutch unfair terms law and has found out that the development is clearly in the direction of the efficient solution.

1 Introduction

Standard terms are a feature of the vast majority of written contracts. Since only one party participates in their formulation, they offer the opportunity for that party to introduce terms that the other might not willingly agree to in negotiations. The European Union has introduced controls over standard terms. It adopted Council Directive 93/13/EEC of 5 April, 1993 on unfair terms in consumer contracts (hereinafter, the Unfair Contract Terms Directive, UCTD).[1] The directive requires member states to have unfair term statutes that meet certain minimum standards. It directs member states to give courts the authority to decline to enforce 'unfair' terms, through the invalidation of such terms. Also in the context of the UCTD, the European Court of Justice has developed the obligation of the national judge to apply consumer law on his own motion in order to protect the weaker party in civil

[1]Council Directive 93/13/EEC of 5 April 1993 on unfair terms in consumer contracts, OJ 1993, L 095/29.

A.-S. Vandenberghe (✉)
Rotterdam Institute of Law and Economics (RILE), Erasmus School of Law, Rotterdam, The Netherlands
e-mail: vandenberghe@law.eur.nl

K. Mathis, A. Tor (eds.), *Consumer Law and Economics*, Economic Analysis of Law in European Legal Scholarship 9, https://doi.org/10.1007/978-3-030-49028-7_6

proceedings.[2] This obligation has been described as the 'ex officio application' of EU consumer law. An EU directive is not the same as an EU regulation. The Directive sets certain aims, requirements and concrete results that must be achieved in every member state. Respective national institutions are then tasked to integrate the directives in the country's legal system and to come up with their own rules to achieve the essence of the directives. In the Netherlands, for example, the requirements of the UCTD were implemented within the rules of the Civil Code that deal with 'general terms and conditions.'[3] Different Member States have taken different measures to implement the Directive.[4] Moreover, unfair terms law further develops under the influence of the decisions taken by national courts. How to evaluate these developments? To the law and economics scholar developments in unfair terms laws can be employed as data to test the grand efficiency theory of law. An approach typical of comparative law and economics is to build a model of an efficient legal institution and then compare it with the real world alternatives of different legal systems.[5] In his 2016 contribution to the Springer Encyclopedia of Law and Economics, Gerrit De Geest compares four theoretical legal solutions to the signing-without-reading problem and concludes that a 'duty to draft efficient terms' imposed upon the drafter of standard terms, is the best solution from an economic point of view.[6] If the efficiency hypothesis of law is true, one would expect the developments of real-world alternatives of legal systems to move in a direction which corresponds with the efficient solution. The aim of this contribution is to test this hypothesis for Dutch standard terms law. Section 2 explains the use of comparative law and economics methodology as a test of the grand efficiency theory of law. Section 3 reproduces De Geest's conclusion that a duty to draft efficient terms is the best solution for the signing-without-reading problem. Section 4 analyses the development of Dutch standard terms law following the implementation the UCTD and concludes that the development is directed towards the more efficient solution.

2 The Method of Comparative Law and Economics

The comparative study of law is primarily aimed at discovering similarities and divergences among legal systems. The comparative methodology presupposes a plurality of legal rules and it compares them in order to determine to what extent they are identical or different.[7] Its aims are at the same time highly practical—

[2]Beginning with ECJ judgment of 27 June 2000, Joined cases C-240/98 to C-244/98 – *Océano Grupo Editorial SA v. Murciano Quintera* [2000] ECR I-04941.

[3]Title 5 (Contracts in general), section 3 (General terms), articles 231–247 Dutch Civil Code.

[4]Schulte-Nölke et al. (2008).

[5]Mattei (1995), p. 430.

[6]De Geest (2016).

[7]Mattei and Monti (2001), pp. 1–2.

facilitation of compliance with foreign law—and highly scientific—improved comprehension of the issues and approaches available to deal with particular legal issues.[8] Law & economics can enrich comparative study of this kind by its building of efficient model rules, which work as uniform terms of comparison for the different solutions adopted by the actual legal systems compared, in order to allow proper measurement of the distance that separates them from the theoretically efficient solution.[9] The enrichment between comparative law and Law & Economics is mutual. In a legal process style comparison of alternative legal solutions comparative law may offer to economic analysis a reservoir of legal alternatives not merely theoretical but actually tested by legal history.[10] Comparative lawyers have often concluded that legal rules seem different at first blush but that, in spite of differences in the substantive and procedural rules across jurisdictions, different legal systems reach similar outcomes. This functional comparative method, which starts from the assumption that rules have the same function, is very well suited to be employed as a test of the grand theory about the efficiency of law.[11] An approach typical of comparative law and economics is to build a model of an efficient legal institution and then compare it with the real world alternatives of different legal systems.[12] Typically, when faced with departures from the efficient model, the comparative legal and economic analyst will try to establish whether the legal system under analysis possesses institutions that can work as efficiency-restoring attributes. If the efficiency hypothesis is confirmed, the comparative method deserves its place, next to other empirical tests, in the catalogue of empirical methods in Law and Economics. If the efficiency hypothesis is falsified, the research outcome of the comparative legal analysis may signal the need for an improved economic theory. The study of institutions may invite economists to re-examine their theories, adapt the underlying assumptions and develop a more nuanced theory. By taking account of the data provided by comparative legal research, Law and Economics may be enriched to the mutual benefit of both disciplines.[13]

[8]Maxeiner (2003), p. 112.

[9]Mattei and Monti (2003), p. 6.

[10]Mattei and Monti (2003), p. 6.

[11]Van den Bergh (2018), pp. 22–23.

[12]Mattei (1995), p. 430.

[13]Van den Bergh (2018), p. 23.

3 The Economically Optimal Legal Solution for the Signing-Without-Reading Problem

3.1 Introduction

In order to develop the economic optimal model rule (the uniform term of comparison) we first need to define the cause of the problem for which the law seeks a solution. This is an essential part of the law & economics approach to law which adopts an instrumental view of the law. The Unfair Contract Terms Directive (the Directive or UCTD) offers consumers in the European Union protection against pre-formulated imbalanced contract terms.[14] According to the European Court of Justice of the European Union (ECJ) the Directive's system of protection assumes that the consumer is in a weak position vis-à-vis the trader as regards both her bargaining power and her level of knowledge. It is not always clear what courts mean by the term 'unequal bargaining' power but the closest economic concept is that of market or monopoly power. The problem with the unequal bargaining rationale for reviewing unfair terms is that a take-it-or-leave-it characteristic is not the fundamental cause of the unfair contract terms.[15] Buyers who sign standard form contracts when they are still in a position where they can freely compare the terms of different competing sellers are not better off. If it is not the take-it-or-leave-it characteristic of contracts that causes the problem, what does? It is the signing-without-reading problem. The overwhelming majority of standard terms contracts are never read. This is confirmed by recent empirical studies which find that very few people even bother to look at the contracts they sign, and even fewer people spend enough time to understand them.[16] This gives contract drafters an incentive to insert one-sided, inefficient terms in the standard term contract. The problem of signing-without-reading is that it may lead to inefficient terms. How to reconcile the economic description of the problem to be solved, i.e. that the signing-without-reading problem may lead to inefficient terms, with the legally expressed aim to protect consumers against unfair terms? The relationship between efficiency and fairness is often presented as if there is a trade-off between them, i.e. 'fairness versus efficiency', but it does not have to be presented in that way. (In)efficiency may also be a way to explain why a term is (un)fair. This latter approach in which the efficiency criterion is used as a way to define fairness is adopted in this contribution.

---

[14]Council Directive 93/13/EEC of 5 April 1993 on unfair terms in consumer contracts, OJ 1993, L095/29.

[15]Marotta-Wurgler (2009).

[16]Bakos et al. (2014) and Ben-Shahar and Schneider (2014).

3.2 *In the Absence of a Signing-Without-Reading Problem, Only Efficient Terms Are Adopted*

The tenet to which all law and economics scholars hold is that in the absence of a signing-without-reading problem, only efficient terms will be adopted. This follows directly from the Coase theorem. Here is an example of how the Coase theorem works, taken from Daniel Friedman's law and economics handbook "law's order":

> You and I are drawing up a contract for a joint business project. It occurs to me that a particular term is inefficient. Giving you an additional month to perform the first stage of the contract would save you a hundred thousand dollars, cost me fifty thousand, and thus increase our net gain by fifty thousand dollars. My first thought is that I should keep my mouth shut, since the change will leave me fifty thousand dollars worse off. But there is a better alternative. I propose to write the change in the contract along with a seventy-five thousand dollar increase in the amount you will pay me for my participation. This simple example demonstrates a very general point, one that underlies the Coase theorem. As long as there exists a change in the terms of our deal that would produce a net benefit, there is a way of making that change that benefits both of us. Hence we would expect rational bargainers to come up with contract terms that maximize the net gain. If our objective is economic efficiency, that is both an attractive outcome and an argument for enforcing contracts as written.[17]

The term which gives the promisee an extra month to perform is, in the example given, an efficient term according to the standard definition of an efficient term. The standard definition of an efficient term is as follows: it is a term that increases the contractual surplus by creating obligations that generate a higher benefit to the promisee than they cost to the promisor. In the example, giving you one extra month to perform is an efficient term because it generates a higher benefit to the promisee (hundred thousand dollars) than it costs to the promisor (fifty thousand dollar). In the absence of a signing-without-reading problem efficient terms will be adopted because they increase the contractual surplus and therefore it is possible to find a price adjustment that will make both parties better off. In the example given, a price increase of seventy five thousand dollars makes both parties better off. Is it also correct to say that in the absence of a signing-without-reading problem, inefficient terms will not be adopted? When the circumstances of the case are such that giving you an additional month to perform would cost me hundred thousand dollar and save you only fifty thousand dollar, the extra month to perform is inefficient. The standard definition of an inefficient term is a term that costs the promisor more than it benefits the promisee. In the absence of a signing-without-reading problem, inefficient terms will not be adopted because such terms decrease the contractual surplus and therefore it is not possible to find a price adjustment that will make both parties better off. Now that empirical evidence has shown that the signing-without-reading problem does exist and assuming that this gives standard contract drafters an incentive to insert inefficient terms, the next question to be asked is which legal solution is best to solve the problem.

[17]Friedman (2000), p. 148.

3.3 Theoretical Solutions to the Signing-Without-Reading Problem

De Geest disentangles four theoretical legal solutions to the signing-without-reading problem:[18]

(1) *Give the standard contract user a duty to draft efficient terms*. The party who uses general conditions (standard contract user) has a duty to draft efficient terms. The sanction for not complying with this duty is that inefficient terms are non-binding. The evidentiary burden is on the standard contract user (drafter).
(2) *Give the standard contract signer a duty to read*. The party who signs standard form contracts has a duty to read the standard contract terms. The contract user (drafter) has to make sure that the contract signer has a reasonable opportunity to become informed about the standard contract terms. The sanction for not reading is that contract terms are binding even when a party has not read them. A duty to read tries to solve the drafter's incentive problem in an indirect way; if a sufficient number of people read the contract, the benefit of inserting inefficient terms may disappear.
(3) *Standard contract terms are never binding*.
(4) *A duty to read with an unconscionability exception*. Terms in standard contracts are binding even when the signer has not read them, unless they are unconscionable. The evidentiary burden that terms are unconscionable are on the contract signer, i.e. on the one who invokes the exception.

One value in law, whether or not it's the leading value, is to find the cheapest way to solve problems, and then to give people incentives to use them.[19] So what is the cheapest way to solve the signing-without-reading problem? De Geest has argued that solution (1) 'Give the standard contract user a duty to draft efficient terms' is the superior solution.[20]

3.4 Standard Terms Are Never Binding (Solution 3)

Theoretically, one solution to the signing-without-reading problem is to stipulate a rule which says that standard contracts are never binding. This solution is, however, generally considered as undesirable.[21] It invalidates all unread terms, even the efficient ones. The legal importance of standard term contracts is that they alter default solutions provided by law. According to the default rule system the law

[18]De Geest (2016).
[19]Farnsworth (2007), p. 18.
[20]De Geest (2016).
[21]De Geest (2016).

provides one solution that applies unless the parties agree otherwise. In standard terms the parties 'agree' otherwise. Invalidating all standard terms in practice means that the legal default rules are always binding—as a matter of fact, all default rules then become mandatory rules in contracts that are not individually negotiated. This would be fine if default rules were always efficient. It is hard to see why this is the case for two reasons. First, they are chosen by legislators and courts on the basis of an analysis that may be wrong. Lawmakers can learn from the market for contract terms, but only if they allow a market for legal terms in the first place. Second, they are not perfectly adapted to individual situations. Even if default terms are efficient for a majority of contracting parties, they may be inefficient for a minority. By allowing this minority to contract away from the default setting, inefficient allocations are prevented.

3.5 A Duty to Draft Efficient Terms (Solution 1) Versus a Duty to Read (Solution 2)

De Geest asks the question whether it is better to give the drafter a duty to draft efficient terms or to give the signer a duty to read? To answer this question he frames the problem in three different ways. Under all three approaches, his conclusion is that a 'duty to draft efficient terms' is a better solution than a 'duty to read'.[22] The first way in which De Geest frames the problem is by asking whether it is a unilateral care or a bilateral care problem. This distinction goes back to Calabresi's work on accident law.[23] If one party is clearly in a better position to avoid accidents than another, incentives should be put on that party to take care according to the least-cost-avoider principle. Applied to the signing-without-reading problem we have to ask which party is in the best position to avoid the inclusion of inefficient terms in contracts? Should the drafter abstain from inserting inefficient terms, should the signer read the contract, or should both do their share of the work to solve the problem? A legal system which requires the drafter to offer signers a reasonable possibility to become informed about the terms and imposes upon the signer a duty to read implicitly assumes that it is a bilateral care problem. An yet, a careful analysis tells us that it is a unilateral care problem.[24] There would be no need to read the contract if the drafter would not insert inefficient terms in the first place. With individually negotiated contracts the duty to read has a social benefit since it allows parties to adapt the contract terms to the particulars of their situation. But with standard term contracts, no such benefit exists since the standard terms are meant to be applied in all dealings with all customers.

---

[22]De Geest (2016).

[23]Calabresi (1970).

[24]De Geest (2016).

The second way in which De Geest frames the problem is by analyzing it in terms of *ex ante* versus *ex post* monitoring. *Ex ante* monitoring takes place before the 'wrongdoing' may occur; *ex post* monitoring takes place after the 'wrongdoing' occurred. Reading a contract before signing is a form of *ex ante* monitoring. The drafter's work is inspected before the wrongdoing takes place. Reading a contract after a dispute has arisen (and refusing to honor one-sided terms), is a form of *ex post* monitoring. A pure duty-to-read rule permits *only ex ante* monitoring: if a one-sided term is discovered after the contract has been signed, it is too late. A pure duty to draft efficient terms permits *ex post* monitoring: if a one-sided term has been discovered after the contract has been signed, the term will not be enforced. The legal system should not make *ex post* monitoring of contract terms impossible.

Finally, the problem may be framed in terms of self-protection versus legal protection against wrongdoing.[25] A pure duty-to-read regime can be viewed as an instance in which the legal system refuses to intervene when it observes socially undesirable behavior (i.e. the drafter inserting inefficient terms into a contract) but instead requires potential victims to protect themselves by walking away before the socially harmful behavior takes place. It can be seen as expressing a policy preference for the virtue of self-reliance, by providing that even if one party has been (or is likely to be) injured by the action of the other in some way that otherwise might merit relief, such relief will nevertheless be denied to the extent that the injured party might with prudent actions have reasonably avoided or minimized the harm resulting from that conduct. But in modern legal systems there is no longer a clear policy preference for the virtue of self-reliance. A clear example is the movement away from the *caveat emptor* principle.

3.6 A Duty to Read with an Unconscionability Exception (Solution 4)

The difference between solution 1 (a duty to draft efficient terms) and solution 4 is chiefly a matter of evidentiary burdens. Indeed solution 1 holds that terms are binding, only if they are efficient and solution 4 holds that terms are binding unless they are clearly inefficient. Who should bear the burden of proof of (in)efficiency? There are two main considerations, according to De Geest: the relative evidence costs to the parties and the likelihood of the hypothesis. They both lead to the conclusion that the drafter should have the burden of proof.[26] First, the drafter has more information on why the terms are efficient or inefficient. After all the drafter is the expert, who also has economies of scale, and drafting is at its core the determination of which terms are efficient. Accordingly, when the drafter drafted in good faith, she only deviated from default rules when she had reasons to believe that a

[25] De Geest (2016).

[26] De Geest (2016).

change of terms created more joint surplus; she already knows the reasons so she can reveal them at little costs. In sum, the drafter is the least-cost-evidence gatherer. Unlike with individually negotiated contracts, there is no *a priori* reason to presume that unread standard terms will be efficient. No one believes anymore that economic self-interest will largely prevent standard terms drafters from overreaching. Therefore, there is no reason to enforce them when a drafter cannot proof their efficiency.

4 Dutch Standard Terms Law: Towards a Duty to Draft Efficient Terms?

When you ask a Dutch lawyer to explain Dutch standard terms laws, he will start by saying that parties are easily bound by them. A Dutch company should offer its customers a reasonable possibility to become aware of the general terms and conditions. Once this obligation has been fulfilled, lack of awareness is not an excuse! Under Dutch contract law rules, a party who has accepted the applicability of a set of general terms and conditions without reading them, is bound by these terms and cannot employ the excuse that he was not aware of their content. Article 6:232 Dutch Civil Code states: "Where the counterparty has accepted the applicability of the user's standard terms and conditions, he is also bound by them if the user understood or ought to have understood that his counterparty, at the moment on which the contract was entered into, did not really know the content of the terms and conditions."

Example. A person accepts an offer made by an online bookshop to buy three books for 25 Euro. A few weeks later the bookshop notifies him that he is obliged to buy books for a value of at least 10 Euro each quarter. The consumer objects by saying that he was not aware of the obligation, but the bookshop tells him that the obligation is written down in the general conditions and that he should have read the general conditions.

There is a duty to read under Dutch contract law. The duty to read is not a duty imposed by contract, but rather a statement about how parties should behave during the contract-forming process.[27] Although in theory it could apply to both parties, the effect of its application will nearly always be to demand a certain standard of conduct from the one who assents to—in most cases, literally 'signs on to', an agreement the terms of which have been prepared and presented by the other. The duty to read is imposed not on the drafter but on the adhering party. The duty to read is an example of what is called in German legal terminology an 'obliegenheit'. It does not impose upon one party an obligation to perform for which a remedy would be available to the other party if that duty were not performed. It does not literally impose a contractual duty to read, but it affects a party's legal position in case of a presumed breach of contract. In the ordinary case, the signer's failure to read comes at a time

[27] Knapp (2015).

before she has any duties at all to the other party; the 'breach' for which she might become liable is her failure to perform as required by the written contract, not her initial failure to read and understand it. Presumably this is a contract that the drafter is willing to perform, but that the signer in some respect does not want to perform. At that point, the failure to read will affect the parties' position in the dispute. The signer will object against the enforcement of the term, but the other party will respond: "You should have read the contract before signing it. It is not my fault that you did not read it, so you have to bear the consequences of your own negligence. You are bound to perform the contract as written and if not, you are liable for breach of the contract".

The 'duty to read' rule has similarities with the *caveat emptor* principle. *Caveat emptor* is an ancient maxim that tells buyers to beware of sellers. Buyers are responsible for collecting all information during the contract-forming process and are at their own peril when they rely on false statements. The buyer has the duty to take all precautionary measures to avoid being mistaken. If he fails to take sufficient precautions, he has to bear the consequences of his negligence. He will be denied a legal claim based on mistake and be bound to the contract. There are many exceptions to the *caveat emptor* rule under Dutch contract law: the rule does not apply when the seller gave incorrect information whereas the buyer could reasonably rely on the information given to him and it is not applied when the seller has a duty to inform about the characteristics of the goods sold.[28] These exceptions follow from the application of the standard of good faith in the pre-contractual stage.[29]

Similarly, there are exceptions under Dutch law to the 'duty to read' rule: standard terms are not binding when they are clearly unreasonable. Article 6:233 Dutch C.c. states: "A stipulation of the terms and conditions is voidable if it is unreasonably burdensome for the counterparty, having regard to the nature and content of the contract, the way in which these standard terms and conditions have been formed, the interests of each party, as evident to the other, and the other circumstances of the case." It means that when the presumed breach of contract concerns an unfair term, the drafter of the standard term will not be able to win the case by simply saying: "You should have read the contract". Instead the court has the authority to invalidate a term which is clearly unreasonable. Article 6:233 Dutch C.c. is the implementation in Dutch contract law of the European UCTD. Article 6 (1) of the UCTD stipulates: "Member States shall lay down that unfair terms used in a contract concluded with a consumer by a seller or supplier, shall as provided for under their national law, not be binding on the consumer (. . .)." In principle it is the party opposing the term which must show that the term is invalid or unenforceable, i.e. typically this is the consumer. Dutch basic standard terms law can be summarized as follows: standard terms are binding unless they are clearly unreasonable.

[28] Article 6:228 Dutch Civil Code.

[29] Case decided by Dutch Supreme Court on 15 November 1957 (*Baris/Riezenkamp),* NJ 1958, 67; Case decided by Dutch Supreme Court on 30 November 1973 (*Van der Beek/Van Dartel),* NJ 1974, 97.

On its face, Dutch standard terms law corresponds with De Geest's fourth solution. As was stated above, this is not the superior solution for the signing-without-reading problem since it imposes the evidentiary burden upon the signer of the standard terms contract to prove that the term is inefficient whereas it is the drafter of the standard term who is the least-cost-evidence gatherer. In order to test the efficiency hypothesis of law, it has to be investigated whether Dutch law has adopted efficiency-restoring devices which bring the outcome in unfair contract cases more in line with the efficient outcome, which is, a duty to draft efficient terms which imposes the evidentiary burden of the efficiency of terms upon the drafter.

In addition to the open norm of article 6:233 Civil Code, Dutch law provides a black list and a grey list of contract clauses, which are usually regarded as regulations of the content of the standard form contract. Upon closer examination, black and grey lists are also ways to implement a duty to draft efficient terms. The black list (article 6:236 Dutch Civil Code) contains clauses that when included in the general terms and conditions, are regarded as not reasonable by law. If the term which the consumer is opposing is on the black list his task is easy. The consumer has the burden to prove that he is a consumer and that the term is on the black list. Evidence wise the black list is consistent with the duty to draft efficient terms since it reduces the standard of proof for the signer significantly. Content wise it is consistent with a duty to draft efficient terms if it contains terms which are inefficient in all cases and for all parties. An example is article 6:236a C.c. which puts on the black list 'a stipulation which deprives the counterparty entirely and unconditionally from his right to claim the performance to which the user has engaged himself'. Such a clause is inefficient because it is a wildcard for opportunistic and destructive behavior. Moreover, the clause is inherently inefficient in the sense that there are no cases in which the adoption of such a term is desirable. The grey list of general terms and conditions (article 6:237 of the Dutch Civil Code) contains clauses that are legally assumed to be unreasonably burdensome. These clauses are not per definition unreasonably burdensome. The clauses are legally presumed to be unreasonably burdensome. If the term which the consumer is opposing is on the grey list his task is also not very difficult. He has the burden of proof that he is a consumer and that the term is on the grey list. The user who wants to make successfully use of such a clause has to prove that there are conditions which make the clause not unreasonably burdensome. The grey list system is evidence wise consistent with the duty to draft efficient terms because it puts on the drafter of the term the burden of proof that a term is efficient. Content wise, consistency with the duty to draft efficient terms exists when the terms on the grey list are terms which are inefficient in the majority of cases. To be able to show such correspondence (or de absence thereof) an in-depth economic analysis of each of these terms is required, which is an interesting undertaking but one that falls outside the scope of this contribution. To conclude, the use of black and grey lists has brought the results of Dutch standard terms law more in line with the efficient solution and this has been achieved by making changes in the rules of evidence. The legal instruments of the black and grey list of unfair contract terms reduce the standard of proof for the consumer significantly. If the party bearing the burden of proof (i.e. the consumer) fulfills the reduced standard of proof, the burden of rebutting the allegation made falls upon the other party, i.e. the drafter.

And there is more. As regards standard contracts falling within the scope of the applicability of the UCTD, the European court of justice has decided that the burden of proof may not be put on the consumer. Rather it is the duty of the national courts to investigate on their own motion whether a standard clause is in conformity with the requirements of the Directive.[30] This justifies shifting the burden of proof to the party using standard terms, i.e. the drafter, a result which corresponds with the efficient model rule.

The results of this analysis contribute to the more general discussion about the improvement of European consumer law in the following way. Legal scholars who argue for better consumer laws in Europe often suggest more public enforcement or harsher sanctions for firms that adopt unfair contract terms. This contribution suggests that much can be gained by focusing on the rules of evidence.

5 Conclusion

The research tests the efficiency hypothesis of law by using the method of comparative law & economics applied to unfair terms law. There are four theoretical legal solutions to the signing-without-reading problem and from an economic point of view a 'duty to draft efficient terms' imposed upon the drafter of the standard form contract is the best solution. The research has looked at the development of real-life Dutch standard terms law and found out that the development is clearly in the direction of the more efficient solution.

References

Bakos Y, Marotta-Wurgler F, Trossen DR (2014) Does anyone read the fine print? Testing a law and economics approach to standard form contracts. J Leg Stud 43:1–35

Ben-Shahar O, Schneider CE (2014) More than you wanted to know: the failure of mandated disclosure. Princeton University Press, Princeton

Calabresi G (1970) The costs of accidents: a legal and economic analysis. Yale University Press, New Haven

De Geest G (2016) Signing without reading. In: Marciano A, Ramello G (eds) Encyclopedia of law and economics. Springer, New York

Farnsworth W (2007) The legal analyst. A toolkit for thinking about the law. The University of Chicago Press, Chicago

[30]ECJ judgment of 27 June 2000, Joined cases C-240/98 to C-244/98 – *Océano Grupo Editorial SA v. Murciano Quintera* [2000] ECR I-04941.

Friedman D (2000) Law's order: what economics has to do with law and why it matters. Princeton University Press, Princeton

Knapp CL (2015) Is there a "duty to read"? Hast Law J 66:1083–1112

Marotta-Wurgler F (2009) Are 'pay-now, terms later' contracts worse for buyers? Evidence from software license agreements. J Leg Stud 38:309–343

Mattei U (1995) The comparative law and economics of penalty clauses in contract. Am J Comp Law 43:427–444

Mattei U, Monti A (2001) Comparative law and economics: borrowing and resistance. Glob Jurists Front 1(2):1–24

Mattei U, Monti A (2003) Comparative law and economics. Societa italiana di economia publica XV Conferenza. Pubblicazione internet realizzata con contributo della Compagnia di San Paolo

Maxeiner JR (2003) Standard-terms contracting in the global electronic age: European alternatives. Yale J Int Law 28:109–182

Schulte-Nölke H, Twigg-Flesner C, Ebers M (eds) (2008) EC consumer law compendium. The consumer acquis and its transposition in the Member States. Sellier, European Law Publishers, Munich

Van den Bergh R (2018) The roundabouts of European law and economics. Eleven International Publishing, The Hague

Ann-Sophie Vandenberghe Rotterdam. Associate Professor at the Rotterdam Institute of Law and Economics (RILE), Erasmus School of Law. Burgemeester Oudlaan 50, Sanders Building (L) area 7.21, P.O. Box 1738, 3000 DR Rotterdam, The Netherlands, Tel + 31 (0)10 4082186. vandenberghe@law.eur.nl. Fields of Interest: Contract Law and Economics, Employment and Consumer Contracts in particular.

Ex-Post Fairness Controls and Contract Design: The Spanish Experience

Fernando Gómez and Mireia Artigot

Abstract The application of the ex post unfairness controls of the Directive 93/13 in consumer financial contracts in Spain has resulted in a litigation wave that has had a significant impact in terms of financial as well as judicial costs. The terms involved in this litigation range from those allocating risks among the contracting parties to terms setting between the parties their share of the mandatory taxes and fees accompanying a mortgage loan. Spanish courts and the Court of Justice of the European Union (CJEU) have held many of these standard terms as unfair and hence, non-binding on consumers. A collateral effect of this litigation has touched contract design. Some of the cost impact of these terms are now included—without specification—as part of the overall contract price. Directive 93/13 on unfair contract terms arguably aimed at maximizing consumer welfare through, among others, enhancing transparency in consumer contracts. This chapter analyzes whether the litigation on consumer mortgage contracts and its impact in contract design has resulted in an increase of contract transparency and discusses whether the resulting contract design regarding some contract dimensions—such as exogenous costs in mortgage financing—has actually served the interests of consumers.

1 Introduction

In the European legal landscape, Directive 93/13 of the 5th of April 1993 on unfair terms in consumer contracts[1] constitutes the most important piece in the legal framework dealing with standard contract terms. Since its adoption, this Directive had always been deemed—and rightly so-, as a relevant ingredient of consumer

[1]Directive 93/13/EEC of 5 April 1993 on unfair terms in consumer contracts, OJ L 95, 21.4.1993, pp. 29–34 (hereinafter Directive 93/13).

F. Gómez · M. Artigot (✉)
Faculty of Law, Universitat Pompeu Fabra, Barcelona, Spain
e-mail: fernando.gomez@upf.edu; mireia.artigot@upf.edu

K. Mathis, A. Tor (eds.), *Consumer Law and Economics*, Economic Analysis of Law in European Legal Scholarship 9, https://doi.org/10.1007/978-3-030-49028-7_7

policy, but it is in recent years when the recognition of its importance and the active use of its provisions by the national courts and the European Court of Justice have peaked.[2] In EU Law, legal controls over standard contract terms are today widely held to be the cornerstone of consumer protection, at least in the contractual sphere.

Far-reaching legal intervention over standard terms may, in the presence of certain conditions, generate a wave of private lawsuits that may reach very significant proportions. When standard terms are used in contracts that are individually sizable—in quantitative and perhaps even in qualitative terms, a mortgage loan is arguably the most substantial contract that a consumer would typically sign, leaving aside their employment contract—, and when standardization of terms leads to clauses that spread over millions of contracts in an economy, a litigation wave may be the outcome.

This has been the case in Spain in recent years—and continues to be that way to a large degree. The stakes of the litigation over various standard terms in mortgage contracts are extremely high, since, in their aggregate, the total amount being claimed is roughly equivalent to 2% of the entire Spanish GDP.[3] In other words, a sizeable chunk of the Spanish GDP lies before the courts in one single group of cases, and has to be decided on the basis of broad and perhaps largely indeterminate notions such as that of "unfair term", which are applied through tests that are openly designed, and have been subject to extensive re-interpretation by the Court of Justice of the EU (CJEU) and by courts in the Member States.[4] As a commentator put it, the unfairness concept under Directive 93/13 is a highly ambiguous formula open to innovative interpretation.[5]

Moreover, doctrines have emerged expanding the scope of ex-post fairness assessments under Directive 93/13. Notably, on the basis of the mandate that terms should be drafted in plain, intelligible language (arts. 4(2) and 5 of Directive 93/13), the CJEU has introduced a test of substantive transparency of non-negotiated terms, at least when the terms refer to the main subject-matter of the contract or the price-quality relationship.[6] The substantive transparency assessment will look into the actual degree of awareness and knowledge of the consumer concerning the implications of the contract term for the overall impact of the transaction on their welfare. If the standard term is considered not to meet the required threshold as to its material or substantive transparency, the term in question may be deemed unfair and thus non-binding on the consumer pursuant to art. 6(1) of Directive 93/13. In Spain,

---

[2]Riesenhuber (2013) and Micklitz and Reich (2014), p. 771.

[3]The Spanish GDP was in 2017 around 110,000 million EUR in constant prices of 2010 (http://sdw.ecb.europa.eu/quickview.do?SERIES_KEY=139.AME.A.ESP.1.0.0.0.OVGD). The disputed amount regarding unfair standard terms in mortgage contracts may total 25,000 million EUR.

[4]Pursuant to art. 3.1 Directive 93/13, a standard term will be deemed unfair if "[..] contrary to the requirement of good faith, it causes a significant imbalance in the parties' rights and obligations arising under the contract, to the detriment of the consumer."

[5]Jansen and Zimmermann (2018), p. 939.

[6]Cases RWE Vertrieb, C-92/11 and especially Gutiérrez Naranjo, C-154/15, C-307/15 and C-308/15.

many but not all cases brought under Directive 93/13 resort to the lack of substantive transparency as the cause of action supporting the consumer claim.

As one would expect, the costs and the disruption of the justice system brought about by this litigation are also enormous—for the parties but, more importantly, for society at large. Given the number of expected (and actual) claims being filed and flooding the civil courts, the Spanish government was forced to hastily create and staff new courts specialized in these kinds of cases.[7] In fact, during 2017 around 1000 claims were filed daily.[8]

This massive litigation has had—and still has—a profound effect on contract design. The goal of this paper is to analyze how the uncertainty created by the litigation and the findings of unfairness have largely resulted in turning contract terms reflecting and allocating contract costs among the contracting parties that were reasonably salient and openly presented to consumers into more opaque elements of the contract price.

2 Ex-Post Fairness Controls in Financial Contracts: The Case of Spain

The effects of ex-post fairness (including substantive transparency as described above) controls in consumer contracts in Spain are particularly noticeable in the context of financial contracts, specifically mortgage contracts where a broad range of contract clauses involving both the main subject matter of the contract—such as floor clauses[9]—and other aspects of the contract—such as taxes and fees arising from mortgage contracts, for example—have been the object of litigation that has resulted in a shift in the way lenders structure their contracts in mortgage finance.

The Spanish real estate market shows one of the highest rates of homeownership compared to rental in Europe.[10] Most of the real estate purchases in Spain have been (and still are) financed through mortgage loans, although the number of loans

[7]See El Economista, 14-11-2017, Los jueces de "cláusulas suelo¨ solo han resuelto el 7% de las demandas. http://www.eleconomista.es/empresas-finanzas-ss/noticias/8742041/11/17/Los-jueces-de-clausulas-suelo-solo-han-resuelto-el-7-de-las-demandas-.html.

[8]See Cinco Días, 17 November 2017. Los españoles presentan 1000 demandas contra la banca cada día (https://cincodias.elpais.com/cincodias/2017/11/16/midinero/1510850222_349769.html).

[9]Floor clauses, generally accompanied by caps, are contract terms that introduce limits on adjustable interest rates (which in Spanish practice are generally based on the Euribor plus a spread). Adjustable interest rates were by far and until very recently the most widely used interest rate alternative in Spain.

[10]In Spain, roughly around 75% of the households are homeowners, while over 10% of the households rent their primary residence. The percentage of households living in rental housing has increased these last years to reach around 17% of all households. However, the proportion of ownership of residential properties over total dwellings, with some slight variation, ranges from 75% to 80%. Source: Instituto Nacional de Estadística (http://ine.es/jaxiT3/Datos.htm?t=4566).

granted decreased very significantly after the housing bubble burst and the resulting crisis erupted.[11]

The aftermath of the financial crisis saw a sharp increase in the number of defaults in mortgage contracts,[12] and home foreclosures by banks and savings banks, which in turn gave rise to large numbers of lawsuits by financial consumers. These lawsuits essentially challenged the various kinds of contract clauses on the basis of the unfairness notions of Directive 93/13, and often ended up before the CJEU.

In the Spanish mortgage market (as well as in others, but clearly not all European markets, as may be illustrated by the cases of Germany or the Netherlands where fixed rates prevail), variable or adjustable rates have dominated the supply of residential credit by the banking sector, as well as the actual loan contracts.[13]

The avalanche of lawsuits on this matter urged the Spanish government to create new courts to handle just these kinds of cases. During 2017 there were 54 courts specialized in unfair contract terms in mortgage contracts with 60 judges allocated to them. Since these courts began their judicial activity around 400,000 claims have been filed before them.[14] The speed at which claims were being filed was initially well above the initial forecast,[15] but it seems to have slowed down in recent quarters. However, the new courts have a resolution rate of only 35%.[16]

What is all this litigation about? Let us identify and briefly present what is being discussed in these numbers about standard terms in loans with mortgage security, and then we will show how this has resulted in a redesign of mortgage contracts.

---

[11] In the years of the housing and credit bubble (up to 2008) there were over 1 million new mortgage loan contracts signed in Spain each year. Since 2009 this number decreased up to a minimum in 2013 and 2014 of less than 300,000 mortgage contracts. In 2018, there were around 315,000 new residential mortgage loan contracts.

[12] The number and the social and economic impact of mortgage foreclosures went down after its peak in 2012–2013, due to improved economic and employment conditions in the Spanish economy. Moreover, some legal relief was offered in 2013 to low-income defaulting debtors. The diminishing trend has accelerated, since in 2018 the average quarterly number of foreclosures on consumers due to mortgage default was around 2200, whereas the equivalent figure was 10,000 in 2015. In this dramatic reduction, decisions by the Spanish Supreme Court against acceleration clauses in mortgage contracts have surely played a role. This litigation is also ongoing, and the last item in it has been the recent decision by the CJEU in *Abanca*, C-70/17 and C-179/17.

[13] See for an international comparison of the use of variable rates in mortgages, Badarinza et al. (2016). In Spain, as in other mortgage markets (Australia, Finland, Ireland, Italy, UK) variable rates have been and are pervasive in the mortgage market, albeit in others (Germany, Netherlands, US), fixed rates dominate mortgage finance.

[14] See http://www.poderjudicial.es/cgpj/es/Poder-Judicial/En-Portada/Los-Juzgados-de-clausulas-abusivas-dictaron-30-744-sentencias-en-el-primer-trimestre-del-ano%2D%2Dun-126-2-por-ciento-mas-que-en-el-mismo-periodo-de-2018.

[15] The governing body of the judiciary, the *Consejo General del Poder Judicial* (CGPJ), estimated that during the first year of activity of these new specialized courts around 190,000 claims would be filed. Judges, lawyers and court staff will be necessary to handle the amount of cases.

[16] See http://www.poderjudicial.es/cgpj/es/Poder-Judicial/En-Portada/Los-Juzgados-de-clausulas-abusivas-dictaron-30-744-sentencias-en-el-primer-trimestre-del-ano%2D%2Dun-126-2-por-ciento-mas-que-en-el-mismo-periodo-de-2018.

2.1 *Litigation on Mortgage Floor Clauses*

As noted earlier, most mortgage contracts in the Spanish financial market have been structured around adjustable interest rates. Given that variable or adjustable rates are riskier (since there is a risk of variation of the interest rates that determines the final rate to be paid, be it Euribor, or some other floating rate) than fixed rates, the opportunity of setting some limits to the variability of final rates to be paid by the debtor emerged as potentially desirable.

Thus, mortgage loan contracts marketed by a substantial fraction of Spanish financial institutions started to include floors, generally accompanied by caps, on adjustable interest rates. In-between the floor and the cap, the interest rate on a mortgage would fluctuate—generally based on Euribor plus a spread agreed by the parties—and that would determine the actual annual rate to be paid by the consumer. The fluctuation, however, would be limited by the range defined by the floor and cap, compared to a contract with no floor and cap.

These last years, interest rates in the Euro-zone have decreased dramatically and reached historically minimum rates.[17] However, many debtors saw how their mortgage payments decreased but only limitedly so, resulting in monthly payments higher than the ones they would have faced had they been paying their monthly dues solely based on Euribor plus the spread, with no lower bound. Some consumers started to claim they had not been (properly, at least) informed of the introduction of the floor clause in their mortgage contract, and were not aware of the economic consequences of the floor. Thus, the clause containing the floor term should be deemed unfair.

The Spanish Supreme Court, in a landmark decision on the 9th of May 2013 declared that floor clauses, though not unfair by their content alone, were typically inserted in mortgage contracts in a way that did not allow consumers to be fully aware of their existence or, at least, prevented consumers from properly grasping the full economic consequences of having one in the contract. In other words, floor clauses did not meet the substantive transparency requirements that could be read in Directive 93/13.[18] The consequences from this judgment were very substantial, and floor clauses, although not per se unfair, disappeared almost completely from the Spanish mortgage market.[19] The Spanish Supreme Court had tried to halt the foreseeable lawsuits in large numbers to be brought by borrowers who had been paying extra amounts to their lenders after 2009–2010 due to the floor clause in their

---

[17]Since 2009 the interest rates established by the European Central Bank in the Euro-zone have been steadily decreasing. https://www.ecb.europa.eu/stats/policy_and_exchange_rates/key_ecb_interest_rates/html/index.en.html.

[18]Art. 3.1 Directive 93/13, provides that a standard term will be deemed unfair if "[..] contrary to the requirement of good faith, it causes a significant imbalance in the parties' rights and obligations arising under the contract, to the detriment of the consumer."

[19]The new Law 5/2019 of March 15 which, among others, implements Directive 201/17 on residential credit contracts has banned floor clauses entirely in residential mortgages.

contracts. The Spanish Court tried to accomplish this by allowing restitution only of the amounts paid after its own decision, and not what consumers had paid in excess before the date of the judgement. The Court argued that the unfairness of the clauses was a close call and, moreover, massive restitution would endanger the then very fragile Spanish financial system.[20]

This attempt at curtailing litigation failed, since a number of lower courts raised the issue before the CJEU who, in the Gutierrez Naranjo decision of 2016, held that the time limit set by the Spanish Supreme Court to restitution claims resulting from a finding of unfairness of a standard term was not compatible with art. 6(1) of Directive 93/13, which is interpreted to require full restitution following a finding of unfairness, with the sole limits of *res judicata* and reasonable periods of statute of limitations. Naturally, lawsuits by borrowers piled up in large numbers even if the Spanish Government set up and encouraged consumers and banks to use a specially created Alternative Dispute Resolution[21] mechanism to process these restitution claims.[22]

2.2 Acceleration Clauses

A different type of standard term that has also been highly litigated with respect to mortgage contracts in Spain is the acceleration clause in case of borrower's default in payments. Acceleration clauses allow the bank, upon the debtor's default, to rescind the loan and require immediate payment of the entire outstanding amount—and not just of the installments the debtor defaulted upon.

Prior to 2013, the Spanish law allowed lenders to accelerate upon the debtor's default of any monthly payment as long as the acceleration clause was registered in the Property Registry. There was no legal minimum in terms of the number of instalments or size of default in order for the creditor to trigger the acceleration clause. Banks, hence, could insert in their mortgage contracts terms providing that as little as one monthly default would trigger the acceleration of the entire loan.[23]

This was the legal scenario until 2013, when the CJEU, in its *Aziz*[24] case, required the Spanish legislator to amend the rules of civil procedure in compliance with European consumer protection. In 2013, the Spanish Law of Civil Procedure was

[20]The finding of unfairness of floor clauses in mortgage contracts in Spain could alone represent up to 4.7 billion euros for the financial industry. See https://cincodias.elpais.com/cincodias/2017/01/27/mercados/1485543849_878448.html.

[21]Hereinafter ADR.

[22]The ad hoc ADR mechanism has received until August 2018 (last officially reported figures) 1,166,000 claims, 517,000 of which have been compensated.

[23]See Miquel (2017).

[24]Mohamed Aziz v Caixa d'Estalvis de Catalunya, Tarragona i Manresa (Catalunyacaixa), C-415/11. In this case the CJEU did not find standard contract terms providing for acceleration clauses to be per se unfair, but held that an acceleration clause upon just one monthly default to be unfair. The

amended[25] to accommodate the Aziz doctrine, and the statute was amended again in 2015.[26] This later reform preserved the registration requirement for acceleration clauses, but required that the debtor defaulted, at least, on three mortgage installments, or that, regardless of the number of installments defaulted, the default was equivalent to at least three monthly portions of total amounts due.

As a consequence of Aziz and its progeny in the Spanish Supreme Court, mortgage foreclosures initiated on the basis of an acceleration clause (the vast majority of foreclosures) were stayed or significantly delayed (a factor behind the observed drastic reduction in foreclosures after 2015). Now, after the decision of the CJEU in Abanca[27] in March of 2019, the ball is again in the court of the Spanish Supreme Court, who has to decide whether mortgage foreclosures based on some loan acceleration term can move on, or no acceleration-based foreclosures are feasible and lenders need to resort to ordinary execution proceedings (that are longer and more costly than mortgage foreclosure proceedings).

2.3 *Taxes and Fees*

Real estate purchases and mortgage loan contracts in the Spanish legal system involve a number of fees and are subject to taxes.

First, parties have to incur notaries' and property registrar's fees, since both the purchase and the mortgage need to be notarized and registered for the entire transaction to be secured.

The regulation of notarial fees, in addition to setting the amounts, vaguely allocates the payment of the fees to the party requesting such services or, when the request cannot be ascertained, on the party interested in those services being provided. Similarly, the fees to be paid to the Property Registry are also regulated as to their amount, but the obligation to pay is placed upon the party acquiring the right being registered.

In addition to notary's and registrar's fees, typically there are other fees to be paid to other parties who have a role to play in the transaction: the independent appraiser who values the property for the purposes of estimating the loan-to-value ratio, and

Spanish Supreme Court has consistently applied this criterion since 2015: STS 23.12.2015; STS 18.12.2016.

[25]Article 639.1 and 2 of the Spanish Law of Civil Procedure were amended in 2013 by the Law 1/2013 of May 14, of measures to reinforce the protection of debtors in mortgage contracts, debt restructuring and public rental contracts.

[26]Law 19/2015 of July 13 of measures reforming the Administration of Justice and the Civil Registry.

[27]Joined cases *Abanca Corporación Bancaria SA v García Salamanca Santos (Case C-70/17) and Bankia SA v Lau Mendoza and Rodríguez Ramírez (Case C-179/17) EU:2019:250. Here,* the European Court of Justice (ECJ) considered the conditions for a national court to replace an unfair contract term with default rules.

the paralegal who handles the paperwork in order to pay the relevant taxes (separate ones on the purchase and on the mortgage) and register both the property and the mortgage loan.

With respect to the fees and taxes arising from the purchase contract for the sale of real estate, there have never been serious doubts that consumers who buy the property have to face them in full. With respect to the mortgage loan, which is a separate contract generating a separate set of fees and taxes, the background legal rules have always been remarkably vague.

Mortgage loan contracts typically contained a term allocating all taxes and fees incurred as a result of the loan contract being agreed, formalized and registered, to the borrower. Very often, the loan contract only contained this general provision on cost allocation, without providing detail on the type, let alone the amount, of the costs to be covered by such clause. However, it is also true that banks were constrained by regulation to provide an estimate of the total amount of taxes and fees, and such estimated amount would be deducted, at the time of signing the mortgage loan, from the sum that the borrower would receive from the lender to pay the seller of the property.[28]

Consumers started to challenge these clauses as unfair, given the general and indiscriminate imposition on the borrower of all taxes and fees incurred as a consequence of the mortgage loan. The Spanish Supreme Court, in a string of decisions, agreed with this claim and held those terms (at least those with a broad formulation covering "all" taxes and fees) to be unfair.[29]

Since the contract term allocating all taxes and fees to the borrower had been struck down, Spanish courts had to painstakingly and separately allocate them to one or the other party or proportionately divide them between both parties.

In a series of decisions, the Spanish Supreme Court has attempted to provide guidance with respect to the allocation of all fees resulting from the mortgage loan.[30] With respect to notaries' fees, the Supreme Court considers that both parties—the financial institution as well as the consumer—are interested in the notarial services related to the mortgage loan and, thus, both should "reasonably" and equally contribute to cover them. As a result, given that under the contract term held unfair the consumer had covered the full amount of the notary's fees, they would now be entitled to be reimbursed by the bank of 50% of the amount of the notarial fees (plus interest).

With respect to registrar's fees, the Supreme Court has determined that, given that the registration of the mortgage contract provides financial institutions with an

[28]Typically, what would happen is that the amount of the loan would go up to cover these taxes and fees: if the price of the property to be financed was X, and the estimated taxes and costs was 10% of X, then the nominal amount of the loan to the borrower would be (X+10% of X). The borrower would get X to pay the seller, and the Bank would use 10%X to pay all costs (taxes and fees) on behalf of the borrower.

[29]STS, 23.12.2015; STS 15.3.2018 (two identical decisions of the same date).

[30]Spanish Supreme Court decisions 44/2019, 46/2019, 47/2019, 48/2019 and 49/2019 all dated 23.1.2019.

enforceable right *in rem* (the mortgage) and a collateral security, those fees should be borne entirely by the lender. Thus, these fees have to be reimbursed in full, plus interest, to all consumers.

With respect to appraisal fees, a similar analysis has led the Spanish Supreme Court to allocate them entirely to the borrower, since in the absence of appraisal a mortgage could not be granted, and the borrower benefits from the lower interest rates applied to a secured loan *vis-à-vis* and unsecured one. As to fees for paralegals and paperwork, the Court has split the amounts equally among the parties, as it did with notarial fees.

The most controversial issue in this area, however, has been that of the taxes on the mortgage loan. Not just because taxes are the bulk of the total amounts at stake (fees plus taxes) in this litigation. It is also because the solution to the conundrum involved not only civil courts, but also the tax courts, who had to interpret the relevant tax provisions and conclude whether the party legally burdened with the tax was the lender or the borrower. Before the contract terms allocating the payment of all taxes incurred directly as a result of the mortgage to the borrower were deemed unfair, this was not an issue with practical importance, since tax authorities would in any case receive payment from the bank on behalf of the borrower, and thus there was no need to make a determination of who should be liable in front of the tax authorities for the payment of the tax.

When those contract terms were wiped out, the issue became crucial, since it was now unclear who had to pay. Moreover, civil courts, confronted with reimbursement claims against banks arising from the unfairness of the tax allocation contract clause, had to determine now who, in the absence of a clause (now gone due to its unfair character) would have been under the legal duty to face the payment of the relevant tax.

Tax regulations (albeit not tax legislative provisions) and the case law from tax courts had considered for a long time that the party subject to the payment of the tax on the mortgage loan was the borrower.

Echoing the pro-consumer position of the Civil Chamber of the Spanish Supreme Court, the tax section of the Administrative Chamber of the Spanish Supreme Court reversed its previous case law, and in a landmark decision dated 16th of October 2018 held that the lender was, under applicable tax law, responsible for the tax on mortgage loans. This was anticipated to generate a tsunami of reimbursement claims by consumers against banks, since this interpretation was considered to be the proper one at the time the mortgage contracts had been signed, and thus, after the contract term allocating payment of the tax to the borrower was held non-binding, the issue had to be resolved by the applicable tax provisions, now receiving the new interpretation. Taken by surprise, and without a clear estimate of the total cost of such mass of reimbursement claims for the mortgage loan tax, the stock market value of the Spanish financial sector crashed, and lost Eur. 5.5 billion in a single day.

Millions of lawsuits were foreseen, and alarms were raised with respect to the financial standing of some institutions on the verge of this litigation wave. However, shortly after these events, the Administrative Chamber of the Spanish Supreme Court, sitting *en banc*, reversed with a narrow majority the change of course adopted by the tax section in October 2018, and in three very controversial decisions dated 27 November 2018, held that it was the borrower under the applicable tax provisions the party who had to pay the mortgage loan tax.

To complicate the picture, the Spanish government adopted on 8th of November 2018 a new piece of legislation clearly stipulating that the lender was the party burdened with the tax on mortgage loans. However, the new Law only applied to future mortgage loans, and lacked any retroactive effects. For the past, it was the *en banc* decision of the Administrative Chamber that prevailed, and thus, no reimbursement in favour of consumers could take place. This portion of the litigation wave was averted.

Not surprisingly, when the government announced the adoption of the new (and non-retroactive) law, the stock market value of the financial institutions remained unaffected. Investors knew that the amount of the tax could be passed-on to borrowers through higher fees or interest rates, as we will show in the next section. What had terrified investors in October 2018 was the large stock of past mortgage contracts, for which fees and interest rates could not be changed, but could give rise to a massive transfer to the existing borrowers through the reimbursement claims covering the tax that had been paid by borrowers but could have been considered to always had been the duty of the lenders to bear.

3 The Effects of Ex-Post Controls in Contract Design: The Case of Spanish Mortgage Contracts

The multitude of lawsuits concerning the unfairness of various standard terms in mortgage contracts in Spain has produced different effects and on different levels. Inducing changes in contract design by the lenders who draft the contract terms is surely one of the most important.

To be sure, a general consequence of the litigation wave, although a difficult one to precisely characterize, let alone to quantify, is legal uncertainty regarding the validity of mortgage contract terms generally in place in Spain for the last 20 years. Three factors seem to make uncertainty a serious problem here: (i) the type and extent of challenges to prevailing terms (from acceleration clauses to default interest rates, from allocation of costs and taxes to floor clauses) has been large; (ii) the outcomes of tests and standards to be applied by courts to solve the disputes are hard to predict; (iii) the number of contracts potentially affected is extremely high. The value of the existing stock of mortgage contracts, and how to design these contracts in the future so as to avoid similar challenges are not easy to manage, and consequently one would expect large costs induced by the legal uncertainty.

Clearly, in some cases we observe effects of the courts' role in appreciating unfairness of contract terms—even on their own motion as the CJEU tells national courts to do—under the Directive 13/93 that are predictable, although the ultimate consequences are not easy to discern and evaluate.

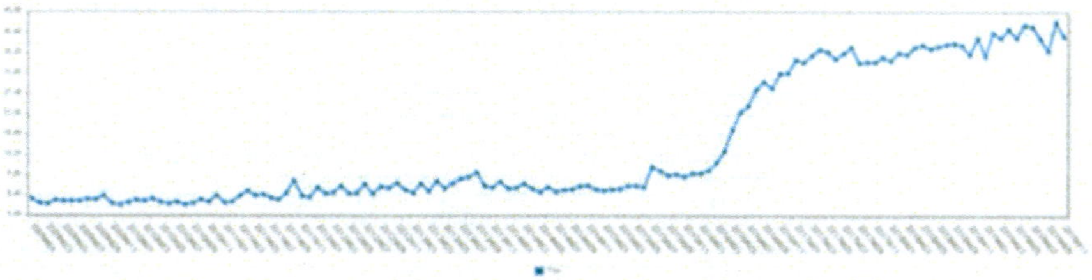

Fig. 1 Percentage of fixed rate mortgages in the Spanish market (Source: Spanish Statistical Office (INE)) (See https://www.ine.es/jaxiT3/Datos.htm?t=24456)

For instance, floor (and ceiling) clauses, after they were frowned upon by the Spanish Supreme Court, have almost but disappeared from the mortgage market, even before they were outlawed by new legislation in March 2019. Despite the fact that the rulings from Spanish courts did not condemn them per se, and only found their transparency wanting, lenders seem to have opted to play a sure hand and ceased to have them in mortgage contracts to mitigate interest rate risk on borrowers. Thus, the market is now dominated by adjustable rate mortgages with no floor or ceiling, and by fixed interest rates (a special form of floor and ceiling where both coincide, although legally they are not seen as such). The following figure shows the enormous growth of fixed rate mortgages in the Spanish market after 2015. Although it is hard to attribute causality to the outcome of the litigation on floor clauses, it is not a wild conjecture to think that it was a contributing factor (Fig. 1).[31]

Also, the litigation on acceleration clauses seems to have substantially decreased the number of foreclosures on mortgaged property. Lower courts reacted to the Supreme Court decision in December 2015 which found that clauses allowing acceleration after just 1 month default were unfair and therefore void, by staying foreclosure proceedings resulting from such acceleration clauses. Again, we cannot make a causal claim here, but the trend is also unmistakable (Fig. 2).

We will now focus on how financial institutions redesign their mortgage contracts in the aftermath of the litigation concerning terms allocating payment of taxes and fees.

The uncertainty created by the thorough (and also hard to predict in its outcome) ex-post fairness scrutiny of standard terms in mortgage contracts has resulted in altering the way in which exogenous costs arising from the contract are allocated. Contracts drafted by lenders used as allocation devices terms that imposed all

[31] Minimum—and even negative—Euribor rates since mid 2012 (http://sdw.ecb.europa.eu/quickview.do?SERIES_KEY=143.FM.M.U2.EUR.RT.MM.EURIBOR3MD_.HSTA) might have been an important driving factor to the increase in the amount of fixed interest rate mortgage contract loans. In light of the ever in history lowest euribor and hence minimum financial costs of variable rate mortgage contracts since 2012, the expectation of this type of variable structure can only be in the mid-long term to increase their financial cost. Hence, fixed interest rates appear as an appealing alternative that eliminates the risks of the surely mid-long term future—perhaps slow—increase in euribor interest rates and hence of financial costs for debtor/consumers.

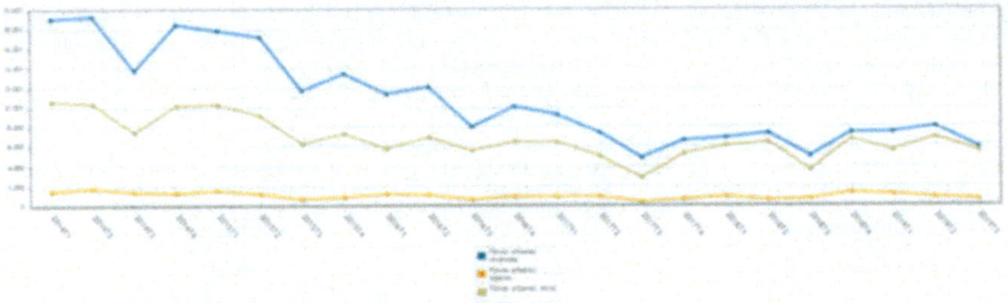

Fig. 2 Number of foreclosure proceedings initiated per quarter (Source: Spanish Statistical Office (INE)) (See https://www.ine.es/jaxiT3/Datos.htm?t=7709)

exogenous costs to borrowers at the time of signing the loan agreement. Fairness controls ended up with those terms being struck down and the allocation being entrusted to courts' interpretation of the background legal rules, regulations or contracts that gave rise to those costs. We have presented in the previous section how the final allocation was made for each separate ingredient of the total exogenous costs of providing and receiving mortgage financing.

Lenders have shifted strategy in contract design and have mostly opted to absorb the exogenous costs initially, and then to pass them on to borrowers through the contract price, in the form of higher initial fees and/or higher interest rates (either higher fixed rates or higher spreads in adjustable interest mortgage contracts).

This shift in the channel used to allocate exogenous costs—from contract terms imposing them at the outset to lenders to an increase in one or more of the components of the contract price—requires further analysis in order to determine its impact on overall contract transparency, one of the major goals of ex-post controls laid down in Directive 13/93.

From a general perspective, having the contract price (fees and/or interest rates or spreads) include elements such as the exogenous costs arising from the contract and previously passed on at the outset through an explicit contract term might be judged positively since it enables them to compare more easily the total economic sacrifice that the mortgage loan implies. Regardless of whether the consumer is aware of the various elements included in the contract price, having the exogenous cost within the price terms (fees and/or interest rates and spreads) might make them more salient and conducive to better consumer decision-making. From this perspective, the inclusion in the price of elements that previously were allocated through a separate contract term may appear as inducing positive effects.

However, in a more nuanced analysis of the different ingredients that find their way into the price terms, the favorable perception of the shift in contract design does not necessarily stand. In order to conduct this analysis, two dimensions of the costs involved in these contracts should be considered. First, the fact that we are dealing with an exogenous and not an endogenous cost from the contract. Second, whether the cost is fixed and can be calculated accurately at the time of entering into the contract.

3.1 Exogenous Costs: A Reasonably Salient Contract Term or Another Ingredient of the Price Term

Some contract costs are endogenous—depend on the actions of the parties to a contract, the contingencies they face and how the contract specifies them for the parties. Others are exogenous, that is, independent of parties' choices and actions, but determined by third parties, most notably, the government. This is clear with respect to taxes, but also to other fees that may be directly or indirectly the by-product of requirements (notarization, registration) imposed by legal rules across the board.

This difference is relevant because endogenous costs can be influenced by the supplier of goods and services (the lender, here) and a comparison between them allows the consumer to compare between different suppliers and choose the one who has the most efficient cost structure and can make the most attractive offer to consumers. In contrast, exogenous costs are by definition homogeneous across suppliers. That is, the taxes, or other third-party fees are the same across suppliers (financial institutions, here) and thus cannot be different and potentially more or less appealing.

Comparing exogenous costs across lenders is moot. These are costs that are determined by third parties. Terms about these costs do not provide additional valuable information to the consumer since all transactions, whoever the lender and the borrower are, generate identical costs. The only important information for the borrower refers to the existence and the amount of such exogenous costs, in order to be able to understand the overall economic sacrifice that entering into mortgage financing will entail compared to other alternatives (no financing, unsecured financing, foregoing the property acquisition, etc.).

Under this light, the inclusion of exogenous costs as part of price terms instead of in an ad hoc standard term allocating those costs would not seem to decrease contract transparency. It could even be considered to enhance overall awareness of those costs if the *ad hoc* term remained largely unnoticed by borrowers. This would be, in general, a fair assessment of the alternatives. Considering the particulars of the Spanish case, however, the salience of the exogenous cost imposition to the borrower was promoted by the requirement to specifically inform the consumer of the estimated amount of those exogenous costs, and the knowledge that such amount would be deducted from the nominal amount of the loan at the time of signing the contract.

3.2 Behavioral Insights: Awareness of Immediate Certain Costs v. Long Term and Uncertain Costs

Behavioural analysis is of great importance to contract economics, since the latter, in a fundamental way, has individual choice at its disciplinary core. At the same time, behavioural considerations are also crucial for the law of contracts and consumer law. How individuals actually decide, the parameters affecting which choices are made and how, and the individuals' awareness regarding the potential outcomes of their decisions, are all fundamental when drafting laws and assessing their potential impact.[32] Reality and legal practice shows that, on a daily basis, the decisions and actions of individuals (and not just consumers) diverge, not unsystematically, from the predictions grounded in the standard rational choice approach traditionally used in economics and in law and economics.

Behavioural considerations suggest that the presentation of a lump-sum cost to be incurred at the moment of entering into the contract has different effects for the consumer's decision than including it in the price and hence turning this cost into an uncertain, long term variable.

It is a well-known general finding of the behavioural law and economics of consumer contracting that

> [..] while people accurately perceive immediate and certain costs, they tend to underestimate deferred and contingent ones.[33]

Does this general result hold in our case?

The impact on transparency and consumer awareness of presenting the exogenous contract costs as a lump-sum cost to be faced upfront or as a component of the contract price to be paid throughout the life of the contract (a long one, in the case of consumer mortgage finance for the acquisition of residential property, typically 30 or more years) hinges upon a number of cognitive biases that may afflict consumers, such as the projection bias, overconfidence, self-control limits or bounded willpower, and hyperbolic discounting.

The projection bias refers to the frequent (mistaken, as it turns out) assumption by individuals that their preferences will not change over time. When taking decisions agents assume that their choices, regardless of whether they are adopted in the present or will be adopted in the future, will be ordered in the same way assuming that future preferences of the individual will be identical as the current ones.[34]

The projection bias is particularly relevant for decisions that are adopted at a specific moment in time, but with an impact at later times when the individuals' preferences might change in the meantime.

The assessment of future events—even in the near future—is an area in which important behavioural biases afflicting individuals are shown in action. Individuals tend to be overly confident about their capacities, abilities, and about the level, quality and reliability of information available to them. As a result, they tend to underestimate the probability and magnitude of negative events impacting their welfare. In this sense, overconfidence refers to the underestimation of negative

[32] Jolls et al. (2000), pp. 13–58. The fact that very often legal education and analysis, and even lawmaking itself, has paid more attention to other dimensions (both normative and technical) does not weaken this view, we believe.

[33] Zamir and Teichman (2018), p. 299.

[34] Loewenstein et al. (2003), pp. 1209–1248.

potential future events at a higher degree than the one they should have using available statistical information.

At the same time, individuals tend to react to immediate events more forcefully than to future events. Individuals tend to overestimate their valuation of the present over the future, so whatever decisions might provide short-term reward seem to be preferred to potential positive events in the future. For that reason, mechanisms to implement commitment are important and relevant for individuals in order to ensure that the short-term rewards might not be the ultimate decisive element, but their long-term interests will be consistently pursued.[35]

Hyperbolic discounting focuses on the direction of the distorted valuation of future events when evaluated from the perspective of the present. Individuals discount the impact on its welfare of future events but they discount it at a hyperbolic rate. Hyperbolic discounting refers to the effect of individuals being impatient in the short term, and very patient when thinking about the long term.[36] That is, immediate events are preferred to the immediate future, that is very heavily discounted, but events that could take place in the far future are discounted very lightly over immediately previous future events.

These behavioural insights point in the direction that direct and upfront passing-on of exogenous costs to be paid at the beginning of the life of the contract might generate enhanced awareness, and may impact consumers' choices more than simply the alternative of passing-on as a (small, presumably) increase in the future mortgage payments over 30 or 40 years.

The second alternative would clearly be one of a "deferred cost" that is more easily ignored, and thus distorts consumer behaviour in a way that immediate costs are less likely to do. With deferred assumption of exogenous costs through long-term payments it is easier for consumers to ignore or downplay the costs and to be allured by the lower initial costs into a transaction that is truly more costly than what it looks like to the behaviourally biased consumer.[37]

Obviously the behavioural argument in favour of immediate and not deferred costs does not imply that having a large number of such upfront costs and fees cannot be used to obscure the perception of the true costs for the consumer, and may call for remedial action on the side of contract law or financial regulation.[38] This, however, does not seem to have been the case with the exogenous costs term given that lenders

---

[35]Della Vigna and Malmendier (2006), pp. 694–719. Penalties for lack of funds or overdrafts, or for overextended credit card spending, or annual fees—with no per-use charges—for a gym might be conceptualized as commitment devices. See Bar-Gill (2004), pp. 1373–1434. It should be noted that these commitment devices might not be effective or have the same impact for all types of consumers—for example, for sophisticated and for naïve consumers.

[36]Della Vigna and Malmendier (2006), pp. 694–719 illustrating hyperbolic discounting through the overconfidence about the future in certain contractual decisions.

[37]Bar-Gill (2012), p. 21.

[38]Sarin (2018), at https://scholarship.law.upenn.edu/faculty_scholarship/2010); Zamir and Mendelson (2017) pp. 1–20, examine the policy in Israel towards a reduction in the number and complexity of bank fees.

had to provide specifically a total amount covering all of them, and remind the borrower that such amount would be deducted from the nominal amount of the loan.

In sum, the Spanish litigation in mortgage contract terms seems to have produced a profound impact on contract design in mortgage loan contracts. It is not at all obvious that some of the changes brought about by how the Spanish courts (and also, not to a small extent, the CJEU) have accomplished the ex post controls over standard terms, are actually for the benefit of consumers. Specially with respect to the exogenous contract costs involved in mortgage financing, replacing *ad hoc* terms (even if non-negotiated) coupled with the obligation to provide an estimate upfront, with price terms that in the long-term pass-on those same costs unto consumers, may prove detrimental to consumers in the presence of cognitive biases.

4 Conclusion

Unfairness controls established by the Directive 13/93 have had a remarkable impact in Spain regarding financial costs and judicial costs in litigation over standard terms in mortgage contracts. However, in all likelihood, the implementation of Directive 13/93 has also had less noticeable effects upon, among others, contract design. Spain, perhaps dramatically so, illustrates these effects.

The uncertainty created by the litigation over standard terms in mortgage contracts impacted many—if not most—of the standard terms that allocated costs among the contracting parties. Litigation ranged from contract terms allocating tax payments, fees involved in entering into a mortgage contract—such as notarial and property registrar's fees—as well as terms allocating variable interest rate risks—such as floor clauses—among the contracting parties. The outcome of this litigation before Spanish courts (and also often before the CJEU) has been to consider that most of this standard terms were unfair or non-transparent under the Directive because they imposed an undue imbalance on the consumer or because they did not allow him for an adequate assessment of the actual economic content involved in the contract.

One of the results of this litigation has been a change in contract design. Some of these costs, that initially were allocated contractually, are now included as an addition—and not separately—to the price terms. This chapter has presented the impact on contract design of mortgage loans of financial litigation and the application of ex-post unfairness controls using the Spanish case as an illustrative—if dramatic—example. The litigation outburst has resulted in a change in the design of consumer financial contracts that, in certain respects, most notably the allocation of exogenous contract costs, raises questions on whether it will ultimately increase consumer welfare.

References

Badarinza C, Campbell JY, Ramadorai T (2016) International Comparative Household Finance, National Bureau of Economic Research Working Paper No, 22066

Bar-Gill O (2004) Seduction by plastic. Northwest Univ Law Rev 98(4):1373–1434

Bar-Gill O (2012) Seduction by contract. Law, economics and psychology in consumer markets. Oxford University Press

Della Vigna S, Malmendier U (2006) Paying not to go to the Gym. Am Econ Rev 96(3):694–719

Jansen N, Zimmermann R (eds) (2018) Commentaries on European contract laws. Oxford University Press, p 939

Jolls C, Sunstein C, Thaler R (2000) A behavioral approach to law and economics. In: Sunstein C (ed) Behavioral law and economics (Cambridge Series on Judgment and Decision Making). Cambridge University Press, Cambridge, pp 13–58

Loewenstein G, O'Donoghue T, Rabin M (2003) Projection bias in predicting future utility. Q J Econ 118(4):1209–1248. https://doi.org/10.1162/003355303322552784

Micklitz H, Reich N (2014) The court and sleeping beauty: the revival of the unfair contract terms directive (UCTD). Common Mark Law Rev 51(3):771

Miquel JM (2017) Las cláusulas de vencimiento anticipado en el contrato de préstamos hipotecario. In: Albentosa LP, Martínez GT (eds) Culpa y responsabilidad. Thomson-Aranzadi

Riesenhuber K (2013) EU-Vertragsrecht, Mohr Siebeck

Sarin N (2018) The salience theory of consumer financial regulation. Faculty Scholarship at Penn Law, at https://scholarship.law.upenn.edu/faculty_scholarship/2010

Zamir E, Mendelson T (2017) Three modes of regulating price terms in standard-form contracts -the Israeli experience. Hebrew Univ Jerus Legal Stud Res Pap Ser 17(40):1–20

Zamir E, Teichman D (2018) Behavioral law and economics. Press, Oxford University

Regulation

Directive 93/13/EEC of 5 April 1993 on unfair terms in consumer contracts, OJ L 95, 21.4.1993, p. 29–34

Law 5/2019 of March 15, on residential credit contracts has banned floor clauses entirely in residential mortgages, Official Gazette (BOE) num. 65

Law 1/2013 of May 14 of measures for enhancing the protection of mortgage debtors, debt restructuring and social tenancy, Official Gazette (BOE) num. 116

Law 19/2015 of July 13 of measures reforming the Administration of Justice and the Civil Registry, Official Gazette (BOE) num. 167

Case Law

Court of Justice of the European Union Judgment in joined cases C-70/17 Abanca Corporación Bancaria SA v García Salamanca Santos and C-179/17 Bankia SA v Lau Mendoza and Rodríguez Ramírez of 26 March 2019

Court of Justice of the European Union Judgment in joined cases C-154/15 and C-307/15 Gutiérrez Naranjo v Cajasur Banco SAU, Ana María Palacios Martínez v Banco Bilbao Vizcaya Argentaria SA (BBVA), Banco Popular Español SA v Emilio Irles López and Teresa Torres Andreu of December 21 2016

Court of Justice of the European Union Judgment C-92/11 RWE Vertrieb AG v Verbraucherzentrale Nordrhein-Westfalen eV of March 21 2013

Court of Justice of the European Union Judgment in case C-415/11. Mohamed Aziz v Caixa d'Estalvis de Catalunya, Tarragona i Manresa (Catalunyacaixa), of March 14 2013
Spanish Supreme Court decisions 44/2019, 46/2019, 47/2019, 48/2019 and 49/2019 of January 23 2019
Spanish Supreme Court Judgment 849/2019 of March 15 2018
Spanish Supreme Court Judgment 79/2016, of December 18 2016
Spanish Supreme Court Judgment 705/2015 of December 23rd 2015

Fernando Gómez Barcelona. Professor of Civil law and Law and Economics at Universitat Pompeu Fabra. Ramon Trias Fargas 25, Barcelona 08005, Tel. +34 542 2000; fernando.gomez@upf.edu. Fields of Interest: contract law, tort law, product liability and consumer law from an economics perspective.

Mireia Artigot Barcelona, Lecturer of Civil Law at Universitat Pompeu Fabra. Ramon Trias Fargas 25, Barcelona 08005, Tel. +34 542 2000; mireia.artigot@upf.edu. Fields of Interest: contract law, tort law, product liability, digital networks and consumer law from an economics perspective.

Correcting Information Asymmetry Via Deep Consumer Information; Compelling Companies to Let the Sunshine In

Danny Friedmann

Abstract Consumers that want to make ethical purchasing decisions and governments that want to make policy decisions to stimulate ethical manufacturing, are left in the dark. Many products are composed of several constituting parts, with or without negative externalities, manufactured by often separate producers, which increases the general perplexity about their degree of ethicality. In 'More Than You Wanted to Know: The Failure of Mandated Disclosure', Professors Ben-Shahar and Schneider have exposed systemic challenges to mandated disclosurite systems. Building upon their work, and applying their lessons, this paper explores the possibility of a disclosurite system, "Deep Consumer Information", which does not mandate, but nevertheless compels companies, due to market forces, to disclose information about the ethicality of their products. Combining Neoclassical Economics (giving consumers the opportunity to make rational choices about the relative weights they want to give to certain ethical issues, for example via intuitive sliders on an app) and Behavioral Economics (notifying the aggregate ethicality ranking of the constituting parts of a product, that can be displayed on the screen of a phone or at digital supermarket shelves), Deep Consumer Information is trying to correct the asymmetry between on the one hand; company and consumer, and on the other; company and government.

1 Introduction

Virtus ipsa pretium sui—Virtue is its own reward[1]

The title alludes to Brandeis' expression: "Sunlight is said to be the best of disinfectants; electric light the most efficient policeman." Brandeis (1914), Chapter V.

[1]Ovidius, Tristia, V. xiv, 19–46.

D. Friedmann (✉)
School of Transnational Law, Peking University Shenzhen, Shenzhen, Hong Kong

K. Mathis, A. Tor (eds.), *Consumer Law and Economics*, Economic Analysis of Law in European Legal Scholarship 9, https://doi.org/10.1007/978-3-030-49028-7_8

> There is a huge element of trust and a leap of faith in virtually every purchase we make, which is why we are so desperate to find, and pay a premium for, any signals of reassurance.[2]

Consumers that want to make ethical purchasing decisions and governments that want to make policy decisions to stimulate ethical manufacturing and ethical products, are left in the dark. Many products are composed of several constituting parts, with or without negative externalities, manufactured by often separate producers, which increases the general perplexity about their degree of ethicality.

In 'More Than You Wanted to Know: The Failure of Mandated Disclosure',[3] Professors Ben-Shahar and Schneider have exposed systemic challenges to mandated disclosurite systems. Building upon their work, and applying their lessons, this chapter explores the possibility of a disclosurite system, "Deep Consumer Information", which does not mandate, but nevertheless compels companies, due to market forces, to disclose information about the ethicality of their products. For consumers, Deep Consumer Information can function as choice-architecture for ethical purchasing decisions, for companies it can signal a degree of ethicality of their products or manufacturing process, and for governments it can help create a level playing field for companies with ethical products and manufacturing processes.

Combining Neoclassical Economics (giving consumers the opportunity to make rational choices[4] about the relative weights they want to give to certain ethical issues, for example via intuitive sliders on an app) and Behavioral Economics (notifying the aggregate ethicality ranking of the constituting parts of a product, that can be displayed on the screen of a phone or at digital supermarket shelves),[5] Deep Consumer Information is trying to correct the asymmetry between on the one hand; company and consumer, and on the other; company and government. In accordance with libertarian paternalism, a term coined by Sunstein and Thaler,[6] people can be furthered in the goals they set themselves. In the same vein as a 'Nudge',[7] Deep Consumer Information is furthering the consumers' own ethical preferences when purchasing products. Of course, despite a consumer's ethical preference, price can trump ethicality. According to Ariely, the question is whether consumers are willing to pay for a social good or whether they make a trade-off in regard to the price.[8] If one's rule is not to buy anything produced by child labour then one cannot make these trade-offs. However, if one allows trade-offs, "a little bit

---

[2]Sutherland (2011), p. 4.

[3]Ben-Shahar an Schneider (2014).

[4]Rational choice is here interpreted as one's rational decision to give substance and effect to one's possibly irrational preferences.

[5]With Information of Things (IoT) a chip can be embedded to the natural "face" of the product, the trademark, which signifies the underlying goodwill of the company. Friedmann (2018), p. 679.

[6]Thaler and Sunstein (2008), pp. 4–6.

[7]Thaler and Sunstein (2008), pp. 4–6.

[8]Ariely D, professor of psychology and behavioural economics at the Center for Advanced Hindsight, Duke University, Durham, N.C.: "Our perception of value is dramatically subjective. It comes from lots of things from the environment." Real Value, documentary by Jesse Borkowski 2013. Available at: https://www.youtube.com/watch?v=ez3CWXQrgVo.

more child labour, for a little bit more saving", becomes a possibility. However, with complete opaqueness about a product's ethicality no trade-offs can be made with price, let alone a comparison between two similarly priced products based on their ethicality.

1.1 Company and Consumer

Certification organizations can rank the manufacturing of the constituting parts and the end-product in regard to their ethical degree. The Internet of Things (IoT) makes it possible that each constituting part of a product will be assigned extra information about its ethicality and which data can be harvested by the ranking algorithm. The ranking of ethical manufacturing can be looked at from different or aggregate dimensions. If companies do not want to disclose information about the ethicality of their products, Deep Consumer Information will make assumptions, so that their ranking will be lower than companies that do cooperate. Ethicality rankings can enable consumers to compare between similar products and make more informed purchasing decisions based on intuitive one-number rankings that take negative externalities with their hidden societal costs into account.

1.2 Company and Government

Deep Consumer Information provides societies the possibility to create a level playing field for ethically manufactured products with those products that caused negative externalities. Governments can tax the unethically manufactured products by adding the hidden costs of the negative externalities, to reduce or remove the unfair price difference and cure this market imperfection in the process. This can lead to a virtuous cycle of ever higher levels of ethical products and manufacturing.

The problem of information asymmetry is not unique to the People's Republic of China. However, the Chinese government has experimented since 2015 with comprehensive methods to rank citizens but also companies to nudge and sanction them into model participants of society in regard to China's specific standard of trustworthiness. In 2020, this Social Credit system must be implemented. Although some commentators expect this to lead to a dystopian future, ranking systems applied to the ethicality of products and manufacturing processes could have beneficial implications for society.

This paper describes how Deep Consumer Information could tackle some problems of mandatory disclosurite systems, correcting the information asymmetry between company and consumer (Sect. 2), company and government (Sect. 3), but is facing other daunting challenges about what is an ethical product and who certifies the certifications (Sect. 4). The Concluding Section will provide an outlook into possible solutions (Sect. 5).

2 Company and Consumer

There is a poignant information asymmetry between companies and consumers. For many companies the ethical dimension of production and their products often lose out on the market, or their labour unions.[9] Plus they want anything related to their products and manufacturing process to be confidential to prevent competitors to take advantage of proprietary knowledge and avoid piercing eyes of governments, NGOs and the public at large to learn about aspects of their products and manufacturing process of which they are less proud, and who can make doing business difficult by regulation. In some cases, this unwillingness has lead to regulatory capture, which decreases the possibility of accountability.[10] Examples include the ag-gag laws in the U.S.[11] If companies are willing to share such information it is only selectively and sparingly if this directly benefits their image.

However, for companies that are not willing to share information about their products and manufacturing process a perfect storm is imminent: transparency will dramatically increase due to a combination of technological, socio-economic and demographic developments. The rise of the IoT, big data, artificial intelligence and transparency in society (also due to a demise of consumers' privacy), more stringent labelling requirements and increasing engagement from the newest generations and in their wake the older generations.

The privacy of consumers off and on the internet, in regard to what you buy, personal data including medical and reputational data in regard to employment, credit, insurance and other vital economic factors are increasingly invaded by companies' algorithms and data, impermeable to inspection.[12] After collection by search engines, ad networks, social media, the data is shared by data brokers, credit bureaus and financial and insurance companies.[13]

---

[9]Volkswagen aims plans to sell 70 models of electric cars. For the production of electric cars it needs fewer workers than for gasoline cars. This is leading to a conflict with the labour unions. VW's newish boss is going full-steam ahead with electric cars, Economist, 14 March 2019. Available at: https://www.economist.com/business/2019/03/16/vws-newish-boss-is-going-full-steam-ahead-with-electric-cars.

[10]Regulatory capture is a form of government failure which occurs when a regulatory agency, created to act in the public interest, instead advances the commercial or political concerns of special interest groups that dominate the industry or sector it is charged with regulating. See in general, Dal Bó (2006) Oxford Review of Economic Policy, 22:2, pp. 203–225.

[11]Ag-gag (Agricultural gag) laws criminalize undercover whistleblowing at factory farms in multiple states of the U.S. (Iowa, Utah, Missouri, Idaho, Wyoming, which impose criminal penalties; and North Carolina, which impose a civil sanction), which makes it impossible to hold factory farms accountable for their actions. Ganzler (2019). Cohen (2019).

[12]Pasquale (2015).

[13]Pasquale refers to the research by Robert Gelman and Pam Dixon: There is legislation in the U.S. for consumers to inspect, annotate and correct the three big credit bureaus in the U.S. [Fair Credit Reporting Act, 15 U.S.C. § 1681, effective 26 October 1970] to make sure that the right information is used. However, there are at least 4000 data brokers who make consumer scores based on different dimensions; which means that correcting information for consumers has become a full-

From a moral point of view, it is uneven that companies can have access to big data on consumers' behaviour, but consumers cannot have access to big data on companies' behaviour. Historically, business self-regulation has preceded government regulation.[14] One can argue that with the Corporate Social Responsibility (CSR) movement, which commenced in the 1950s,[15] companies started to share some information about their welfare enhancing activities. These were either prompted by the idea that it would improve business interests, namely avoid labour unrest, attract people for recruitment and retain employees, or enhance social ideals, or all of these.[16] In 1962, Milton Friedman argued that

> few trends could so thoroughly undermine the very foundations of our free society as the acceptance by corporate officials of a social responsibility other than to make as much money for their stockholders as possible.[17]

However one can respond that "social responsible" products, in other words ethical products, make much sense from a business perspective, also for stockholders, if consumers care about ethicality and are willing to pay a premium for them, which might not have been a large contingent in 1962. But times have changed. According to Moon, in the 1990s, the concept of CSR was embedded in corporations using standards and codes, increased social reporting, and growing partnerships between companies and NGOs or governmental organizations.[18] Even though these companies might have incorporated CSR, or the partly overlapping concept of Business Ethics, or are reporting about some ethical activities for the transparency requirements of their investors or stock exchanges, this does not necessarily mean that they are willing to share information about how ethically their products are nor how ethically these products have been manufactured.

There are examples of companies with arguably intrinsically unethical products or unethical manufacturing processes, which do use CSR systems. An example is McDonald's, a company that is on the one hand a contributor to the obesity epidemic (which induces all kinds of health issues such as diabetes),[19] carbon dioxide emissions, animal cruelty,[20] massive deforestation of rainforests to grow soybeans for animal feed.[21] On the other hand, it "gives back to the community" via, for

---

time job which is not feasible and thus can have severe consequences. Looking at The Black Box Society, A USPIRG Education Fund/Center for Digital Democracy Event, YouTube video. Available at: https://www.youtube.com/watch?v=hkXdxYG_lFA.

[14]The medieval guilds are a case in point. Vogel (2010), p. 70.

[15]CSR has its roots in the time of the Industrial Revolution in the 1800s. Carroll (2008), pp. 19–20.

[16]Carroll (2008), pp. 20–21.

[17]Friedman (1962), p. 133.

[18]Moon (2005), pp. 56–57.

[19]Devitt (2018).

[20]The Secret Ingredient in Chicken McNuggets: Animal Cruelty, Mercy for Animals. Available at: http://mcdonaldscruelty.com/.

[21]Neslen (2017).

example, the Ronald McDonald House Charities.[22] Another example is Royal Dutch Shell, which is connected to the oil spills in Nigeria in 2008, which damage has increased in the last decade, because they have not been cleaned up,[23] which is at odds with Shell's CSR mission: "We aim to be a good neighbour wherever we work, by contributing to the well-being of communities."[24] Such practices of making unsubstantiated or misleading claims about the environmental benefits of a product, service, technology or company practice is called greenwashing.[25] Mandalaki and O'Sullivan introduced an interesting explanation and categorisation of such behaviour, derived from Catholic doctrine: by dividing such behaviour into three categories: proper indulgence (genuinely attempting to offset bad behaviour and preventing it will happening again); abuse of indulgence (no real effort to eliminate a harmful activity and instead hopes to compensate for it by carrying out "good works" in another area); organizational impostorism (business makes claims about its "morally upright" behavior in certain of its activities while continuing to behave in an unethical manner in others).[26]

The transmission of stringent standards from developed countries to developing countries has been facilitated by global brands that are vulnerable to threats to their reputation and the emergence of international communications, so that activists can acquire and disseminate information about business practices that deviate from the standard.[27]

When consumers are duped into believing that they are buying a product that is aligned with their ethical value system, even though it is not, Danush calls this identity harm.[28] She points to an example of Hershey's CSR report in 2014, in which the chocolate manufacturer claimed to have zero tolerance for the worst kinds of child labour in its chocolate-supply chain, but before and after releasing press statements which extend deadlines for sourcing child-labour-free cocoa in 2005, 2008, 2010 and 2020.[29]

According to marketing research it seems that newer generations are more engaged with ethics and morals than older generations. The Center for Generational Kinetics provides a classification of generations. Generational Breakdown: Info About All of the Generations: Gen Z, iGen, or Centennials: Born 1996—To be determined; Millennials or Gen Y: Born 1977–1995; Generation X: Born 1965–1976; Baby Boomers: Born 1946–1964; Traditionalists or Silent Generation:

---

[22]McDonald's Corporate Social Responsibility page. Available at: https://www.mcdonalds.com.hk/en/social-responsibility.html.

[23]Kent (2018).

[24]Shell Communities site. Available at: https://www.shell.com/sustainability/communities.html.

[25]Aggarwal and Kadyan (2011), pp. 61–66.

[26]Mandalaki and O'Sullivan (2016), pp. 203–227.

[27]Vogel (2010), p. 71.

[28]Danush (2018), p. 804.

[29]Danush (2018), p. 847.

Born 1945 and before. Thus, Generation Z is more engaged than Millennials, who are more engaged than Generation X, who are more engaged than Baby Boomers.[30]

Why are companies not transparent in regard to the ethicality of their products? They might be laboring under the following assumptions:

- They cannot be too much out of step with their competition.
- They want to satisfy the market demands, instead of shaping the demands in the market.
- It is not the task of a company to raise awareness or to teach consumers about ethicality.
- Consumers care less about where a product is coming from and how it is made. They care most about the quality/price ratio;[31]
- If they do care, they can be fooled into thinking that the product is coming from an ethical source, even though it is not;
- If they do care and cannot be fooled about the source of the product, they cannot distinguish good from evil.
- Only governments can hold companies to account.

2.1 Labelling

> Labelling means any words, particulars, trademarks, brand name, pictorial matter or symbol relating to a foodstuff and placed on any packaging, document, notice, label, ring or collar accompanying or referring to such foodstuff [or other products, DF].[32]

Labelling can be an important counterforce against the opaqueness of the ethicality of products in the eyes of consumers. However, despite labelling most products' ethicality is still shrouded in intransparency.

Labelling can entail information about the source of the product, and about the mode of production, processing or composition.[33] The manufacturing process might consist of different processes and a product might consist of different components, sourced from different jurisdictions. Obviously, product manufacturers are in the best position to provide information about how they manufacture the product and what are the constituting parts of a product. Mandatory information standards are

---

[30]Sullivan (2018). Generational Breakdown: Info About All of the Generations, Center for Generational Kinetics. Available at: https://genhq.com/faq-info-about-generations/.

[31]Quality/Price ratio is a measure of perceived value, of the enjoyment you receive weighed against the price you have to pay.

[32]Article 3(4) Regulation (EU) No 1151/2012 of the European Parliament and of the Council of 21 November 2012 on quality schemes for agricultural products and foodstuffs OJ L 343, 14.12.2012, pp. 1–29. ELI: http://data.europa.eu/eli/reg/2012/1151/oj.

[33]Article 18(1)(a) Regulation (EU) No 1151/2012 of the European Parliament and of the Council of 21 November 2012 on quality schemes for agricultural products and foodstuffs OJ L 343, 14.12.2012, pp. 1–29. ELI: http://data.europa.eu/eli/reg/2012/1151/oj.

introduced to ensure that consumers are provided with important details of a product to enable them to make appropriate personal choices. Information standards require suppliers to give consumers prescribed information when they purchase specified goods for example, ingredient labelling for cosmetics, labelling for tobacco products and care labelling for clothing and textile products. Information standards may or may not relate to safety. However, mandatory consumer product information standards are limited.

Switzerland is one of the jurisdictions with the most stringent compulsory labelling system. The objectives of its Federal Food and Commodities Law are stated in Article 1: to protect the health of consumers from unsafe foods and commodities; ensure hygiene; protect consumers from deception, and most saliently for this chapter's purpose: to provide consumers with the information necessary for the purchase of food or commodities. This chapter argues that the degree of ethicality is germane for consumers so they can make informed purchasing decisions.

The Federal Food and Commodities Law provides the following:

- Article 7(1) only safe products may be placed on the market;
- Article 10(1) those who handle food need to do so in a hygienic way;
- Article 12(1) prescribes the labelling and information obligation for anyone who places pre-packaged food on the market: country of origin, name of the good, and the ingredients.

No explicit ethicality disclosure is prescribed under the Federal Food and Commodities Law, although Article 20(3) Federal Food and Commodities Law is going further than a disclosure obligation,[34] as will be pointed out below. In 2018, it turned out that the Migros and Coop, respectively the biggest and second biggest Swiss supermarket chains, were not in compliance with the labelling requirement in regard to the country of origin.[35] Country of origin, and more specifically, traceability of the components of the end-product is imperative to secure the integrity of the supply chain, which is needed to support the ethicality of the products. Article 28 Federal Food and Commodities Law obligates manufacturers of food and substances intended or foreseeable to be processed into food, commodities, cosmetics, and toys to provide traceability of their products. Traceability and the integrity of the supply chain, made possible by IoT, is a precondition for safeguarding the standard of product ethicality at the level manufactured by the producer.

[34]However, see Art. 20(3) Bundesgesetz über Lebensmittel und Gebrauchsgegenstände (Lebensmittelgesetz, LMG) vom 20. Juni 2014 (Stand am 1. Mai 2017). "Er kann das Inverkehrbringen kosmetischer Mittel, deren endgültige Zusammensetzung oder deren Bestandteile mit Tierversuchen getestet worden sind, zur Einhaltung der Bestimmungen der Lebensmittelgesetzgebung, einschränken oder verbieten." Available at: https://www.admin.ch/opc/de/classified-compilation/20101912/index.html#a20.

[35]Swiss supermarkets selling products with no country of origin on label, Le News, 13 December 2018. Available: https://lenews.ch/2018/12/13/swiss-supermarkets-selling-products-with-no-country-of-origin-on-label/.

If a dimension of ethicality is not on the label, consumers need to do their own research for each product, which is time-consuming, burdensome and cannot be expected from consumers. For example in regard to cosmetics, in Australia, the Trade Practices (Consumer Product Information Standards) (Cosmetics) Regulations 1991[36] prescribes to disclose the list of ingredients, but does not disclose information about whether or not they are tested on animals. In comparison, Article 20(3) of the Swiss Federal Food and Commodities Law takes a proactive role in this regard and may restrict or prohibit the placing on the market of cosmetic products whose final composition or their ingredients have been tested on animals.[37]

Standards are ubiquitous in most jurisdictions. Standards are published documents setting out specifications and procedures designed to ensure products, services and systems are safe, reliable and consistently perform as intended. Snyder states that in global value chains, product standards, together with intellectual property rights and rules of origin are the principal normative devices to ensure product quality and safety.[38] Sometimes the standards concern the ethicality of products; for example China and the EU had conflicting standards in regard to the environment. Genetically modified organisms (GMOs) are a case in point. Despite the WTO Dispute cases against the then European Communities' moratorium on GMOs,[39]—which was partially won by the U.S., Canada and Argentina—the EU continued to ban GMOs. But, as Snyder clarifies there was a persistent pressure by pro-trade actors for "standardisation, harmonisation of national standards or at least mutual recognition of equivalence".[40] From a product ethics perspective, this search for the greatest common denominator in standards, for example via multilateral structures, could lead to a race-to-the-bottom.

Voluntary standards establish a common language defining quality and safety criteria, which the government can use as basis for the development of a mandatory standard. Like most mandatory safety standards, those of Australia only address essential safety features.[41] One can determine that current product information, with

---

[36]From 1 January 2011, a prescribed consumer product information standard made under the Trade Practices Act 1974 which is still in force on 1 January 2011 continues in force as if it were an information standard made under the ACL.

[37]Art. 20(3) Bundesgesetz über Lebensmittel und Gebrauchsgegenstände (Lebensmittelgesetz, LMG) vom 20. Juni 2014 (Stand am 1. Mai 2017). "Er kann das Inverkehrbringen kosmetischer Mittel, deren endgültige Zusammensetzung oder deren Bestandteile mit Tierversuchen getestet worden sind, zur Einhaltung der Bestimmungen der Lebensmittelgesetzgebung, einschränken oder verbieten." Available at: https://www.admin.ch/opc/de/classified-compilation/20101912/index.html#a20.

[38]Snyder (2016), p. 1.

[39]WTO DS291, 292, and 293 European Communities—Measures Affecting the Approval and Marketing of Biotech Products, One-page case summary, 21 November 2006. Available at: https://www.wto.org/english/tratop_e/dispu_e/cases_e/1pagesum_e/ds291sum_e.pdf.

[40]Snyder (2016).

[41]Aquatic toys, baby bath aids, baby dummies, baby walkers, balloon blowing kits, basketball rings and backboards, bean bags, bicycle helmets, bicycles; blinds, curtains and window fittings; bunk beds, care labelling for clothes and textiles, child restraints for use in motor vehicles, cigarette

regards to its ethicality, is inadequate. In the absence of this, consumers have turned to social media to gain information and experiences by others of the products. This is a suboptimal solution, which actually can amplify non-ethical purchases.[42]

In general, the Swiss Federal Food and Commodities Law improves the transparency for consumers. However, Article 24(4) Federal Food and Commodities Law prescribes that some information is not accessible to the public, such as:

a. official control reports and the documents containing conclusions on the findings and information obtained during the inspection (Article 32 (1));
b. Results of research and surveys (Article 40), to the extent that they permit conclusions to be drawn from the manufacturers, distributors or products concerned;
c. the risk classification of companies by the enforcement authorities.

One can argue that this information is relevant for consumers if they want to be able to make an informed purchasing decision. The reason for this might be that the Swiss legislator wanted the administrative authorities to judge companies and not the media or the public at large. Thereby retaining the control over when information about these companies will be shared with the media and the public at large.

One can argue that in most cases there is insufficient labelling with regards to the ethicality of products to guide consumers. Most are about public health and safety. For example, with regards to food products, most labels are to provide the source of the goods, and the ingredients, to avoid food allergies.

2.2 *Certifications*

Next to mandatory and voluntary labelling, certification can provide extra information about ethicality, for example certifications about energy efficiency,[43] wood from responsibly managed forests,[44] child labor free products,[45] products manufactured in

lighters, cigarettes, cosmetics, cots, exercise cycles, fire extinguishers, hot water bottles, jacks, luggage straps, motorcycle helmets, nightwear for children, portable swimming pools, prams and strollers, ramps for motor vehicles, recovery straps for motor vehicles, soccer goals, sunglasses and fashion spectacles, support stands for vehicles, swimming and flotation aids for water familiarization and swimming tuition, tobacco health warnings, toys, toys and finger paint containing lead and other elements, toys containing magnets, toys for children up to and including 36 months, treadmills. Mandatory Standards, Australian Competition & Consumer Commission. Available at: https://www.productsafety.gov.au/product-safety-laws/safety-standards-bans/mandatory-standards.

[42]If, for example, Friend A is perceived by of most of her or his social connections as an ethical person, and nevertheless buys a non-ethical product, this purchasing behaviour can be followed by her or his social connections.

[43]ENERGY STAR Overview. Available at: https://www.energystar.gov/about.

[44]FSC Certification. Available at: https://us.fsc.org/en-us/certification.

[45]Child Labor Free, How it Works. Available at: https://www.childlaborfree.com/.

a company with gender equality,[46] and vegan products.[47] Then there are specific rules and guidelines of how to label products, for example foodstuffs using the PDO and PGI certificates.[48]

Certifications can be protected via two subspecies of trademarks: certification marks or collective marks. Belson defines certification marks as "principally indicia of conformity of goods or services to particular standards, stipulated by the proprietor of the mark,"[49] and collective marks as "mark[s] owned by an association or 'collectivité' for the use of its members."[50] A significant difference between certification marks and collective marks is that only the certifier of certification marks cannot sell or trade the certified goods. This is to ensure that the certifier will more objectively maintain the standard set. Whether this objectivity of the certifier, who is paid by those who use the certificates, is guaranteed is questionable. In contrast, the collective that is using collective marks, can sell and trade their certified goods.

It is not inconceivable that certifications for ethical products that are important to a minority will be dominant for the products offered to the majority. In particular for products where the majority paradoxically does not care about the certification.[51] Examples are Halal and Kosher certifications in case they certify that a product does not have pork as ingredient of the product, for example toothpaste. However, these religiously-oriented certifications become controversial for at least a part of the majority if they certify that the animals used for the products were ritually slaughtered, *i.e.* a Halal or Kosher certificate on meat products. In Switzerland, since a plebiscite of 1893, the slaughter of animals without prior stunning before the withdrawal of blood is prohibited without exception for every type of slaughter and every species of animal, except for poultry.[52]

However, certifications on products are a first step, but they are not a sufficient solution. There is a panoply of certifications on products. Many products have one or more certifications. A case in point is *quinoa*, a kind of grain that is considered to be very healthy. *Quinoa* of 'I HEART KEENWAH' has five certifications: Non GMO Verified (non-genetically modified organism); Fair Trade Certified; USDA Organic (organic backed by the US Department of Agriculture); K Pareve (K stands for Kosher, and Pareve means it will be considered Kosher when it is either used with dairy or meat, since it has neither of these ingredients); Vegan (containing no animal products). To make it more complex, in between the row of certificates it says

---

[46] Why Edge Certification? Available at: http://edge-cert.org/.

[47] What is the Certified Vegan Logo? Available at: https://vegan.org/certification/.

[48] Commission Communication—Guidelines on the labelling of foodstuffs using protected designations of origin (PDOs) or protected geographical indications (PGIs) as ingredients OJ C 341, 16.12.2010, pp. 3–4. Available at: https://eur-lex.europa.eu/legal-content/EN/TXT/?uri=CELEX:52010XC1216(01).

[49] Belson (2017), p. 30.

[50] Belson (2017), p. 36.

[51] Taleb (2016).

[52] Art. 21(1-2) Tierschutzgesetz [Animal Welfare Act] 16 December, 2005. Available at: https://www.admin.ch/opc/de/classified-compilation/20022103/201705010000/455.pdf.

'Gluten Free', as if it is also a certificate issued by a certifier, which is not the case here, and which is not needed, since *quinoa* naturally does not have any gluten, which is relevant for people with a gluten allergy. To estimate the value of each of these certificates would require quite some research. Are they trustworthy? Do the objectives of the certifiers align with one's ethical preferences? The current constellation of certificates can indeed be confusing to consumers.

If one is comparing two competing products for about the same price, and each has a certain amount of certificates, and these certificates are different from each other, how to compare these certificates and weigh each of these certificates in a timely manner? This would lead to comparing apples and oranges. Deep Consumer Information would make it possible to apply the same ethical preferences setting for all products, which would make a comparison of an apple and another apple possible.

Thus, a one-number ranking based on pre-set ethical preferences would be superior to studying each single certificate on the package. If one uses the latter option, one can climb the learning curve, that is, if the ethicality of the product would be static, which often is not the case, over time one can do repeat-purchasing, but without being able to compare it to new products on the market. A better solution is to have a one-number ranking which is dynamic and will adapt in real-time to any changes in the ethicality of the product.

2.3 Fraud

Besides not providing information about product ethicality, some firms deliberately and maliciously provide the wrong information. Counterfeit and pirated products, where companies based on bad faith are passing off the genuine source of the goods or adding a certification on an uncertified good as their own, deceive and confuse the consumers. Another problem of certification is that the standards set by the certifying organization are not met, but that the products can still be sold with the certificate, due to insufficient assessment or enforcement. Food fraud (intentional deception using food for economic gain), including substitution (replacing a low value ingredient for a high value ingredient), addition (adding unapproved and undeclared enhancements to improve product attributes), dilution (mixing a low quality liquid with a high quality liquid), concealment (hiding ingredients of low quality) tampering or misrepresentation of food, food ingredients or food packaging, includes false statements made about a product, counterfeiting (copying the brand name, packaging concept, recipe, processing method etc. of food products for economic gain).[53] Salient examples include horsemeat sold as beef, pork sold as lamb, and adding

[53]Food Fraud Vulnerability Assessment and Mitigation, PwC, November 2017. Available at: https://www.pwc.com/gx/en/services/food-supply-integrity-services/assets/pwc-food-fraud-vulnerability-assessment-and-mitigation-november.pdf.

growth hormones to meat. Professor John Spink, Director of the Food Fraud Initiative MSU estimates food fraud is worth US$40 billion globally each year.[54] In comparison: illegal trade in heroin is worth an estimated US$30 billion and firearms US$8.5 billion a year.[55]

According to Wight, humans have a deep-set human instinct, which he calls 'the reputation reflex': strong, ingrained biological reasons why we are drawn to a partner or conduct business with people with resources to spare.[56] We are attracted to those who build long-term relationships, which are mutually profitable over time.

> The desperate and the hungry play a short game, their need for their next meal trumping any desire to build a reputation for probity in the long-term.[57]

Therefore, from a game theory perspective, in the long-term it pays off for companies to take responsibility for their products and ethically produce ethical products.

The asymmetry between the product manufacturer on the one hand and the consumer, and government on the other hand (see next Section), can lead to adverse selection and misallocation of resources in society.[58] Unethical purchases can have unexpected drawbacks or lead to perverse results.[59] For example buying "dirty" rare-earth elements or "blood" diamonds from conflict zones can intensify these conflicts,[60] since the parties involved can buy weapons from the revenues earned, which can lead to a proliferation of criminal behaviour, which leads to victims, both humans and gorillas.[61]

3 Company and Government

Guiding the invisible hand[62]

---

[54]Food Fraud Vulnerability Assessment and Mitigation, PwC, November 2017. Available at: https://www.pwc.com/gx/en/services/food-supply-integrity-services/assets/pwc-food-fraud-vulnerability-assessment-and-mitigation-november.pdf.

[55]Sampson (2017).

[56]Wight (2008).

[57]Wight (2008).

[58]Akerlof (1970), pp. 488–500.

[59]Merton (1936), pp. 894–904. See also negative externalities that burden society in the next Section.

[60]In July 2018, the U.S. trade commission expanded its definition of diamond to include lab grown diamonds. "As of January 2019, Tiffany and Co., the biggest jeweler in the world by sales, will disclose the origin of all of its diamonds. It could force a new wave of transparency across the jewelry world. Are lab-grown diamonds the future?", 1843 The Economist YouTube video, 19 March 2019. Available at: https://www.youtube.com/watch?v=s1h4gze_ktk.

[61]Reilly (2019).

[62]This subheading was inspired by the Guiding the Invisible Hand: Economic Liberalism and the State in Latin American History, by Love and Jacobsen (1988).

In 1776, Adam Smith argued that "[b]y pursuing his own interest he frequently promotes that of the society more effectually than when he really intends to promote it."[63] Smith was, however a child of his time, and negative externalities would only start to manifest themselves more clearly a few years into the Industrial Revolution.[64]

Consumers are often guided by the quality/price ratio[65] of a product, instead of taking the ethical dimensions into account. This quality maximization and price minimization might be a rational strategy in the short-term,[66] in the long-term however, and in the aggregate of all consumers together, this leads to negative externalities which does not only affect consumers but also non-consumers. Instead of the premise that the consumer is completely rational, the better view is to see him or her as boundedly rational.[67] In purchasing decisions, the rationality of consumers is limited by the information that they have, their cognitive limitations and time restraints.

Quality/price ratio[68] in combination with brands is often used to short-cut the search process. The brand, and its underlying goodwill, can be protected via trademarks, including non-traditional trademarks, such as three-dimensional marks, colour marks and sound marks. The trademark distinguishes the source of the goods of one undertaking from those of other undertakings. A geographical indication identifies that a certain agricultural good is coming from a certain place and possesses qualities or a reputation that are essentially due to that origin. Both trademarks and geographical indications are granted by administrative agencies. One can argue that, at least some geographical indications could reveal something about the ethicality of such products. For example in the EU, geographical indications are divided in two main categories, Protected Geographical Indications (PGI) and Protected Designations of Origin (PDO),[69] that are created to promote economic, social and environmentally sustainable rural development and foster ethical, *i.e.*

---

63 Smith (1776), Book IV, Chapter II, para IX.

64 The industrial revolution started around 1760 to somewhere between 1820 and 1840. Source Wikipedia.

65 Quality/price ratio is a measure of perceived value weighed against the price.

66 Sutherland is skeptical about the consumer as a rational being: "Decisions are actually taken down in the basement [amygdala DF] and the brain issues hasty post-rationalisations to explain why you adopted the course you did." Sutherland (2011), p. 42.

67 Most people are partly rational in their actions. Simon (1962), pp. 177–182.

68 Quality/price ratio is a measure of perceived value weighed against the price.

69 Regulation (EU) No 1151/2012 of the European Parliament and of the Council of 21 November 2012 on quality schemes for agricultural products and foodstuffs OJ L 343, 14.12.2012, pp. 1–29. Available at: ELI: http://data.europa.eu/eli/reg/2012/1151/oj.

extensive, and diverse agricultural products. The requirements for PDOs[70] are more stringent than for PGIs.[71]

Recital 18 Regulation (EU) No 1151/2012
The specific objectives of protecting designations of origin and geographical indications are securing a fair return for farmers and producers for the qualities and characteristics of a given product, or of its mode of production, and providing clear information on products with specific characteristics linked to geographical origin, thereby enabling consumers to make more informed purchasing choices.

Article 4 Regulation (EU) No 1151/2012
A scheme for protected designations of origin and protected geographical indications is established in order to help producers of products linked to a geographical area by: (a) securing fair returns for the qualities of their products; (b) ensuring uniform protection of the names as an intellectual property right in the territory of the Union; (c) providing clear information on the value-adding attributes of the product to consumers.

Fischler speaks of local methods that "create a bond of trust between the consumer, the product, the place from which it originates, and the people living there who develop it."[72] The EU also wants to protect Traditional Expressions,[73] which are traditional terms connected to products with a PDO or PGI, or used for production or ageing methods[74] colour,[75] type of place,[76] quality or for a particular event linked to the history of the product with a PDO or PGI.[77] PDOs, PGIs and Traditional Expressions can be registered on the EU's electronic register,[78] for wine

[70] For the PDO there needs to be a relation between the product and its origin, marked by many specifically established natural and human factors. The product cannot be reproduced outside its area of origin. Production, processing and preparation phases should be carried out in the same geographical area in which the natural and human factors are located. Blakeney (2014), 3.37, 78. See also Friedmann (2017), p. 278.

[71] A PGI is the name of a region, specific place or, in exceptional cases, a country used to describe an agricultural product or a foodstuff originating in that region, specific place or country, which possesses a specific quality, reputation or other characteristics attributable to that geographical origin and the production and/or processing and/or preparation of which take place in the defined geographical area. Friedmann (2017), p. 278.

[72] Fischler (2004).

[73] Gaeta and Corsinovi (2015).

[74] Hors d'âge; Vin jaune.

[75] Ambré; Clairet; Caret.

[76] Château; Clos.

[77] Cru artisan, Cru bourgeois, Cru classé, whether or not supplemented by Grand; Premier Grand; Deuxième; Troisième; Quatrième; Cinquième; Grand cru; Villages.

[78] Article 104 Regulation (EU) No 1308/2013 of the European Parliament and of the Council of 17 December 2013 establishing a common organisation of the markets in agricultural products and repealing Council Regulations (EEC) No 922/72, (EEC) No 234/79, (EC) No 1037/2001 and (EC) No 1234/2007 OJ L 347, 20.12.2013, pp. 671–854. ELI: http://data.europa.eu/eli/reg/2013/1308/oj.

these registrations by EU members and non-EU members can be found on the EU database called e-Bacchus.[79] In addition, the EU is also using the so called Traditional Specialties Guaranteed (TSG) for agricultural products intended for human consumption or foodstuff with a traditional composition, or produced according to a traditional production method.[80]

In the absence of information about the ethicality of products, consumers that value ethics use different heuristics, short-cuts, and intuition in their purchasing decisions.[81] Traditional trademarks, certification or collective marks and geographical indications are such short-cuts. After an ethical conscious consumer has made a purchasing decision based on heuristics or intuition, and the product has not disappointed him or her, the consumer will continue to buy it without much second thought, unless the consumer's attention was drawn to negative news about the ethicality of the product. Once this habit has established itself, it is difficult to change the purchasing pattern of the consumer due to path dependency and humans' nature as creatures of habit.

Just as there is an information asymmetry between companies and consumers,[82] there is one between companies and government. For example, even though a government has the policy that the polluter pays, it is difficult for the government to assess whether the product has been manufactured in a polluting way, or whether the product will pollute during or after its lifespan. Governments often only levy tax on any market activity that generates negative externalities (costs not internalized in the market price),[83] such as eco tax, fat tax, and ethax (ethics tax). This Pigouvian tax is intended to correct an inefficient market outcome, and does so by being set equal to the social cost of the negative externalities.[84] However, due to globalization, so that the elements of the product originate from different places, each under different

---

[79]e-Bacchus consists of the Register of designations of origin and geographical indications protected in the EU in accordance with Regulation (EU) No 1308/2013; lists non-EU countries' geographical indications and names of origin protected in the EU in accordance with bilateral agreements on trade in wine concluded between the EU and the non-EU countries' concerned; lists the traditional terms protected in the EU in accordance with Regulation (EU) No 1308/2013. Available at: http://ec.europa.eu/agriculture/markets/wine/e-bacchus/.

[80]Council Regulation (EC) No 509/2006 of 20 March 2006 on agricultural products and foodstuffs as traditional specialities guaranteed. OJ L 93 of 31.3.2006. Available at: https://eur-lex.europa.eu/legal-content/EN/TXT/?uri=LEGISSUM:l66043.

[81]According to Gigerenzer and Selten, heuristics are an excellent way to make decisions in a world of uncertainty. Gigerenzer and Selten (2001).

[82]"There are many markets in which buyers use some market statistic to judge the quality of prospective purchases. In this case there is an incentive for sellers to market poor quality merchandise, since the returns for good quality accrue mainly to the entire group whose statistic is affected rather than to the individual seller. As a result there tends to be a reduction in the average quality of goods and also in the size of the market." Akerlof (1970), pp. 488–500.

[83]In many jurisdictions livestock farmers receive subsidies for products that generate negative externalities, (carbon dioxide, ground water contamination, inefficient use of water, health risks for consumers).

[84]Pigou (1920).

environmental protection regimens makes it opaque for governments and oftentimes impossible to tax at the source. Therefore, it is preferable to tax the end-product. Since both domestic and imported products are taxed, there is no discrimination between these categories. However it could give friction since internationally recognised minimum standards under the WTO Agreement would be taxed. On the one hand these taxes for ethically challenged goods can be justified, on the other hand some would characterize these taxes to be non-tariff-barriers to trade and investment. The question is whether the interests of public health and safety *etc.* weigh against this. One can argue that if internationally recognised minimum standards generate negative externalities, these standards are too low.

3.1 Goodness Is the Default, Evilness the Deviation

Ethical products are often more expensive than non-ethical products. The majority of consumers focus predominantly on the quality/price ratio of products. Therefore, there is no level playing field for products with a high degree of ethicality, which results in a race to the bottom with ever cheaper and less ethical products. To increase fair competition, a government can give subsidies to manufacturers of ethical products or tax the manufacturers of unethical products. The latter option is principally preferable, since it corrects the negative externalities caused by the manufacturers of unethical products and goodness is the default, evilness the deviation, and gives manufacturers of ethical products a fighting chance. The reward for manufacturers of ethical products should be provided by the market and not the government. The Swiss Fair-Food-Initiative proposed to reorder the market by promoting regional farmers, environmentally friendly products, and fair trade products.[85] It also wanted to proscribe information if animal products originate from intensive farming.[86] The labels would be defined and controlled by Bio Suisse and

[85]Eidgenössische Volksinitiative "Für gesunde sowie umweltfreundlich und fair hergestellte Lebensmittel (Fair-Food-Initiative)", Argumentarium, 2. Available at: https://fair-food.ch/wp-content/uploads/2018/08/ffi_argumentarium_d.pdf.

[86]"Leider hat es die Politik bisher versäumt, den Konsumentinnen und Konsumenten eine echte Wahlmöglichkeit zu geben. Die Anbieter und Hersteller sind heute nicht verpflichtet, auf den verarbeiteten Produkten zu deklarieren, woher die wichtigsten Zutaten kommen und welche Produktionsmethoden angewendet wurden." [Unfortunately, politics has failed to give consumers a real possibility to vote. Now, the supplier and manufacturer are not obligated to declare on the products where the most important ingredients are coming from and which production methods are being used.]

Eidgenössische Volksinitiative Für gesunde sowie umweltfreundlich und fair hergestellte Lebensmittel (Fair-Food-Initiative)", Argumentarium, 2. Available at: https://fair-food.ch/wp-content/uploads/2018/08/ffi_argumentarium_d.pdf.

IP-Suisse.[87] However, the Swiss Federal Popular Initiative was rejected in the Autumn of 2018.[88]

The result of taxing the unethical products combined with a higher ethical ranking could lead to a virtuous cycle of ever higher standards of ethicality: a Darwinian survival of the most ethical.[89]

3.2 *Social Credit for Companies*

Deng Xiaoping's decision to open up the People's Republic of China for international trade has transformed the country in less than 30 years from a faltering planned economy to a thriving market economy supplemented with state companies. Although the mixture of market and planned economy in China has contributed to lifting more than a half billion people out of poverty, it is far from perfect. One such imperfection of the market economy is seen with the manufacturing of a product creates negative externalities, for example air pollution that is degrading the environment and causes cardiovascular and respiratory diseases and non-smoking lung cancer.[90] Because the way products and their constituting components are produced is not transparent, it is impossible for consumers to make fully informed purchasing decisions. For this reason, it is impossible for governments to create a level playing field for the ethical manufacturing of products. Although this problem is not unique to the People's Republic of China, the Chinese governmental structure is exceptionally well positioned to resolve these challenges, precisely because a significant part of its economy is planned.

The Chinese government has experimented since 2015 with comprehensive methods to rank citizens but also companies to nudge and sanction them into model participants of society in regard to China's specific standard of trustworthiness.

Since April 2016, the Chinese government is applying a social credit system for the liquor industry in Luzhou, Sichuan Province.[91] Baijiu-producing companies are

[87] Eidgenössische Volksinitiative "Für gesunde sowie umweltfreundlich und fair hergestellte Lebensmittel (Fair-Food-Initiative)", Argumentarium, 8. Available at: https://fair-food.ch/wp-content/uploads/2018/08/ffi_argumentarium_d.pdf.

[88] Federal Popular Initiative. Available at: https://www.bk.admin.ch/ch/d/pore/va/20180923/det621.html.

[89] Herbert Spencer wrote about the "survival of the fittest" after having read Darwin's On the Origin of Species of 1859. Spencer (1864), p. 444. Darwin started to use the term in the 5th edition of On the Origin of Species in 1869.

[90] David Stanway, China lung cancer on rise, smog suspected—China Daily, Reuters, 11 August 2017. Available at: https://uk.reuters.com/article/uk-china-health-pollution/china-lung-cancer-on-rise-smog-suspected-china-daily-idUKKBN1AR09U.

[91] Mareike Ohlberg, Shazeda Ahmed, Bertram Lang, Central Planning, Local Exoerunebts, The complex implementation of China's Social Credit System, Merics, 12 December 2017. Available

monitored for compliance with regulations. The implications of companies' rankings range from their eligibility to receive subsidies and access to public procurement, to their position in case of land distribution, credit conditions, investment opportunities, access to online retail platforms and social media. For the company representatives, the companies' rankings can influence their own, which has implications for their career and travel privileges.[92]

In 2020, the Social Credit system must be implemented throughout China. Although many commentators expect this to lead to a dystopian future, ranking systems applied to the ethicality of companies and especially products could have beneficial implications for society.

4 Ethical Product and Certifier of Certifiers

4.1 What Is an Ethical Product?

The first consequential decision Man ever took, got him and his wife expelled from the Garden of Eden. Ever since, people have debated about what is Good and what is Evil. Deep Consumer Information is based on the notion that libertarian paternalism recognises that consumers have different value systems, and therefore have different ethical priorities. Deep Consumer Information is in that sense value-free.

Deep Consumer Information lets consumers choose along different ethical dimensions, such as environmental rights, fair trade, labour rights, children's rights, women's rights, human rights, animal rights, *etc*. This can be done, in one go, for example via an application on a digital devise. With intuitive sliders the consumer can set his or her ethical preferences. On a scale of 1 to 10, one can for example put the slider of fair trade to 9; for women's right to 8, for animal rights to 6, *etc*. Based on these settings, each product will be ranked according to these ethical dimensions. If one changes the settings, one will get different rankings. This means that if two consumers compare the same two products, they could have a different ranking based on their ethical preferences. Nevertheless, the combined rankings of Deep Consumer Information will favour some products, and disfavour other products. From this perspective, one can argue that Deep Consumer Information is a most direct form of democracy. Those who did not set their ethical preferences will get the average of the settings of all who did set their ethical preferences.

Consumers are able to set their preferences once, or they can change their settings as many times as they want, or never set any preferences and defer to the settings of

at: https://www.merics.org/sites/default/files/2017-12/171212_China_Monitor_43_Social_Credit_System_Implementation.pdf.

[92]Mirjam Meissner, China's Social Credit System, A big-data enabled approach to market regulation with broad implications for doing business in China, Merics, 24 May 2017. Available at: https://www.merics.org/en/microsite/china-monitor/chinas-social-credit-system.

the average consumer. The first requires a reasonably small amount of effort, the latter minimises the required effort to zero. According to Sutherland:

> it is believed by environmentalists that in order for people to adopt good environmental behaviour it is first necessary to convert them into committed environmentalists who share exactly the same motivations as their own. This is very painful and involves a huge amount of very annoying preaching which generally makes people resentful. The trick is to change behaviour first then the attitudes will follow.[93]

In the same vein, it should be made easier for consumers to make other ethical choices.

4.2 *Ranking Ethicality*

Many a product has several constituting parts, which are manufactured by other producers. Each end-product or its constituting components are manufactured with or without negative externalities. Consumers that want to make ethical purchasing decisions and governments that want to make policy decisions to stimulate ethical manufacturing are left in the dark. However, the rise of IoT enables to add information, including information about ethicality along different dimensions, to each separate element of a product; and on the basis of these separate elements, the ethicality of the aggregate elements of a product; *i.e.* the end-product, can be determined by a ranking algorithm. Blockchain, which are distributed, immutable databases, and IoT, which are embedded chips with a private key that cannot be replicated, can guarantee the integrity and traceability[94] of the supply chain and make it transparent in regard to product ethicality.

4.3 *Ranking Algorithm*

A lot has been written about ethical algorithms, but not much about algorithmic ethics. The ranking algorithm falls within this second category and is an important tool in the hands of choice-architects to further the goals of ethical consumers. A simple ranking algorithm is aggregating the weighted values of the separate elements of a product along the different ethical dimensions, as set by the consumer. A more advanced ranking algorithm will take into account some other factors such as lifespan, recyclability, biodegradability, and transport/storage[95] of the end-product.

---

[93] Sutherland (2011), p. 6.

[94] Friedmann (2019), p. 17.

[95] A counterintuitive example from ETH Center for Ecological System Design: the impact on the environment of imported apples from New Zealand, which means shipping them over more than 20,000 km, was lower than for Swiss apples during a few weeks in Summer, when Swiss apples are

Companies can provide information about the ethicality of their products. Of course this information needs to be assessed by certifiers. If companies provide the wrong information, their ranking will be downgraded. NGOs such as Greenpeace, Fair Trade organizations, and governmental organizations can also provide information about the ethicality of products if they have assessed them.

If manufacturers of products are not willing to share information about the ethicality of their products, the algorithm will downgrade the ranking relative to products of manufacturers that have shared information. In the absence of cooperation from a company, the ranking algorithm will approximate, use heuristics, and make assumptions based on for example the point of origin of the product: if a product originates from Belarus it will be ranked lower in regard to the environment than when it comes from Switzerland, due to the different levels of environmental protections in the respective jurisdictions. These kinds of heuristics can be made accurately with deep learning software. Deep learning are neural networks, where in between input layers (such as sources of origin of a product) and output layers (the degree of ethicality of a product), there are artificial neurons. After the software (a framework of different machine learning algorithms) is trained with sufficient data, it can figure out what the artificial neurons should be computing so that it will completely automatically learn the most accurate function mapping from the input (source of indication of a product) to the output (the degree of ethicality of a product). Using algorithms that can orchestrate decentralized networks of real-time data feeds ("oracles") to draw on multiple sources of data from the internet so that one does not have to rely on a single one, significantly increases the validity of the data, which can be fed to a blockchain.[96] The more layers you add to a neural network and the more data one can feed it, the more accurate it will become. The billions of data generated by IoT,[97] will significantly contribute to this accurateness.

The ranking algorithm can be fed with real-time information about scandals,[98] safety recalls, for example outbreaks of food safety scares, and information that directly influences the ethicality of the products. Article 23 Swiss Federal Food and Commodities Law[99] provides the legal ground for the competent federal authorities to order the enforcement authority to restrain the market release or to order the withdrawal from the market in case of a product that is in compliance with legal requirements but which directly endangers consumers according to new scientific

stored for up to half a year and the New Zealand fruits are fresh harvested were shipped. Federal Popular Initiative, 10. Available at: https://www.bk.admin.ch/ch/d/pore/va/20180923/det621.html.

[96]Orcutt (2018).

[97]"8.4 billion IoT devices were in use in 2017, up 31 percent from 2016, and this will likely reach 20.4 billion by 2020." Ranger (2018).

[98]For example Dieselgate which affected German car brands. Report on the inquiry into emission measurements in the automotive sector (2016/2215(INI)) 2.3.2017. Available at: http://www.europarl.europa.eu/doceo/document/A-8-2017-0049_EN.html?redirect.

[99]Article 23 Swiss Federal Food and Commodities Law. Available at: https://www.admin.ch/opc/de/classified-compilation/20101912/index.html#a23.

insights. The disclosurite system of Deep Consumer Information tries to tackle such a problem via the consumer side.

4.4 *Certifier of Certifiers*

Different certifiers uphold different standards, and enforce compliance differently. The organic food industry is, just as many other industries, sometimes plagues by fraud[100] and value-chain integrity challenges.[101] Ceres, a German inspection agency tested 232 samples from Chinese organic farms, 37 percent showed more than traces of pesticide residue. It also depends on how the tests are performed.[102] These examples severely damage the trust of consumers in certificates of certifiers such as USD Organic, which is a U.S. government-backed certifier.

The optimal solution would be to have certifiers that are well-paid and chosen for life, and therefore presumably incorruptible, and who recuse themselves in case of a possible conflict of interest, just as Supreme Court judges in the U.S. To guarantee trustworthy certifiers might be the most vulnerable part of the concept of this disclosurite system. Then again, this Achilles heel could be fortified by the rise of deep learning,[103] which will help approximate reasonable rankings.

5 Conclusions

What consumers buy has real consequences for consumers, traders in the value-chain and society at large. To be precise, in the absence of information about a product's ethicality moral consumers frequently become unwittingly complicit in sustaining unethical products and manufacturing processes, increasing negative externalities to themselves and society at large.

It is ineluctable that in the age of increasing transparency, companies will try to distinguish themselves in regard of their products' ethicality from other companies. As pointed out above, a small minority of consumers can impose its standard on a majority of consumers and companies who do not care much about it. In case of ethical rankings that could cure society of negative externalities this is auspicious.

[100] Whoriskey (2018).

[101] Whoriskey reports about a shipment of 36 million pounds of soybeans that were fumigated by pesticide and sailed in 2016 from Ukraine to Turkey to California and along the way transformed into USDA Organic soy. Whoriskey (2017).

[102] Whoriskey (2017).

[103] Deep Learning is used in layers to create an Artificial "Neural Network" that can learn and make intelligent decisions on its own. Deep Learning can be applied to the algorithmic ethics, hence the name Deep Consumer Information. Patidar (2018).

The world's most comprehensive behavioural algorithmic system is being developed in the People's Republic of China. This "Social Credit" system is already being implemented and is aimed to increase the degree of Chinese socialist morality of its citizens and companies. The disclosurite system of Deep Consumer Information advocates the ranking of products based on their ethicality, using algorithms and data harvested via IoT, so that consumers at last can make informed purchasing decisions (several ethical dimensions weighted according to their individual choice). Deep Consumer Information enables clueless consumers, metamorphosing into sovereign and ethically responsible citizens, to vote with their wallets. A principle which could lead to ever more ethical methods of manufacturing, phasing out negative externalities.

In the eighteenth century, Hume argued that the moral imagination diminishes with distance. Moral imagination is envisioning the full range of possibilities in a particular situation in order to solve an ethical challenge, according to Mark Johnson.[104] It is the goal of Deep Consumer Information to diminish the distance, from the rainforests to the supermarket shelves, so that moral imagination can be magnified.[105]

A consumer that has pre-set his or her preferences of the different ethical dimensions (environment, labour rights, women's rights, *etc.*) with sliders on an app, can use that same app to scan a QR-code[106] on the package of a product in the supermarket.

The application on the phone[107] consults, at lightning speed, the ranking algorithm which provides the consumer a one-number ranking of that particular product that can be read on the phone, together with a bar chart on which one can see the rankings per ethical dimension. One could make this one-number product ethicality ranking even more intuitive to add a certain colour; more green in case it is in alignment to one's pre-set preferences, and more red in case it is not. If one is shopping for a friend, one could download that person's profile settings, so that you shop according to his or her preferences. Furthermore, for those who cannot make up their mind about their ethical preferences, they could download existing profile settings of well-renown ethicists, such as Professor Peter Singer, or other exemplary figures consumers respect and trust.

[104]Johnson (1993).

[105]Inspired by Hume's saying that '*the moral imagination diminishes with distance.*' Hume (1738–1740), 2.3.7.3, SBN 429.

[106]QR stands for Quick Response.

[107]According to Swiss Federal Food Safety and Veterinary Office FSVO, the future of (nutrition) labelling can be found in making smart use of the phone: "Make (more) use of smartphone technology to allow tailored information?" Compulsory labelling on food and nutritional labelling in Switzerland: current state and international cooperation, 2017. Available at: https://www.wto.org/english/tratop_e/tbt_e/9_Switzerland_e.pdf.

Ariely said that "[w]hen you stand at the shelf, the most salient thing is price, it is easy to look at, it has decimals."[108] The concept of Deep Consumer Information is to provide a one-number ranking of the product ethicality, which is at least as easily understandable as a product price.

Blockchain, IoT and artificial intelligence can help guarantee the integrity of the supply chain, consumer information and the traceability of the constituting elements of the end-product. A more perfect world provides consumers with information, such as an ethical ranking, to make more fully informed ethical purchasing decisions.

Acknowledgement The author thanks Samuel Becher, Omri Ben-Shahar, Tobias Gesche and Thibault Schrepel and the participants of the 8th Law and Economics Conference 'Consumer Law and Economics' for their comments and discussion at the Faculty of Law, University of Lucerne, 29-30 March 2019.

References

Aggarwal P, Kadyan A (2011) Greenwashing: the darker side of CSR. Indian J Appl Res 4 (3):61–66. Available at: https://www.researchgate.net/publication/275755662_Greenwashing_The_Darker_Side_Of_CSr

Akerlof G (1970) The market for "Lemons": quality uncertainty and the market mechanism. Q J Econ 84(3):488–500. Available at: http://www.jstor.org/stable/1879431

Ariely D, Real Value, YouTube documentary by Jesse Borkowski 2013. Available at: https://www.youtube.com/watch?v=ez3CWXQrgVo.

Belson J (2017) Certification and collective marks. Edward Elgar, Cheltenham

Ben-Shahar O, Schneider C (2014) More than you wanted to know: the failure of mandated disclosure. Princeton University Press

Blakeney M (2014) The protection of geographical indications, law and practice. Edward Elgar, Cheltenham

Brandeis L (1914) Other People's Money and How the Bankers Use It (Cosimo, Inc. 2009). Available at: https://louisville.edu/law/library/special-collections/the-louis-d.-brandeis-collection/other-peoples-money-chapter-v

Carroll A (2008) A history of corporate social responsibility: concepts and practices

Cohen I (2019) Ag-gag laws stifle first amendment freedoms. Harv Polit Rev, 19 February 2019. Available at: http://harvardpolitics.com/united-states/ag-gag-laws/

Crane A, McWilliams A, Matten D, Moon J, Siegel D. (eds) The Oxford handbook of corporate social responsibility. OUP. Available at: https://dl.bsu.by/pluginfile.php/66249/mod_resource/content/1/A_History_of_Corporate_Social_Responsibility.pdf

Danush S (2018) The law of identity harm. Washington Univ Law Rev 96:804. Available at: https://ssrn.com/abstract=3260260

Darwin C (1869) On the origin of species in 1869 (5th edn)

---

[108] Ariely said that it difficult to express the value to avoid child labor or obesity in an exact number. That is the very objective of Deep Consumer Information.

Ariely D, professor of psychology and behavioural economics at the Center for Advanced Hindsight, Duke University, Durham, N.C.: "Our perception of value is dramatically subjective. It comes from lots of things from the environment." Real Value, documentary by Jesse Borkowski 2013. Available at: https://www.youtube.com/watch?v=ez3CWXQrgVo.

Devitt M (2018) New Report Shows U.S. Obesity Epidemic Continues to Worsen. AAFP, 15 October 2018. Available at: https://www.aafp.org/news/health-of-the-public/20181015obesityrpt.html

Fischler F (2004) Quality Food, CAP Reform and PDO/PGI, Congress Fondazione Qualivita Siena, 17 April, 2004. Available at: http://europa.eu/rapid/press-release_SPEECH-04-183_en.pdf

Friedman M (1962) Capitalism and freedom. University of Chicago Press, Chicago

Friedmann D (2017) TPP's Coup de Grâce: how the trademark system prevailed as geographical indication system. In: Chaisse J, Gao H, Lo C-F (eds) Paradigm shift in international economic law rule-making, TPP as a new model for trade agreements? Springer, New York. Available at: https://ssrn.com/abstract=3090172

Friedmann D (2018) The accountability of trade marks. J Intell Prop Law Pract 13(9):679. Available at: https://academic.oup.com/jiplp/article/13/9/679/5063292

Friedmann D (2019) Protecting the integrity of consumer information and the supply chain of Wine in China. In: Simões FD (ed) The legal protection of consumers: developing a market economy in China. Routledge, forthcoming

Gaeta D, Corsinovi P (2015) Traditional Terms and Appellation wines: debates insight of TTIP negotiation. Paper prepared for the 145th EAAE Seminar "Intellectual Property Rights for Geographical Indications: What is at Stake in the TTIP?" Parma, Italy April 14-15 2015. Available at: http://iogt.org/wp-content/uploads/2015/03/D.-Gaeta-P.-Corsinovi-2015-Traditional-Terms-and-Appellation-Wines-Debates-in-Sight-of-TTIP-Negotiation.pdf

Ganzler M (2019) Judge Overturns Iowa's Ag-Gag Law in Victory for Good Business. Forbes, 14 January 2019. Available at: https://www.forbes.com/sites/maisieganzler/2019/01/14/judge-overturns-iowas-ag-gag-law-in-victory-for-good-business/#6b04ea343d8c.

Gigerenzer G, Selten R (eds) (2001) Bounded rationality: the adaptive toolbox. MIT Press

Johnson M (1993) Moral imagination: implications of cognitive science for ethics. University of Chicago Press

Kent S (2018) Pollution Worsens Around Shell Oil Spills in Nigeria. Wall Street Journal, 25 May 2018. Available at: https://www.wsj.com/articles/pollution-worsens-around-shell-oil-spills-in-nigeria-1527246084.

Love J, Jacobsen N (eds) (1988) Invisible hand: economic liberalism and the State in Latin American history. Praeger Publishers, New York

Mandalaki E, O'Sullivan P (2016) Organisational indulgences or abuse of indulgences: Can good actions somehow wipe out corporate sins? M@n@gement 2016/3, 19:203–227. Available at: https://www.cairn.info/revue-management-2016-3-page-203.htm#

Merton R (1936) The unexpected consequences of purposive social action. Am Sociol Rev 1 (6):894–904

Moon J (2005) An explicit model of business-society relations. In: Habisch A, Jonker J, Wegner M, Schmidpeter R (eds) Corporate social responsibility across Europe. Springer, pp 51–65

Neslen A (2017) Burger King animal feed sourced from deforested lands in Brazil and Bolivia. The Guardian, 21 August 2017. Available at: https://www.theguardian.com/environment/2017/mar/01/burger-king-animal-feed-sourced-from-deforested-lands-in-brazil-and-bolivia

Orcutt M (2018) Blockchain smart contracts are finally good for something in the real world. Technol Rev, 19 November 2018. Available at: https://www.technologyreview.com/s/612443/blockchain-smart-contracts-can-finally-have-a-real-world-impact/.

Ovidius (43 BCE–17 CE), Tristia. Ex Ponto. Available at: https://archive.org/stream/ovidtristiaexpon011949mbp/ovidtristiaexpon011949mbp_djvu.txt

Pasquale F (2015) The black box society, the secret algorithms that control money and information. HUP, Cambridge

Patidar S (2018) Machine Learning vs. Deep Learning. DZone, 18 August 2018. Available at: https://dzone.com/articles/comparison-between-deep-learning-vs-machine-learni

Pigou A (1920) The economics of welfare. Macmillan, London

Ranger S (2018) What is the IoT? Everything you need to know about the Internet of Things right now. ZDNet, 21 August 2018. Available at: https://www.zdnet.com/article/what-is-the-internet-of-things-everything-you-need-to-know-about-the-iot-right-now/

Reilly K (2019) The Congo's civil war is wiping out gorilla populations. Time, 5 April 2019. Available at: http://time.com/4282616/the-congos-civil-war-is-wiping-out-gorilla-populations/

Sampson A (2017) Food fraud: high roller of the crime scene. The Weekly Times, 28 May 2017. Available at: https://www.weeklytimesnow.com.au/agribusiness/decisionag/food-fraud-high-roller-of-the-crime-scene/news-story/a9837a9f2232ec5c520e2997f03bb617

Simon H (1962) Models of man: social and rational-mathematical essays on rational human behavior in a social setting. J Philos 59(7):177–182

Smith A (1776) An Inquiry into the Nature and Causes of the Wealth of Nations. EconLib electronic edition. Available at: https://www.econlib.org/library/Smith/smWN.html

Snyder F (2016) The EU, China and product standards. In: Wei S, Gottwald J-C, Brown K, Cottey A (eds) Routledge handbook on EU-China relations. Routledge, London (2021, forthcoming). Available at: https://ssrn.com/abstract=2843008

Spencer H (1864) 1 Principles of Biology, 444

Sullivan L (2018) Millennials: ethics and morals become identity markers for brands. MediaPost, 16 July 2018. Available at: https://www.mediapost.com/publications/article/322250/millennials-ethics-and-morals-become-identity-mar.html

Sutherland R (2011) The 11th Brands Lecture, Accountability is not enough. Available at: http://www.britishbrandsgroup.org.uk/upload/File/Lecture%202011.pdf

Taleb N (2016) The most intolerant wins: the dictatorship of the small minority. Incerto, 14 August 2016. Available at: https://medium.com/incerto/the-most-intolerant-wins-the-dictatorship-of-the-small-minority-3f1f83ce4e15

Thaler R, Sunstein C (2008) Nudge, improving decisions about health, wealth, and happiness. Yale University Press, New Haven

Vogel D (2010) The private regulation of global corporate conduct. Bus Soc, 49. Available at: https://iow.eui.eu/wp-content/uploads/sites/28/2017/04/Beckers-03-Vogel.pdf

Whoriskey P (2017) The labels said 'organic.' But these massive imports of corn and soybeans weren't. Washington Post, 12 May 2017. Available at: https://www.washingtonpost.com/business/economy/the-labels-said-organic-but-these-massive-imports-of-corn-and-soybeans-werent/2017/05/12/6d165984-2b76-11e7-a616-d7c8a68c1a66_story.html?utm_term=.8a177583d739

Whoriskey P (2018) USDA officials said they were guarding against organic food fraud. Congress decided they need help. Washington Post, 20 December 2018. Available at: https://www.washingtonpost.com/business/2018/12/20/usda-officials-said-they-were-guarding-against-organic-food-fraud-congress-decided-they-need-help/?noredirect=on&utm_term=.d03e548762cf

Wight R, The Arts & Business Lecture 2008 The Peacock's Tail and the Reputation Reflex: the Neuroscience of Art Sponsorship, Engine 2008. Available at: https://digitalwellbeing.org/downloads/PeacockTail.pdf

Danny Friedmann Shenzhen/Hong Kong. Visiting Assistant Professor of Law of the Peking University, School of Transnational Law. Room 513 School of Transnational Law. Peking University Shenzhen Graduate School, University Town, Xili, Nanshan District, Shenzhen, China 518055. Shenzhen Tel. + 86 13714357910; Hong Kong Tel. + 852 9324 5292. dannyfriedmann@gmail.com. Fields of Interest: Trademark Law, Geographical Indications, Copyright Law, Patent Law, Internet Intermediate Liability, Algorithmic Justice.

Part III
Data Protection Regulation

Law in Books and Law in Action: The Readability of Privacy Policies and the GDPR

Shmuel I. Becher and Uri Benoliel

Abstract The most systematic legislative attempt to make more order in the chaotic world of privacy is the EU General Data Protection Regulation (GDPR). The primary objective of the GDPR is to level the playing field and give individuals more control over their personal data. Among other things, the GDPR aspires to force companies to be more transparent around data collection and usage. Along these lines, the GDPR requires firms to clearly communicate privacy terms to end users by using "clear and plain language" in their privacy agreements. In this study we ask whether, half a year post-GDPR, firms offer users online privacy agreements that are written in a readable manner. To that end, we empirically examine the readability of privacy policies of 300 highly popular websites. The results indicate that in spite of the GDPR's requirement, users often encounter privacy policies that are largely unreadable. After presenting the empirical results we further discuss the legal and policy implications of our findings.

1 Introduction

The political economy of digital capitalism is largely premised on a new exchange. On the one hand, individuals can enjoy free communications and relatively cheap services and goods. On the other, individuals allow firms to collect and analyse

Alluding to Pound (1910).

S. I. Becher (✉)
School of Accounting and Commercial Law, Victoria University of Wellington, Wellington, New Zealand
e-mail: samuel.becher@vuw.ac.nz

U. Benoliel
School of Law, College of Law and Business, Ramat Gan, Israel

K. Mathis, A. Tor (eds.), *Consumer Law and Economics*, Economic Analysis of Law in European Legal Scholarship 9, https://doi.org/10.1007/978-3-030-49028-7_9

extensive data.[1] Put simply, individuals often pay online, consciously or unintentionally, with their data and privacy.

Firms hold unimaginable information on consumers, and consumers allegedly agree to that practice. Google, for example, knows where its users have been, and it has years' worth of photos. Google knows what users have searched for, the music they listened to, and the videos they watched. It further knows the activities users partake when visiting third parties' websites, and all the apps they have been using. It also knows users' bookmarks, contacts and emails. In addition, Google can know every event its users attended or the items they purchased.

Likewise, Facebook maintains every message one has sent or been sent, and it knows the contacts on our phones. Facebook also stores the information regarding users logging in: where, when and what device they used. Armed with all this information, these and other firms can typically share users' information with other third parties. Presumably, consumers agree to that as well.

Privacy experts have been well aware of this reality for some years,[2] and numerous discussions and debates have ensued. The general public, however, is much less aware of, and concerned about, privacy issues. Having said that, privacy issues are becoming more and more salient. This, in part, is due to manifold privacy scandals that have occurred in recent years. These scandals demonstrate that (sometimes unauthorised) third parties can access and use private information that powerful firms hold.

Consider the following examples. Uber's data was breached in 2016, affecting 50 million riders and 7 million drivers, as well as disclosing some 600,000 U.S. driver license numbers. In September 2018, the company reached a settlement, agreeing to pay $148 million that was distributed among the U.S. states. In the same month, Google confirmed that "Hundreds of apps are able to scan and share data from the email inboxes of Gmail accounts". Perhaps most conspicuously, a huge public protest erupted earlier that year as a response to the Facebook-Cambridge Analytica data scandal, where the data of millions of people's Facebook profiles was harvested. Thereafter, Facebook's CEO Mark Zuckerberg testified about the firm's privacy practices before two Senate committees.

Privacy, and especially online privacy, is becoming a hot topic in public talks, mass media, popular books and social media. Given growing public awareness and recent large-scale privacy scandals, it is now also at the forefront of policymaking. Notably, the most systematic legislative attempt to make more order in the chaotic world of privacy is the EU General Data Protection Regulation (GDPR). In general, the GDPR reflects the European attempt to carefully plan for "every aspect of interaction with data".[3]

[1] Cf. Balkin (2018).

[2] Tene (2008).

[3] Hoofnagle et al. (2018), p. 2.

The fact the European legislature was breaking the ground in this domain did not take the world by surprise. The EU has a strong focus on citizens' rights,[4] it recognises privacy as a human right, and it is specifically committed to data protection.[5] Moreover, data privacy is blended with consumer protection. Consumer protection, in turn, is considered to be "one of the most important and significant identifying signs of European Union policies."[6]

The GDPR seeks to standardize data protection laws across EU member countries. One of the primary objectives of the GDPR is to level the playing field and give individuals more control over their personal data. According to Article 1.2, the GDPR "protects fundamental rights and freedoms of natural persons and in particular their right to the protection of personal data". The GDPR also aspires to force companies to be more transparent around data collection and usage. Among other things, it generally requests companies erase personal data on request and forces them to take better care in managing clients' data.

There is yet another interesting dimension to the GDPR, which received less scholarly and public attention: the requirement to clearly communicate privacy terms to end users. Simply put, the GDPR requires firms to use "clear and plain language" in their privacy agreements. This, in turn, provides quite a unique opportunity to examine the readability of legal texts that are subject to a recently-enacted plain language rule. In accordance, this chapter asks whether, half a year post-GDPR, firms present users with online privacy agreements that are written in a readable manner, which users can understand.

The remainder of this essay is organised as follows: Sect. 2 presents a quick overview of the GDPR, putting it in context and focusing on the concept of plain language. Section 3 then moves to succinctly discuss empirical measures and tools designed to systematically examine text readability. Section 4 reviews prior empirical findings that shed some light on the language of privacy policies. Section 5, which constitutes the main contribution of this chapter, empirically examines the readability of current privacy policies. Section 6 proposes policy recommendations and discusses the limitations of our research. Concluding remarks follow.

2 Privacy Policies, GDPR and Plain Language

2.1 General Background

Technology and modernisation radically alter our environment. The digital age and the Internet of Things create new forms of data flow, data sharing, data collection and data analysis. Firms are constantly collecting information about individuals and

---

[4]Schwartz and Peifer (2017).

[5]Hoofnagle et al. (2018), pp. 2–3, and 6.

[6]Abril et al. (2018), p. 30.

monitoring their behaviour. This leads to privacy, big data and data protection related concerns.

As we become a data-driven society, the privacy landscape is changing. Significant attempts to protect privacy and security are undertaken. Some of these attempts are led by businesses. Others are fuelled by growing social outrage and academic literature. Naturally, this is reflected in, and supplemented by, privacy law and policy.

The GDPR, which came into full effect on May 25, 2018, strives to protect individuals from privacy and data breaches in the era of large-scale analytics. The GDPR applies across all Member States, including the UK. Once the UK leaves the EU, the Data Protection Bill "will help ensure that the standards of the GDPR are enshrined in UK law".[7]

The GDPR is an expansive piece of legislation, applicable also to any non-European entities that process personal data of EU consumers. It protects the personal data of those who reside in the EU, as well as tourists and temporary visitors to the EU. For this and other reasons, it impacts numerous companies and organisations beyond the EU borders, many of which "have been scrambling to become GDPR compliant".[8]

Overall, the GDPR is an extensive piece of legislation which replaces, and builds on, the previous Data Protection Directive 95/46/EC. The GDPR includes eleven chapters, 99 articles, and 173 recitals. Scholars argue that it "covers an immense landscape of potential informational problems", attempting "to answer all information questions ex ante".[9] The GDPR is regarded as a cornerstone of modern privacy law,[10] which "will fundamentally reshape the way in which data is handled across every sector".[11] Undoubtedly, the GDPR has the potential to significantly impact the regulatory framework around privacy and data collection.[12]

The GDPR seeks to empower individuals by granting them rights to access, while also acknowledging the 'right to be forgotten'. Moreover, it introduces data portability, and it calls for privacy by design.[13] It also mandates breach notifications, while establishing various mechanisms aimed at facilitating effective enforcement. To enhance its effectiveness, severe fines can be imposed for breaches of the GDPR.[14] In accordance, it has been reported that firms around the world agreed to comply with the GDPR.[15]

---

[7]Markram (2018).

[8]Rustad and Koenig (2018), p. 68.

[9]Hoofnagle et al. (2018), p. 3.

[10]Rustad and Koenig (2018).

[11]https://eugdpr.org/.

[12]https://eugdpr.org/the-regulation/.

[13]Rustad and Koenig (2018).

[14]Hoofnagle et al. (2018), pp. 2, 4, 6, 32–33.

[15]Rustad and Koenig (2018).

In many ways, the GDPR further exemplifies that the U.S. levels of privacy protections are inadequate when compared to the EU.[16] Some scholars have further raised the provocative question of whether the GDPR signals the end of tech giants, such as Google and Facebook.[17] Other commentators wondered whether the GDPR may facilitate a move towards "splinternet"—where the internet is broken into "national and regional networks".[18] Yet others predicted a battle between authorities and tech titans, where the latter try "to blunt the GDPR's effect".[19] At the same time, some have pointed out that many countries are revising their privacy laws, so to comply with the GDPR.[20]

Finally, the GDPR requires firms to use "clear and plain" language when communicating with end users. To be sure, plain language rules are not a novel invention and the GDPR is not the first attempt to enhance the readability of legal documents. We now turn to provide some examples and concisely discuss the plain language movement.

2.2 *The Plain Language Movement and Plain Language Rules*

Plain language rules can be found in different domains, employed by a range of countries and states. Conspicuously, plain language rules have been enacted in the U.S. in various contexts, generating a Plain English Movement.[21] The movement aims to ensure that legal texts are written in a readable manner so that laypeople can read and easily understand them.[22]

For instance, the Franchise Rule that governs the franchise industry[23] requires franchisors to provide disclosure documents that are written "clearly", "legibly", and in "plain English".[24] Furthermore, it requires that the language be "understandable by a person unfamiliar with the franchise business," and that it incorporates "short sentences" and "everyday language".[25] Many other examples exist in various

---

[16] Bignami and Resta (2015), Schwartz (2013) and Hoofnagle et al. (2018), p. 6.

[17] Houser and Voss (2018).

[18] https://www.economist.com/the-economist-explains/2016/11/22/what-is-the-splinternet.

[19] Hoofnagle et al. (2018), p. 5.

[20] Rustad and Koenig (2018), p. 88.

[21] Felsenfeld (1982–1983), p. 408; Serafin (1998), p. 694; Kimble (1992), p. 3.

[22] Schiess (2003–2004), p. 53.; Friman (1994–1995), p. 108.

[23] https://www.ftc.gov/enforcement/rules/rulemaking-regulatory-reform-proceedings/franchise-rule.

[24] 16 C.F.R. § 436.6(b).

[25] 16 C.F.R. § 436.1(o).

disclosure domains, such as securities,[26] employment,[27] consumer law,[28] privacy,[29] consumer credit and the like.[30]

U.S. Plain English rules are also in place with respect to consumer contracts, potentially promoting consumers' ability to make informed decisions.[31] Several U.S. states have adopted statutes—varying in coverage and standards—that mandate readability.[32] Some statutes provide only general guidance on readability standards.[33] Other statutes, however, detail a set of objective syntactic requirements.[34]

The plain language movement is not limited to the U.S. For instance, Canada has also been implementing plain language initiatives. In 1979, the Bank of Nova Scotia and the Royal Insurance of Canada produced a plain language loan forms and insurance policy (respectively).[35] More recently, in March 2000 the Canadian Bankers Association announced that its members were "committed to providing customers with banking information which they can easily understand and use."[36] The initiative focused on mortgages, adopting plain language as a standard.[37]

Similarly, several voluntary commitments have been made by Canada's financial sector in respect of plain language. While following these non-legislation commitments is not mandatory, this helps financial institutions meet their obligations under new federal disclosure requirements. Doing so also makes it easier for consumers to understand credit cards and other loan agreements.[38] Along similar lines, the New Zealand Bankers Association also commits to making information about their products and services "readily available and in plain language".[39]

With respect to contracts, several Canadian provinces have passed legislation requiring certain types of contracts to be written in plain language, or in language that is comprehensible or intelligible.[40] In Australia, the National Consumer Credit Protection Act 2009 requires contracts and notices by credit providers to be "easily

[26] 17 C.F.R. § 230.421.

[27] 29 U.S.C. § 1022(a).

[28] 12 C.F.R. § 205.4; 15 U.S.C. § 2302(a).

[29] 45 C.F.R. 164.520(b)(1).

[30] 15 U.S.C. § 1632(a); 12 C.F.R. § 213.3(a) (Consumer Leasing Act); 12 C.F.R. § 1024.32(a)(1) (Real Estate Settlement Procedures Act of 1974); 12 C.F.R. § 1030.3(a) (Truth in Savings Act).

[31] Timm and Oswald (1985), p. 33.; Ross (1981), p. 331.

[32] Lloyd (1986), p. 687.

[33] See, for instance, Mont. Code Ann. § 30-14-1103 (West 2015).

[34] See, for instance, Con. Gen. Stat. Ann. § 42-152(c)(1), (2) & (5) (West 2015).

[35] Asprey (2005), p. 62.

[36] https://www.bmo.com/pdf/9243738PlainLangMortDocs_en.pdf.

[37] https://www.bmo.com/pdf/9243738PlainLangMortDocs_en.pdf.

[38] https://www.cba.ca/voluntary-commitments-and-codes-of-conduct?l=en-us.

[39] http://www.nzba.org.nz/wp-content/uploads/2018/05/Code-Of-Banking-Practice-A4-PDF-FINAL.pdf.

[40] Asprey (2005), p. 9.

legible" and "clearly expressed."[41] Furthermore, the New South Wales Legal Profession Uniform Law Application Act states that a conditional cost agreement must be written in plain language.[42]

In the EU, the Unfair Contract Terms Directive 1993 specifies that contracts should be drafted in "plain, intelligible language". Following the principle of *contra proferentem*, ambiguities should be interpreted in the consumer's favour and against the drafter; further incentivising the use of clear language.[43] Lastly, courts in New Zealand are instructed to examine whether a term in a consumer contract is "transparent" in determining whether the term is "unfair".[44] In evaluating a term's transparency, courts should consider the extent to which it is "expressed in plain language".[45]

2.3 Consent and Plain Language

The GDPR requires the use of plain language in a few contexts. One of these contexts is consent. Generally speaking, consent is a foundation of information privacy laws. Indeed, a significant part of privacy law and policy is grounded on this notion.[46]

Arguably, firms can ask users to consent to information processing. If users are sufficiently aware of the consequences of data usage, privacy concerns are largely mitigated. However, it is rather unlikely that users can indeed provide firms with meaningful and informed consent. Users are unaware of data collection practices. They cannot grasp the scope and depth of this phenomenon. They are also unable to absorb and internalise the immense amount of information involved. Furthermore, users may suffer from cognitive biases and limited attention span, which can prevent them from systematically considering the issue. To be sure, scholars have noted the futility of achieving meaningful "consent" in today's information society.[47]

Consent is one of the GDPR's cornerstones. The GDPR strengthens its conditions in an attempt to advance meaningful and freely given consent. Generally speaking, this reflects the GDPR's suspicion toward consent as a basis for data collection. As Hoofnagle et al. note:

> The GDPR is constitutionally skeptical of... consent, particularly of the low-quality or "take it or leave it" variety. The GDPR's architects realized that if low-voluntariness consent could justify data activities, the GDPR would just become another exercise in clicking "I agree" to

[41] National Consumer Credit Protection Act 2009, s 184(1).

[42] Legal Profession Uniform Law Application Act 2014 (NSW), s 181(2)(a).

[43] Article 5.

[44] Fair Trading Act 1986, s 2 (1), the definition of "transparent".

[45] Fair Trading Act 1986, s 46L....

[46] Zarsky (2019).

[47] Zarsky (2019).

> unread, unnegotiable terms. . . . In many contexts, the burdens the GDPR places on consent makes it impossible as a mechanism to make data use legal.[48]

Under the GDPR, consent becomes the least attractive option as a legal basis for data processing. This is so due to the GDPR's requirements for validity of obtaining and managing consent. It is also due to the fact that individuals can easily withdraw their consent at any moment. It is therefore generally agreed that the GDPR's requirements around consent can significantly limit its usability and practicability as a basis for data processing.[49]

Furthermore, the GDPR requires firms to use "clear and plain language" when basing its data processing on consent.[50] Article 7, titled "condition to consent", states that (emphasis added):

> 1. Where processing is based on consent, the controller shall be able to demonstrate that the data subject has consented to processing of his or her personal data.
> 2. If the data subject's consent is given in the context of a written declaration which also concerns other matters, the request for consent shall be presented in a manner which is **clearly distinguishable** from the other matters, **in an intelligible and easily accessible form, using clear and plain language.**

The requirement to employ clear and plain language in the context of consent is further strengthened by GDPR recital 42. This recital requests that where the basis for collecting information is the subject's consent, "a declaration of consent pre-formulated by the controller should be provided in *an intelligible and easily accessible* form, *using clear and plain language*".

2.4 The Contractual Basis and Plain Language

Consent is merely one of six bases for processing personal data under the GDPR.[51] One additional legal basis for data collection, which is related to our context and is central to businesses,[52] is contractual. According to the GDPR, contractual agreements can serve as a legitimate basis for information processing.

Notably, a contract can be a legitimate basis only when information processing is "necessary for the performance of a contract to which the data subject is party. . . .".[53] Additionally, firms must meet the principle of "purpose limitation." Under this

[48] Hoofnagle et al. (2018), p. 5.

[49] Schwartz and Peifer (2017), p. 144.

[50] Data Protection Working Party (2018), p. 14.

[51] https://gdpr-info.eu/issues/consent/.

[52] Hoofnagle et al. (2018), p. 17.

[53] GDPR, Article 6, 1(b).

principle, the use of information cannot be "incompatible with the initial purposes" for which the contract was formed.[54]

Here again, the GDPR does not allow firms to employ vague, ambiguous or illegible terms full of legalese. In order to enhance transparency, firms are expected to use clear and plain language. Under Article 12.1, data controllers should provide information to data subjects "in a concise, transparent, intelligible and easily accessible form, using *clear and plain language*...".

Along these lines, GDPR recital 39 clarifies that "...transparency requires that any information and communication relating to the processing of those personal data be easily accessible and *easy to understand*, and that *clear and plain language* be used". The recital further notes that "Natural persons should be made aware of risks, rules, safeguards and rights in relation to the processing of personal data...". In a similar vein, recital 58, which discusses the principle of transparency and 'ease', clarifies that "transparency requires that any information addressed to the public or to the data subject be concise, easily accessible and *easy to understand*, and that *clear and plain language*... be used".

Like in other contexts, the clear and plain language requirement regarding privacy policies attempts to counteract firms' practice to draft inaccessible privacy policies, loaded with legalese. Just before the GDPR came into effect, Givanni Buttarelli, the supervisor of the EU data protection authority, was also cited complaining about privacy policies. According to Buttarelli, these policies "are written in perhaps a long and vague approach, perhaps in legalese, and this does not help people so they must be scrutinised carefully."[55] Buttarelli further noted that firms have the ability to harness data mining and artificial intelligence, as well as their access to excellent legal advice. Such firms, contended Buttarelli, should be expected to be ethically oriented and provide consumers with clearer and more accessible privacy policies.[56]

To summarize, the idea of mandating or otherwise encouraging plain language has been exercised in a variety of contexts. Using plain language makes legal documents more accessible. It therefore has the potential to advance trust in markets and reduce information asymmetries, and as a result—improve overall market efficiency. This is perhaps most valuable when the information's recipient is not likely to have necessary knowledge, experience, sophistication or understanding to make informed decisions.

In theory, the idea of using plain language has a lot of promise. However, realising its potential requires effective enforcement and a clear framework. If one cannot measure clearly text readability, enforcing plain language rules becomes challenging and complicated. In the next Part, we explain how text readability can be measured in an objective and consistent way.

[54]GDPR, Article 5, 1(b).

[55]https://www.wired.com/story/how-a-new-era-of-privacy-took-over-your-email-inbox/.

[56]https://www.wired.com/story/how-a-new-era-of-privacy-took-over-your-email-inbox/.

3 Text Readability from an Empirical-Linguistic Perspective

Readability reflects a reader's ability to understand a text. Readability measures are based on linguistic variables such as length of sentences, word count and the average number of syllables per word. Generally speaking, there is a significant body of literature discussing readability. There are also a few commonly-used readability tests.

The field of text readability assessment is evolving, and no test is absolutely accurate. In this study we employed two different readability tests: (1) the Flesch Reading Ease (FRE) test; (2) the Flesch-Kincaid (F-K) test.[57] These two tests are highly correlated with other readability test formulas,[58] are considered reliable,[59] and are often used together in empirical studies.[60]

The FRE test, developed by Rudolph Flesch, is based on two factors. The first is the average sentence length in a text. The second is the average number of syllables per word in that text. The test is based on the assumption that longer sentences, and words with many syllables, are harder to read. To be specific, the formula that underlines the FRE test is as follows: 206.835 – (1.015 × average sentence length) – (84.6 × average number of syllables per word).

The score of the FRE formula ranges from 0 to 100. The higher the FRE score the more readable the text. According to readability literature, an FRE score lower than 60 means that the text is not understandable by consumers.[61] In line with this literature, regulators sometimes employ this benchmark as a requirement. For instance, a score of 60 or higher is often used by U.S. government agencies to ensure that documents are readable.[62]

The second readability test applied in this study is the F-K test, developed by Rudolph Flesch and John P. Kincaid. Similar to the FRE test, the F-K test is based on the average number of words per sentence and the average number of syllables per word. However, the coefficients of the F-K formula, among other things, differ from those of the FRE formula. The F-K formula is as follows: (0.39) × (average number of words per sentence) + (11.8) × (average number of syllables per word) – 159.

This formula, which was derived by testing a large sample of readers,[63] produces a score that estimates the grade level required to understand the text. For example, an

[57]The FRE and F-K tests were executed, as in many other empirical readability studies, using Microsoft Word software. See https://support.office.com/en-us/article/test-your-document-s-readability-85b4969e-e80a-4777-8dd3-f7fc3c8b3fd2.

[58]Calderón and Smith (2007), p. 21.

[59]Alexander (2000), p. 938.

[60]Rogers et al. (2007), p. 185; Long and Christensen (2011), p. 147.

[61]See for instance, Lloyd (1986), p. 689 ('Plain English' is defined as a text with a score of 60 or better).

[62]See for instance, Narwani et al. (2016), p. 603.

[63]McClure (1987), p. 12.

F-K score of 7 indicates that only a 7th grader and above will be able to easily understand the text. When the formula results in a number greater than 12, it indicates the overall number of years of education needed to understand the text. Accordingly, the higher the number, the harder it is to understand the text.

Of course, readability is not only a function of text characteristics. Text's readability also depends on the readers themselves. Factors such as educational and social background, or interests and expertise, can impact readability. Given that the policies in our sample are the most popular 300 sites in England and Ireland, it encompasses a large and heterogeneous population. We therefore make no unique or strong assumptions regarding the pool of readers of privacy policies.

4 The Readability of Privacy Policies: Prior Findings and Complaints

In an attempt to comply with the GDPR, users have been bombarded in 2018 with emails, alerting them of changes made to privacy policies.[64] Firms were notifying users of their updated policies in order to obtain their consent before collecting data. In response, the media has complained about "consent fatigue", arguing that the GDPR "is burdensome" and does not really serve users' interests.[65] Some opined that even if consumers wanted to seriously engage with these notices and policies this would be rendered impossible. Metaphorically, these notices allegedly generated a "tsunami of emails" that threaten to "crush" consumers.[66]

The media has also been discussing the actual impact of the GDPR on the content of privacy policies themselves. One recent report attempted to examine how the GDPR effected such policies drafted by ten leading and popular firms such as Google, Facebook, Amazon, Twitter, eBay, Instagram and Netflix.[67] According to this study, post-GDPR, the length of these policies increased, on average, by nearly 26%, as did their complexity. The total reading time for the ten policies studied totalled over 3 h. Some policies required more than 25 min to read.[68] This is in line with a recent study, which examined a large sample of privacy policies, mainly of Americans firms that are affected by the GDPR.[69] The study found that most privacy policies in that sample have been revised in 2018. It also found that this revision resulted in significantly longer privacy policies.

A 2017 report—post-GDPR enactment but prior it came into effect—looked into some privacy agreements employed by a few large UK companies, measuring their

[64] https://www.valuewalk.com/2018/07/privacy-policy-updates-gdpr/.

[65] https://www.wired.com/story/how-a-new-era-of-privacy-took-over-your-email-inbox/.

[66] https://www.wired.com/story/how-gdpr-affects-you/.

[67] https://www.valuewalk.com/2018/07/privacy-policy-updates-gdpr/.

[68] https://www.valuewalk.com/2018/07/privacy-policy-updates-gdpr/.

[69] Marotta-Wurgler and Davis (2019).

readability.[70] The study found that firms tended to use lengthy policies (over 2500 words). At the same time, the content of privacy policies required a grade level that ranged "from grade 11 to grade 19". Based on these findings, the author opined that "... all of these companies need to rewrite their privacy statements in 'clear and plain language'. Otherwise, they will fall foul of the GDPR."[71]

These reports are in line with other evidence, suggesting that privacy policies are generally written in levels that dissuade individuals from reading. Evaluating the readability of online privacy notices across two periods, a 2006 study found that privacy notices have become longer and less readable.[72] The study concluded that privacy policies in the U.S. are not equivalent to the average consumers levels of education, and therefore their "readability needs to improve".[73]

A more recent BBC study reviewing privacy policies of 15 high-profile companies reported that "Social site terms [are] tougher [to read] than Dickens", and are in fact written at a university level.[74] The study also found that reading the privacy policies and the terms and conditions of these companies would require "almost nine hours in total".[75]

Similarly, a 2002 study examined 80 websites of internet healthcare providers. The study found privacy policies readability to range from "very difficult" to "fairly difficult".[76] Being able to read and comprehend the average privacy policy, it was found, would require approximately 2 years of university education, clearly "beyond the reading level of most adults".[77] The authors thus concluded that the studied privacy statements are inadequate as a means to inform consumers.

These findings are consistent with another study, which argued that the average reading level required for reading the privacy policies was significantly higher than "the average American adult reading level", which is "between 7th and 8th grade".[78] Overall, roughly 75% of the policies examined in this study were above the average reading level. Along these lines, it has been argued that "realistically, most privacy policies will still not be human readable and will be hiding the needles in a haystack of legalese".[79]

It has also been opined that privacy policies are getting longer.[80] While this does not in and of itself make the policies more difficult to read, it may dissuade users

---

70 https://www.visiblethread.com/2017/09/the-gdpr-and-plain-language-how-to-be-compliant/.

71 https://www.visiblethread.com/2017/09/the-gdpr-and-plain-language-how-to-be-compliant/.

72 Milne et al. (2006), p. 243.

73 Milne et al. (2006), p. 245.

74 https://www.bbc.com/news/business-44599968.

75 https://www.bbc.com/news/business-44599968.

76 Graber et al. (2002), p. 644.

77 Graber et al. (2002), p. 645.

78 https://www.commonsense.org/education/blog/its-not-you-privacy-policies-are-difficult-to-read.

79 https://www.wired.com/story/how-gdpr-affects-you/.

80 Milne et al. (2006).

from reading. Long and complicated policies come with a clear cost.[81] In fact, researchers have found that reading one's privacy policies would require hundreds of hours to complete. In the U.S. alone, this amounts to a national loss of 781 billion USD in opportunity cost.[82]

Likewise, a Norwegian consumer advocate recently echoed these complaints. Specifically, he and his team found that the privacy policies on an average person's phone are 900 pages long. Reading these policies out loud takes more than 31 h. In essence, they submitted that people do not read their privacy agreements; that the agreements are too long, and that they are written in an inaccessible language.[83]

Interestingly, researchers have started toying with new technological tools, so-called transparency-enhancing technologies, as a means to analyse privacy policies. Employing such an App, a group of Canadian researchers "found that a large fraction of privacy policies are written at a language level that is above that of many smartphone users."[84]

Remarkably, a European team reported on preliminary results after employing artificial intelligence (machine learning) techniques to assess privacy policies of 15 major companies—such as Google, Facebook, Amazon, Uber, Airbnb and Netflix—post-GDPR.[85] Analysing the content of these policies, the team concluded that "none of the analysed privacy policies meets the requirements of the GDPR." In terms of clear and plain language, 11% of the examined sentences were found to contain unclear language.

5 The Empirical Test

5.1 Data-Set

Our initial sample was based on 300 highly popular websites in two major European English-speaking countries: the U.K. and Ireland. This sample consisted of two sub-samples: (1) the 200 most popular websites in the U.K., such as Google.co.uk and Amazon.co.uk; (2) the 100 most popular sites in Ireland, such Rte.ie and Independent.ie.

Our source of data was the Alexa Top Sites web service, which provides a ranked list of the most popular websites by country. According to Alexa, a site's popularity ranking "is based on a combined measure of Unique Visitors and Pageviews."[86] The

---

[81]Becher and Unger-Aviram (2010).

[82]McDonald and Cranor (2008–2009).

[83]https://www.ted.com/talks/finn_myrstad_how_tech_companies_deceive_you_into_giving_up_your_data_and_privacy/up-next?language=en.

[84]Austin et al. (2018).

[85]Contissa et al. (2018).

[86]See https://support.alexa.com/hc/en-us/articles/00449744.

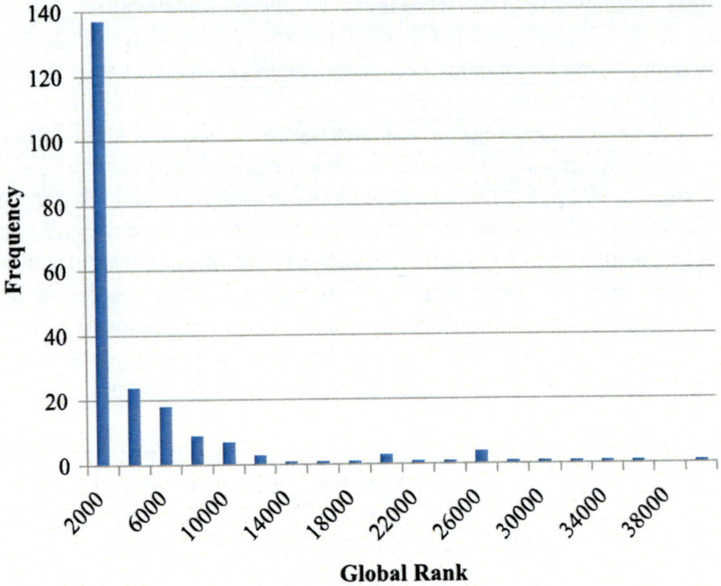

Fig. 1 Frequency distribution histogram for global rank (n = 216)

Alexa Top Sites service is a powerful website traffic measurement tool,[87] which is based on millions of internet users.[88] It is built on one of the largest samples of internet users available in the world.[89] It is therefore widely used as a source of data for empirical research.

While our initial sample was based on 300 websites, our final sample comprised a somewhat smaller sample of 216 websites. This is for two major reasons: first, there were some duplicates. Some of the websites located via the Alexa Top Site service, such as Facebook.com and Youtube.com, appeared under both the U.K. and Ireland's most popular website sub-samples. Second, we were unable to locate an English-written privacy policy for a few websites.

It is important to note that according to Alexa's global index, many websites in our sample are highly popular not only in the U.K. and Ireland but also globally. For example, Google, YouTube, and Facebook are globally ranked first, second the third (respectively). More generally, the global rank of our sample websites ranged between 1 and 38,826 (Debenhams.ie). The mean global rank was 3729 and the median global rank was 455. The distribution of the global rank is highly asymmetric, as is seen in the frequency distribution histogram in Fig. 1.

[87]Reidenberg et al. (2015), p. 54; Marine-Roig (2014), p. 386.

[88]https://blog.alexa.com/top-6-myths-about-the-alexa-traffic-rank/.

[89]https://aws.amazon.com/alexa-top-sites/.

We also attempted to gain an insight into the potential impact of the GDPR on readability levels. For that reason, we sought to locate the privacy policies that were in use before the GDPR came into force. Of the 216 sampled websites, 24 sites provided access to their pre-GDPR policies, which is a relatively small sample size. However, we believe that the readability results of this sample can, and should, serve as a preliminary indication of the potential effect of the GDPR. Yet, we should be rather cautious before making any extrapolations about the overall influence of the GDPR on the readability of privacy policies. We return to this point below.

5.2 *Methodology*

We tested the readability of each of the sample websites privacy policies as of January 2019. For that end, we employed the FRE and F-K tests. The tests were executed in our study via Microsoft Word,[90] which has been used in many empirical readability studies.

Notably, Microsoft Word tests the readability of sentences that end with a punctuation mark.[91] However, we located in our sample privacy policies that included, inter alia, a list of many statements with no punctuation mark at the end. To illustrate, the following text from Google's privacy policy included four statements with no punctuation mark at the end:

To delete your information, you can:

- Delete your content from specific Google services
- Search for and then delete specific items from your account using My Activity
- Delete specific Google products, including your information associated with those products
- Delete your entire Google Account

We manually added a punctuation mark—in this case a period (.)—at the end of each statement. This enabled Microsoft Word to better test the readability of these statements.

Likewise, Microsoft Word's readability test ignores phrases that end with a semicolon and are part of a vertical list of phrases. Ignoring these phrases seems reasonable, given their ambivalent readability consequences. Although phrases that end with a semicolon in vertical lists normally do not play a dominant role in privacy agreements, we decided to conduct another stringent readability test on a sample of 25 policies. In each of these policies, we replaced semicolons at the end of phrases in vertical lists, where applicable, with periods. The results of the test, as reported below, show that this did not significantly change readability levels.

[90] https://docs.microsoft.com/en-us/office/vba/api/word.readabilitystatistics.

[91] https://support.microsoft.com/en-us/help/292069/readability-statistics-incorrect-or-missing-in-word.

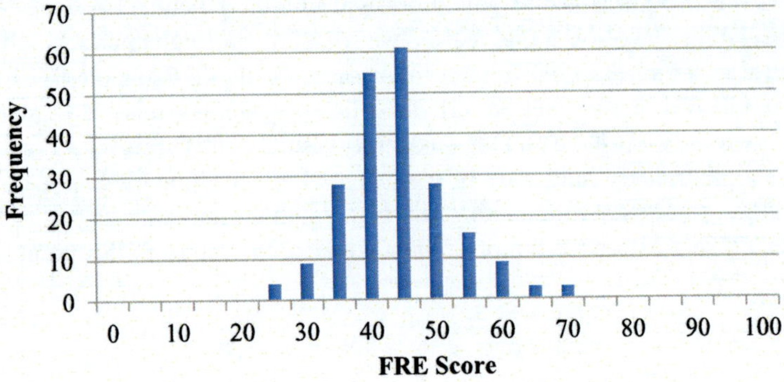

Fig. 2 Frequency distribution histogram for FRE scores (n = 216)

6 Results

This Section begins by presenting the fundamental empirical results using FRE and F-K scores. It then examines the statistical relationships between three website variables: (a) the global popularity rank; (b) the FRE score; (c) the F-K scores. The readability scores of current privacy policies indicate that these policies are often unreadable.

7 Readability of Privacy Policies

As noted, the recommended FRE score for consumer-related information should be 60 or higher. However, the median FRE score in our sample is 41.20, and the mean FRE score is 41.53. To put this average FRE score in context, it is comparable to the usual score of articles in academic journals,[92] which do not target the general public.

Furthermore, almost all of the privacy policies in our sample, i.e., 96.76% of the policies—209 out of 216 policies, received an FRE score that is lower than the recommended score of 60. The frequency distribution histogram of the FRE scores is represented in Fig. 2. (NB: For the vigilant reader who is not used to reading histograms it is important to clarify that the short blue column in Fig. 1 under the value '60' represents scores ranging from 55 to 60).

Similarly, while the recommended F-K score for consumer-oriented materials is 8th grade, the median F-K score in our sample is 13, and the mean F-K score is 12.78. Almost all the privacy policies, namely 209 out of 216 (96.76%), received an F-K score that is higher than the recommended score of 8th grade. This means, as in

[92] Payne et al. (2000), p. 1792; Health and Safety Executive, Evaluation of Product Documentation Provided by Suppliers of Hand Held Power Tools, p. 14 available at http://www.hse.gov.uk/research/rrpdf/rr714.pdf.

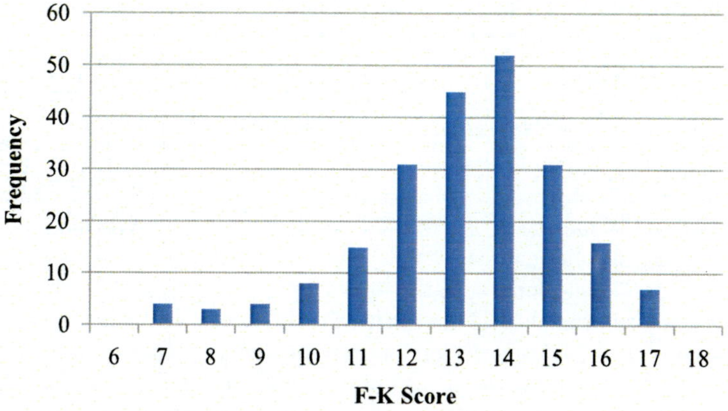

Fig. 3 Frequency distribution histogram for F-K scores (n = 216)

Table 1 The readability scores of Pre-GDPR vs. current privacy policies

	Pre-GDPR Privacy policies (n = 24)		Current privacy polices (n = 24)	
	Mean	Median	Mean	Median
FRE	38.20	39.30	41.68	42.35
F-K	13.62	13.10	12.36	12.35

the case of the FRE test, that 96.76% of the policies are unlikely to be understood by the average user. Figure 3 represents the frequency distribution histogram for the F-K scores.

Did privacy policies become more readable post GDPR? Interestingly, the readability results of the old privacy policies tested in this study hint that their readability indeed improved, at least to a degree. For the 24 websites that published their pre-GDPR privacy policies, the results of our study show that current privacy policies are slightly more readable than the older policies.

For example, while the average FRE score of pre–GDPR privacy policies is 38.20, the FRE score of the current policies is 41.68. Similarly, while the average F-K score of pre–GDPR policies is 13.62, the F-K score of current policies is 12.36. In line with that, the average words per sentence dropped from 23.7 for the pre-GDPR policies, to 20.3 for the post-GDPR policies. However, this is a marginal improvement. As Table 1 indicates, the post-GDPR privacy policies are still beyond the reading abilities of the average user.

Our decision to compile the 216 privacy policies in our sample in one group may raise an additional concern. This is so, since these 216 policies come from two different countries. However, this decision does not distort the findings. Slightly restated, separately examining the readability of U.K. and Irish policies did not yield any significant differences. In essence, while the policies used in Ireland might seem a bit less readable, the differences are quite negligible. Table 2 illustrates.

Table 2 Readability scores per country

	U.K. privacy policies (n = 182)		Ireland privacy polices (n = 96)	
	Mean	Median	Mean	Median
FRE	41.70	41.20	40.71	40.30
F-K	12.77	13.10	12.89	13.10

Another important clarification relates to a potential confusion regarding the number of policies in our sample. Recall, that some of the websites in our sample, such as Google.com, appeared under both the U.K. and Ireland's most popular website sub-samples. This explains the difference between the overall size of our sample (n = 216) and the total number of websites reported in Table 2 (n = 276).

Lastly, we tested the impact of removing semicolons and replacing them with periods. As noted, this did not yield a notable difference. We examined a random sample of 25 policies, and after removing semicolons the average FRE score changed from 39.184 to 39.084. Similarly, and the average F-K score changed from 13.284 to 13.276. This is in line with another study on the readability of sign-in-wrap contacts of 500 highly popular websites in the U.S.,[93] in which we also found that such a replacement had merely a negligible effect.

8 Statistical Relationships

In order to quantify the statistical relationships between a website's global popularity rank, FRE score, and F-K score, we calculated the Spearman's rank correlation coefficient between these variables. The Spearman coefficient is a nonparametric measure that is based on ranks rather than on the actual values. It is, therefore, robust to outliers and deviations from normal distributions, as in our global rank data (See Fig. 1 above).

The results of the bivariate analysis are troubling from a consumer policy perspective. The correlations between the global popularity rank and the FRE and F-K scores were weak but statistically significant, meaning that they could not be attributed merely to chance ($r = 0.21$, $p = 0.002$ and $r = -0.17$, $p = 0.01$ for FRE and F-K, respectively). These results may imply that websites that are less globally popular than the sites tested in this study are likely, to some degree, to have even poorer readability scores than the websites in our sample.

Unsurprisingly, the correlation between the FRE and F-K scores was strong and negative ($r = -0.91$, $p < 0.001$). This implies that the two measures quantify readability in a comparable way. Figure 4 is a scatterplot for the FRE and F-K scores that illustrates the linear negative relationship between these two variables.

[93]Benoliel and Becher (2019).

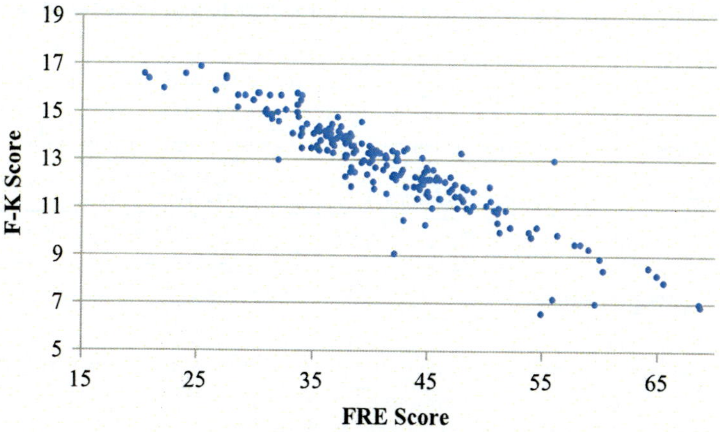

Fig. 4 Scatterplot for FRE and F-K Scores (n = 216)

9 Discussion and Policy Recommendations

Under the GDPR, firms are required to draft their privacy policies using plain language. Testing the readability of privacy policies allows us to see whether these policies are indeed readable, as required by the GDPR. Our study empirically indicates that privacy policies are still very often unreadable. Apparently, at least at the time this study was conducted, the general duty to use plain language under the GDPR often does not result in readable policies. The improvement in readability, since the GDPR came into effect, seems rather scant and slow.

This, in turn, raises an obstacle for those users who wish to become familiar with the content of their privacy policies. Unreadable policies also denote that fewer users are able to make informed decisions based on what these policies say. It also inflicts higher costs for third parties–such as pro-consumer organizations and online review websites and platforms that may be interested in studying, ranking or commenting on privacy policies.

Some may believe believe that privacy policies contain complex information and arrangements, and as such require complex language. This is, no doubt, true to some degree. Yet, the readability of legal texts can typically be improved, thus enhancing both people's tendency to read and their comprehension of such texts.[94] Generally speaking, complex issues do not necessary justify excessively long sentences and complicated jargon.

According to readability literature, sentences should be kept relatively short. It is generally recommended that the average sentence length of a text should be no more

[94]Masson and Waldron (1994); Kelley et al. (2010); Seizov et al. (2019), p 161.

than 20–25 words.[95] Beyond that, the text is likely to be hard to read.[96] Yet, the policies in our sample had an average sentence length of 22.19 words. This makes the typical privacy agreements we examined difficult to read for the average user.

As one anecdotal illustration, consider the following sentence—which contains no less than 91 words—taken from one of the policies in our sample (vice.com):

> You may also choose to participate in a third party application or feature on our Sites (such as posting to your page on a third party service or otherwise linking the Sites with another web site or interactive service) or on a third party web site or service (such as one of our Facebook applications or a similar application or feature on a third party web site or service) through which you post content or allow us to collect (or the third party to share) information about you, including Personal Information.

However complicated, the policies we examined in this study are relatively more readable than U.S. consumer online contracts, which we examined elsewhere.[97] Remarkably, they were more readable even before the GDPR came into effect. However, it is hard to make any comparison between the two, since they involve different types of legal texts in different regimes.

Where to from here? As a first step, we propose that the general duty to employ plain language will be accompanied by clear guidelines. Accordingly, we suggest that privacy policies will be aligned with the FRE and F-K standards. These standards are easy to employ and verify, and they are commonly recommended for consumer-oriented materials.

According to this proposal, a privacy policy that targets the general pool of consumers—such as the ones we examined in this study—should not receive an FRE score under 60 or an F-K score above 8th grade. We propose that if it does, the drafter would be presumed to be in breach of the GDPR. Whether courts will be allowed to excuse drafters in exceptional cases is an important question to be considered in the future, once similar suggestions take shape.

Our proposal hence paves the way for courts to impose fines on unscrupulous firms who draft unreadable policies. Hefty fines can serve as an excellent tool for deterring and disciplining firms. Empirical findings indicate that firms are generally sensitive to litigation outcomes, and that they tend to draft–and sometimes change–their consumer/user agreements accordingly.[98]

While the FRE and F-K standards may serve as a good starting point, such tests should be used only as a prerequisite legal standard for examining the readability of privacy agreements. True, poor readability scores of texts with long sentences and multisyllable words may typically indicate that the text is difficult to read. However, firms might manipulatively generate good readability scores that do not necessarily mean that the text is indeed easy to understand. A privacy policy with short sentences and monosyllabic words may receive acceptable readability scores under

---

[95]Wydick (2005), Garner (2013) and Kimble (2002).

[96]McIntyre (1996) and Nirmaldasan (2012).

[97]Benoliel and Becher (2019).

[98]Marotta-Wurgler and Taylor (2013).

the FRE and F-K tests. Yet, such a policy might be unreadable since its grammatical structure is flawed or through the use of legal terms of art.

Furthermore, our study examines only those popular privacy policies in the U.K. and Ireland, which are written in English. We do not examine readability of privacy policies in other countries and languages. In light of the scope of the GDPR, it is of course important to measure readability of policies is other languages. At the same time, readability standards should be made mandatory once firm can use the relevant linguistic tools in order to check their privacy agreements. Keeping in mind the twenty-three official languages of the EU, this might require the development of additional linguistic, legal or regulatory tools.

Moving beyond the immediate results of our study, the end purpose of the plain language requirement in the GDPR is not to increase readability per se. Rather, it is to promote the likelihood that users understand these policies. Therefore, policymakers should consider moving beyond the common FRE and F-K readability standards.

One possible approach to consider in this context is to require firms to ensure that a large segment of their consumers indeed understand key terms, rights and obligations incorporated in their privacy policies. Firms have been using a variety of tools to increase users' engagement and understanding in many other contexts. Such tools—which may include standardisation, videos, tutorials, infographics, humour, prizes and much more—can be utilized to promote consumers' comprehension of legal texts.

Interestingly, such an approach seems to be in line with the European Court of Justice case law. According to this case law, the contractual requirement to use 'plain language' is interpreted in a broad way. With respect to unfair terms in standard form contracts, the court noted that the meaning of plain language goes beyond grammatically correct sentences. Rather, the court reasoned, it also requires

> that the contract should set out transparently the specific functioning of the mechanism [determining the price], so that that consumer is in a position to evaluate, on the basis of clear, intelligible criteria, the economic consequences for him which derive from it.[99]

Yet another potential path is technological. Complex texts might not pose such a challenge to machines, and detecting flaws in privacy agreements can be facilitated by using machine learning platforms. In this context, artificial intelligence platforms and apps are now being used for automating the reading of legal texts, such as privacy policies.[100] These attempts, therefore, merit further attention and consideration.

Policymakers, app developers and other intermediaries may also consider other approaches that can supplement the ones noted here. One idea, which has been exercised in other contexts, is the use of one overall and easy-to-understand signal. Such a signal could advise consumers of the relative level of risk of the privacy

---

[99]ECJ, *Árpád Kásler, Hajnalka Káslerné Rábai v OTP Jelzálogbank Zrt*, Judgement [2014] Case C-26/13, 30 April 2014 [(*Kásler*)], para.75.

[100]Austin et al. (2018) and Contissa et al. (2018).

policy. For instance, consider a red-amber-green colour-coding system, which has been implemented in the domain of food health labelling.[101] Applied in our context, a red code would signal high privacy risks; an amber code would denote medium privacy risks; and a green code would indicate low privacy risks. Such signals, which should be placed in a conspicuous place, would be intuitively understood and hence better aligned with human psychology.[102]

Users' privacy is a thorny and complex issue, and readability is obviously not an all-cure response. Our recommendations should not be misinterpreted as suggesting as if making privacy policies readable is a panacea. Users may well agree to one-sided and biased policies, even if drafted in a readable way. Making these policies readable yet excessively long, written in small font or hard to find may present some serious challenges. Furthermore, re-drafting privacy policies comes with costs, and these costs may be passed, at least in part, on to consumers.

To be sure, our analysis should not rest other privacy concerns with relation to the way firms collect, handle and use private information. Of course, we hope that making privacy policies more readable will yield further pressure on firms to draft clear and balanced agreements. Nonetheless, there is no guarantee that this scenario will unfold. Legislatures and courts must stay vigilant, even if a privacy agreement is found to be readable.

Finally, our results can also serve as an important and humbling reminder as to the limited power and impact of legal change more generally. Too often, it is hard to promote significant, efficient and immediate change via legislation.[103] The law is just one component of a complex reality. Change, if it indeed occurs in the desired direction, is often likely to be limited and gradual.

10 Conclusion

In spite of the GDPR's requirement, European citizens often encounter privacy policies that are largely unreadable. Making privacy policies readable may bring about a few notable benefits. For starters, drafting readable policies better respects users' autonomy.

Beyond that, readability can contribute, to a degree, to better comprehension of legal texts.[104] This, in turn, can make such texts more salient, leading firms to compete over terms. True, complex and technical ideas may require sophisticated language. Nevertheless, an effort can be made to simplify legal texts. Indeed,

---

[101] Becher et al. (2019).

[102] Becher et al. (2019).

[103] For a recent more general analysis see Reidenberg et al. (2019).

[104] Masson and Waldron (1994) and Kelley et al. (2010).

anecdotal evidence suggests that simplifying legal documents, such as consumer contracts, may well be accompanied by more balanced terms.[105]

The European legislature believed that using plain language in privacy agreements can be part of a better, holistic approach to users' privacy. We credit this approach and believe it is an idea worth exploring. While not a magic bullet, readability can prove to be important for users' privacy. But merely having a law in books is not likely to yield the anticipated change.

Acknowledgement We thank William Britton for excellent research assistance. We are also grateful to Anne-Lise Sibony, Tal Zarsky and the participants at the Consumer Law and Economics Conference at University of Lucerne (2019) for important comments and discussions on a previous draft.

References

Abril P, Blázquez F, Evora J (2018) The right of withdrawal in consumer contracts: a comparative analysis of American and European law. Indret 3:1–56

Alexander R (2000) Readability of published dental educational material. J Am Dent Assoc 131 (7):937–942

Asprey M (2005) Plain language for lawyers, 3rd edn. Federation Press, Sydney

Austin LM, Lie D, Sun P et al (2018) Towards dynamic transparency: the AppTrans (transparency for android applications) project. SSRN Electr J:1–51

Balkin J (2018) Fixing Social Media's Grand Bargain. Hoover Working Group on National Security, Technology, and Law, Aegis Series Paper No. 1814:1–20

Becher S, Unger-Aviram E (2010) The law of standard form contracts: misguided intuitions and suggestions for reconstruction. DePaul Bus Commer Law J 8:199–223

Becher S, Gao H, Harrison A et al (2019) Hungry for change: the law and policy of food health labeling. Wake Forest Law Rev 54:1305–1360

Benoliel U, Becher S (2019) The duty to read the unreadable. Boston College Law Rev 60:2255–2296

Bignami F, Resta G (2015) Transatlantic privacy regulation: conflict and cooperation. Law Contemp Probl 78:231–266

Calderón J, Smith S (2007) FONBAYS: a simple method for enhancing readability of patient information. Ann Behav Sci Med Educ 13(1):20–24.

Contissa G, Docter K, Lagioia F et al (2018) Claudette meets GDPR: automating the evaluation of privacy policies using artificial intelligence. SSRN Electr J:1–64

Data Protection Working Party (2018) Guidelines on consent under Regulation2016/679. WP259 rev.01:1–33

Felsenfeld C (1982–1983) The plain English movement in the United States. Can Bus Law J 6:408–421

Friman M (1994–1995) Plain English statutes: long overdue or underdone? Loyal Univ Consum Law Rev 7:103–112

Garner B (2013) Legal Writing in Plain Language English 27

[105] Hoffman (2018).

Graber M, D'Alessandro D, Johnson-West J (2002) Reading level of privacy policies on Internet health Web sites. J Family Pract 52:642–645
Hoffman D (2018) Relational contract of adhesion. Chicago Law Rev 85:1395–1461
Hoofnagle C, van der Sloot B, Borgesius F (2018) The European general data protection regulation: what it is and what it means? UC Berkeley Public Law Research Paper, pp 1–40
Houser K, Voss G (2018) GDPR: the end of Google and Facebook or a new paradigm in data privacy? Richmond J Law Technol 25:1–109
Kelley P, Cesca L, Bresee J et al (2010) Standardizing privacy notices: an online study of the nutrition label approach. In: CyLab SIGCHI Conference on Human Factors in Computing Systems, New York, pp 1573–1582
Kimble J (1992) Plain English: A Charter for Clear Writing, Thomas M. Cooley Law Rev 9:11–14
Kimble J (2002) The elements of plain language. Mich Bar J Oct. 2002-44
Lloyd H (1986) Plain language statutes: plain good sense or plain nonsense? Law Library J 78 (683):696
Long L, Christensen W (2011) Does the readability of your brief affect your chance of winning an appeal? J Appellate Pract Process 12(1):145–162
Marine-Roig E (2014) A webometric analysis of travel blogs and review hosting: the case of Catalonia. J Travel Tour Market 31:381–396
Marotta-Wurgler F, Davis K (2019) Contracting for data. N Y Univ Law Rev 94:662–705
Marotta-Wurgler F, Taylor R (2013) Set in Stone? Change and innovation in standard-form contracts. N Y Univ Law Rev 88(1):240–245
Masson M, Waldron M (1994) Comprehension of legal contracts by non experts: effectiveness of plain language redrafting. Appl Cogn Psychol 8:67–85
McClure G (1987) Readability formulas: useful or useless? IEEE Trans Prof Commun 30(1):12–15
McDonald A, Cranor L (2009) The cost of reading privacy policies. J Law Policy Inf Soc 4:543–568
Mcintyre B (1996) English News Writing 19
Milne G, Culnan M, Greene H (2006) A longitudinal assessment of online privacy notice readability. J Public Policy Mark 25(2):238–249
Narwani V, Nalamada K, Lee M et al (2016) Readability and quality assessment of internet-based patient education materials related to laryngeal cancer. Head Neck 38(4):601–605
Payne S, Large S, Jarrett N et al (2000) Written information given to patients and families by palliative care units: a national survey. Lancet 355:1792–1792
Pound R (1910) Law in books and law in action. Am Law Rev 44(1):12–36
Reidenberg J, Breaux T, Carnor L et al (2015) Disagreeable privacy policies: mismatches between meaning and users' understanding. Berkeley Technol Law J 30(1):39–68
Reidenberg JR et al (2019) Trustworthy privacy indicators: grades, labels, certifications and dashboards. Wash Law Rev 96:1409–1460
Rogers R, Harrison KS, Shuman DW et al (2007) An analysis of miranda warnings and waivers: comprehension and coverage. Law Human Behav 31(2):177–192
Ross S (1981) On legalities and linguistics: plain language legislation. Buffalo Law Rev 30:317–362
Rustad M, Koenig T (2018) Towards a global data privacy standard. Florida Law Rev 71:365–453
Schiess W (2003–2004) What plain language really is. Scribes J Legal Writ 9:43–75
Schwartz P (2013) The EU-US Privacy collision: a turn to institutions and procedures. Harv Law Rev 126:1966–2009
Schwartz P, Peifer K (2017) Transatlantic data privacy. Georgetown Law J 106:115–179
Seizov O, Wulf A, Luzak J (2019) The transparent trap: a multidisciplinary perspective on the design of transparent online disclosures in the EU. J Consum Policy 42:149–173
Serafin A (1998) Kicking the legalese habit: the SEC's plain English disclosure proposal. Loyola Univ Chicago Law J 29:681–717

Tene O (2008) What Google knows: privacy and internet search engines. Utah Law Rev 4:1433–1492
Timm P, Oswald D (1985) Plain English laws: symbolic or real? J Bus Commun 22:31–38
Wydick R (2005) Plain English for Lawyers 36
Zarsky T (2019) Privacy and manipulation in the digital age. Theor Inq Law 20:157–188

Websites

Amazon. AWS | Alexa Top Sites - Up-to-date lists of the top sites on the web. Available at https://aws.amazon.com/alexa-top-sites/. Accessed 12 February 2019
Calver T, Miller J (2018) Social site terms tougher than Dickens. BBC News. Available at https://www.bbc.com/news/business-44599968. Accessed 28 November 2018
Canadian Bankers Association (2000) Plain Language Mortgage Documents. Available at https://www.bmo.com/pdf/9243738PlainLangMortDocs_en.pdf. Accessed 30 November
Canadian Bankers Association (2015) Voluntary commitments and codes of conduct. Available at https://www.cba.ca/voluntary-commitments-and-codes-of-conduct?l=en-us. Accessed 30 November 2018
EUGDPR. The EU General Data Protection Regulation (GDPR) is the most important change in data privacy regulation in 20 years. Key Changes with the General Data Protection Regulation. Available at https://eugdpr.org/. Accessed 26 November 2018
Fergal (2018) The GDPR & Plain Language – What You Need To Do To Comply. VisibleThread. Available at https://www.visiblethread.com/2017/09/the-gdpr-and-plain-language-how-to-be-compliant/. Accessed 26 November 2018
Federal Trade Commission (2017) Franchise Rule. Available at https://www.ftc.gov/enforcement/rules/rulemaking-regulatory-reform-proceedings/franchise-rule. Accessed 26 November 2018.
GDPR Key Changes. Key Changes with the General Data Protection Regulation – EUGDPR. Available at https://eugdpr.org/the-regulation/. Accessed 26 November 2018
General Data Protection Regulation (GDPR). Consent. Available at https://gdpr-info.eu/issues/consent/. Accessed 26 November 2018
Lee I (2018) It's Not You; Privacy Policies Are Difficult to Read. Common Sense Education. Available at https://www.commonsense.org/education/blog/its-not-you-privacy-policies-are-difficult-to-read. Accessed 26 November 2018
Markram R (2018) What is the data protection bill? Available https://www.markellaw.co.uk/insights/what-is-the-data-protection-bill/. Accessed 17 June 2020
Myrstad FL-H (2018) How tech companies deceive you into giving up your data and privacy. ted. Available at https://www.ted.com/talks/finn_myrstad_how_tech_companies_deceive_you_into_giving_up_your_data_and_privacy/up-next?language=en. Accessed 26 November 2018
Microsoft. Readability Statistics object (Word). Available at https://docs.microsoft.com/en-us/office/vba/api/word.readabilitystatistics. Accessed 12 February 2019
Microsoft. Readability statistics incorrect or missing in Word. Available at https://support.microsoft.com/en-us/help/292069/readability-statistics-incorrect-or-missing-in-word. Accessed 12 February 2019
Microsoft. Test your document's readability. Available at https://support.office.com/en-us/article/test-your-document-s-readability-85b4969e-e80a-4777-8dd3-f7fc3c8b3fd2. Accessed 12 February 2019
New Zealand Bankers Association (2018) What you can expect from your bank The Code of Banking Practice. Available at http://www.nzba.org.nz/wp-content/uploads/2018/05/Code-Of-Banking-Practice-A4-PDF-FINAL.pdf. Accessed 30 November 2018
Nirmaldasan (2012) Longer the Sentence, Greater the Strain, Readability Monitor. Available at https://strainindex.wordpr ess.com/2012/04/30/longer-the-sentence-greater-the-strain/. Accessed 26 April 2019

Orelind G (2017) Top 6 Myths about the Alexa Traffic Rank. In: Alexa Blog. https://blog.alexa.com/top-6-myths-about-the-alexa-traffic-rank/. Accessed 12 February 2019

Raza S (2018) GDPR Has Changed Privacy Policies Updates at Google, Reddit, Facebook. ValueWalk. Available at https://www.valuewalk.com/2018/07/privacy-policy-updates-gdpr/. Accessed 24 November 2018

S L (2016) What is the "splinternet"? The Economist. Available at https://www.economist.com/the-economist-explains/2016/11/22/what-is-the-splinternet. Accessed 24 November 2018

Tiku N (2018) Why Your Inbox Is Crammed Full of Privacy Policies. Wired. Available at https://www.wired.com/story/how-a-new-era-of-privacy-took-over-your-email-inbox/. Accessed 26 November 2018

Yeomans L (2009) Evaluation of product documentation provided by suppliers of hand held power tools. Health and Safety Executive. Available at http://www.hse.gov.uk/research/rrpdf/rr714.pdf. Accessed 12 February 2019

Shmuel I. Becher School of Accounting and Commercial Law, Victoria University of Wellington. Fields of Interest: Contract Law, Consumer Law, Economic Analysis of Law, Behavioural Analysis of Law, Law and Wellbeing, Empirical Legal Studies, Legal Education, Negotiation and Dispute Resolution.

Uri Benoliel School of Law, College of Law & Business. Fields of Interest: Contract Law, Franchise and Distribution Law, Empirical Legal Studies, Economic Analysis of Law.

'Your DNA Is One Click Away': The GDPR and Direct-to-Consumer Genetic Testing

Miriam C. Buiten

Abstract In the last decade, a wide variety of direct-to-consumer (DTC) genetic tests has become available that allow consumers to learn about their ancestry, genetic traits and propensity to genetic diseases. DTC genetic testing companies encourage consumers to share their data for research purposes. The reason is that these companies operate on two-sided business models, generating revenue primarily through selling genetic data to pharmaceuticals and research institutions. This chapter considers possible reasons for concern about consumers sharing their genetic data. It discusses various market failures that may arise in this two-sided market, ranging from information asymmetries to externalities and market power. This chapter asks whether the General Data Protection Regulation (GDPR) is able to mitigate these market failures, or whether specific laws for genetic data processing are in order. This chapter concludes that the broad research exemption in the GDPR leaves a regulatory vacuum for DTC genetic testing companies and biobanks alike.

1 Introduction

Rapid advances in DNA sequencing technology combined with decreasing costs of computing power are opening up new possibilities for using genomic data. In the last decade, a wide variety of direct-to-consumer (DTC) genetic tests has become available. Commercial companies such as 23andme allow individuals to order a genetic test online, obtain information about their DNA and ancestry and share it with others on a social network.

M. C. Buiten (✉)
Law School, University of St. Gallen, St. Gallen, Switzerland
e-mail: miriam.buiten@unisg.ch

K. Mathis, A. Tor (eds.), *Consumer Law and Economics*, Economic Analysis of Law in European Legal Scholarship 9, https://doi.org/10.1007/978-3-030-49028-7_10

These companies declare that they comply with the General Data Protection Regulation (GDPR) when collecting and sharing data.[1] Nevertheless, DTC genetic testing has been met with concern regarding privacy and security protection. 23andme, in possession of genetic data of 5 million customers[2] and backed by Google as one of its principal investors, sells the genetic data, web behavior and self-reported information of its customers to third parties for the purposes of scientific research and commercial applications.[3]

This chapter considers why it may be problematic that people voluntarily share their genomic data. It discusses how the GDPR may contribute to addressing these problems, particularly in light of the research exemption it contains for handling genetic data. Acknowledging that a well-balanced policy for genomic data requires joints efforts from policy makers, technical experts and ethics communities, this chapter considers how the GDPR may contribute to respecting individuals' privacy with regard to their genomic data, and in what respects it falls short.

From a (behavioural) economics perspective, there are several reasons for regulating DTC genetic services, despite consumers using them voluntarily. The primary reason is the existence of information problems: since we have yet to discover everything there is to know about DNA, consumers cannot be aware of all possible consequences of sharing their genomic data on the internet. Ten years from now, the genome of an individual may reveal considerably more information about them than we know now, for instance regarding their disease susceptibility risks. Even for known genome-health risk associations, consumers may not be aware of these when sharing their genomic data online. Cognitive biases may exacerbate the information problems, as consumers may underestimate uncertain future risks as compared to the immediate benefits they receive from learning about their ancestry. In a 2012 study, users of DTC services described their motivations for sharing their genomic data as 'curiosity' and 'fun'.[4] Additional problems in the market may arise, since companies such as 23andme exploit a two-sided business model.[5] This may create network effects, which can lead to market concentration or market power, and consequently to less privacy-friendly alternatives for consumers.

This chapter considers why these problems, which are common in consumers markets, may have particularly severe consequences in case of genomic data. First, genomic data cannot be revoked. Unlike a credit card that can be cancelled once its number has been compromised, an individual cannot change their genome. Second,

[1]Regulation (EU) 2016/679 of the European Parliament and of the Council of 27 April 2016 on the protection of natural persons with regard to the processing of personal data and on the free movement of such data, and repealing Directive 95/46/EC (General Data Protection Regulation). 4 May 2016 OJ L 119/1.

[2]See M. Herper (Forbes, 2015), "Surprise! With $60 Million Genentech Deal, 23andMe Has A Business Plan", www.forbes.com/sites/matthewherper/2018/07/25/23andme-gets-300-million-boost-from-glaxo-to-develop-new-drugs/#2fcdbc293213.

[3]Stoeklé et al. (2016), p. 3.

[4]Vayena et al. (2012).

[5]Stoeklé et al. (2016).

genomic data does not only pertain to the person to whom it belongs: to some extent, it also contains information about their family.[6] An individual may thus impose a negative externality on their family members by sharing their genomic data, which can reveal familial relationships as well as disease susceptibility risks of family members. Leakage of genomic data may have serious implications, including genetic discrimination by insurance companies or employers. The data may even have forensic applications and criminal implications. These consequences may arise not only as a result of deliberate sharing of genomic data, but also through security breaches, for instance by the IT of a hospital.

One way of mitigating the problems associated with sharing genetic data is to limit its processing in data protection law. The GDPR that took force in 2018 lays down rules for data processing in general and processing sensitive personal data in particular. The EU data protection law reform spurred an intense debate about its potential effect on medical research.[7]

The GDPR only partially addresses the problems associated with consumer genetic testing. While the GDPR contains special rules concerning 'sensitive data'—which includes genetic data—it also stipulates a research exemption, relieving researchers of some of the stricter requirements concerning the processing of data.[8] For good reasons, this exemption aims to ensure that data protection law does not foreclose valuable research projects that rely on genomic data. However, it is unclear if the scope of the research exemption reaches beyond that, potentially including commercial actors such as 23andme. This may cause confusion among consumers and lead them to take poor decisions regarding their genomic data.

Given the sensitivity of genomic data and the unknown future applications, one might consider limitations on the commercial use of this data altogether. In the EU, uncertainty for consumers may be exacerbated since national laws vary in their rules on direct-to-consumer genetic testing.[9] Additionally, the member states are to specify the details of the GDPR in terms of the type and form of consent that is required (specific or broad). This chapter argues that, given the security and privacy risks involved, a clear and consistent policy approach regarding DTC genetic testing on the European level may be desirable.

---

[6]Azencott (2018), p. 2.

[7]Mostert et al. (2016), p. 956.

[8]Article 9(2)(j) GDPR provides that sensitive personal data, including genetic data, can be processed without adhering to the strict consent requirements in Article 9(2)(a) GDPR for research purposes.

[9]Kalokairinou et al. (2018).

2 Business Model of Consumer Genetic Testing

2.1 *Services*

Direct-to-Consumer (DTC) Genetic Testing Companies offer a variety of different services. These companies allow consumers to trace back their ancestry or to discover certain traits rooted in their DNA (such as athletic or musical abilities). Aside from these rather recreational types of tests, some companies also offer to test consumers' propensity to certain diseases (such as Parkinson's or Alzheimer's disease).

In the United States, DTC testing for genetic diseases seems to be widely offered and accepted. Despite some setbacks with the Food and Drug Administration,[10] in 2017 the FDA allowed DTC genetic testing companies to provide genetic risk information for certain conditions to their customers.[11] In Europe, DTC genetic testing companies primarily offer genealogy tests. This may be due to some stricter regulation regarding the conduct of genetic tests for diseases. In Germany, for example, genetic tests for medicinal purposes can only be conducted by a doctor.[12]

2.2 *A Two-Sided Business Model*

2.2.1 The Consumer Side

For a price of €69–99, consumers can order a DNA kit (a saliva collection test).[13] The test includes a container that the consumer is meant to fill with a saliva sample and send back to the DTC genetic testing company. The company tests and sequences the DNA sample, making the results available to the consumer on its website with a password. Results may include information on ancestry, genetic traits (e.g. athletic skills) and, depending on national rules on delivering medical test results, the propensity to diseases (e.g. Alzheimer's).

DTC genetic testing companies aim to attract consumers by promoting their genetic testing service as a fun way to learn more about yourself, your family and your ancestry. As the company AncestryDNA put it in December 2018, their service is "the best last-minute Christmas gift", with customers getting "inspired to explore new parts of the world" and potentially finding "a Scandinavian cousin".[14]

[10] Herper (Forbes, 2015).

[11] FDA News Release, April 06, 2017, www.fda.gov/news-events/press-announcements/fda-allows-marketing-first-direct-consumer-tests-provide-genetic-risk-information-certain-conditions.

[12] § 7 German Genetic Diagnostics Act (Gendiagnostikgesetz). However, the Act does not apply to genetic tests conducted for research purposes.

[13] On the available offers and pricing structures, see further Plöthner et al. (2017).

[14] See www.ancestry.com.

Providing consumers with genetic information, however, is not the primary business model of DTC genetic testing companies. Almost all of the companies providing DTC genetic testing ask consumers purchasing their tests to also opt into their "research program". By opting in, consumers allow the company to use their genetic test results for further research. Consumers may be asked to fill out questionnaires regarding different health and lifestyle aspects. The majority of consumers purchasing DTC genetic testing appears to be open to letting the company use their data for "scientific purposes". In 2017, more than 80% of 23andMe opted into the company's research program.[15]

2.2.2 The Research Side

For DTC genetic testing companies, selling consumers' data through their research programm is the primary business model. To encourage consumers to participate in the research program, companies such as 23andme establish a 'participatory culture'.[16] They advertise joining the research program by telling consumers they will be part of something bigger by actively contributing to valuable research. While participation in surveys is always voluntary, it is also always encouraged.

The true gold mine for DTC genetic testing companies is thus to create a large biobank that is of interest for medical and pharmaceutical research. The anonymised collection of gene scans represents a vast sample of genetic profiles from which researchers hope to decipher connections between DNA and disease. For instance, pharmaceutical companies could quickly identify some 15,000 people to study Parkinson's through 23andMe, or nearly 300,000 with depression or high blood pressure, and ask them to complete additional surveys or recruit them to participate in clinical trials.[17]

DTC genetic testing companies capitalise on personal data by collaborating with research institutions. Research partners of DTC genetic testing companies include non-profit organisations and academic institutions as well as commercial companies.[18] For example, 23andMe concluded a $60 million deal with Genentech worth $10 million upfront and up to $50 million if further milestones are reached.[19] 23andMe also shared (anonymously) the DNA data it collected on 650,000 individuals with pharmaceutical giant Pfizer.[20]

[15] A. Bluestein (FastCompany 2017), "After a Comeback, 23andMe Faces its Next Test", www.fastcompany.com/40438376/after-a-comeback-23andme-faces-its-next-test; Geiger and Gross (2019), p. 12.

[16] Harris et al. (2013), p. 241.

[17] FastCompany (2017).

[18] See www.23andme.com/en-int/research/.

[19] FastCompany (2017).

[20] FastCompany (2017).

3 Concerns Regarding DTC Genetic Testing

3.1 Concerns

Despite the evident benefits that this medical research can produce, the business model of DTC genetic testing companies raises several concerns. First, the results provided by DTC genetic testing companies may have a profound effect on people's lives. Besides any psychological effects of having knowledge of genetic propensity to certain diseases, customers of DTC genetic testing companies may experience consequences in other aspects of their lives. The consequences of a data breach would be considerable, especially in the case of 23andme, which possesses genetic data of 5mil customers and has Google as its primary investor. Consumers could face genetic discrimination by insurers or employers when genetic risks are exposed. Forensic applications and criminal implications have also become apparent, with enforcement authorities tracking down criminals by signing up on genealogy websites using suspects' DNA.[21] Notwithstanding the obvious importance of capturing criminals, applications in law enforcement illustrate the need to consider more broadly the consequences of DNA sharing for relatives. Genetic data contains not only information about the person providing the data, but also about the relatives of that person.

A second concern of DTC genetic testing related to consumers being the product rather than the customers in this market, possibly without these consumers being aware of that. The exchange of testing kits for results is presented as the main transaction but instead serves as a means to achieve the primary exchange, namely the sale of genetic data to pharmaceuticals and research institutions.

Third, genetic data is a particularly sensitive type of data. Genetic data is unchangeable and it does not become outdated. Moreover, the amount of information that can be gained from genetic data will only increase in the future while costs for testing are decreasing. Anonymisation is nearly impossible: in many cases, only very little extra information is needed to identify the person the genetic data belongs to.[22]

3.2 Market Failures

As a result of these concerns, the market for consumer genetic testing may not function efficiently without regulatory intervention. That is, consumers may share more data than they would like to because of several market failures.

---

[21] See e.g. The Washington Post, 'Hunt for Golden State Killer led detectives to Hobby Lobby for DNA sample', www.washingtonpost.com/news/post-nation/wp/2018/06/02/hunt-for-golden-state-killer-led-detectives-to-hobby-lobby-for-dna-sample/.

[22] Hogarth et al. (2008).

3.2.1 Information Asymmetries

First, consumers may not be aware that anonymisation of genetic data is nearly impossible and that only very little extra information is needed to identify the person to whom the genetic data pertains. Consumers may also not be aware of the scope of their consent (i.e. sale to commercial companies).[23] Additionally, consumers may not realise that the information to be gained from genetic data may increase considerably in the future, while costs may decrease. As a result of asymmetric information, consumers may share more data than they would if they were fully informed.

An individual's genome cannot be altered. This means that genetic data will retain a permanent link with the particular individual.[24] Against this background, the consumer genomics industry has been embroiled in controversies from the start. The industry encountered scepticism from medical professionals around the provision of misleading information to consumers without medical support.[25] In the literature, strategies of DTC genetic testing companies to obscure scientific uncertainties have been discussed extensively.[26]

3.2.2 Cognitive Biases

Second, consumers may underestimate the risks of future applications and may suffer from hyperbolic discounting when it comes to these future risks. Consumers may also fail to grasp that genetic data is unchangeable (in case of a data breach).

As with asymmetric information, cognitive biases may lead consumers to share more data than they would if these biases were absent.

3.2.3 Externalities

Third, genetic data also contains information about blood relatives who have not chosen to share their genetic data. Consumers may fail to take into account the interests of these relatives, who may not want their data to be shared or who may be affected in case of a data breach.

An individual may thus impose a negative externality on their family members by sharing his or her genomic data, which can reveal familial relationships as well as disease susceptibility risks of family members. In a U.S. case, researchers published the genome of a woman who had died five decades earlier from cervical cancer. Her

---

[23]Laestadius et al. (2017) find that DTC genetic testing companies do not consistently meet international transparency guidelines related to confidentiality, privacy, and secondary use of data.

[24]Quinn and Quinn (2018), pp. 1003–1004.

[25]Geiger and Gross (2019), p. 3; Rockwell (2017).

[26]West (2019). Geiger and Gross (2019), p. 19.

descendants complained that the sequence contained information about them and asked for the data to be taken down from public databases.[27]

Leakage of genomic data may have serious implications, including genetic discrimination by insurance companies or employers. A U.S. aspiring army helicopter pilot was rejected for the position as soon as she revealed that genetic testing, done as part of a research study, had shown she had a mutation for a specific type of cancer.[28]

As a result of negative externalities, consumers may share more genetic data than they would if sharing data would affect only themselves. This effect should be balanced against the positive externalities associated with sharing data. Society can benefit from sharing genetic data if this leads to scientific breakthroughs regarding the cause or treatment of diseases.

3.2.4 Network Effects and Market Power

Finally, DTC genetic testing firms operate through a platform model, on two-sided markets with indirect network effects. Typically, these companies serve two sets of customers: consumers who buy the DNA kits in exchange for money and genetic information, and pharmaceuticals or research institutes that buy the genetic datasets.

The platform controls the flow of value across these exchanges. The first value flow is the price consumers pay for the genetic testing. While on the surface this value flow is a relatively straightforward commodity trade, it provides the basis for the revenue stream on the research side of the market. DTC genetic testing companies often erect a large smoke screen between these sides of the market.[29]

The second revenue stream stems from the sale of accumulated data to research laboratories and pharmaceutical companies.[30] On average, a single individual contributes to 200 different research studies.[31] Consumers do not share in the research profit made off their genetic data.[32]

Network effects are key to this business model: the more consumers are willing to share their genetic data for research purposes, the more pharmaceutical companies are willing to pay for the datasets. When network effects are present, a self-reinforcing process may emerge in which already large platforms become ever larger. As a result, two-sided markets with network effects may become concen-

[27] Naveed et al. (2015), p. 6.

[28] Lindor (2012).

[29] Geiger and Gross (2019), p. 12.

[30] Stoeklé et al. (2016).

[31] Geiger and Gross (2019), p. 12.

[32] See further Weichert (2019), p. 152–3.

trated. The leading firms may have market power, allowing them to impose higher prices or unfavourable terms and conditions, for instance with respect to data collection.[33]

4 Genetic Data in the GDPR

In light of these market failures, regulatory intervention into the market for DTC genetic testing may be warranted. Data protection law can help mitigate the problems associated with sharing genetic data.

The EU adopted the GDPR in 2016 after an intense debate on data protection law reform, stipulating general principles for data processing. The GDPR lays down specific rules for processing sensitive data, while allowing more leeway for processing data for research purposes.

4.1 Processing Sensitive Data

Article 9 GDPR lists genetic data as a type of "sensitive data".[34] It defines genetic data as

> personal data relating to the inherited or acquired genetic characteristics of a natural person which give unique information about the physiology or the health of that natural person and which result, in particular, from an analysis of a biological sample from the natural person in question.

The fact that the GDPR explicitly mentions genetic data as a type of sensitive data is a novelty—the fact that genetic data is considered "sensitive data", however, is not. Even before the GDPR took force, most genetic data could be categorised as sensitive data under Article 8 of the Data Protection Directive[35] by defining them as health data.[36] Nonetheless, by explicitly including genetic data, the GDPR provides clarity and does away with remaining uncertainties regarding the categorisation of genetic data.

The processing of the special categories of personal data listed in Article 9 (1) of the GDPR is prohibited, unless an exception listed in Article 9 (2) is fulfilled. First,

---

[33]Buiten (2018).

[34]Article 9 GDPR. Specifically, the GDPR refers to special categories of personal data.

[35]Directive 95/46/EC of the European Parliament and of the Council of 24 October 1995 on the protection of individuals with regard to the processing of personal data and on the free movement of such data.

[36]See Schild (2019), para. 138; Pormeister (2017b), Schweighofer et al. (2017), p. 5.

genetic data may be processed if the data subject has given their explicit consent to the processing for one or more specified purposes.[37] However, the GDPR allows the member states to rule out the possibility to give consent to the processing of sensitive data. Second, genetic data may be processed if processing is necessary to protect vital interests, for the purposes of preventive or occupational medicine or for scientific purposes.[38] According to Article 9 (4) GDPR, member states are free to maintain or introduce further conditions, including limitations with regard to the processing of genetic data, biometric data or data concerning health.

Aside from the special provisions of Article 9, the general provisions of the GDPR regarding the processing of personal data apply. This includes the safeguards listed in Art. 89(1) GDPR, such as to respect principles relating to processing of personal data of Article 5 that include storage limitation and data minimisation.

In short, if data is processed for research purposes, one either needs consent or to benefit from the research exemption.

4.2 Consent

Consent can only be given for specific purposes that have been determined beforehand.[39] This is meant to enable the data subject to estimate the scope of their consent.[40] The purposes for which the consent is to be given therefore have to be as specific as possible.

In the research context however, it is often not possible to clearly identify the scientific research purpose of personal data processing at the time of data collection. Accordingly, Rec. 33 GDPR allows for a broad consent for data processing for research purposes. Consent can be obtained for "certain areas of scientific research", meaning that it is sufficient to determine the area of scientific research rather than having to provide a detailed description of the research pursued.

It is unclear how widely or narrowly one should interpret 'certain areas of scientific research'. Rec. 50 GDPR indicates that retrospective use of genetic databases is allowed. There is no requirement to obtain consent for further or re-use of earlier obtained data in research. Arguably, DTC genetic testing companies could sell genetic data to pharmaceuticals by asking customers to consent to 'future research'. However, it has been suggested to interpret the wording of Rec. 33 in a restrictive manner, especially regarding the processing of sensitive data.[41]

[37] Art. 9 (2) (a) GDPR.

[38] Art. 9(2)(j) GDPR.

[39] Articles 2 no. 11; 5 (1) (b); 6 (1) (a) and 9 (2) (a) GDPR.

[40] Stemmer (2018), para. 74.

[41] Stemmer (2018), para. 78.

4.3 Research Exemption

4.3.1 Scope

DTC genetic testing companies may collect data without consent insofar they benefit from the GDPR's research exemption. The research exemption applies if data processing can be said to have a research purpose. Rec. 159 GDPR calls for a broad interpretation of 'research' that includes privately funded research. This means that commercial research could fall under the research exemption, allowing DTC genetic testing companies to sell data to pharmaceutical companies.[42]

Art. 6 GDPR states that processing of personal data without consent must be necessary for the purposes of the legitimate interest pursued. According to Art. 5(1) (b) GDPR, further processing for research purposes without consent must be compatible with the initial purpose of collection (regardless of what purpose).

4.3.2 Privileges

The research exemption offers several privileges. First, personal data processed for research purposes are exempted from the principle of storage limitation. According to Article 5 (1) (e) GDPR, personal data may not be stored for longer than necessary for the purposes for which the data is processed. However, if the data is stored solely for scientific purposes it is possible to keep it stored for a longer period as long as the storage is in accordance with Article 89 (1) GDPR.

A second concession in favour of scientific research concerns further processing of the data beyond the initial purpose. In general, personal data may only be collected for specified, explicit and legitimate purposes and may not be further processed in a manner that is incompatible with these purposes. The criteria for compatibility, listed in Article 6 (4) GDPR, include the link between the purposes for which the personal data have been collected and the purposes of the intended further processing; the nature of the personal data and the context in which the personal data have been collected; the possible consequences of the intended further processing for data subjects; and the possibilities to encrypt or anonymise the data. According to Article 5 (1) (b) GDPR, further processing for scientific purposes is always considered to be compatible with the purposes for which the personal data has been collected, thus enabling researcher to make use of data that has been (lawfully) collected for other purposes.

[42]On the scope of the research exemption, see further Werkmeister and Schwaab (2019).

4.3.3 Limitations

The GDPR makes it possible for the member states to create a legal basis for processing sensitive data for scientific reasons in accordance with Article 89 (1) GDPR. National provisions allowing the processing of sensitive data for such purposes must be proportionate to the aim pursued and must contain suitable and specific measures to safeguard the fundamental rights and the interests of the data subject.

In the context of processing personal data for scientific purposes, member states may also limit the data subject's rights to access and rectify their data or to restrict or object to its processing.[43] Member states may however only limit these rights insofar they are likely to seriously impair the achievement of the specific purposes of the data collection, and insofar these derogations are necessary to fulfil these purposes. Any such derogations would need to be introduced by the member state via national legislation.

The GDPR moreover provides an exception from the data subject's right to erasing the data if the processing is necessary for scientific purposes, and insofar as the use of that right is likely to render impossible or seriously impair the achievement of the objectives of that processing.[44] It also provides that the duty to inform the data subject when processing personal data that has not been obtained from the data subject themselves does not apply when providing the information proves impossible or would involve a disproportionate effort, particularly regarding processing for scientific reasons. The duty to inform does not apply if it is likely to render impossible or seriously impair the achievement of the objectives of the scientific processing.[45] In such cases, data subjects must be properly informed about their rights and interests. Should the data be processed for multiple purposes, then these derogations can only apply for the processing for research purposes.[46]

Article 89 (1) GDPR requires data processing to be subject to appropriate safeguards for the rights and freedoms of the data subject. These safeguards are to ensure that technical and organisational measures are in place to ensure the respect for the principle of data minimisation. Said measures can include the pseudonymisation of the data, given that the scientific purposes can be fulfilled with pseudonymised data. The same goes for the anonymisation of the processed data: if the processing of anonymised data is sufficient for fulfilling the scientific purposes, only anonymised data may be processed. Data processing for scientific purposes can only benefit from the privileges discussed above if it is conducted in a manner corresponding with Article 89 (1). In this way, the GDPR balances the fundamental rights of Article 13 of the EU Charter of Fundamental Rights (EUCF),

---

[43] Germany has introduced such provision in its new privacy law.

[44] Article 17 (3) (d) GDPR.

[45] Article 14 (5) (b) GDPR.

[46] Article 89 (4) GDPR.

the freedom of scientific research, with Articles 7 and 8 EUCF, which form the basis of European Data Protection Law.[47]

Summarising, the GDPR provides several privileges for the processing of personal data if the purpose is scientific research. Some of these privileges are governed by national transpositions, possibly leading to different conditions for the processing of personal data for scientific purposes across the EU. Member states especially have leeway to regulate sensitive data, which could lead to forum shopping by data processors looking for the most lenient rules.[48]

4.3.4 Implications for DTC Genetic Testing

Under the GDPR, DTC genetic testing companies will be able to process genetic data either by obtaining consent or by benefiting from the research exemption.

The difficulties in obtaining consent for the use of personal data for largely undetermined future research purposes have been discussed extensively in the literature.[49] Legally valid consent would have to be specific explicit and freely given. It is questionable whether such legally valid consent can be obtained upfront, if the possible consequences of consenting are impossible to foresee.[50] Such a one-time consent might be insufficient to ensure meaningful individual control over personal data.[51] At the same time, obtaining specific consent for every time the data is further processed could be prohibitively burdensome.[52]

The GDPR has taken the approach of a 'broad consent', covering a broad range of future data uses for research purposes. However, the legal validity and ethical acceptability of broad consent has been debated.[53] In any case, obtaining a broad consent will allow DTC genetic testing companies to use consumers' data for research purposes.

If DTC genetic testing companies do not obtain consent, they could nevertheless process the genetic data for research purposes in line with the GDPR's research exemption. In the literature, varying positions have been put forward as to the appropriate scope of the research exemption for medical research. While some argue its use should be kept to a minimum in favour of obtaining consent,[54] others view it as an acceptable alternative to obtaining consent when data are further processed in biobanks.[55] Given that data could be stored for an indefinite period of

[47]See Geminn (2018), p. 641; Pauly (2018), para. 3.

[48]Pormeister (2017a), p. 140.

[49]Nuffield Council (2015) and Mittelstadt and Floridi (2015).

[50]Mostert et al. (2016), p. 957; Boddington et al. (2011) and McGuire and Beskow (2010).

[51]Caulfield and Kaye (2009).

[52]Steinsbekk et al. (2013), Casali (2014) and Petrini (2010).

[53]Laurie and Postan (2013), Master et al. (2012), Kaye (2012) and Allen and McNamara (2011).

[54]Abbing (2015).

[55]Ruyter et al. (2010).

time in respect of research purposes, a broad consent allows for further processing a long time after the individual has given his consent.

Next to obtaining consent or benefiting from the research exemption, another alternative to protect data could be to anonymise the personal data. However, there seems to be a broad consensus that it is impossible to guarantee anonymity.[56] Irreversible anonymisation of data requires extensive stripping of the datasets and largely excludes data linkage. This makes most large research projects impossible, especially when genetic data are processed further in different contexts.[57] The more associated data relating to non-genetic factors e.g. lifestyle variables or socioeconomic data is combined with genetic data, the easier it is to identify an individual.[58]

4.4 Biobank Regulation as a Blueprint?

Whereas DTC genetic testing is a relatively new phenomenon, many of the associated problems with processing genetic data are not new. In essence, DTC genetic testing companies build a large biobank, selling datasets to research laboratories and pharmaceutical companies. The novelty is merely the source of information in these biobanks—biobanks themselves have been around for a long time.

Biobanks typically collect and store biological materials, which are used not only for current research projects, but also for future, not yet specified, research projects. Biobanks generally apply anonymisation to assure donor privacy, while allowing, under specific conditions, that participants remain re-identifiable in order to provide clinically relevant information back to the donor. They employ governance structures such as ethics review committees that serve to protect donors' rights.[59]

Given the sensitive nature of data stored in biobanks, several countries have introduced specific regulations for biobanks. These regulations differ greatly and have had varying success. Some countries set up one publicly funded biobank, such as Estonia, Hungary, Sweden, Iceland, Spain and Belgium. In Estonia, the project to establish a national biobank remains in place after several setbacks, whereas in Iceland it ultimately came to a halt.[60]

In other countries, such as France and the United Kingdom, provisions on biobanks or bio-collections are integrated into broader administrative and legislative instruments. The UK law has been criticised for being too complex to effectively guide researchers who wish to share data.[61]

---

[56]Mostert et al. (2016), p. 958; Sethi and Laurie (2013), Heeney et al. (2011), Mascalzoni et al. (2014), McGuire et al. (2008), Rodriguez et al. (2013) and Gymrek et al. (2013).

[57]O'Brien (2009), Knoppers et al. (2012) and Tene and Polonetsky (2012).

[58]Quinn and Quinn (2018), p. 1003.

[59]European Commission (2012), p. 13.

[60]Vossenkuhl (2013), p. 105 seq. Eensaar (2008) and Pálsson (2008), Pormeister (2017a), p. 134.

[61]Thomas and Walport (2008).

Other countries have no specific rules for biobanks in place, but do regulate genetic data (e.g. Switzerland). Yet other countries only have general rules in place for data processing, such as Germany and the Netherlands.[62] Similarly, in Denmark biobanks are explicitly subject to data protection legislation and no specific regulations are in place.[63] In Germany, a biobank act has been debated several times, but this did not culminate into a specific biobank regulation. While some stress the need for such a specific law,[64] others find that existing rules are mostly sufficient.[65]

Overall, in many countries biobanks are governed by a mosaic of legal instruments, regulatory bodies and informal governance tools. Researchers may face considerable uncertainty when sharing or merging research data, especially in cross-border contexts. Biobank managers have expressed concerns that the current regulatory framework for human biobanks within Europe creates uncertainty and inhibits the building of biobank infrastructure.[66] Some have called for creating coherent European rules for biobanks in order to better address the legal challenges raised by research involving biomedical data.[67] In 2012, the European Commission issued an Expert Group Report on governing biobanks. It recommends, among other things, to ensure effective governance of biobanks and to improve collaboration between national oversight bodies.[68]

Despite the varying regulatory landscape, some commonalities in regulations for biobanks can be listed. First, biobanks usually need to notify competent national authorities and obtain accreditation. Second, government authorities, such as data protection agencies, generally supervise the biobanks. Third, management of biobanks is typically limited to medical or biomedical professionals. Fourth, security measures are mandatory as a means to secure human tissue samples or data pertaining to these samples stored at the facility.[69]

Many countries have ethics committees or institutional review boards in place to oversee the biobanks. These bodies have become one of the main gatekeepers for research data processing. Researchers typically have to submit a proposal to the research ethics committee for approval, explaining the risks and benefits to the individual participants of involvement in the research protocol as well as providing the informed consent forms and information sheets that will be used in the study. If approved, research participants are asked to sign an informed consent form before the project commences.[70] In practice, broad consent is obtained that allows further processing of the data in future projects. With respect to biobanks, as with DTC

[62]European Commission (2012), p. 39; Pormeister (2017a).

[63]Zika et al. (2010), p. 42.

[64]Albers MedR (2013), p. 483 seq.

[65]Taupitz and Schreiber (2016), p. 309.

[66]European Commission (2012), p. 34.

[67]Briceño Moraia et al. (2014), p. 190.

[68]European Commission (2012), p. 7.

[69]European Commission (2012), pp. 40 seqq. (with references to the corresponding legislation).

[70]Kaye (2011) p. 379.

genetic testing, there is an ongoing debate as to whether this is ethically sound and legally valid.[71]

5 Conclusion

As the regulatory experience with biobanks shows, the peculiarities of biomedical research, including the use of biomedical data and its often international nature, call for clear and coherent rules. The rise of direct-to-consumer genetic testing only amplifies the need for such rules.

Whereas the GDPR has clarified some issues with respect to sensitive data, it leaves many gaps as to the possibilities for processing genetic data for research purposes. The GDPR lays down rules that rightfully aim to ensure that data protection law does not hamper research. At the same time, adequate safeguards need to be provided for consumers against the risks of genetic testing. It is questionable if the GDPR rules were intended to go as far as to include pharmaceutical deals of DTC genetic testing firms. Nevertheless, as the GDPR stands this seems to be possible, even without consent.

The GDPR allows continuing processing of research data based on a one-time and general consent. In light of the information asymmetries and cognitive biases that may be present with DTC genetic testing, this may lead consumers to share more data than they would like to if fully informed. The GDPR leaves considerable room for research processing of genetic data. This may be problematic in light of negative externalities on family members who did not choose to share their DNA, especially if the data is shared with commercial third parties.

It appears that transparency measures are warranted, particularly where consumers may have difficulty finding out who uses their genetic data and for what purposes the data is being used.[72] There are several options for mitigating the problems associated with consumers sharing genetic data, both within and outside the GDPR. The GDPR could limit the scope of the research exemption to exclude commercial research. This, however, may be difficult to enforce in practice. Member states are given considerable room to impose stricter rules in this area than the GDPR provides, which they may use to limit the scope of 'research'.

Other solutions may lie outside data protection law. Several countries already limit the services that DTC genetic testing companies are allowed to offer. In Germany, for instance, genetic risks may only be communicated by a medical doctor.

---

[71] Caulfield and Kaye (2009).

[72] See further Kulynych and Greely (2017) on increasing information to patients on the use of their genomic data.

Another possibility would be to introduce controlled-access or managed-access models for biobanks.[73] This would allow maintaining a level of control on downstream uses of the research databases through review by specialised committees that oversee the incoming data access requests.

Acknowledgement The author gratefully acknowledges financial support from Deutsche Forschungsgemeinschaft (DFG) through CRC TR 224.

References

Abbing HD (2015) EU cross-border healthcare and health law. Eur J Health Law 22:1–12

Albers M (2013) Rechtsrahmen und Rechtsprobleme bei Biobanken. MedR 31:783–791

Allen J, McNamara B (2011) Reconsidering the value of consent in biobank research. Bioethics 25:155–166

Azencott CA (2018) Machine learning and genomics: precision medicine versus patient privacy. Philos Trans R Soc A 376(2128):20170350. Available at https://doi.org/10.1098/rsta.2017.0350

Boddington P, Curren L, Kaye J et al (2011) Consent forms in genomics: the difference between law and practice. Eur J Health Law 18:491–519

Briceño Moraia L et al (2014) A comparative analysis of the requirements for the use of data in biobanks based in Finland, Germany, the Netherlands, Norway and the United Kingdom. Med Law Int 14(4):187–212

Buiten MC (2018) Regulating data giants: between competition law and data protection law. In: Mathis K (ed) New developments in competition law and economics, Series economic analysis of law in European legal scholarship. Springer

Casali PG (2014) Risks of the new EU Data protection regulation: an ESMO position paper endorsed by the European oncology community. Ann Oncol 25:1458–1461

Caulfield T, Kaye J (2009) Broad consent in biobanking: reflections on seemingly insurmountable dilemmas. Med Law Int 10:85–100

Eensaar R (2008) Estonia: Ups and downs of a biobank project. In: Gottweis H, Petersen A (eds) Biobanks: governance in comparative perspective. Routledge, New York, pp 56–70

European Commission DG for Research and Innovation, Gottweis H, Kaye J (2012) Biobanks for Europe: A Challenge for Governance. https://publications.europa.eu/en/publication-detail/-/publication/629eae10-53fc-4a52-adc2-210d4fcad8f2

Geiger S, Gross N (2019) A tidal wave of inevitable data? Assetization in the consumer genomics testing industry. Bus Soc, 0007650319826307

Geminn ChL (2018) Wissenschaftliche Forschung und Datenschutz Neuerungen durch die Datenschutz-Grundverordnung. Datenschutz und Datensicherheit

Gymrek M, McGuire AL, Golan D, Halperin E, Erlich Y (2013) Identifying personal genomes by surname inference. Science 339:321–324

Harris A, Wyatt S, Kelly SE (2013) The gift of spit (and the obligation to return it) how consumers of online genetic testing services participate in research. Inf Commun Soc 16(2):236–257

Heeney C, Hawkins N, de Vries J, Boddington P, Kaye J (2011) Assessing the privacy risks of data sharing in genomics. Public Health Genomics 14:17–25

Hogarth S et al (2008) The current landscape for direct-to-consumer genetic testing: legal, ethical, and policy issues. Ann Rev Genomics Hum Genet 9:161–182

[73]On technical solutions for protection of genome data, see further Wang et al. (2017). On organizational safeguards and a broader discussion of governance of DTC genetic testing, see Shabani and Borry (2018) and Phillips (2016).

Kalokairinou L, Howard HC, Slokenberga S, Fisher E, Flatscher-Thöni M, Hartlev M, van Hellemondt R et al (2018) Legislation of direct-to-consumer genetic testing in Europe: a fragmented regulatory landscape. J commun Genet 9(2):117–132

Kaye J (2011) From single biobanks to international networks: developing e-governance. Hum Genet 130:377–382

Kaye J (2012) The tension between data sharing and the protection of privacy in genomics research. Annu Rev Genomics Hum Genet 13:415–431

Knoppers BM, Zawati MH, Kirby ES (2012) Sampling populations of humans across the world: ELSI issues. Annu Rev Genomics Hum Genet 13:395–413

Kulynych J, Greely HT (2017) Clinical genomics, big data, and electronic medical records: reconciling patient rights with research when privacy and science collide. J Law Biosci 4(1):94–132

Laestadius LI, Rich JR, Auer PL (2017) All your data (effectively) belong to us: data practices among direct-to-consumer genetic testing firms. Genet Med 19(5):513

Laurie G, Postan E (2013) Rhetoric or reality: what is the legal status of the consent form in health-related research? Med Law Rev 21:371–414

Lindor NM (2012) Personal autonomy in the genomic era. In: Video Proceedings of Mayo Clinic Individualizing Medicine Conference

Mascalzoni D, Dove ES, Rubinstein Y et al (2014) International Charter of principles for sharing bio-specimens and data. Eur J Hum Genet 23:721–728

Master Z, Nelson E, Murdoch B, Caulfield T (2012) Biobanks, consent and claims of consensus. Nat Methods 9:885–888

McGuire AL, Beskow LM (2010) Informed consent in genomics and genetic research. Annu Rev Genomics Hum Genet 11:361–381

McGuire AL, Caulfield T, Cho MK (2008) Research ethics and the challenge of whole-genome sequencing. Nat Rev Genet 9:152–156

Mittelstadt BD, Floridi L (2015) The ethics of big data: current and foreseeable issues in biomedical contexts. Sci Eng Ethics; e-pub ahead of print 23 May 2015; https://doi.org/10.1007/s11948-015-9652-2

Mostert M, Bredenoord AL, Biesaart MC, van Delden JJ (2016) Big Data in medical research and EU data protection law: challenges to the consent or anonymise approach. Eur J Human Genet 24(7):956

Naveed M, Ayday E, Clayton EW, Fellay J, Gunter CA, Hubaux JP et al (2015) Privacy in the genomic era. ACM Comput Surv (CSUR) 48(1):6

Nuffield Council on Bioethics: The collection, linking and use of data in biomedical research and health care: ethical issues, 2015. Available at http://nuffieldbioethics.org/wp-content/uploads/Biological_and_health_data_web.pdf

O'Brien SJ (2009) Stewardship of human biospecimens, DNA, genotype, and clinical data in the GWAS era. Annu Rev Genomics Hum Genet 10:193–209

Pálsson G (2008) The rise and fall of a biobank: the case of Iceland. In: Gottweis H, Petersen A (eds) Biobanks: Governance in comparative perspective. Routledge, New York, pp 41–55

Pauly D (2018) Kommentierung zu Art. 89 DSGVO. In: Paal BP, Pauly D (eds) Datenschutzgrundverordnung Bundesdatenschutzgesetz

Petrini C (2010) 'Broad' consent, exceptions to consent and the question of using biological samples for research purposes different from the initial collection purpose. Soc Sci Med 70:217–220

Phillips AM (2016) Only a click away—DTC genetics for ancestry, health, love… and more: a view of the business and regulatory landscape. Appl Transl Genomics 8:16–22

Plöthner M, Klora M, Rudolph D, von der Schulenburg JMG (2017) Health-related genetic direct-to-consumer tests in the German setting: the available offer and the potential implications for a solidarily financed health-care system. Public health Genomics 20(4):203–217

Pormeister K (2017a) Genetic data and the research exemption: is the GDPR going too far?. International Data Privacy Law 7(2):137–146

Pormeister K (2017b) The GDPR and big data: leading the way for big genetic data?. In: Annual privacy forum. Springer, Cham, pp 3–18

Quinn P, Quinn L, (2018) Big genetic data and its big data protection challenges. Comput Law Secur Rev 34(5):1000–1018

Rockwell KL (2017) Direct-to-consumer medical testing in the era of value-based care. J Am Med Assoc 317:2485–2486

Rodriguez LL, Brooks LD, Greenberg JH, Green ED (2013) Research ethics. The complexities of genomic identifiability. Science 339:275–276

Ruyter KW, LOuk K, Jorqui M, Kvalheim V, Cekanauskaite A, Townend D (2010) From research exemption to research norm: recognising an alternative to consent for large scale biobank research. Med Law Int 10:287–313

Schild HH (2019) Commentary to Article 4 GDPR. In: Brink S, Wolff HA (eds) BeckOK Datenschutzrecht. C.H. Beck Muenchen, para. 138

Schweighofer E et al (2017) Privacy Technology and Policy; Data Protection Working Party. Working document on genetic data. 12178/03/EN WP 91

Sethi N, Laurie G (2013) Delivering proportionate governance in the era of eHealth: making linkage and privacy work together. Med Law Int 13:168–204

Shabani M, Borry P (2018) Rules for processing genetic data for research purposes in view of the new EU General Data Protection Regulation. Eur J Hum Genet 26(2):149

Steinsbekk KS, Kåre Myskja B, Solberg B (2013) Broad consent versus dynamic consent inbiobank research: is passive participation an ethical problem? Eur J Hum Genet 21:897–902

Stemmer (2018) Commentary to Article 7 GDPR. In: Brink S, Wolff HA (eds) BeckOK Datenschutzrecht. C.H. Beck Muenchen, para. 74

Stoeklé H-C, Mamzer-Bruneel M-F, Vogt G, Hervé C (2016) 23andMe: a new two-sided data-banking market model. BMC Med Ethics 17:19

Taupitz J, Schreiber M (2016) Biobanken - zwischen Forschungs- und Spenderinteressen. Bundesgesundheitsbl Gesundheitsforsch Gesundheitssch 59(3):1–7

Tene O, Polonetsky J (2012) Privacy in the age of big data: a time for big decisions. Stanford Law Rev 64:63–69

Thomas R, Walport M (2008) Data sharing review (UK) http://www.justice.gov.uk/reviews/docs/data-sharing-review-report.pdf

Vayena E, Gourna E, Streuli J, Hafen E, Prainsack B (2012) Experiences of early users of direct-to-consumer genomics in Switzerland: an exploratory study. Public Health Genomics 15:352–362

Vossenkuhl C (2013) Der Schutz genetischer Daten. Unter besonderer Berücksichtigung des Gendiagnostikgesetzes. Schriftenreihe Medizinrecht, Springer, Heidelberg

Wang S, Jiang X, Singh S, Marmor R, Bonomi L, Fox D, Dow M, Ohno-Machado L (2017) Genome privacy: challenges, technical approaches to mitigate risk, and ethical considerations in the United States. Ann N Y Acad Sci 1387(1):73–83

Weichert T (2019) Genetische Genealogie und Datenschutz. Datenschutz und Datensicherheit-DuD 43(3):149–153

Werkmeister C, Schwaab M (2019) Auswirkungen und Reichweite des datenschutzrechtlichen Forschungsprivilegs. Computer und Recht 35(2):85–90

West SM (2019) Data capitalism: redefining the logics of surveillance and privacy. Bus Soc 58:20–41

Zika E, Paci D, Schulte T, Braun A, RijKers-Defrasne A, Deschênes M, Fortier I, Laage-Hellman J, Scerri CA, Ibarreta D (2010) Biobanks in Europe: prospects for harmonisation and networking. http://ftp.jrc.es/EURdoc/JRC57831.pdf

Miriam C. Buiten Assistant Professor of Law and Economics, University of St. Gallen, Law School. Bodanstrasse 3, CH-9000 St. Gallen, Tel. +41 71 224 32 22, miriam.buiten@unisg.ch, www.ls.unisg.ch. Fields of Interest: Internet & Technology Law, Competition Law, Data Protection Law, Economic Analysis of Law.

Part IV
Further Applications

The Poisonous Fruit of Foreign Currency Loans for Consumers in Selected Central European States: The Dilemma for Macroeconomic Policy

Jarosław Bełdowski and Wiktor Wojciechowski

Abstract This chapter is devoted to the analysis of the determinants and shape of public intervention in selected transition CEE countries within the foreign currency loan market through legislative and executive branches of government. The study is limited to three CEE countries that have taken different regulatory paths with extreme (Hungary), moderate (Croatia) and limited approach (Poland). The public authorities in these countries faced a dilemma whether to step into private contractual provisions in order to ease the consumers' burden or to save the stability of domestic banking sector. We show that the shape of public interventions depended heavily on the situation in which the financial sector and macroeconomic stability were located. The better macroprudential supervision, the smaller the need for intervention after the crisis, because the smaller scale of the problem.

1 Introduction

The topic of foreign currency loans within transition economies attracted various literature attention from different angles.[1] However, our research focuses on the topic neglected within Law & Economics literature, namely Law and Macroeconomics.[2] Due to the rapid expansion of foreign currency loans in transition countries some consumers were exposed to numerous risk to which they were not accustomed previously. For instance, at that time the currency risk could not be mitigated through typical means, e.g. hedging instruments, as such instruments were not available or

[1] Dübel and Walley (2010), Brown et al. (2011), Brown and De Haas (2012), Yeşin (2013), Brzoza-Brzezina et al. (2017).

[2] Gordon (2000).

J. Bełdowski (✉) · W. Wojciechowski
Department of International Comparative Studies, Warsaw School of Economics, Warsaw, Poland
e-mail: wiktor.wojciechowski@sgh.waw.pl

K. Mathis, A. Tor (eds.), *Consumer Law and Economics*, Economic Analysis of Law in European Legal Scholarship 9, https://doi.org/10.1007/978-3-030-49028-7_11

just started to be implemented.[3] As a result of global financial crisis in 2008 various stakeholders have been faced with the dilemma whether to step into private contractual provisions in order to ease the consumers' burden or to save the stability of domestic banking sector with no or limited public intervention. The former approach could be supported by the political economy argument[4] as well as Law & Economics through least or cheapest cost avoider's concept.[5] In contrast, the "preserving stability approach" goes along with some macroeconomics' arguments underlying the sacrifice of individual interest to reduce potential detrimental effects to the domestic financial system in general. In other words, it is the matter or not to intervene for public stakeholders.

Our chapter focuses on public intervention in selected transition CEE countries within the foreign currency loan market through legislative and executive branches of government. We omit the judicial branch's approach as it is disputable in our opinion whether it is possible to forge a public policy through judicial means. Consequently, we do not take into account some developments in this matter within domestic judicial systems (in particular the recent judgement of Supreme Court of Croatia on the topic) as well as the European Court of Justice jurisprudence (in particular the judgment in Case C-260/18). Our analysis is limited to three CEE countries which belong to the European Union, namely Hungary, Croatia and Poland. All of them have taken different regulatory paths with extreme (Hungary), moderate (Croatia) and limited approach (Poland). To better understand local peculiarities we describe the market of foreign currency loans within each country from its infancy up to the implementation of ultimate regulatory solution. We contribute to the existing literature by overlooking at the consequences of different regulatory paths on domestic economies.

This chapter is organized as follows. In the first section we briefly discuss existing literature on the matter. The second section is devoted to the description of conditions and some developments of foreign currency loan market in each country. The third section aims to analyze the foreign currency loan market in Hungary, Croatia and Poland from the macroeconomic point of view. We conclude in the last section.

[3]Dübel and Walley (2010).

[4]Political economy is focused on the distribution of benefits from economic activity, especially who gains and who loses from a particular policy or reforms. For surveys of the relevant literature see e.g. Rodrik (1996) or Drazen (2000).

[5]The concept of 'least cost avoider' has been introduced into Law & Economics in its beginning and it could be summarized generally that it is focused on the burden of responsibility which is shifted towards the party which could prevent an accident at the lowest cost. For further reading see Calabresi (1970). See also Gilles (1992). Critically Dari-Mattiacci and Garoupa (2009), Carbonara et al. (2016).

2 Literature Overview

Foreign currency lending and borrowing has not been invented in Central Eastern Europe but it has been present before in many regions of the world. In general it could be noted that household borrowing in foreign currency is negatively impacted by financial sector development.[6] It could also be reiterated that whenever the difference between domestic and foreign interest rates is positive, this channel biases borrowers' choices towards foreign currency, even if the exchange rate is known to depreciate as implied by the interest parity condition.[7] Both demand and supply factors play an important role in loan currency decisions. For instance, banks are also more likely to grant loans in foreign currency that are large and long-term.[8]

In addition, household deposit 'dollarization' (covering situation when a foreign currency is used in addition to or instead of the domestic currency as legal tender; further as "currency substitution") increases interest rate spread in the economy and pushes firms to borrow in foreign currency. Furthermore, such currency substitution increases currency mismatch in the non-financial sector and creates balance sheet effects after exchange rate movements.[9] In other words high credit dollarization creates balance sheet risks in the economy, because firm revenues are denominated in local currency and when the exchange rate depreciates, firms need to pay higher interest rate costs, which deteriorates their balance sheets, and leads to lower investment and wages. For instance, it has been stated that credit 'euroization' in Croatia (currency mismatch with regard to Euro currency) appears to have been a by-product of a complex political and economic environment in the country during the last twenty years. The last decade appears to be strongly influenced by the monetary and financial policies of the central bank, in conjunction with banks' efforts to minimize the regulatory costs of holding liabilities through regulatory arbitrage.[10]

The academic literature has approached the topic of foreign currency borrowing in CEE broadly.[11] More detailed are papers that focus on the cases of Hungary, Croatia and Poland separately. For instance, Pellényi and Bilek (2009) point at unhealthy mix of public policy which most likely contributed to the foreign currency borrowing in Hungary. In relation to Croatia it has been shown the policymakers should not focus only on 'prescribed' tools and policy options, but they should think broader, as it is the only way to increase the chances of successfully managing systemic risks. Last, but not least the case of Poland restructuring of mortgage loans in CHF according to the original rate may undermine the stability of the banking

[6]Corrales and Imam (2019).

[7]Kolasa (2016).

[8]Beckmann et al. (2015).

[9]Dalgic (2018).

[10]Galac and Kraft (2010).

[11]Buszko and Krupa (2015) and Novák and Vámos (2017).

system and become a dangerous precedent in the market economy.[12] In contrast, reverse dependence of foreign exchange rate and interest rate of foreign currency loans has already helped to avoid materialisation of credit default risk in the banking system. Therefore global fluctuations of economy are possibly not a danger for Polish borrowers provided that Swiss and Euro areas remain stable economies.[13]

3 Main Drivers of the Surge of Foreign Currency Loans in Hungary, Poland and Croatia

The main drivers of an upsurge of foreign currency denominated loans in the analyzed countries were:

- higher interest rates of loans denominated in domestic currencies than in foreign ones,
- observed appreciation of domestic currencies against those in which the loans were denominated,
- accepted expectation that the domestic currencies would experience further appreciation due to process of economic convergence.

However, the increased demand for loans denominated in foreign currencies has not been met unless the considered countries have abandoned limits on capital flows associated with their accession to the EU.

The increase of foreign currency loans has posed significant challenges for the macroeconomic policy and stability. One can point at least three main channels through which they affect economic performance. Firstly, the higher volume of foreign currency loans, the bigger is the magnitude of the economic fluctuation associated with changes of foreign currency rates. Prior to the global financial crises, a relatively unconstrained access to foreign currency loans boosted domestic demand, especially on the housing market. Due to gradual appreciation of domestic currencies observed at that time, households that took foreign currency loan to buy properties experienced income effect associated with lowering cost of servicing their debt. On the contrary, after burst of the global financial crises and sudden depreciation of domestic currencies, costs of instalments dramatically rose which in effect dampened domestic demand.

Secondly, high volume of foreign currency loans lowers effectiveness of domestic monetary policy. When foreign currency loans are easily available, a decision of monetary authority to increase domestic interest rates in order to dampen domestic demand may turn out to be counterproductive: instead of hampering aggregate demand, it may strengthen demand of domestic households for foreign currency loans and thus surge aggregate demand. In a similar vein, a decrease of domestic interest rates aimed at strengthening domestic demand may lead to domestic

[12]Olszewska (2018).

[13]Wośko (2013).

currency depreciation, then to an increase of costs of debt servicing and thus to unintended fall of aggregate demand in the economy.

Thirdly, high volume of foreign currency loans poses significant risk for the stability of the financial sector. Although banks usually hedge against foreign currency rates fluctuations, borrowers are usually not accustomed to this kind of risk. A substantial domestic currency depreciation, as it was the case in the analyzes countries after a burst of the global financial crises, leaded to a huge growth of loan instalments expressed in domestic currencies and thus to an increase of non-repayment ratio and considerable worsening of banks' foreign currency loan portfolio. A poorer quality of banks' loan portfolio requires creation of additional reserves, deteriorates banking sector profitability and ultimately leads to lower ability to grant new loans in times of economic slowdown accompanied with domestic currency depreciation.

An ultimate impact of measures aimed at resolving problem of high foreign currency indebtedness on real economy depends heavily on how their costs are distributed among all involved stakeholders. Taking into account the main channels through which foreign currency debt affects economic policy and stability discussed previously, one can point at the following stakeholders that are potentially the most affected, namely: borrowers (mainly households), banking sector and the authorities responsible for macroeconomic policy: government and central bank. Common wisdom states that maintaining *status quo* in the three analyzed CEE countries involved putting all debt servicing burden almost entirely on the borrowers' shoulders. In fact, it is not true since the high volume of foreign currency loans associated with an increasing share of non-performing loans resulting from domestic currency depreciation posed a significant systematic risk on the financial sector with all possible adverse consequences for economic growth prospects and limited ability of domestic fiscal and monetary economic policy to counteract possible economic fluctuations and limit their impact on the real economy. Depending on the magnitude of the foreign currency problem, determined to much extent by the effectiveness of the measures implemented so far that should have limited growth of foreign currency loans, the analyzed countries decided to take different steps. Figure 1 presents the main channels through which a considered conversion of foreign currency loans into domestic currency credits could affect real economy.

Assuming that conversion of the foreign currency loans would result in a decrease of loan instalments expressed in domestic currency, it is likely households would increase their purchases and thus strengthen aggregate demand and government revenue. On the contrary, if the costs of foreign currency loans conversion were levied mainly on the banking sector, it would result in lower profits of the financial institutions and possibly also in depressing of government revenue from corporate income taxes. In effect, an outcome of the foreign currency loans conversion for the public finance performance is unclear. The expected growth of households expenditures heavily depends on the exchange rate used for the foreign currency loan conversion. If regulations allow to apply preferential exchange rate resulting in lower loan instalments then a positive impact of loan conversion on household expenditures is more likely than the current exchange rate has to be used.

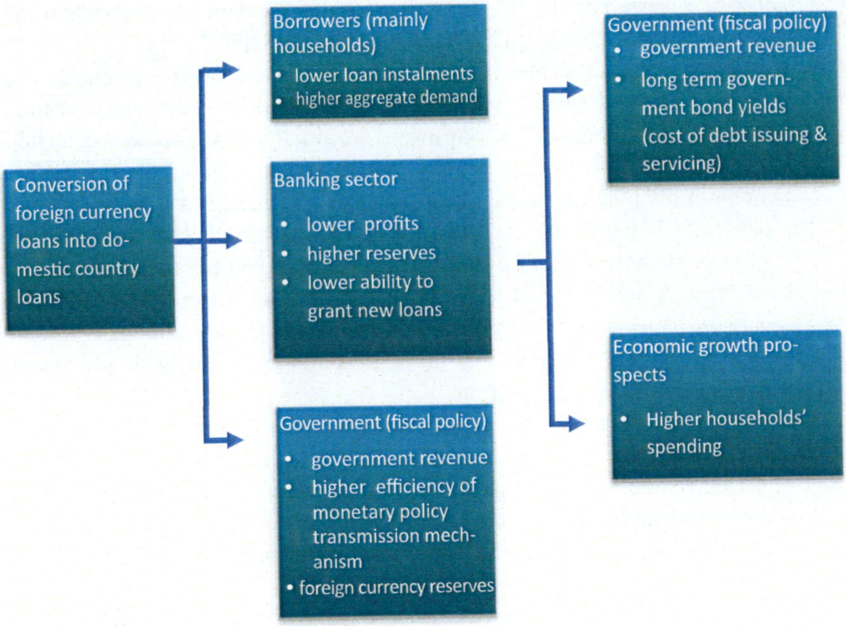

Fig. 1 Main channels through which a conversion of foreign currency loans into liabilities expressed in domestic currency affects economy

Irrespective of the impact of loan conversion on budget performance, one can expect that a decrease of a share of loans denominated in foreign currencies would strengthen effectiveness of countercyclical domestic monetary policy. Another important issue that might be associated with the loan conversion is complementary measures from the central bank that is about to limit imbalances in the financial market arising from currency conversion. Although it involves lowering of the central bank's foreign currency reserves and thus enhances country's vulnerability to the adverse economic fluctuations, on the other hand, it contributes to an increased stability of the domestic financial sector. As it was mentioned before, the ultimate effect of the foreign currency loan conversions on the economic performance is unclear and depends on the initial scale of the problem and the cost distribution among all stakeholders. From this perspective the only certain lesson to be learnt from the past experiences is that solid macroprudential policy is a core requirement that is able to limit dilemma how to spread costs among households, banking sector and taxpayers of restoring financial stability fueled by the uncontrolled surge of foreign currency loans. The more forward looking and thus more efficient macroprudential policy conducted in Poland than in other analyzed CEE countries is believed to play a significant role in limiting growth of foreign currency loans.

4 The Market of Foreign Currency Loans in Hungary, Croatia and Poland

4.1 *Case of Hungary*

Foreign currency loans were available in Hungary before 2000, but their rise was only noticeable in the beginning of twenty-first century. In fact, Hungary experienced a significant deepening of the financial sector after 2000. This hike was achieved through lending which was mainly based on foreign currency loans provided for households (consumers), in particular mortgage loans (Fig. 2) as well as companies (Fig. 3).

4.1.1 Actions Between 2009 and 2010

The global financial crises of 2008 led to increased sovereign risk, which in turn brought significant soaring up in risk premiums and contributed to the major depreciation of Hungarian forint (HUF), especially against Swiss franc (CHF) (Fig. 4). In turn, Hungarian households experienced a significant increase of their debt burdens denominated in foreign currencies. Unsurprisingly, increased instalments caused difficulties for a growing number of debtors soon after the global crisis outburst.

However, the first significant executive action came through the Government Decree 361/2009 on the terms of prudent retail lending and the assessment of creditworthiness. According to the decree, the credit institutions in Hungary were only allowed to provide loans to natural persons in foreign currency under strict conditions, namely regular authenticated monthly gross income in the currency of the loan and 15 times higher than the statutory minimal monthly basic wage

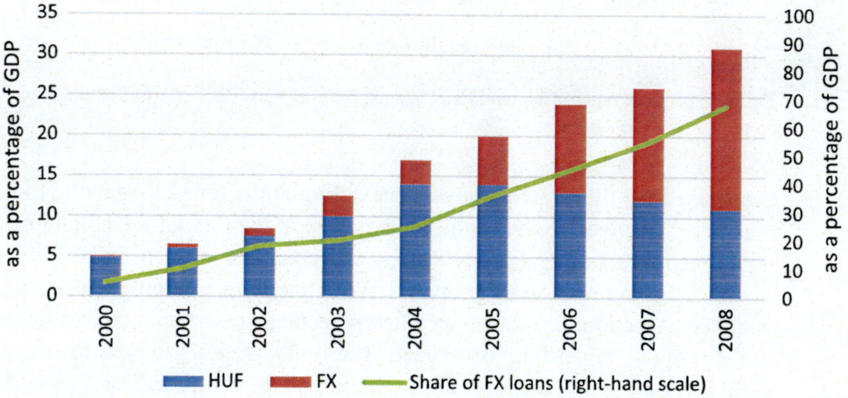

Fig. 2 Currency structure of the household loans in Hungary. Source: Own elaboration based on Krekó and Endrész (2010)

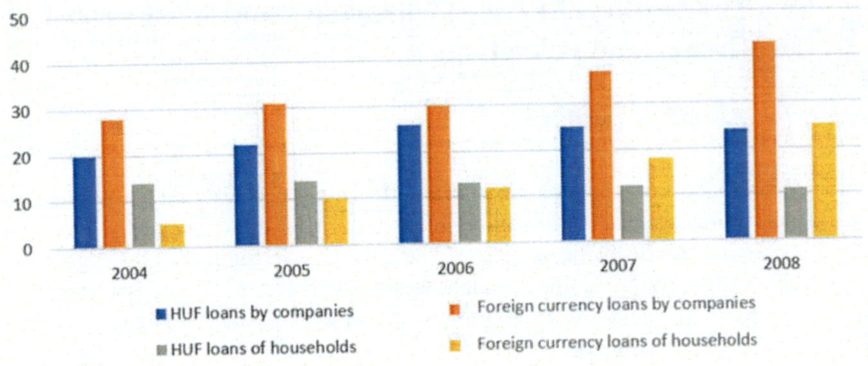

Fig. 3 The corporate and household loans from 2004 to 2008 (percentage of GDP). Source: Own elaboration based on Akos (2015)

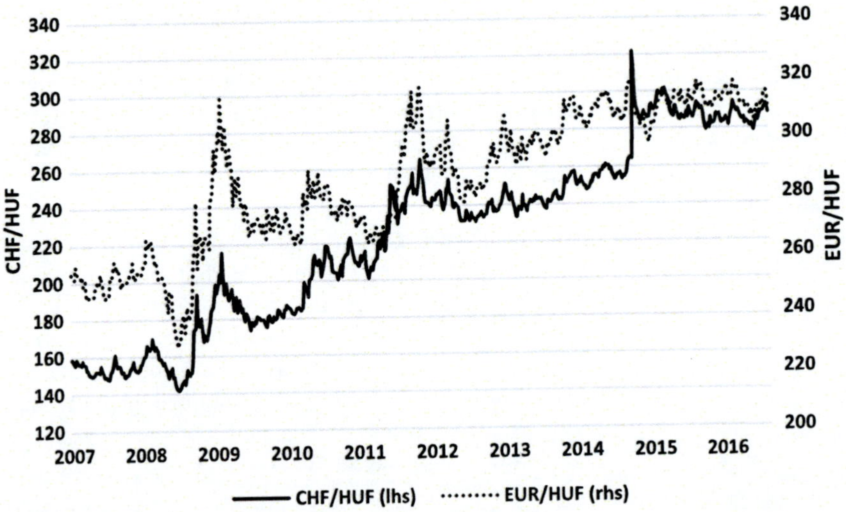

Fig. 4 Exchange rate of CHF and EUR against HUF in years 2007–2016. Source: https://www.xe.com/

determined for full-time employees prevailing at the time of signature of the credit contract. Moreover, the value of the exposure at the time of the commitment could not exceed 80% of the property's market value in case of loans in HUF and secured by mortgage on real estate property. When the loan was provided for a building under construction, the above-specified percentage could apply to the market value of the property when fully completed. The limits were set to have the thresholds of 60% in case of mortgage loans in EUR and 65% in case of financial leasing arrangements in EUR while 45% and 50% in other currencies respectively. The credit institutions were to set up creditworthiness limits for all individual loan applicants defined in proportion to monthly income, i.e. DTI ratio. The assessment of credit eligibility banned purely collateral based lending and requires the credit eligibility check of private person customers on a mandatory basis in each and every case. For instance, the instalments to be paid in a month at the time of the credit approval could not exceed 80% of the credit eligibility limit in case of loans in EUR and 60% of the credit eligibility limit in case of loans denominated in other currencies. In addition, the Government set up the National Asset Management Agency (NET) with the aim to socially support of deprived persons having retail mortgage loans in foreign currency. NET's goal is to purchase mortgaged residential properties of deprived debtors and allow them to stay as tenants. The debtors pay a discounted rental fee, and can stay there, while the lender writes-off the remaining mortgage debt.

Furthermore, the Parliament voted in July 2010 to temporarily ban the provision of foreign currency loans with a mortgage collateral. The purpose of the ban was to prevent the further indebting of the population and to decrease the likelihood of losing their property (the ban was lifted in June 2011 in order to comply with EU regulations). At the time the National Bank of Hungary (MNB) allocated a total amount of EUR 36 million of the central bank reserves to the banking system in order to support it (converted credits worth 0.17% of GDP). In addition, a moratorium on evictions, option of early pay-back of the loans under favorable terms and the possibility of freezing the monthly payments at a lower level for a temporary period had been introduced.

4.1.2 Actions Between 2011 and 2012

It is assumed that the major reform affecting foreign currency debtors and banking sector in Hungary occurred when a reduction of the foreign currency loans' exposure during the period of September 2011 and February 2012 was implemented as the foreign currency debtors were allowed to settle their accounts at a favorable predetermined interest rate[14]. As a result the credit institutions reported conversions of EUR 178.1 million out of the total EUR 438 million foreign exchange loans eligible for that scheme. The rules regarding the sales of residential real estate collaterals were also introduced. Accordingly, the sale of properties serving as a collateral were restricted by quarterly quotas with the aim to limit the number of properties sold by the institutions in order to reduce their impact on the prices of real estate and to limit the number of evicted debtors (between 1st October 2011 and 31st December 2014 collateral properties were allowed to be assigned for a forced liquidation only if they are marked out under the quota system). The credit institutions were obliged to set the list of properties for forced sale quarterly separately in each county. The quotas were gradually increasing (in 2011—2%, in 2012—3%, in

[14]It only applied to households that took out a loan at a rate equal to or lower than introduced in 2011.

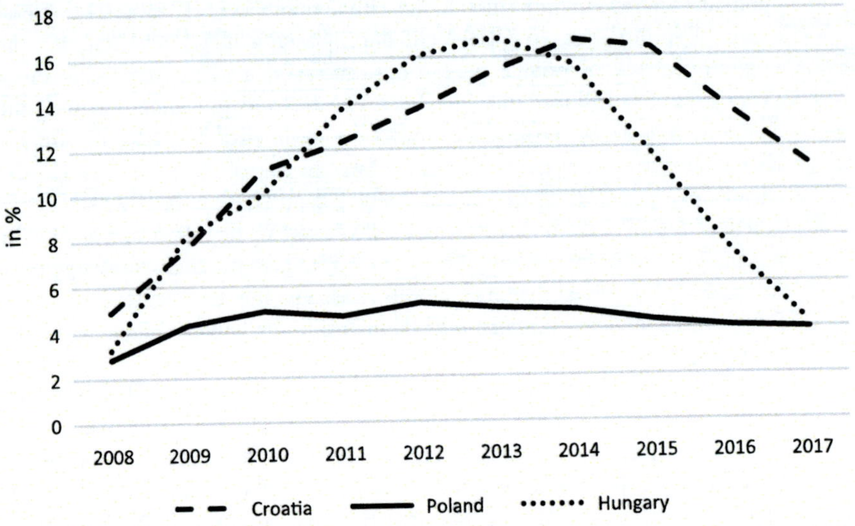

Fig. 5 Non-performing loans (% of total loans in the banking sector). Source: Own elaboration based on the World Bank data

2013—4% and in 2014—5% of the number of mortgage credit agreements past due more than 90 days). At last, those limitations were lifted in the beginning of 2015. Moreover, the Government in its Decree No. 341/2011 on housing interest subsidy introduced the Home Creation Programme to provide social housing subsidy and grants for buying residential properties. Save for conditions to be fulfilled, subsidies were applied to the following purposes: building or purchasing a new home; purchasing or refurbishing used home; purchasing a housing property which was encumbered with a defaulted mortgage or terminated loan; purchasing a smaller home by defaulted debtors; replacing a defaulted foreign currency mortgage secured by a housing property collateral into a loan denominated in HUF and for purchasing back a property from the NET.

4.1.3 Action in 2014

As the CHF/HUF started to rise and the interest rates of loans remained fixed or in some cases became elevated due to a higher interest rate risk (despite a decrease of LIBOR rate), the ability of borrowers to repay had been decreasing, determining the level of all non-performing CHF loans at 26.4% in 2013 and 22.1% in 2014 (Fig. 5). The interest rates for CHF housing (mortgage) loans in the 2013–2014 were oscillating in the range 4–5% as banks in Hungary increased their interest by approximately 1 p.p., and such an elevated cost was maintained in the next years despite decreasing interest rates in Switzerland. In 2014, the Hungarian Parliament adopted a law requiring banks to reimburse borrowers for fees and surcharges levied during the lending period that were deemed to be unfair. Based on that law, banks were required to pay back about 1 trillion HUF to more than 1.3 million Hungarian households. Those families who had already repaid their loans received a cash payment in 2015 whereas others who were still paying a loan had the principal reduced by the corresponding amount. As a result the reductions in principal cut monthly loan payments amounted to 25–30% less on average. However, the estimated costs for banking sector amounted to EUR 2–3 billion (2.84% GDP).

4.1.4 Final Action in 2015

In 2015, Parliament adopted a new law that obliged all banks to convert foreign currency mortgage loans into HUF ones. A significant chunk of those currency loans was denominated in euro (approximately 85% of all mortgage loans denominated in a foreign currency at the time). The amount of foreign currency loans at that point had declined but was still worth approximately 3.6 trillion HUF which was equal to 10% of Hungarian GDP. As a result, the National Bank of Hungary made available to the financial institutions the necessary amount of foreign currency and the forex rates were set according to market exchange rates. In fact, the central bank had allocated EUR 9 billion (of available 36) foreign exchange reserves for this purpose emphasizing no effect on the stability of its central bank reserves.

4.2 *Case of Croatia*

Since 2000, because of dynamic economic growth, savings accumulated in deposits in Croatian banks, both in domestic and foreign currency, have started to increase. Due to the inflow of foreign investment capital, these deposits began to dominate in the structure of banks' portfolios over deposits denominated in *kunas* (HRK). Foreign currency loans in Croatia since 2000 were mostly linked to the euro. The Swiss franc became popular after 2000 as a cheaper alternative to loans in euros or HRK. In late 2014, loans in CHF accounted for 16% of total loans to the household sector and were mostly related to housing (Fig. 6).

4.2.1 Action in 2013

An in-depth analysis of CHF loans by policy stakeholders began when the Swiss franc started to appreciate in 2009 (Fig. 7). The value of loans increased from HRK 23.7 billion to approx. HRK 27 billion, or EUR 3.5 billion, i.e. slightly below 8% of Croatian GDP. Some borrowers with CHF liabilities started to have problems with repayments within the prescribed period. In effect, the Minister of Finance proposed amendments to the law on granting loans (law on crediting), which were accepted by

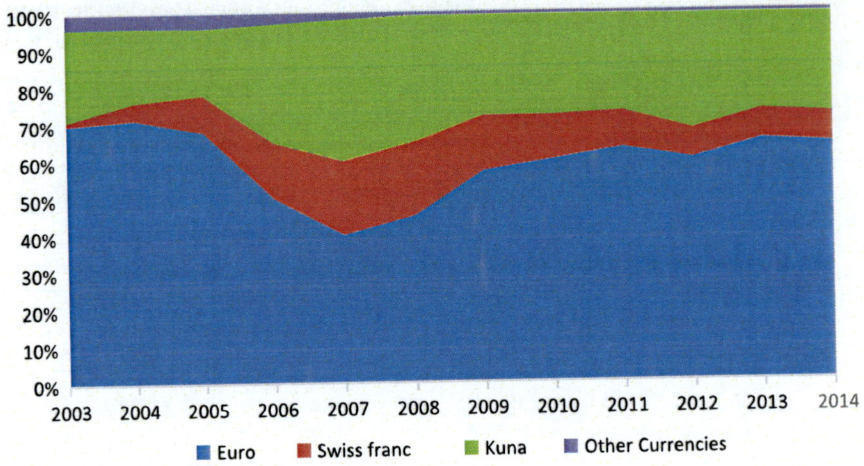

Fig. 6 Currency structure of total net loans in Croatia in 2003–2014. Source: Own elaboration based on CNB (2015)

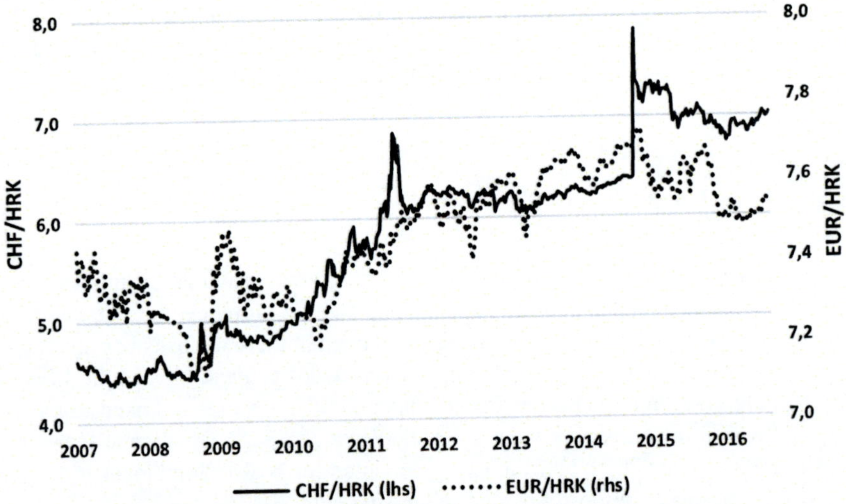

Fig. 7 Exchange rate of CHF and EUR against HRK in years of 2007–2016. Source: ex.com

the Parliament in 2013. The introduced changes required banks to tighten the interest rate in the case of loans granted in CHF, and in extreme cases even to a refund.

4.2.2 Final Action in 2015

When the Swiss National Bank abandoned the CHF/EUR floor on January 15, 2015, the Croatian Parliament temporarily froze the exchange rate for repayments of Swiss franc household loans, but the scope was quickly broadened to cover individual entrepreneurs. The intention was to find a compromise between debtors and banks during the one-year freeze, but it was not achieved. At the end of March 2015, CHF loans represented around 23 billion (EUR 3 billion) or 9% of total banks' loan portfolios in Croatia. Most of these loans (95%) were taken by households out of which 18.6% of total loans belong to households and 35.6% of total housing loans were denominated in CHF.

In September 2015, the Parliament adopted legislation requiring banks to offer their clients to retroactively convert their clients' CHF to EUR (past principal and interest payments on Swiss franc loans were recomputed as if borrowers had been indebted in variable rate euro loans). The cost to banks has been estimated at about 2% of GDP. They have on average remained profitable, even during the prolonged recession, but the conversion resulted in a loss in 2015. Although sizable, this was manageable from a financial stability perspective due to the high bank capitalization. Households with CHF loans reduced their debt and substantial uncertainty was removed. Currency risk, however, has been substituted by interest risk. Following the decision, the National Bank of Croatia intervened in the FX market and provided domestic liquidity with a view to prevent excess volatility. The government was also facing a revenue loss, as banks can deduct these losses from future profits. Moreover, the decision has been challenged in the Constitutional Court and some banks are contemplating filing complaints at the International Centre for Settlement of Investment Disputes.

4.3 *Case of Poland*

The first loans denominated in foreign currencies were available in Poland as early as in the 1990s. However, they started only to gain popularity in 2000 and shortly became to dominate the Polish mortgage loans' market (Fig. 8).

Formally, the possibility of granting loans denominated in foreign currencies was introduced in 2001. In subsequent years, mortgage loans, in particular in Swiss francs, became very popular due to the low interest rates.

4.3.1 Action in 2006

The expansion of foreign currency loans drew some attention of stakeholders in Poland. The first reaction was through an action of Polish Financial Supervisory Authority (the 'PFSA')—a governmental agency exercising supervision over Polish financial market. In 2006, the PFSA issued the so-called Recommendation S—a soft law instrument duly observed by the market within which it was emphasized that "*(...) the bank, when granting loans in foreign currencies, analyzes the creditworthiness of the client assuming that the interest rate for a foreign currency loan is equal to at least the interest rate for a loan in Polish zlotys and the loan capital is*

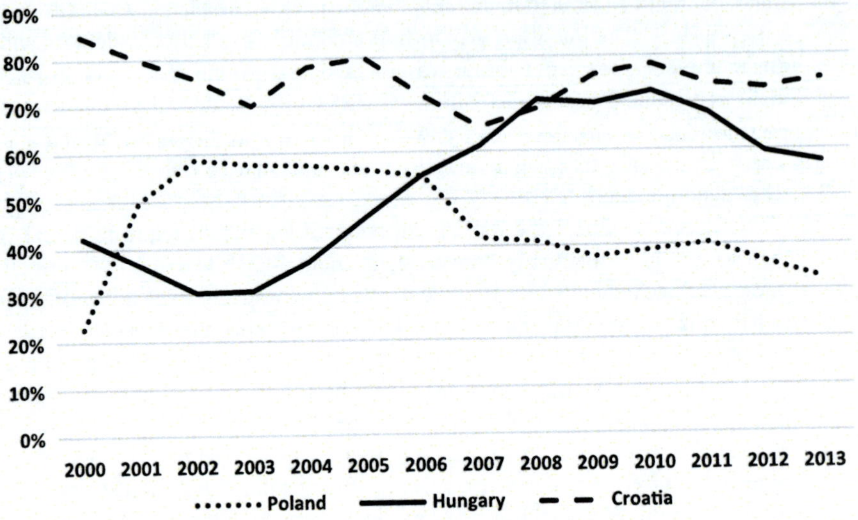

Fig. 8 Share of foreign currency loans in total private sector loans in years 2000–2013. Source: Łaszek (2013)

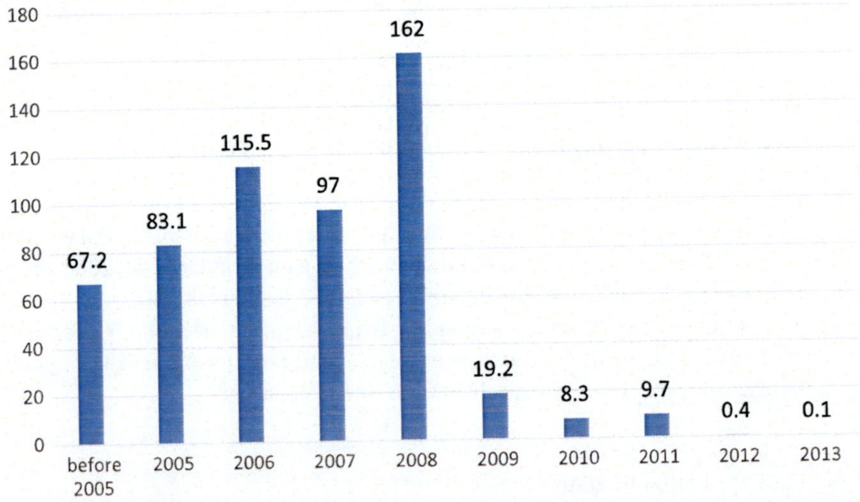

Fig. 9 Number of newly granted mortgage loans in CHF in Poland. Source: Own elaboration based on KNF (2015)

20 percent". Nevertheless, the expansion of foreign-denominated loans were not slowed down as a result. In fact, 162,000 mortgage loans in CHF were further granted in 2008 with their share estimated to be 69% in the total number of newly granted mortgage loans in Poland (Fig. 9).

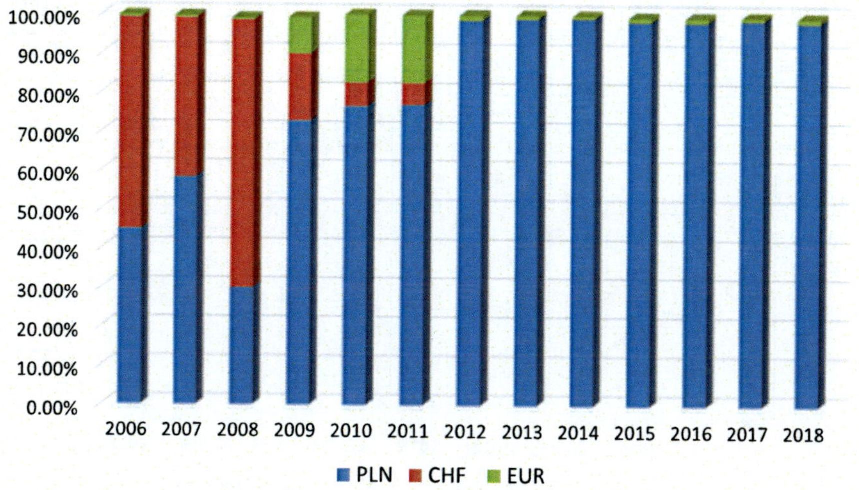

Fig. 10 The currency structure of the value of newly granted mortgage loans in Polandi in years 2006–2018. Source: Quarterly reports of Polish Bankers' Association, 2006–2018

One of the consequences of the global financial crises which started in September 2008 was the strong weakening of Polish zloty. In effect, some banks in Poland stopped providing mortgage loans in CHF while others used a prohibitive margin, demanded a very high own contribution or above-average earnings from potential clients. The number of CHF mortgage loans decreased significantly, but they were shortly replaced by euro ones (Fig. 10).

4.3.2 Actions in 2008

In December 2008, the PFSA introduced the Recommendation S II, which supplemented its previous version from 2006. This time its main goal was to limit the banks' ability to impose the rules on interest rates on foreign currency loans. In more detail, banks were obliged to inform clients in writing about currency risk, interest rate risk as well as the impact of currency spread on loan repayment fee schemes. In the beginning of 2010, the PFSA implemented the Recommendation T, whose main objective was to strengthen the loan risk management. Measures recommended to be taken by Polish banks were several.[15]

[15]For instance, determination of the maximum level of debt service costs (depending on the net income of the applicants, it was 50% or 65% respectively); the assessment of the creditworthiness of loans with a variable interest rate the possibility of changing it (estimation individually, based on the analysis of the volatility of market rates); constant monitoring of the level of loan exposure protection by calculating the loan to value level (LtV); using the available databases to make a reliable assessment of creditworthiness; adequate management of retail indices by introducing internal risk-limiting limits, adequate valuation of collateral and stress tests.

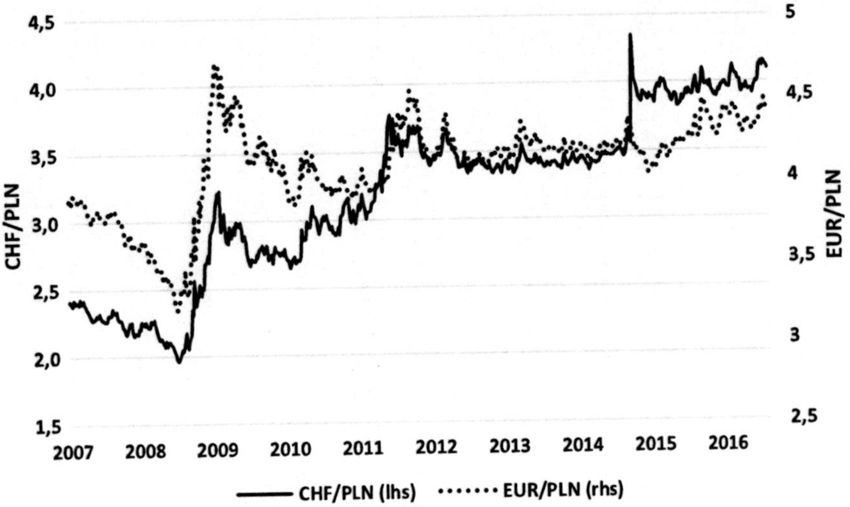

Fig. 11 The exchange rate of CHF and EUR against PLN in years 2007–2016. Source: NBP

In the meantime the Swiss franc grew stronger, which prompted the Swiss National Bank (SNB) to counteract it. In September 2011, a decision was taken to partially tighten the euro exchange rate for the Swiss franc and to maintain the ratio of 1.20 CHF to EUR. Such a corridor was to be maintained at all costs. Nevertheless, on January 15, 2015, the SNB announced to abandon it worsening within seconds the position of Polish consumers who borrowed in CHF (Fig. 11).

4.3.3 Action in 2011

At last, in the beginning of 2011 the PFSA adopted Recommendation S III which introduced the rule that the borrower will not be able to allocate more than 42% of its net income to service his/her loan. Regardless of the loan tenor, a 25-year time period has been adopted for the purposes of assessing creditworthiness for all mortgage loans. In fact, obtaining a loan in a foreign currency turned out to be almost impossible in Poland. But it was not until June 2013 when the PFSA finally barred to grant the foreign currency loans through its final amendment to the Recommendation S which has introduced the rule "*in what currency you earn, in which you will get a mortgage*". In August 2011, the act amending the Polish banking law was adopted. The so-called the anti-spread law stipulated that the borrower in debt in a foreign currency would be able to repay loan installments with the currency purchased individually (in general banks imposed an obligation to purchase the currency through their own channels adding financial burden on the client as the purchase cost was above the market threshold). Moreover, banks have lost the opportunity to request additional fees or commissions for annexes to the loan contracts. The banks were also obliged to insert provisions regarding some detailed rules for determining the methods and dates of setting exchange rates in existing and new loan contracts.

4.3.4 Ultimate Solution?

In 2015, Law on the support of borrowers in financial distress, who took out a housing loan, came into force. The main goal of the act was the introduction of the Borrowers' Support Fund. The Fund's resources came from banks' contributions which were proportional to the size of their portfolio of mortgage loans whose delay in repayment of capital or interest exceeds 90 days, reimbursement of such support and income from investing the Fund's resources. The Fund started to operate in February 2016. Its main task is to help the borrowers, who are in a difficult situation, in the physical repayment of housing loans. Currently, a draft amendment to the act awaits Parliament's approval. Generally speaking it assumes the division of the Borrowers Support Fund into the Supporting Fund and the Restructuring Fund. The former is to be for all borrowers in a difficult financial situation whereas the latter for the process of supporting voluntary and restructuring of the portfolio of housing loans denominated or indexed to currencies other than those in which borrowers earn income. The mechanism of the Supporting Fund will be analogous to the currently in force. The resources of the Supporting Fund will come from: banks' contributions, returns of support or loans for repayment of debt, income from Fund's investments, other paid-in resources. It is worth to mention that the draft amendment has been heavily criticized by the banking sector prompting to the allegations that EU law may be broken in result.

5 The Restructuring of Foreign Currency Loans: An Attempt of the Evaluation

One of the reasons why governments often contemplate debt restructuring are social problems, which arise when households' debts rise. Taking into account lessons learned from the past episodes of households' debt restructuring, it appears that some consensus has emerged in the literature on the key principles that are necessary to ensure that the benefits of the government involvement in debt restructuring outweigh the cost.[16] From the economic perspective, an important argument for the government to get involved into renegotiation of the private debt contracts between households and banks or create framework that eases this process is when the

[16]The comprehensive discussion about the key conditions that have to be met in order to achieve successful debt households' restructuring is laid out for example in Laeven and Lareya (2009) or Baudinio and Yun (2017).

households' indebtedness reaches levels that impede overall macroeconomic performance. The key challenge in design of the households' debt restructuring package is the way how the cost of resolution of distressed loans would be shared among the key shareholders. The successful government intervention that involves covering some burdens by the taxpayers' money should be designed after taking into account the degree of fiscal space available and its potential negative impact on public debt sustainability (Laeven and Lareya 2009).[17] Liu and Rosenberg (2013) point out that the most important elements of the successful government intervention that can help the benefits outweigh the cost are as follows:

- **Appropriate burden sharing**: The scheme should distribute the cost of restructuring between borrowers and lenders while taking into account their respective loss-absorption capacity. This also applies to any share of the cost to be assumed by the government, which should be strictly determined by the available fiscal space.
- **Targeting:** For equity reasons and to avoid moral hazard, the scheme should be time-bound, selective and provide debt relief only to those borrowers whose ability to service their debt is likely to be restored after restructuring.
- **Collaborative approach**:[18] Participation in any government-coordinated scheme should ideally be voluntary. At a minimum, all stakeholders need to be involved in its design. Schemes that retroactively revise existing private contracts need to be avoided as they undermine the rule of law and hurt the investment climate.
- **Managing expectations**: Simply talking about government-sanctioned bailouts may undermine credit discipline. Equally, it may contribute to irresponsible lending behavior. This calls for clear communication, including a firm commitment to abstain from taking further measures once a support scheme has been put in place.

5.1 Hungary

Burden sharing:

- **Ban on unilateral increase of the interest rate:** Mortgage credit contracts allowed banks in Hungary for unilateral adjustment of the interest rates. In effect, prior to the global financial crisis banks often increased the interest rates by even 2–3 percentage points. In 2009 and then in 2010 the implemented regulations limited their ability to raise interest rates on foreign currency denominated household's loans. However, these regulations have not been strict enough and banks often managed to question them and ultimately opted out due to special reasons. The banks' ability to unilateral adjustment of the interest rate on

[17] Laeven and Lareya (2009).

[18] Liu and Rosenberg (2013).

mortgage loans has been finally banned in Home Protection Act, but it applied only to newly granted mortgage loans.

- **Reimbursement of the fees and surcharges**: In 2014 a new law required banks to reimburse borrowers for all fees and surcharges levied during the lending period that were deemed to be unfair. It applied to the households that still had foreign currency denominated loans as well as to those that have already paid all installments. As a result the reductions in principal cut monthly loan payments amounted to 25–30% less on average. However, the estimated costs for banking sector amounted to EUR 2–3 billion (2.8% GDP).
- **Early repayment scheme:** In 2011 debtors were allowed to repay their mortgage burden at the foreign currency rate more favorable than the current market rate. The difference between the actual and the preferential loan payment was shared between the state, the debtor and the banking sector. The debtors who decided to leverage this preferential program (approx. 40% of all debtors) had to repay the principal part of the differential, but what is of great importance the payment was scheduled to start after 2017 (i.e. after 6 years). The scheme implied a debt relief of approx. 20–30% of the total loan burden. As banks were not obliged to offer forint-denominated loans for debtors interested in early repayment of their foreign-currency mortgage loans, the scheme was attractive mainly for the relatively wealthy households that were able to use their private savings for the early repayment (MNB 2012). The burden of interest part payment of the mortgage loan was shared between the state and the banking sector. In effect, banking sector faced a loss of more than HUF 300 billion.
- **Assisting defaulting mortgage debtors:** government established special state agency (NET) that aimed at offering a solution to some of the non-performing debtors in order to help them avoid eviction. According to the regulations, NET was allowed to offer help to only socially disadvantaged debtors. It purchased the real property collateral behind non-performing loans and allows the former debtor to remain in the property as a tenant.
- The ultimate obligatory conversion of the foreign currency debt introduced in 2014 caused substantial losses in the banking sector.

Targeting:

- Although early repayment scheme introduced in Hungary in 2011 aimed at reducing households' exposure to the foreign currency risk, it focused almost entirely on relatively wealthy households that were able to use their private savings for the early repayment of the debt on favorable terms. On the contrary, poorer households without adequate savings and that lack the ability to take a new loan in domestic currency could not take advantage of this program.
- Taking into account the experiences from the early repayment scheme, the authorities established NET that offered support to some of the non-performing debtors in order to help them avoid eviction.
- The ultimate obligatory conversion of the foreign currency debt introduced in 2014 applied to all debtors irrespective of their financial situation.

Collaborative Approach The Government and the Hungarian Banking Association reached an agreement on a number of measures to support lending and address distressed private sector debt.

5.2 *Poland*

Burden sharing:

- **The anti-spread law**: from 2011 on borrowers who have debt in a foreign currency are able to repay loan installments with the currency purchased individually. Previously banks in general imposed an obligation to purchase the currency through their own channels adding financial burden on the client as the purchase cost was above the market threshold.
- **Borrowers' Support Fund**: in 2015 special fund was established to support the borrowers, who are in a difficult financial situation, in the physical repayment of housing loans. The Fund's resources came from banks' contributions which were proportional to the size of their portfolio of mortgage loans whose delay in repayment of capital or interest exceeds 90 days (as well as from the reimbursement of the support and income from investing the Fund's assets). The debtors in distressed financial situation can apply for temporary help in servicing debt repayments, but the support should be then reimbursed in instalments spread over a certain period of time.

Targeting:

- Compared to the other countries analyzed here, the debt relief measures implemented in Poland were limited. The burden for the banking sector involved the obligatory contribution to the Borrowers' Support Fund. Banks were also forced to resign from the revenues they obtained from selling foreign currency to their debtors at less favorable terms than the market rate.
- The Borrowers' support fund was created to help households in distressed financial situation, but this support has to be paid back and thus it did not gain much popularity and was seldom used.

Collaborative approach:

- All measures aimed at easing foreign currency debt prepared by the authorities have been consulted with the banking sectors. Although it is difficult to provide a formal assessment it seems that the association of the banks in Poland played an important role in blocking the introduction of legislation that shifted most of the burden of restructuring foreign denominated loans to banks.

Table 1 The general assessment of the realized or proposed measures aimed at foreign currency debt relief in Hungary, Poland and Croatia

	Targeting	Appropriate burden sharing	Collaborative approach	Managing expectations
Hungary	Yes	No	Yes	Yes
Poland	Yes	Yes	?	Yes
Croatia	Yes	No	No	Yes

5.3 Croatia

- **Burden sharing:** In 2015 banks were forced to retroactively convert their clients' debt denominated in CHF to EUR. It is estimated that it caused a loss of banks of about 2% of GDP.
- **Targeting**: The obligatory loan conversion from CHF to EUR was applied to all banks' clients.
- **Collaborative approach:** The conversion of swiss franc denominated loans into EUR was voluntary for debtors (households) and obligatory for banks (lenders).

Important factor influencing the success of restructuring is close coordination with key market players, who may help to identify a size of necessary public intervention. The process of debt restructuring should not be introduced before macroeconomic policies have stabilized the economy and a bank recapitalization program has been put in place to restore the banking sector to health. It can mean introducing mechanism such as recapitalizations and government purchases of distressed loans. Looking back to previous financial crises, we can conclude that the policymakers should aim to maximize recovery rates and minimize the time and cost involved with debt restructuring. Any private debt restructuring strategy should be embedded in broader financial sector reform. Especially, it should aim at strengthening financial regulations on credit supply that would minimize the risk of a surge of non-performing loans in the future, like e.g. strict limits of the amount of loan to the households' income (LTI) and/or to the value of real property that the credit is going to finance. The experiences of CEE countries indicate also currency mismatch between households' revenue and loans is of great importance (Table 1).

6 Conclusion

Taking into account three selected CEE countries which have struggled with foreign currency loans in the last decade we could draw the following conclusions. The shape of the intervention depended on the effectiveness of activities reducing the creation of credit in currencies before the crisis of 2008. The better macroprudential supervision, the smaller the need for intervention after the crisis, because the smaller scale of the problem. It is worth noting that Poland, albeit gradually, tightened the regulatory grip over foreign currency loans relatively in the begging of their nascence.

Interventions were affected by the situation in which the financial sector and macroeconomic stability were located: Hungary is the most extreme case with the high share of non-performing loans and the substantial currency mismatch between deposits and credits in the banking sector. It is interesting to mention that they completely solved CHF denominated loans before the Swiss National Bank abandoned its limit of 1.2 EUR/CHF in January 2015. However, the impact of conversion of foreign currency loans into liabilities expressed in domestic currency on prospects of economic growth are not unequivocal. Levying the foreign currency conversion costs mainly on the banking sector's shoulders was conducive to an increase in consumer demand and VAT receipts, although it evidently had a negative impact on the condition of the banking sector. At the same time, however, it was a one-time shock, and uncertainty about the quality of the loan portfolio of banks in the event of further depreciation of the domestic currency systematically restrained domestic demand of households. Due to recent occurrence of foreign currency phenomena in three selected CEE countries it is still to be seen the results of different regulatory paths taken by Hungary, Croatia and Poland.

References

Akos E (2015) International Monetary Fund and Hungary (available at https://eurodad.org/files/pdf/5645ece64e8a3.pdf)

Baudino P, Yun H (2017) Resolution of non-performing loans – policy options, Bank for International Settlements, Financial Stability Institute, FSI Insights No. 3

Beckmann E, Roitner A, Stix H (2015) A local or a foreign currency loan? Evidence on the role of loan characteristics, preferences of households and the effect of foreign banks. Focus on European Economic Integration, Oesterreichische Nationalbank (Austrian Central Bank), (1), pp 24–48

Brown G, De Haas R (2012) Foreign banks and foreign currency lending in emerging Europe. Econ Policy 27(69):57–98

Brown G, Kirschenmann K, Ongena S (2011) Foreign currency loans – demand or supply driven?. Working Paper No. 2011-2. Swiss National Bank

Brzoza-Brzezina M, Kolasa G, Makarski K (2017) Monetary and macruprudential policy with foreign currency loan. Grape Working Paper No. 19, 2017

Buszko M, Krupa D (2015) Foreign currency loans in Poland and Hungary – a comparative analysis. Proc Econ Financ 30:124–136

Calabresi G (1970) The costs of accident: a legal and economic analysis. Yale University Press, New Haven

Carbonara E, Guerra A, Parisi F (2016) Sharing residual liability: the cheapest cost avoider revisited. J Legal Stud 45(1):173–201

Corrales J Imam PA (2019) Financial dollarizaton of households and firms: does it differ? IMF Working Paper No. 19/19

Croatian National Bank (2015) Some facts about loans in Swiss francs and some options for government intervention

Dalgic H (2018) Financial dollarization in emerging markets: an insurance arrangement. University of Mannheim

Dari-Mattiacci G, Garoupa N (2009) Least-cost avoidance: the tragedy of common safety. J Law Econ Organ 25(1):235–261

Drazen A (2000) Political economy in macroeconomics. Princeton University Press, Princeton

Dübel H-J, Walley S (2010) Regulation of foreign currency mortgage loans: the case of transition countries in Central and Eastern Europe. Finpolconsult-World Bank

Galac T, Kraft E (2010) Monetary and financial policies for "de-euroization" - a case study of recent Croatian experience. Croatian National Bank, p 2011

Gilles S (1992) Strict liability, and the cheapest cost-avoider. Virginia Law Rev 78(6):1291–1375

Gordon R (2000) Law and macroeconomics. In: Boudewijn B, De Geest G (eds) Encyclopedia of law and economics, vol I. The history and methodology of law and economics. Edward Elgar, Cheltenham, pp 660–693

Kolasa M (2016) Equilibrium foreign currency mortgages. SGH

Komisja Nadzoru Finansowego (Polish Financial Supervisory Authority – KNF 2015) Wpływ silnego osłabienia PLN względem CHF na stabilność polskiego sektora bankowego oraz sytuację finansową kredytobiorców, March 2015

Krekó J, Endrész M (2010) The role of foreign currency lending in the impact of the exchange rate on the real economy. MNB Bulleting 5:29–38

Laeven L, Lareya T (2009) Principles of household debt restructuring. IMF

Łaszek J (2013) Rozwój i finansowanie sektora nieruchomości w Polsce. Bezpieczny Bank 4 (53):19–51

Liu Y, Rosenberg CB (2013) Dealing with private debt distress in the wake of the European financial crisis. IMF

Novák Z, Vámos I (2017) Conversion of Foreign Currency Loans in the CEECs. In: Proceedings of the ENTRENOVA – EnTerprise Research InNOVAtion Conference, Dubrovnik, Croatia, 7-9 September 2017, IRENET – Society for Advancing Innovation and Research in Economy, Zagreb, pp 66–73

Olszewska G (2018) Foreign currency loans and stability of the banking system in Poland. Central Eur Rev Econ Financ 3:67–82

Pellényi G, Bilek P (2009) Foreign Currency Borrowing: The Case of Hungary, Working Paper / FINESS 5.4, DIW Berlin, German Institute for Economic Research

Rodrik D (1996) Understanding economic policy reform. J Econ Lit 34:9–41

Wośko Z (2013) Credit risk of fx loans in poland. Interest and fx rate dependence. University of Łódź

Yeşin P (2013) Foreign currency loans and systematic risk in Europe. Fed Reserve Bank St Louis Rev 95:219–236

Związek Banków Polskich (Polish Bankers' Association), Raporty kwartalne (2006–2018) (Quarterly reports 2006–2018)

Jarosław Bełdowski Warsaw. Associate Professor at the Warsaw School of Economics, Department of International Comparative Studies. 02-554 Warszawa, Al. Niepodległości 162, Poland, Tel. + 48 22 654 93 45; jaroslaw.beldowski@sgh.waw.pl. Fields of Interest: Law and Economics, New Institutional Economics, Labour and Product Market Regulations.

Wiktor Wojciechowski Warsaw. Associate Professor at the Warsaw School of Economics, Department of International Comparative Studies. 02-554 Warszawa, Al. Niepodległości 162, Poland, Tel. + 48 22 654 93 45; wiktor.wojciechowski@sgh.waw.pl. Fields of Interest: Institutional Economics, Labour and Product Market Regulations, Fiscal Policy.

In Search of the Theory of Harm in EU Consumer Law: Lessons from the Consumer Fitness Check

Fabrizio Esposito and Anne-Lise Sibony

Abstract Recently, EU Consumer law has undergone a 'Fitness Check' (or REFIT). We thought that checking the fitness for purpose of a body of law would involve revisiting its purpose. This is why we expected to find in the rich REFIT documentation (over 4000 pages of studies and Commission documents) an explicit discourse on the goals of consumer law. Our aim was to connect this discourse to two lines of scholarship: a doctrinal line pointing out that EU consumer law lacks a clear direction and that, to the extent it does have one, it is too strongly geared towards market integration to the detriment of protection of the weakest, and an economically informed approach seeking to formulate a theory of harm that could underpin the enforcement of consumer law, by analogy with the practice in competition law. We agree that a clearer direction and a stronger conceptualisation of what harms the law seeks to protect consumers against would improve EU consumer law. This paper defines a 'theory of harm', illustrates what a theory of harm for consumer law could look like and analyses the REFIT documentation in search for elements of such a theory. Our findings are largely disappointing. We looked for something that is not there. The REFIT's *tour de force* is to check fitness for purpose without discussing purpose. It does so by adopting a circular approach and defining consumer harm as instances of under-enforcement of the law. This presupposes that all possible harms are already accounted for in the law and only occur when the law is not properly enforced. We uncover an irony instead of a theory of harm. What the REFIT does delineate is a normative space in which to develop a theory of harm for the future. It consists of a virtuous triangle of empowerment, trust and a well-functioning internal market. The REFIT also suggests that an economic-based theory of harm would need to interact with several legal elements. Consumer weakness, empowerment and legitimate expectations constitute ingredients for an economically grounded, behaviourally sensible and legally workable theory of harm.

F. Esposito · A.-L. Sibony (✉)
Faculty of Law, University of Louvain, Louvain-La-Neuve, Belgium
e-mail: fabrizio.esposito@eui.eu; anne-lise.sibony@uclouvain.be

K. Mathis, A. Tor (eds.), *Consumer Law and Economics*, Economic Analysis of Law in European Legal Scholarship 9, https://doi.org/10.1007/978-3-030-49028-7_12

1 Introduction

The EU Internal Market constitutes the largest consumer economy in the world. A 'high level of consumer protection' is a defining feature of this market[1] and the EU has positioned itself internationally as a leading actor when it comes to consumer rights. These circumstances alone would make the European theory of harm in consumer law worthy of attention. In addition, EU consumer law just underwent a 'fitness check' and is being 'modernised', so that it is also timely to consider the fundamental orientation of consumer protection rules in Europe.[2]

As is often the case, legislation does not contain a clear expression of goals or of a theory of harm. It is, of course, possible to ascertain on the basis of existing legal texts what each piece of legislation seeks to protect consumers against (e.g. the unfair contract terms directive seeks to protect consumers against unfair terms), but these piecemeal indications do not amount to a comprehensive view of how market transactions can harm consumers or to what extent the various types of harms consumers suffer are legally relevant. While consumer law scholars have made the point that EU consumer lacks a clear direction,[3] their worry has not yet prompted a conversation on what 'theory of harm' animates or could animate consumer law. Indeed, the phrase 'theory of harm' itself is not familiar to consumer lawyers.[4]

In this chapter, we start from the premise that it would be desirable to equip EU consumer law with a more robust normative and theoretical framework. It would be helpful from at least four points of view. First, from a normative perspective, having a more explicit doctrine of which types of harm the law seeks to prevent would help guide future revisions of legislation, including adaptations to developing online realities. Second, regarding precisely online practices which harm consumers, it would help determine which ones should be tackled with the tools of consumer law and which with other instruments, such as rules on data protection or competition law, as well as clarify how these various sets of rules interact. Third, conceptualising harm is the first step for measuring it and this could help enforcement authorities define their priorities.[5] Finally, an effort to articulate a theory of

[1]Art. 38 Charter of Fundamental Rights of the European Union. See also Art. 169 TFEU and Art 12 TFEU.

[2]At the time of writing, of the two legislative proposals making up the 'New Deal for consumers', it is very likely that one will be adopted: the European Parliament and European Council have reached an agreement on the Proposal for a 'Modernisation directive' (European Commission 2018b). The fate of the companion proposal for a Directive on representative actions for the protection of the collective interests of consumers, (European Commission 2018a) is more uncertain (legislative procedure 2018/0089/COD).

[3]Howells et al. (2018) p. 2; Twigg-Flessner (2007).

[4]The first and notable contribution on this theme is Siciliani et al. (2019) (hereafter 'Consumer Theories of Harm').

[5]It was initially to help the Office of Fair Trading (UK) prioritise enforcement that Siciliani developed the models presented in Consumer Theories of Harm (supra note 4).

harm could open a new dialogue between legal scholars and social scientists—economists and behavioural scientists—in the field of consumer policy.

In our search, we take inspiration from competition law, where the phrase 'theory of harm' is common. At the most general level, it refers to an explanation of why and how a given practice unlawfully harms consumers. With minor adjustments, it offers a useful organizing framework for our enquiry. This framework centres around two questions: (1) What counts as unlawful consumer harm under EU consumer law? (2) When and how can such harm be expected to happen? This chapter searches for answers in the recent fitness check on consumer and marketing law. The motivation for searching for a theory of harm in this particular corpus are linked to the very nature of a fitness check, or 'REFIT' as it is known in the EU jargon.

A REFIT is a retrospective evaluation of a body of legislation. REFITs can be conducted about any set of EU rules and many have been since the early 2000s, when the Better Regulation Agenda of the Commission was first rolled out.[6] In 2016–2017, came the turn of EU consumer law. The exercise aimed to assess whether existing consumer directives were still fit for purpose. As any REFIT, it proceeds from a commitment to gather the 'best available evidence' and to analyse existing law in light of five criteria: effectiveness, efficiency, coherence, relevance, and EU added value.[7] The very mission of a REFIT makes the consumer fitness check particularly relevant to anyone interested in a theory of harm: it seems self-evident that consumer law is only fit for purpose if it adequately protects consumers against those harms that the law sought to avert in the first place. For this reason, we expected to find an elaboration of consumer harm in the REFIT. This expectation was bolstered by the fact that the first two criteria against which the legislation must be assessed are effectiveness and efficiency. Since both these notions express a property of a means-ends relationship, it seemed logical that the REFIT would contain an explicit discourse on ends.

From a Law & Economics perspective, the strong empirical commitment and the explicit identification of efficiency as one of the assessment criteria make the Consumer REFIT an interesting institutional activity. As we explain in more detail below, in competition law, the explicit elaboration on theories of harm formed an integral part of the modernization of enforcement at EU level. The effort to become more transparent as to what counts as legally relevant harm for the purpose of competition law enforcement played an important role in claiming that EU competition law was 'fit for purpose', although this language was not used at the time. In

[6]Communication for the Commission, European Commission (2002). It is difficult to know exactly how many REFITs have been conducted even after the publication in April 2019 of the results of a stock-taking exercise on the Better Regulation Agenda: European Commission (2019a) and accompanying Staff Working Document European commission (2019b). The Commission reports having conducted 'more than 150 REFIT initiatives' in the first 3 years of the Juncker Commission ('initiative' is not defined and seems to be co-extensive with the 150 measures to simplify Union legislation presented during the same period). Cost estimates suggest that 60 to 70 fitness checks are conducted every year, European Commission (2019b).

[7]European Commission (2015b), p. 53; European Commission (2017e), p. 52.

this sense, the 'more economic approach' in competition law may be seen a forerunner of what has since become known as 'evidence-based policy-making'.[8] It can therefore serve as a useful term of comparison in the search for a theory of harm in the Consumer REFIT.

While the comparison with competition law is helpful, we must be wary of not overlooking the differences between the two policy areas. First of all, economic analysis informs EU consumer law significantly less than it does EU competition law (this is true both of the law itself and the corresponding legal scholarship). This is due in part to distinct traditions: consumer law initially grew from national private law, which, in Europe, has not been strongly influenced by economics. The European efforts to harmonise consumer law since the mid 1970s have not changed this relative disconnect between law and economics in the field of consumer protection. Competition law, for its part, emerged as a distinct body of EU rules (even if it had roots in some national traditions)[9] with a distinct identity. It is made up primarily of open textured rules (articles 101 and 102 TFEU), which give the Court ample leeway for interpretation. From the early days, the Court infused the interpretation of these rules with economics (of the time).[10] Later on, when the Commission turned to a more economic approach, the Court increasingly had to respond to economic arguments. Because the Court adjudicates competition law cases (and does not merely respond to requests for interpretation of EU law from national courts by way of preliminary rulings), the growing sophistication of economic argumentation of the Commission and defendants led the Court to a deeper engagement with economics.[11]

By contrast, EU consumer law consists of a large body of directives which have been transposed into national law, sometimes with important variations. For example, a given conduct in a given market context may be considered harmful to consumers in one Member State and not harmful in another.[12] Consumer law is not directly enforced by the Commission but only by the relevant national authorities (which may or may not be the same as those enforcing competition law). This implies that the Court almost exclusively responds to requests for preliminary rulings from national courts, *i.e.* interprets directives without adjudicating cases.[13]

[8] The 'more economic approach' in competition aimed to inform individual decisions rather than new rules, but it nonetheless has a policy component as evidenced in the Communication from the Commission—European Commission (2009).

[9] Gerber (2001).

[10] See e.g. Judgment of the Court of 18 May 1962, C-13/60, Ruhrkohlen-Verkaufsgesellschaft mbH and others v. High Authority of the European Coal and Steel Community, EU:C:1962:15. See also Rueff (1965), p. 13.

[11] Sibony (2008), part II, esp. p. 714.

[12] For example, assessing whether a contract term is unfair requires a comparison between the term and the default rule which would apply under national law in the absence of such term. See e.g. Howells et al. (2018), pp. 141 sq.

[13] The Court can also be called to rule on infringement proceedings, when a Member States does not enforce EU directive properly (in which case the Court also does not adjudicate a case relating to a

Therefore, none of the factors that led to a deeper engagement of the Court with economics in competition law are present in the context of consumer law. Regarding consumer harm in particular, the case-law does shed some light on what constitutes consumer harm, but the Court has never felt the need to turn to economics. In this sense, the current state of consumer law is comparable to that of competition law before the 'more economic approach' offered an economics-based rationalisation and recalibration, but without the same impetus from the Commission towards a greater use of economics.

Against this background, it is fair to recognise that our search for a theory of harm is not prompted by calls from consumer law practitioners. Instead, by choosing to engage with this topic based on an analysis of the Consumer REFIT, we seek to contribute to the conversation prompted by Howells et al., who rightly point to a need to restate the goals of consumer law. In addition, we take the REFIT as a testing ground to assess the prospects of a greater opening of consumer law to economics and behavioural sciences. In order to extract what the Consumer REFIT brings to a theory of harm, Sect. 2 defines what a theory of harm means for EU consumer law, Sect. 3 presents what we found in the 4000 pages of documentation making up the Consumer REFIT that is susceptible to shed light on an underlying theory of harm. Section 4 seeks to make sense of the disappointing findings.

2 What Is a Theory of Harm in Consumer Law?

At the most general level, a 'theory of harm' may be defined as a set of general propositions describing when consumers suffer harm that calls for legal intervention. At present, EU consumer law is in need of a theory of harm (Sect. 2.1). While that theory may well be different from that of competition law, because the two sets of rules pursue different (if complementary) aims, it is nonetheless helpful to turn to competition law for guidance on the concept of theory of harm (Sect. 2.2). On this basis, a recent doctrinal proposal outlining a theory of harm for EU consumer law will be discussed (Sect. 2.3).

2.1 *Why EU Consumer Law Needs a Theory of Harm*

In their book *Rethinking EU Consumer law*, Howells, Twigg-Flessner and Wilhelmsson explain that EU consumer law lacks direction, which is precisely

consumer aggrieved by an alleged violation of consumer rights). In competition law, by contrast, the EU courts review the legality of Commission decisions applying competition provisions to the conduct of undertakings and thus adjudicate cases in the last instance.

why they call for a rethink.[14] Lacking direction is a less than enviable state at any time, but it represents a particular challenge when the legislature needs to assess whether and how existing law needs to be adapted to digital markets. Howells *et al.* recognise that there are reasons why the overarching goals pursued by the EU in this area are not spelt out. Member States sometimes have diverging views, especially when it comes to private law and, for this reason, ambiguity or silence is indispensable to achieve consensus on a directive.[15]

This said, a more explicit statement of the protective aim of EU consumer law would helpful for at least two reasons. First, it is in fact not obvious that consumer law always or only aims to *protect* consumers.[16] This counter-intuitive proposition has animated an EU debate: scholars have argued that, in the development of EU consumer law, the market building objective has taken precedence over protection of the weakest.[17] It is a fact that harmonising national consumer legislation in order to remove the obstacles that regulatory diversity creates for businesses has been at the forefront of the Commission's agenda.[18] In the process, critics argue, emphasis was laid on getting Member States to adopt rules that would enable businesses to roll out uniform marketing strategies throughout the internal market. As a result, the needs of vulnerable consumers were not at the centre of attention. Rather, the legislator focused on the active and competent consumers that are likely to shop around, fuel competition and market integration. They, not the vulnerable consumers most in need of protection, constitute the target constituency of EU consumer law, a development that some consumer law scholars regret.[19] In light of this critique, it would make eminent sense to clarify the measure in which consumer law aims, respectively, to facilitate market integration and to protect consumers—and which group of consumers. In this regard, it should be said that no one disputes—including not critics—that market integration brings benefits to consumers: the benefit of greater choice and lower prices thanks to competition. But, for authors who see consumer law as part of social policy, such benefits are markedly distinct from what they understand as protection of the weakest. Protection is not the right to more choice or greater availability of cheap goods. Rather, it comes from the recognition that some

[14]Cited n. 3.

[15]The Unfair Contractual Terms Directive (UCTD) (Council of the European Union 1993) is a case in point. Howells et al. (2018) 133 sq.

[16]Micklitz (2012), pp. 283–296.

[17]Micklitz (2012), Weatherill (2016), Howells et al. (2018) p. 2 arguing that EU consumer law is at risk of overstating the internal market goal and ought to be rebalanced towards protecting weak consumers).

[18]See, among many other illustrations, Unfair Terms Directive (Dir. 93/13/EC), recital 6; European Commission (2010), p. 2; Directive on certain aspects concerning contracts for the supply of digital content and digital services (2015/0288/COD), recital 1.

[19]Weatherill (2016). Weatherill does not regret *per se* that EU law has not developed a policy targeted at vulnerable consumers, but that, due to the choice of maximum harmonization, Member States have limited leeway to do so.

consumers are not in a position to benefit from the market unless the law affords specific protections.

The second reason why a clarification of the protective aims of EU consumer law is needed is linked to variations in space and time. Legal systems in which consumer law is embedded rest on different priors about what is generally good for consumers. For example, the law in one jurisdiction may reflect a preference for allowing consumers to benefit from low prices to the greatest possible extent (the 'Walmart model'),[20] be it at the expense of what is, in other legal systems, seen as cut-throat competition or inacceptable working conditions. Another legal system may emphasise consumer rights, such as the right of withdrawal or a right to an extended guarantee, be it at the expense of higher prices and less choice (the 'mandatory insurance' model).[21] In other words, what legal system considers at any point in time as the harm(s) to consumer which are to be avoided or reduced is a matter of normative choice. Making these choices explicit is a precondition for meaningful comparisons between EU consumer law and that of other jurisdictions. It also allows to take stock of evolutions which have taken place over time and helps ascertain whether criticism has been overstated or not.

Finally, there is a practical reason why a theory of harm is needed in EU consumer law. As fines for violations of consumer protection rules are set to rise to a maximum of 4% of worldwide turnover,[22] more attention will be paid to how infringement decisions are reasoned and justified. As economic stakes rise, it is likely that these decisions will be increasingly litigated. In this context, both enforcement authorities and courts will need clear guidance.

2.2 *What Is a 'Theory of Harm'? A Definition Inspired by Competition Law*

The definition of 'theory of harm' we offer here is derived from the meaning of the same phrase in EU competition law. In competition law, 'theory of harm' entered the vocabulary of enforcers in the wake of the 'more economic approach'. The Commission embraced this new approach in the 1990s in relation to the enforcement of article 101 TFEU and merger control and, in the mid-2000s, in relation to article 102 TFEU.[23] This turn meant embracing two key ideas: first, that the aim of competition law was to advance consumer welfare (rather than to guarantee equality

[20]Whitman (2007), p. 340.

[21]Howells et al. (2018), pp. 131, 164. On the different orientation of EU and US law on unfair contract terms, Sibony (2019).

[22]Subject to the proposal for a Modernisation directive being adopted, European Commission (2018b).

[23]On article 101: Lianos (2007); on merger control: Vesterdoft (2005); on article 102: Economic Advisory Group on Competition Policy (2005) and European Commission (2009) (cited n. 8).

of market access among competitors) and, second, that any decision to enforce competition law should state why the particular conduct of the undertaking (s) concerned was detrimental to consumers. As part of their duty to give reasons,[24] the Commission or a National Competition Authority (NCA) would now have to explain what 'theory of harm' justifies enforcement. The context of competition litigation allows to distinguish three layers of a theory of harm: (i) the general doctrine of harm, (ii) the accepted explanations of how harm happens and (iii) the case-specific scenarios of harm.

The first layer—the general doctrine of harm—is the received answer to the question: 'when are consumer harmed?'. It constitutes the normative component of the theory of harm and defines what is considered relevant consumer detriment in a legal regime (e.g., EU consumer law, US antitrust). It is a general and abstract description of the type(s) of consumer harm the law seeks to avert or reduce (e.g. high prices, restriction of choice). It expresses the protective aims of the law by spelling out which market outcomes will be considered injurious. In other words, formulating a general doctrine of harm means clarifying the normative benchmark against which firms' conduct will be appraised.

The second layer relates to the question 'what causes harm?'. This component of the theory of harm relates to causation. It is made up of the set of accepted explanations for how harm happens. In competition law, this layer has been developed on the basis of economic analysis. It comprises a typology of causal mechanisms that link certain market practices to consumer harm in certain contexts. The EAGCP report, which laid the ground for the Commission's communication on exclusionary abuses, offers a number of illustrations. Regarding predation, for example, it distinguishes between scenarios of predation based on reputation, on 'signal jamming' and those based on 'capital market imperfections'.[25] Other examples of accepted scenarios of harm include leveraging effect[26] or margin squeeze.[27] Such a typology of circumstances that are conducive to harm and causal mechanisms that produce harm in those circumstances constitutes a repertoire of sufficient explanations of why a given market practice can legitimately be banned or placed under close scrutiny. Competition authorities may use these standard explanations of how consumer harm typically happens as building blocks to structure an enforcement decision. It should be noted that this second layer of the theory of harm expresses the received wisdom and characterises the state of the art of enforcement in any given jurisdiction at any given point in time. Despite efforts to produce international convergence in fora such as OECD or ICN, differences remain alive.

[24]Art. 196, para. 2 TFEU (or similar provisions under national law).

[25]Report by the EAGCP (Economic Advisory Group on Competition Policy (2005)), cited above n. 23.

[26]E.g., Judgment of the Court of 15 February 2005, C-12/03 P, *Commission v. Tetra Laval*, EU:C:2005:87, para. 44.

[27]E.g. Judgment of the Court of 14 October 2010, C-280/08 P, *Deutsche Telekom v. Commission*, EU:C:2010:603, para. 163 (sq). As in *Tetra* (cited above n. 26), the case revolved around the exact circumstances in which the alleged scenario of harm is credible.

Such differences relate to beliefs rather than theory. For example, the difference between the US and EU approach to excessive pricing in case of firms with significant market power is explained by the Israeli competition authority as being based entirely on a disagreement over the comparative advantages of the competitive process and enforcement in policing price levels[28]—a disagreement similar to the one evoked above regarding relative levels of trust in markets and consumer protection.[29]

There is a third even more granular layer of theory of harm, namely the case-specific operationalisation of the (level 2) template explanation of harm. Consider the practice of margin squeezing. A margin squeeze is the imposition of a price of an intermediate good or service (e.g. fee charged to telecom operators to access the local loop owned by a dominant incumbent) that is high enough to have an exclusionary effect on an as efficient competitor in the downstream market in an economic context where the vertically integrated dominant firm also sets another price that constitutes a competitive constrains for other operators on the market. A case in point is *Deutsche Telekom*, where the incumbent telecom operator set the charge to access its network (a cost for new entrants) and the retail price for internet access (a competitive constraints for new entrants) at such levels that the difference between these two prices did not allow for profitable entry.[30] In a margin squeeze case, the Commission (or NCA) will have to explain why the facts do support a finding of margin squeeze.

In EU competition law, the turn to a more economic approach affected all three layers. First, it changed the general doctrine of harm by clarifying that harm to competitors was not what the law sought eliminate and that, rather, the focus was on consumer harm. Second, it shaped the repertoire of standard justifications for enforcement by developing considerably the template explanations for how certain market practices, in certain settings, are likely to cause such harm. Third, it made it easier for competition authorities to model the scenario of harm in a particular case after one of the accepted explanations (or a combination of more than one such template-explanations). Except in relation to restrictions by object, a finding of infringement could in principle only stand if each of these building blocks was fleshed out by case-specific evidence (e.g. an explanation of how margin squeeze works in *this* case).

This led to a clarification of the role of courts in relation to the various components of a theory of harm. The first layer is a matter of interpretation of the law, which is clearly within the remit of courts. The second layer is essentially left to the discretion of the Commission (and NCAs). It is not the job of courts to distil economic theory into a toolbox for enforcement (what we called a repertoire of accepted explanations for consumer harm). In addition, the doctrine of 'limited review of complex economic appraisals' applies and courts will not engage with

---

[28]Israeli Antitrust Authority (2014, 2017).

[29]Text at footnotes 20 and 21.

[30]Deutsche Telekom v. Commission, cited above n. 27.

the authority's choice of a particular anticompetitive scenario in any given case (e.g. the choice to frame the competition concern as a risk of margin squeeze).[31] But courts will conduct a full review of the internal coherence of the scenario of harm and of the case-specific evidence (e.g. are there any findings of facts that contradict the scenario the authority chose to advance? If so, are those findings adequately considered?).[32] In so doing, courts fulfil a mission that is not specific to any particular theory of harm but is the essence of judicial review in a system guaranteeing the rule of law.

As compared to competition law, consumer law has not reached a similar stage of elaboration when it comes to conceptualising harm or adopting a typology of conducts and market circumstances that lead to harm. This is why the discussion needs to centre on the first two layers. In this regard, a recent proposal articulates what could be a level 2 typology of scenarios of harm.

2.3 A Theory of Harm for Consumer Law? A Recent Proposal

In what is, to our knowledge, the first and only attempt to date, Siciliani, Riefa and Gamper propose a general theory of consumer harm. We summarize the results of their inquiry with the aim to illustrate what a theory of consumer harm can look like, to later use their work as term of comparison with what we find in the Consumer REFIT.

In relation to layer one—what is harmful to consumers—Siciliani, Riefa, and Gamper use a modified standard economic approach: consumer detriment is measured in terms of consumer surplus, but the authors add a filter, which consists in giving more significance to the harm to vulnerable consumers. Under this approach, consumer harm consists of a reduction in weighted consumer surplus. Consumer surplus is "a measure of the economic welfare that is gained from purchasing and consuming goods and services".[33] Such a standard carries two main risks, which the authors address properly: first, the risk of being reductionist and, second, the risk of being insensitive to the differences in ability to pay. Consumer surplus can be reductive when elements of what makes the exchange beneficial to consumers are not accounted for. The risk, however, comes mainly from an erroneous understanding of the concept of consumer surplus. This error consists in equating consumer surplus with legal doctrines that limit the legal significance of the damage to economic losses. From an economic perspective, anything influencing a consumer's willingness to pay also influences consumer surplus. The second risk, namely, the risk of distributive insensitivity exists within economic theory and is a well-known

[31] Judgment of the Court of 11 July 1985, C-42/84, *Remia v. Commission*, EU:C:1985:327, para 34.

[32] *Tetra* (cited above n. 26), para 39; Sibony (2007), pp. 747 sq; Castillo de la Torre and Gippini-Fournier (2017), 6.084.

[33] Siciliani et al. (2019), p. 80.

one. Willingness to pay is in part a function of ability to pay. This implies that richer people, having a higher ability to pay, also display a higher willingness to pay than poorer people. The concept of consumer surplus does not allow to take these issues into consideration easily. Siciliani, Riefa, and Gamper address this difficulty by noting that it is important to consider if a practice targets vulnerable consumers. This additional layer of analysis allows to go beyond a mere arithmetic sum of the surplus gained and lost by different groups of consumers, to give superior normative significance to the losses of the vulnerable ones—losses that are therefore more difficult to off-set with benefits to other consumers.

Moving to layer two—how consumers can be harmed—the authors elaborate an analytical framework which outlines four archetypical scenarios of harm.[34] They start by dividing consumers and traders in two categories. Consumers can be naïve or sophisticated, a distinction which the authors relate to the dichotomy between the legal categories of vulnerable and average consumers. Traders can be fair or unfair depending on whether they are "well-intentioned" firms or "unscrupulous" ones.[35] This depends on whether their business strategy is respectful of the interests of consumers or not. The framework also considers the information verifiability—how easy it is for consumers to verify an information and market partition—the extent to which the demand- or supply-side of the market includes predominantly one type of consumer or of traders. Verifiability relates to information about product attributes. In this regard, products attributes are divided into three categories according to how simple it is to verify the truth of an information relating to them: search, experience, and credence attributes. For search attributes, verifications costs are low, and the verification can typically happen before the conclusion of the contract. In case of experience attributes, as the name suggests, it is through experience that the information can be verified. Finally, in case of credence attributes, verification costs are typically prohibitive for consumers, who are therefore incapable of verifying the information. Market partition (our term) focuses on the interaction between sophisticated and naïve consumers on the one hand, and fair and unfair traders on the other. If a practice targets only naïve consumers, the demand-side of the market is partitioned; if fair traders prefer to exit a market, the supply-side is partitioned. Partition is important because sophisticated consumers and fair traders in a non partitioned market contribute to protecting naïve consumers and to keep unfair traders under control, to some extent. On this basis, Siciliani, Riefa, and Gamper describe four 'archetypal theories of [consumer] harm':[36] the scam, the lemon, the shock, and the subsidy.

In the scam scenario, both the demand- and supply-side of the markets are partitioned, to the effect that there are only naïve consumers and unfair traders on the market. The more difficult it is to verify information, the greater the probability of harm. Deception and exploitation are the rule in these markets, such as in the case

[34]Siciliani et al. (2019), pp. 109–136.

[35]Siciliani et al. (2019), p. 110.

[36]The authors call them 'consumer theories of harm (CToHs)'.

of pyramid schemes and fake prize draws. In the lemon scenario, there is a risk of partition of both the demand- and supply-sides. The partition may be the result of a severe information asymmetry problem. As in the path-breaking paper by Akerlof, which inspires the name of this scenario,[37] fair traders and sophisticated consumers may gradually exit the market because of their incapacity to distinguish fair from unfair offers. For example, if it is difficult for consumers to verify the quality of a used car, sellers of high-quality cars fail to obtain an adequate price for their cars and exit the market—for such a low price, they prefer to keep their car instead of selling it. This reduces the market price, pushing the sellers of cars of slightly lower quality to exit too. The process continues until only 'pieces of junk' are available on the market. In the shock scenario, the supply-side is essentially partitioned—the market is colonized by unfair firms. As the demand-side is not partitioned, sophisticated consumers offer some degree of protection to the naïve ones. A crucial example of this scenario are unfair terms in standard terms. As these terms are often non-salient, competition stimulates traders to take advantage of consumers, but to the extent demand is not partitioned, sophisticated consumers offer some protection to the naïve ones.[38] Finally, the subsidy scenario is similar to the shock one. The key difference is that now the demand-side is partitioned, so that sophisticated consumers do not protect the naïve ones; actually, there is a chance that sophisticated consumers benefit from unfair practices against naïve consumers through a mechanism of cross-subsidisation. An example of this would be that of mandatory remedies that naïve consumers pay for but typically do not exercise.

These four scenarios describe typical market dynamics that are considered harmful for consumers and therefore may trigger enforcement. In other words, these scenarios belong to the second layer of a general theory of consumer harm. Just like in competition law, these scenarios are considered as building blocks. More precisely, the four scenarios are not mutually exhaustive or exclusive, but they do represent an attempt to cover the majority of the cases for consumer protection intervention.[39] Accordingly, in light of the specificities of a case, these scenarios can be combined to build tailored explanations of why consumers are harmed in a certain context. These tailored explanations would then belong to the third layer of a theory of consumer harm.

2.4 *Illustration: The Example of Dual Quality Goods*

To illustrate the usefulness of building a theory of harm, let us consider so-called dual quality products, which prompted such vivid political debates in Europe since 2017 that President Juncker mentioned it in his State of the Union address that

[37] Akerlof (1970).

[38] Seminal in this regard, Korobkin (2003). Broad overview in Esposito (2017).

[39] Siciliani et al. (2019), pp. 111–112.

year.[40] Responding to the outrage of several eastern European leaders and Members of the European Parliament, he stated that, 'in a Union of equals, there can be no second class consumers' and called it unacceptable that 'in some parts of Europe, people are sold food of lower quality than in other countries, despite the packaging and branding being identical: Slovaks do not deserve less fish in their fish fingers, Hungarians less meat in their meals, Czechs less cacao in their chocolate". Traders operating in Western Europe can deceive Central-Eastern Europe consumers by offering them products of a quality that is lower to the one in Western Europe—this is at least the concern of predominantly Central and Easter Europe governments.[41] The Proposal of Modernisation Directive "make(s) it explicit" that the commercialization of these goods is an unfair commercial practice.[42] According to the legislative definition, there is a case of dual quality good when goods with "significantly different composition or characteristics" are marketed as identical.

What scenario of harm, if any, would correspond to dual quality goods? The demand-side is geographically partitioned, with Central-Eastern European consumers being victims of deceptive practices—Western brands that supposedly should market products of premium quality *de facto* lower the quality of their products. Local traders can be expected to fight against these practices, while Western consumers might even benefit from some cross-subsidisation. Dual quality products have thus some features of the scam scenario and of the subsidy one. As noted, the circumstance that the real-world problem fits partially in different archetypical scenarios of harm shall not be seen as a problem of the framework built by Siciliani, Riefa, and Gamper. On the contrary, the combination of different template scenarios is to be expected—these are precisely archetypes rather than an exhaustive typology. What matters here is that the framework helps to identify—in a more analytical and less emotional way that was prevalent in the debate—the problematic features of the practice of dual quality goods. A better understanding of the problem will then be helpful to establish enforcement priorities and assess to what extent a particular product shall be considered of dual quality.

Having outlined why a theory of harm would be helpful for consumer policy, this section showed that, similarly to what is observed in competition law, it is possible to construct a typology of harms and market configurations leading to consumer harm that could help justify, rationalise and structure the enforcement of consumer law. We now turn to the REFIT to examine whether it leads to any progress in that direction.

---

[40] European Commission (2017a).

[41] European Parliament (2018a).

[42] Proposal European Commission (2018b), p. 4.

3 The Theory of Harm in the Consumer REFIT

Checking the 'fitness for purpose' of EU consumer law presupposes that one has a clear notion of what the purpose of that body of legislation is. As mentioned, a REFIT is more than a routine policy evaluation. The EU Better Regulation Agenda defines it as an ambitious re-evaluation of a whole body of legislation, examining it in light of five criteria: effectiveness, efficiency, coherence, relevance, and EU added value. Among these criteria, effectiveness and efficiency are of particular interest for eliciting the purpose of consumer protection as each of these criteria describes a property of a means-ends relationship (effectiveness describes a means-ends relationship where means reach the desired end, while efficiency describes one where means reach the desired end at the least possible cost). Moreover, it cannot be excluded from the outset that additional insight can be found under the other three criteria.

The Consumer REFIT conducted in 2016–2017 and the subsequent legislative proposals tabled in 2018 represent a rich source (over 4000 pages) of research, data gathering, and analysis with a direct bearing on the ends and means of EU Consumer Law. This corpus consists of inception documents drafted by the Commission, which outlines the questions to be researched and the methodology to be followed,[43] studies produced by external contractors in response to the Commission's tenders,[44] and the Staff Working Document in which the Commission took stock of all that research.[45] Subsequently, the Commission introduced legislative proposals presented as a follow-up on the REFIT.[46] These proposals were completed with *ex ante* impact assessments, which were submitted to the Regulatory Scrutiny Board, thus giving rise to an additional report.[47] In this paper, we leave out this pre-legislative work because it does not add relevant material for our enquiry. Conversely, we add to our corpus a study which is not formally part of the REFIT but is contemporaneous, widely cited in the REFIT, and of particular importance to

[43]Two documents fall in this category: European Commission (2015a, c) [on file with the authors].

[44]A number of documents fall in this category: the main report (CIVIC 2017), which is based on 28 national reports evaluating the application of existing directives; a separate study on the application of the Consumer Rights Directive written by RPA, CSES and EPRD (European Commission 2017g); a study on the costs and benefits of the minimum harmonisation under the Consumer Sales and Guarantees Directive (European Commission 2017h); a study on the costs and benefits of extending certain rights under the Consumer Sales and Guarantees Directive (European Commission 2017i); a set of empirical studies (survey, mystery shopping field study and lab experiments) designed to test how consumers understand and use information in various contexts: GfK Belgium, Consumer Market Study to support the Fitness Check of EU consumer and marketing law (all available from the Consumer REFIT page: http://ec.europa.eu/newsroom/just/item-detail.cfm?item_id=59332.

[45]European Commission (2017f) and separate report European Commission (2017d) (all available from the Consumer REFIT page, see previous note).

[46]Cited n. 2.

[47]European Commission (2017b).

our enquiry as it focuses on measuring consumer detriment.[48] This REFIT-centred corpus seems apt to study and unpack the normative premises underlying this body of EU legislation and thereby shed some light on the theory of harm underpinning EU consumer law. While none of these documents constitutes a binding source of law, their stated purpose is to inform legislation and enforcement. It is reasonable to think they capture the current thinking within the Commission also in relation to the surveillance of implementation at national level and to the Commission's intervention before the Court (a frequent occurrence when the Court is dealing with a preliminary reference from a national court asking guidance regarding the interpretation of EU consumer law). The theory of harm—if any—expressed in these documents could therefore generate legal effects indirectly, through new EU legislation but also infringement procedures and dialogue with the Court on the interpretation of the law.

In this section, we first outline how the REFIT documents present the goals of EU consumer law and discuss how this may translate as a (level 1) doctrine of harm (Sect. 3.1); we then present what can be found in the voluminous REFIT documentation by way of indications of an emerging (level 2) theory of harm (Sect. 3.2).

3.1 Elements of Doctrine of Harm: Empowerment, Trust, and the Internal Market

One of the most intriguing aspects of the Consumer REFIT relates to the way in which the Commission Report articulates the goals of EU consumer law. According to the treaty, the goals of consumer policy are to "promote the interests of consumers and to ensure a high level of consumer protection".[49] In the REFIT, the "overarching objectives of the Directives" are described as "increasing consumer trust and empowerment while contributing to a better functioning of the internal market".[50] This terminology is not new,[51] but the way in which it differs from the original language of the treaty *prima facie* seems to lend credibility to the critique already mentioned: 'protection' has disappeared.[52] Trust and empowerment are beautiful words. They capture essential elements of what makes a good life. However, in the context of consumer law scholarship, there is a suspicion that those words are used in a reductionist sense. The fear is that the focus on empowerment promotes the vision

---

[48]European Commission (2017c). A similar study had been done a decade before: Europe Economics (2007).

[49]Art 169 TFEU. This provision contains a reference to article 114 TFEU (on measures having as their object the establishment and functioning of the internal market), which also refers to a high level of consumer protection (art. 114, para. 2, TFEU).

[50]European Commission (2017f) p. 18.

[51]See European Commission (2007, 2011).

[52]Micklitz (2012), cited n. 16.

expressed by the average consumer standard, that of a superman or superwoman, when few consumers do in fact fit this image.[53] This concern is documented also in the context of the Consumer REFIT, especially on the side of consumer associations, who lament the detachment from reality of the average consumer standard.[54]

We respect this fear and do not think it should go away. We also think that the new formulation of goals of consumer policy deserves to be considered with an open mind. We acknowledge that REFIT documents seem to be doing just what scholars have warned against, yet we do not read the empowerment language of the Commission as a provocation. Rather, we submit that the way in which the Commission uses "empowerment" to describe an overarching goal of consumer policy is compatible with genuine protection. The language of empowerment does not offer a guarantee that the interests of the weakest will receive more consideration, but it also does not rule it out. The Modernization and Enforcement Directives proposed by the Commission as a follow up to the Consumer REFIT bear testimony to the fact that the empowerment rhetoric does not signify a less intrusive approach to EU consumer law.[55] Indeed, the proposed reform lays emphasis on the procedural side of consumer empowerment and provides for more effective remedies and sanctions.

On the concept of empowerment, it is instructive to look at a 2011 Report,[56] where it is explained that the 2007–2013 European Consumer Agenda was based on the notion of empowered consumers, who can actively participate in the market and make it work for them by exercising their power of choice and by enforcing their rights properly. The 2012 European Consumer Agenda was built around four main objectives designed to increase consumer confidence in the market by: (a) ensuring their safety, (b) providing consumers with information and education on their rights; (c) securing means of redress and stepping up enforcement; and (d) identifying new emerging challenges such as vulnerable consumers and unsustainable patterns of consumption.

Ultimately, consumer empowerment is meant to ensure that consumers "can actively participate in the market and make it work for them by exercising their power of choice and by having their rights properly enforced".[57] In other words, making empowerment a central goal of consumer policy highlights a two-way relationship between consumer law and the internal market project which has always characterised EU law. The internal market serves consumers by offering them "greater choice, lower prices, and the affordability and availability of essential services".[58] Conversely, consumers serve the internal market project (which also benefits businesses) by actively shopping around. Similarly, consumer trust, the other value promoted to the rank of overarching objective in the REFIT, goes both

[53]Weatherill (2016), p. 312.

[54]CIVIC (2017), pp. 41–43.

[55]Intrusive here is meant both with reference to national laws and to business strategies.

[56]European Commission (2011).

[57]European Commission (2012), p. 5.

[58]European Commission (2002), p. 2. See also European Commission (2007), p. 9.

ways: consumers are better off if the market is made trustworthy—by enforcing laws against 'unfair traders'[59] and it is also true that trusting consumers is what the market needs. In particular, in the EU context, the issue is to create greater trust in online cross-border transactions. Boosting such transactions enables consumers to reap more fully the benefits of the internal market *and* open new markets for traders.

What critics point out is that the virtuous triangle between empowerment, trust and internal market works for the active and competent consumers and does not include the weakest consumers or support an agenda of protection that would cater for their needs. This is true but does not imply that the protection of vulnerable consumers is neglected. Rather, it treated as a separate agenda—presumably for the very reason that stakes are different.[60] The really fundamental issue is whether the distinction between naïve and sophisticated consumers can be maintained in light of the finding that vulnerability does not only characterise individual consumers because of their age, handicap or socio-economic characteristics, but can affect any consumer in certain market situations.[61] Bracketing this issue, which is flagged in documents on vulnerable consumers but not considered in the REFIT, it is possible to conclude that the virtuous triangle of empowerment, trust and internal market constitutes the normative background to the REFIT. This has implications for the theory of harm: it is consistent with this framework to consider that any disruption of the harmonious triangular flow is harmful to consumers (notwithstanding the circumstance that the same disruption may also be harmful to the internal market). If we go back to the four archetypical scenarios by Siciliani, Riefa, and Gamper, this means that the main focus is on scenarios where the interests of naïve and sophisticated consumers are aligned, namely the lemon and shock scenarios. Contrary to the scam scenario, in the lemon and shock scenarios the demand-side is not partitioned, and sophisticated consumers provide some degree of protection also to naïve ones. Moreover, contrary to the subsidy scenario, the lemon and shock scenarios do not raise problems in terms of distributive effects between naïve and sophisticated consumers. Accordingly, the lemon and shock scenarios are the ones where it is most understandable for enforcement authorities to focus on the needs of sophisticated consumers. In the next section, we examine if this hypothesis is supported by an analysis of the REFIT documents.

3.2 Is There a Theory of Harm in the Consumer REFIT?

We have explained that we understand a theory of harm as comprising three layers—a typology of the relevant harm, accepted explanations of how it happens, and case-specific explanations that it happens. In this section, we extract from the Consumer

[59]To use the terminology of Siciliani et al. (2019) (See above 1.3).

[60]See in particular European Commission (2016).

[61]See Competition and Markets Authority (2019).

REFIT the main insights we found there in relation to the theory of harm underlying Consumer Law. Regarding the general doctrine of harm (what counts as consumer harm for the purposes of consumer law), the REFIT is elusive. It eschews the need to define harm by opting for a self-referential approach and holding that consumers suffer harm when the law is under-enforced.

3.2.1 Layer 1: An Elusive Typology of Harm

In the Consumer REFIT, little is said in relation to what types of harms EU consumer law protects consumers against. What is found is however sufficient to conclude that the notion of harm is rich and multidimensional, and it cannot be reduced to a simple economic notion such as that of (loss of) surplus as compared to some ideal situation (e.g. perfect competition). This is evidenced in particular by the references to psychological harm, which a 2017 study on revealed personal consumer detriment ("2017 Study") makes no attempt to quantify in monetary terms.[62]

In relation to the types of harm consumers are exposed to, the most important insights in the Consumer REFIT are found in the discussion under the efficiency criterion, collecting information on the benefits and costs of EU consumer law for consumers. However, for the most part the collected information is of little help for current purposes. This is because the Consumer REFIT simply reports the results of a survey asking how much consumers have *benefitted* from EU consumer law. The counterfactual is the situation before the introduction of EU consumer law.[63] This framing expresses the Commission's focus on legitimising EU action and documenting the 'added value' of EU law. The focus therefore is on the law rather than on harmful market conducts. In addition, the survey attempts to quantify the benefits of EU law, but without unpacking what kinds of benefits they might be or what the counterfactual is (national law prior to harmonisation?). Consequently, the information collected does not help clarify what "benefit" means nor, relatedly, what "harm" means in EU consumer law.

An important exception, very useful for current purposes, is the reference to the "2017 Study".[64] This study is often cited in the Consumer REFIT and presents a discussion of the "Dimensions of consumer detriment".[65] It distinguishes between four types of detriment: financial detriment, time loss, psychological detriment, and adverse effects on health. Financial detriment consists in "the monetary costs and losses incurred . . . as a result of a problem" and relates to excessive prices, the costs of repairing the good or obtaining redress.[66] "Time loss refers to the total amount of time a consumer has spent either as the direct result of a problem or from trying to

[62]European Commission (2017c).

[63]European Commission (2017f), pp. 72–73.

[64]European Commission (2017c).

[65]European Commission (2017c), p. 38.

[66]European Commission (2017c), pp. 38–39.

sort a problem out".[67] The psychological detriment is the "emotional cost" imposed on the consumer because of a problem.[68] Little is said on what an adverse effect on health is, with the discussion focusing on the measurement problems that this type of harm raises. The 2017 Study found that, in 2015, EU consumers suffered a monetized post-redress consumer harm in six markets ranging between EUR 20.3 and 58.4 billion, in addition to psychological detriment, which was not monetized.[69] This evaluation shows that consumers need better protection, which justifies further EU action. For our purposes, it confirms that the notion of consumer harm is broad and not limited to surcharge or deception, though it includes both. Consistently with the separation between 'mainstream' consumer protection and specific vulnerability intervention, the typology of harm proposed in this study does not distinguish between harm suffered by 'naïve' and 'sophisticated' consumers. However, there is no conceptual difficulty in considering that all four types of harm can be experienced both by vulnerable and by 'average' consumers. In addition, if one acknowledges that anyone can be vulnerable depending on the situation, this framework is also compatible with the idea that, certain contexts increase the likelihood and/or the magnitude of harm.

Another way to approach the underlying conception of harm posited in the REFIT consists in searching for expression of a benchmark or counterfactual. To establish that harm occurred, one necessarily needs a term of comparison: harm can be represented as a discrepancy between what the consumer obtained in fact and what she should have obtained in a normatively relevant scenario. In the Consumer REFIT, the implicit counterfactual is what would have happened absent the illegal business practice such as scams or other unfair practices. In other words, the benchmark is a fully effective EU consumer law: consumers are only harmed when the law is under-enforced. Although not explicitly articulated, this choice of comparator is revealed by the circumstance that, throughout the REFIT, the degree of non-compliance of traders with the law constitutes the primary benchmark for consumer harm.[70] The same benchmark also emerges from the discussion of both the effectiveness and the efficiency of EU consumer law. In relation to effectiveness, the central concern is related to traders' compliance with EU consumer law and with the contribution of different dispute resolution mechanisms to it.[71] Even the level of consumer awareness of their rights is analysed for its contribution to ensuring that

[67]European Commission (2017c), p. 39.

[68]European Commission (2017c), p. 40.

[69]The difference between pre- and post-redress harm reveals that compensation reduced harm of an amount between EUR 5.8 and 14.606 billion. It would be of interest to compare these data with the turnover and profit level in the studied industries, but the relevant data are not available on Eurostat (https://ec.europa.eu/eurostat/web/short-term-business-statistics/data/database).

[70]See, in particular, European Commission (2017f), p. 74: "The Fitness Check shows that there has not been significant progress on traders' compliance with consumer protection rules .... On the other hand, this is still an overall positive outcome, as infringements happening online can now harm more consumers across the EU at the same time".

[71]European Commission (2017f), pp. 18–33.

consumers act when their rights are breached.[72] Perhaps even more clearly, the discussion of both the benefits and the costs of EU consumer law for consumers focuses on the benefits that legislation is delivering, and how better enforcement would reduce consumer harm cause by the infringement of EU consumer law. Arguably, the following quote summarizes the whole discussion appropriately: "Non-compliance with consumer protection rules can lead to costs for consumers".[73]

This circular construction eschews any reflection on the primary sources of harm in terms of market conducts and market configurations. It pre-supposes that all the harms consumers are exposed to are already correctly and completely defined in the law as it stands. In other words, our question is circumvented by referring to the harms existing directives target (insufficient information, unfair practices, unfair terms…) without any attempt to conceptualise them further. There is some irony in this purely internal perspective: it lives precious little space for the consideration of potential regulatory failures—failures that could properly be considered in a fitness check, whose aim it is to improve the regulatory framework. Taking effective consumer law as a benchmark to identify consumer harm and assess if consumer law is fit for purpose is circular, if not paradoxical.

Next to the central self-referential benchmark which defines harm as instances of under-enforcement, the 2017 Study introduces two additional benchmarks. One consists of the optimal state characterised by the absence of regulatory failures *or market failure* ('first-best benchmark').[74] Compared to the self-referential benchmark just discussed, the first-best benchmark re-introduces market realities into the definition of harm. The other benchmark introduced in this study stands somewhere between the law and reality outside the law: it consists in a reference to the reasonable expectations of consumers ('expectation benchmark').[75] Under the expectation benchmark, consumers are considered to be harmed when business practices fail to meet their reasonable expectations. The actual expectations of consumers exist outside the law and are a matter for empirical enquiry, but it falls to the law to define what expectations deserve to be considered legitimate. This benchmark is consistent with scholarly accounts of the function of consumer law in general[76] and is explicitly referred to in some directives, for example on product liability (which was left outside the scope of the REFIT). More broadly, many rules may be read as expressing what the law considers legitimate expectation of consumers, whether in terms of pre-contractual information, fair commercial practices or fair contractual clauses. In this regard, the 2007 Study focuses explicitly on reasonable expectations, but then observes that "in practical terms," applicable legal norms play a pivotal role in determining what expectations are reasonable.[77]

[72]European Commission (2017f), pp. 31–33.

[73]European Commission (2017f), p. 35.

[74]European Commission (2017c), p. 24.

[75]European Commission (2017c), p. 24.

[76]Howells et al. (2018), p. 163; Micklitz (2012).

[77]Europe Economics (2007) pp. 42–58.

For this reason, while we find more appropriate to speak of legitimate expectation, it also seems that the alternative between 'reasonable' and 'legitimate' expectations is mostly a semantic one. However, the criterion of legitimate expectations is not much used as such in the case law of the Court and scholars have pointed to its potential to further develop the law, in particular in relation to unfair contract terms.[78] It will therefore be interesting to see if the Commission chooses to rely on the 2017 Study to push for such a development when it intervenes before the Court.

Both of these benchmarks are operationalised in the 2017 Study. They underpin the distinction between personal and structural detriment, initially proposed in a 2007 study and adopted in various following studies.[79] Personal detriment derives from the "specific problems for individual consumers relative to a benchmark of reasonable expectations"[80] and therefore refers to the expectation benchmark. Structural detriment "focuses on welfare loss due to market or regulatory failure"[81] and therefore refers to the first-best benchmark. Defective product illustrates the category of personal detriment; only few products of that type are defective, and consumers are entitled to expect that the products they buy are not defective. Cartel overcharges offer an illustration of the category of structural detriment: when firms collude to artificially raise the price above the competitive level, there is a market failure; therefore, the harm caused to consumers by overcharges is an instance of structural detriment. The distinction between personal and structural detriment reminds of the important distinction between situational and structural bargaining power introduced by Trebilcock.[82] As Trebilcock's distinction is categorical, it is at least tempting to conceive of personal and structural detriment as distinct concepts in the sense that overall consumer harm would be the sum of personal and structural detriment. The 2017 Study points out that these two broad categories of detriment "overlap", but then outlines a test to establish whether a particular concern falls "within the scope of structural or personal detriment"—thereby suggesting again that the concepts are distinct. A similar ambiguity can be found also in the 2007 study on consumer detriment introducing the distinction ("2007 Study").

A closer look reveals that this simple conceptual distinction is, however, poorly founded. The problem lies in forgetting that the grounds for the distinction were epistemic: both the 2007 and the 2017 Studies aimed to provide metrics for consumer detriment. In this perspective, it was crucial to define what component of consumer harm could be measured with what tool. In fact, the definitional task of the 2007 Study was the "establishment of sound operational benchmarks".[83] The choice of two definitions was animated by a (commendable) pluralistic attitude stemming

---

[78] Howells et al. (2018), pp. 132 and 163 make a case for the principle of protection of legitimate expectation to be given greater consideration in the development of the law.

[79] Europe Economics (2007).

[80] European Commission (2017c), p. 26.

[81] European Commission (2017c), p. 26.

[82] Trebilcock (1997).

[83] Europe Economics (2007), p. 11.

from "the fact that economists and psychologists view consumer detriment in different ways".[84] Accordingly, the 2007 Study did not deal with the question of when consumers are harmed; more pragmatically, the authors tried to establish which elements of harm could be measured reliably with a certain technique—showing along the way their sensitivity to the risk of a reductionist understanding of what constitutes consumer harm ('if it cannot be measured, it does not exist'). In fact, the distinction based on whether there is a market or regulatory failure (structural detriment) or a disappointment of consumer expectations (personal detriment) is not a sharp one. For example, an unfair commercial practice can be said to cause personal detriment.[85] Yet, one can say equally accurately that non-compliance with the Unfair Commercial Practice Directive causes "significant aggregate loss to European consumers".[86] Similarly, with an anti-competitive overcharge, it depends what consumers' expectations are taken as benchmark. If one takes the price consumers actually paid as representative of consumer expectations, then they suffered structural detriment only.[87] However, if the legitimate consumer expectations are competitive prices,[88] the overcharge causes also personal detriment. The distinction between personal and structural detriment remains useful for practical purposes because it helps to understand how consumer harm can be identified and measured. However, for our endeavour to typify the components or categories of consumer harms, the distinction is of little help.

Our analysis shows that the harm taken in consideration in the Consumer REFIT covers various aspects of human welfare. This is in line with the broad definitions of benefits and costs one finds in the Better Regulation Toolbox—the document that gives practical insights to Commission officers on how to conduct Better Regulation activities. Moreover, the 2017 Study surely provides a clearer picture of what types of harm EU consumer law seeks to protect consumers against than do the directives. Obviously, however, one has to keep in mind that neither the Commission nor the EU and national enforcement authorities or courts are bound in any way to utilize these categories in the law-making and adjudicatory practices. In relation to the benchmark against which harm may be appraised, we found three approaches. The first is circular: it takes non-compliance with legislation as benchmark, thus eschewing the need to define harm and, in so doing, making it impossible to assess whether EU consumer legislation is truly fit for purpose (i.e. whether it catches all counts of harm that deserve to be included). This approach cannot be useful for enforcement as this notion of consumer harm adds nothing to the notion of infringement and thus could not direct enforcers' attention to any specific facts or question that they are not already considering. The first-best benchmark focuses on structural detriment. It has the merit of envisaging the possibility of regulatory failure, which is

[84]Europe Economics (2007), p. 41.

[85]European Commission (2017c), p. 27.

[86]European Commission (2017f), p. 35.

[87]Europe Economics (2007), p. 46.

[88]European Parliament and Council (2009), paras. 1 and 45 and Art. 3(3).

welcomed in the context of a fitness check, but requires the articulation of a very complex theory to identify the best possible legal intervention. As its name suggests, the first-best benchmark can thus be conceived of the ultimate result to which a theory of consumer harm shall aspire. Its main drawback comes from the complexities of articulating, operationalizing, and applying such benchmark. The expectation benchmark focuses on personal detriment, which is a criterion enforcers could consider and this would alter current practice if done more systematically. To do so, a thorough reflection on what expectations consumers are entitled to have would be needed. In conclusion, the self-referential benchmark is ostensibly modest and limited in scope, but also simpler to apply in comparison to the first-best and expectation benchmarks. One is however left to wonder to what extent a fitness check using the self-referential benchmark can be really said to rely on the best available evidence.

3.2.2 Layer 2: Scenarios of Consumer Harm

The layer 2 of the theory of harm identifies causal mechanisms that lead to consumer harm. The Consumer REFIT rests on a concise but sophisticated account of the 'intervention logic' of the evaluated directives. This is a valuable source of information to identify the causes of harm EU consumer law seeks to neutralise. It is, however, less useful to describe how these causal mechanisms work (let alone measuring their effects). This causal aspect, which is at the heart of an ambitious theory of harm remains largely opaque in the Consumer REFIT.

The Consumer REFIT breaks down the sequence of a consumer transaction in three main phases: promotion and marketing; conclusion of the contract; performance of the contract.[89] Each phase is connected with one or more directive covered by the Consumer REFIT, thereby clarifying, for example, that pre-contractual information—regulated under the Consumer Rights Directive—relates to the second phase (conclusion of the contract) not first phase (promotion and marketing). During both the first and second phases, EU consumer law intends to help consumers take better decisions. To this end, it makes certain information mandatory and it imposes a duty to write terms in plain and intelligible language. In this context, the relevant consumer harm results from ill-informed choices and can be economic, psychological or both. It would seem to be caused by practices that exploit consumer weakness, inattention or bounded rationality. During the conclusion of the contract, consumers are also protected against standard terms causing a significant imbalance in the performance of the parties. Therefore, in can be inferred that significant inequality in the respective performances causes harms to consumers. During phase 3, consumers are granted specific remedies in relation to defective goods; a defective goods is thus a source of harm. Throughout the transaction, consumers are further protected

[89] European Commission (2017f), p. 7; also European Commission (2017d), p. 9. There is no elaboration of what these phases describe, they are indeed quite intuitive.

against commercial practices that are likely to materially distort their economic behaviour. Importantly, vulnerable consumers—the naïve consumers in Siciliani, Riefa, and Gamper's framework—receive tailored protection. The general benchmark for assessing consumer harm is one in which consumers make informed decisions and are protected against unfair behaviour by traders. Accordingly, harm is caused by poor decisions and unfairness. Admittedly, this finding is hardly innovative. It could have been be derived from a textual analysis of the directives and the related case-law in the absence of the REFIT. More importantly and disappointingly, it is of little significance for illuminating what causal mechanisms lead to poor decisions or unfairness (and therefore harm).

The Consumer REFIT is not entirely silent on the matter of what causes harm. On several occasions, consumer law is justified by reference to the notion of consumer weakness. This is entirely consistent with the case-law of the Court of Justice, which has ruled that, "in relation to a trader, the consumer is in a weaker position, in that he must be deemed to be less informed, economically weaker and legally less experienced than the other party to the contract".[90] In relation to layer 2 of the theory of harm, the notion of consumer weakness could provide a starting point for developing scenarios of harm by following a two-step procedure. First, weakness is broken down into its various dimensions, such as imperfect information, bounded attention, bounded cognitive abilities, bounded rationality, bounded willpower. Second, on these grounds, it becomes possible to construct a typology of business conducts which opportunistically take advantage of these traits and thereby cause consumer detriment. From a broad Law & Economics perspective, the explicit references to information asymmetries and unequal bargaining powers is noteworthy. These references show that the concept of consumer weakness already welcomes economic considerations to some extent in the Luxemburg courtrooms and could potentially constitute the locus of more elaborate constructs.[91] In other words, the concept of weakness is porous enough accommodate legal arguments inspired by economics and behaviours sciences. In addition, concepts and typologies borrowed from psychology can inspire and help structure scenarios of exploitation of known consumer weakness (susceptibility to influence as studied in psychology).[92] The conceptual work of building on economic and behavioural analysis to produce an analytical grid and guide the enforcement of consumer law was not the object of the REFIT and stands to be undertaken.

At the end of Sect. 3.1, we formulated the hypothesis that the predominantly important scenarios of harm we would find in the Consumer REFIT are those scenarios where the interests of naïve and sophisticated consumers are most aligned, namely the lemon and shock scenarios. The evidence we found is largely inconclusive but also weakly supportive of the hypothesis. The hypothesis is supported to the extent that the Consumer REFIT typically does not distinguish between categories of consumers, arguably under the implicit assumption that they all have similar needs.

[90] Judgment of the Court of 4 October 2018, C-105/17, *Kamenova*, EU:C:2018:808, para. 34.

[91] Esposito (2018).

[92] Sibony (2014), pp. 903–942.

At the same time, on occasion, the specific vulnerabilities of some consumers do emerge and receive specific attention. This was seen to be the case in relation to unfair commercial practices, and when we analysed the case of dual quality products in Sect. 2.4, we found that such market practice had features of the scam scenario, in flat contradiction with the hypothesis that the primary focus is on the lemon and shock scenarios.

The gap between our initial question and the focus of the REFIT calls for some additional discussion in order to make sense of the disappointing findings.

4 Making Sense of Our Findings

4.1 A Surprising Omission: Harm Caused by Regulatory Failures

By essentially saying 'harm happens when the law is violated', the Consumer REFIT starts from the premise that the law perfectly identifies circumstances which are conducive to consumer harm. In other words, referring to consumer harm as (only) instances where the law is not properly enforced amounts to saying that the law is perfect as it is. This approach makes it singularly difficult to uncover a theory of harm in the REFIT because there is no need to articulate one: it is deemed to be already contained in the law and its accuracy is placed outside the scope of the retrospective evaluation. This self-referential benchmark takes the law as the ultimate parameter of consumer detriment and leaves no room for considering regulatory failures. Instead, the focus is solely on enforcement failures, which, curiously, are discussed neither in relation to the effectiveness nor the efficiency of EU consumer law.[93] What is ostensibly missing is an explicit discussion of the regulatory failures of EU consumer law.

This is a significant omission because optimal institutional design requires to select the form of market governance that minimizes the sum of costs of market failure and regulatory failures. This REFIT acknowledges this in principle,[94] but does not elaborates on market failure and says only very little on regulatory failures. Any elaboration on regulatory failures has to be read between the lines because the emphasis is strongly on regulatory success. Examples of regulatory failure alluded to include uncertainty about the scope and content of the *ex officio* doctrine—whereby national courts are under a duty to raise *ex officio* the unfair character of a term in a

[93]European Commission (2017f), pp. 65–66.

[94]CIVIC (2017), p. 245: "efficient implementation of EU consumer and marketing law across Member States ... requires striking a balance between the gains from flexibility and the costs arising from the failure to realise the full potential gains from trade across the borders of Member States", referring to the trade-off between the effectiveness of EU consumer law and the chilling effects that legal uncertainty may cause on trading activities within the Internal Market.

consumer contract—and of various provisions of the Unfair Commercial Practices Directive, as well as problems of overlap between different information duties.[95] None of these regulatory imperfections however is considered as sources of consumer harm.

Discussions of compliance costs provide another indirect entry into the REFIT discourse of regulatory failure. As part of the fact-finding for the REFIT, stakeholders were asked if certain regulatory burdens were either unnecessary—because they do not bring real benefits to consumers—or disproportionate—because they place excessive burdens on traders. An example of the former type is the duty to disclose a fax number for sending complaints, which is perceived as obsolete. An example of disproportionate duty powerfully advocated by business in the stakeholder consultations concerned certain aspects of the right of withdrawal under the Consumer Rights Directive. The Commission deferred to the business view in its proposal but faced significant pushback in the European Parliament.[96] Unsurprisingly, consumer associations were against any limitation of the right of withdrawal.[97] They also criticised the fact that compliance costs had been evaluated on grossly insufficient data.

In sum, regulatory failure is not seriously investigated in the REFIT and could not be in the absence of any benchmark of consumer harm external to the law. It is ironic in an exercise whose *raison d'être* is to check the fitness for purpose of the law—i.e. identify market and regulatory failures and solutions to ameliorate them. It is probably the case that the Consumer REFIT was sur-determined by a Commission priority, namely to close two long-standing dossiers: the lack of individual remedies under the UCPD and the lack of collective redress for consumers. Taking effective legislation as benchmark for harm is circular and unhelpful in many ways but allowed the Commission to build the narrative necessary to legislate on enforcement. Had the Commission wanted to focus more on the substantive dimension of EU consumer law, it would probably have prioritized the analysis of structural detriment caused by market and regulatory failures.

4.2 *Towards a Clearer Theory of Consumer Harm: Empowerment as Overarching Principle?*

As is clear from our analysis, this Consumer REFIT contributes very little to clarifying what the law considers as constituting consumer harm or how it understands causes of consumer harm. However, the REFIT language maps out the normative space in which this doctrine has to emerge. A cardinal point of this

[95]European Commission (2017f), p. 28 (*ex officio* doctrine), pp. 89–90 (UCPD) and pp. 58–62 (overlapping information duties).

[96]European Parliament (2018b), p. 38.

[97]BEUC (2018), pp. 8–9.

space is the notion of legitimate expectations. It radiates in many directions: consumers can legitimately expect to reap the benefits of the internal market, to receive accurate, sufficient and understandable information, to be offered fair contract terms, not to be misled or aggressively pushed to enter a transaction. Another densely charged normative concept, which is as yet under-used, is consumer empowerment. It too has many dimensions: consumers can be empowered through education, through information—though this form of empowerment has well documented limitations–,[98] through access to redress mechanisms, through naming and shaming (in the media or social media), through algorithmic assistance.[99]

At this point, we suggest a simple and, in our view at least, conceptually convincing way forward for building a theory of harm for EU consumer law having empowerment as its overarching principle. Consumers in the European Union have the legitimate expectation of being empowered. Accordingly, the harm EU law has to eliminate comes from the market conducts and the legal frameworks that disempower consumers. This would be a comprehensive framework. It would identify market configurations and behaviour conducive to consumer detriment, but also draw attention to the various types of empowerment that consumers need, and how EU consumer policy may help provide them or facilitate their emergence. It is thus understandable why the Consumer REFIT emphasizes so much the potential of collective redress for improving the position of consumers in markets. Collective redress would make it easier for consumers to vindicate their rights, with obvious effects in disciplining firms. The empowerment framework should strive to be normatively and methodologically inclusive. Normatively, it should recognise that different consumers have different empowerment needs in different circumstances—without ruling out that all may have the same basic needs in some circumstances. Methodologically, empowerment as a notion is not strongly associated with a particular discipline. It may therefore lend itself to an integrated approach drawing on both economic and behavioural insights, integrating the currently dominant information paradigm while offering space to develop consumer protection along other lines of investigation. Enriching and structuring the notion of consumer empowerment would not disrupt the important connection between empowered consumers and the internal market, which characterises EU consumer law. A richer understanding of what empowers consumers may, if anything, reinforce the internal market narrative. Effectively empowered by consumer policy according to their respective needs, consumers of various descriptions could trust the internal market as a safe place and benefit from the opportunities it creates.

[98]Howells (2005).

[99]Gal and Elkin-Koren (2017).

5 Conclusion

In this chapter, we tried to bring together two lines of questioning about EU consumer law which converge in a call for clarification of its orientation. One line is doctrinal: EU consumer law scholars find that EU consumer law lacks direction and oscillates in an unsatisfactory way between the aim of market building (favourable to business as much as consumers) and that of a high level of protection. The other line is more economic: taking inspiration from competition law, where a theory of harm has come to structure enforcement activities, other scholars sought to outline a theory of harm for consumer law. For our part, we thought it interesting to confront these scholarly proposals with the Consumer REFIT. We had good reasons to think that the REFIT would contain an expression of the EU view on aims and on harm: because the REFIT aims to check whether the law is fit for purpose, it should restate its purpose; because the REFIT has to appraise the effectiveness and efficiency of the law, it should contain a discourse on the means-ends match or mismatch and, therefore, on what the ends are. From there, it should be possible to ascertain what is the underlying theory of harm, which states which harms the law seeks to protect consumers against.

Our findings are disappointing. The REFIT eschews the clarification scholars call for. It does restate aims and it does not elaborate on what harms are legally relevant. It largely circumvents these two related questions by adopting a circular approach. When consumer harm is discussed, it is equated with instances of under-enforcement. This presupposes that the law is perfect: that it contains a complete and up-to-date characterisation of circumstances in which market interactions harm consumers—which needs not be restated—so that harm only ever happens when the law is not enforced. This is ironic given that the *raison d'être* of a REFIT is to check whether legislation is still fit for purpose.

In this sense, the REFIT does not represent an institutional contribution to the scholarly enterprise of clarifying the direction of EU consumer law or constructing a theory of harm suited for guiding enforcement in this area of law. The endeavour will have to remain a scholarly one for the time being. This said, the REFIT does contain scattered indications that scholars need to consider when reflecting about EU consumer law.

First, it is clear from the REFIT that EU law would not welcome an overly restrictive notion of consumer harm, limited to loss of economic surplus. Second, the REFIT names a normative space in which a theory of harm can be developed. It consists of a virtuous triangle of empowerment, trust and a well-functioning internal market. Empowered consumers benefit from the internal market and, in turn, further integration through cross-border shopping, provided they trust such transactions to be safe.

We looked for something that is not there: a theory of harm. What we found is a background for a theory to be developed. The pioneering work discussed in this chapter is an excellent starting point. The next step in our view is to integrate the dimension of empowerment, which is not new but is salient in the post-REFIT documents. This notion, together with the notions of consumer weakness and legitimate expectations present in the law, seem to be the ingredients for an economically grounded, behaviourally sensible, and legally workable theory of harm.

References

Akerlof GA (1970) The market for "Lemons": quality uncertainty and the market mechanism. Q J Econ 84(3):488–500

BEUC (2018) Proposal for A Better Enforcement and Modernisation of EU Consumer Protection Rules – "Omnibus Directive" - The BEUC view. https://www.beuc.eu/publications/beuc-x-2018-081_omnibus_directive.pdf [https://perma.cc/Z7GL-94TW]

Castillo de la Torre F, Gippini-Fournier E (2017) Evidence, proof and judicial review in EU competition law. Edward Elgar, Cheltenham

CIVIC (2017) Study for the Fitness Check of EU consumer and marketing law Final report Part 1 – Main report. https://ec.europa.eu/newsroom/just/item-detail.cfm?item_id=59332

Competition and Markets Authority (2019) Consumer vulnerability: challenges and potential solutions. https://assets.publishing.service.gov.uk/government/uploads/system/uploads/attachment_data/file/782542/CMA-Vulnerable_People_Accessible.pdf [https://perma.cc/8SBU-H62W]

Council of the European Union (1993) Directive 93/13/EEC on Unfair Terms in Consumer Contracts, OJ L 95, 21.4.1993, pp 29–34

Economic Advisory Group on Competition Policy (2005) An economic approach to Article 82, July 2005. http://ec.europa.eu/dgs/competition/economist/eagcp_july_21_05.pdf

Esposito F (2017) A dismal reality: behavioural analysis and consumer policy. J Consumer Policy 40(2):193–216

Esposito F (2018) Conceptual foundations for a European consumer law and behavioural sciences scholarship. In: Micklitz H-W, Sibony A-L, Esposito F (eds) Research methods in consumer law a handbook. Edward Elgar, Cheltenham, pp 38–76

Europe Economics (2007) An analysis of the issue of consumer detriment and the most appropriate methodologies to estimate it Final Report for DG SANCO by Europe Economics. http://www.europe-economics.com/publications/study_consumer_detriment.pdf

European Commission (2002) Action plan "Simplifying and improving the regulatory environment", COM(2002) 278 final. http://www.europarl.europa.eu/meetdocs/committees/juri/20040218/020278EN.pdf

European Commission (2007) EU consumer policy strategy 2007–2013. Empowering consumers, enhancing their welfare, effectively protecting them, COM (2007) 99 final. https://eur-lex.europa.eu/legal-content/EN/ALL/?uri=COM%3A2007%3A0099%3AFIN

European Commission (2009) Communication, Guidance on the Commission's enforcement priorities in applying Article 82 of the EC Treaty to abusive exclusionary conduct by dominant undertakings, OJ C 45 of 24.2.2009, 7-20 ('priority paper')

European Commission (2010) Green paper on policy options for progress towards a European Contract Law for consumers and businesses, COM(2010)348 final

European Commission (2011) Staff Working Paper, Consumer Empowerment in the EU, SEC (2011) 469 final. https://ec.europa.eu/info/sites/info/files/consumer_empowerment_eu_2011_en.pdf

European Commission (2012) A European Consumer Agenda - Boosting confidence and growth, COM(2012) 225 final. https://ec.europa.eu/commission/sites/beta-political/files/consumer_agenda_2012_en.pdf

European Commission (2015a) Evaluation and Fitness Check (FC) Roadmap. http://ec.europa.eu/smart-regulation/roadmaps/docs/2016_just_023_evaluation_consumer_law_en.pdf [https://perma.cc/T7U8-HAV4]

European Commission (2015b) Staff Working Document, Better Regulation Guidelines, SWD (2015) 111 final. http://ec.europa.eu/smart-regulation/guidelines/docs/swd_br_guidelines_en.pdf

European Commission (2015c) Study to support the fitness check of EU consumer law JUST/2015/RCON/PR/CO02/0112. https://ted.europa.eu/TED/notice/udl?uri=TED:NOTICE:461153-2015:TEXT:EN:HTML

European Commission (2016) Consumer vulnerability across key markets in the European Union Final report https://ec.europa.eu/info/sites/info/files/consumers-approved-report_en.pdf (March 26th 2019) [https://perma.cc/F9JR-YLSX]

European Commission (2017a) President Jean-Claude Juncker's State of the Union Address. http://europa.eu/rapid/press-release_SPEECH-17-3165_en.htm [https://perma.cc/Q8S4-UJKV]

European Commission (2017b) Regulatory scrutiny board opinion (Ares (2017) 2254646 - 02/05/2017) https://ec.europa.eu/info/sites/info/files/consumerlawfcopinion.pdf [https://perma.cc/8DMZ-WCZV]

European Commission (2017c) Study on measuring consumer detriment in the European Union. https://ec.europa.eu/info/publications/study-measuring-consumer-detriment-european-union_en

European Commission (2017d) Staff working document Evaluation of the Consumer Rights Directive, SWD(2017) 169 final. https://ec.europa.eu/newsroom/document.cfm?doc_id=44874

European Commission (2017e) Staff working document, Better Regulation Guidelines, SWD (2017) 350. https://ec.europa.eu/info/sites/info/files/better-regulation-guidelines.pdf

European Commission (2017f) Staff Working Document Report on the Consumer Fitness check, SWD(2017)209/F1. http://ec.europa.eu/newsroom/document.cfm?doc_id=44639

European Commission (2017g) Study on the application of the Consumer Rights Directive 2011/83/EU Final Report ec.europa.eu/newsroom/document.cfm?doc_id=44637

European Commission (2017h) Study on the costs and benefits of minimum harmonisation under the Consumer Sales and Guarantees Directive 1999/44/EC and of potential full harmonisation and alignment of EU rules for different sales channels. https://publications.europa.eu/en/publication-detail/-/publication/358f6bb9-9ac0-11e8-a408-01aa75ed71a1/language-en/format-PDF

European Commission (2017i) Study on the costs and benefits of extending certain rights under the Consumer Sales and Guarantees Directive 1999/94/EC. https://publications.europa.eu/en/publication-detail/-/publication/4d120ad5-deee-11e7-9749-01aa75ed71a1/language-en/format-PDF

European Commission (2018a) Proposal for a Directive of the European Parliament and of the Council on representative actions for the protection of the collective interests of consumers, COM (2018) 184. https://eur-lex.europa.eu/legal-content/EN/TXT/?uri=CELEX:52018PC0184

European Commission (2018b) Proposal for a Directive of the European Parliament and of the Council amending Council Directive 93/13/EEC of 5 April 1993, Directive 98/6/EC of the European Parliament and of the Council, Directive 2005/29/EC of the European Parliament and of the Council and Directive 2011/83/EU of the European Parliament and of the Council as regards Better Enforcement and Modernisation of EU Consumer Protection Rules ('Modernisation Directive"), COM(2018)185. https://eur-lex.europa.eu/legal-content/EN/TXT/?uri=CELEX%3A52018PC0185

European Commission (2019a) Better regulation: taking stock and sustaining our commitment, COM(2019)178. https://ec.europa.eu/info/sites/info/files/better-regulation-taking-stock_en_0.pdf

European Commission (2019b) Staff Working Document, Taking Stock of the Commission's Better Regulation Agenda, SWD(2019) 156 final. https://ec.europa.eu/info/sites/info/files/better-regulation-taking-stock-swd_en.pdf

European Parliament (2018a) Report on Dual Quality of Products in the Single Market, A8-0267/2018 (2018/2008(INI)) of 19.7.2018. http://www.europarl.europa.eu/doceo/document/A-8-2018-0267_EN.html [https://perma.cc/2EQ9-P5MZ]

European Parliament (2018b) Draft Report by Daniel Dalton on the proposal for a directive as regards better enforcement and modernisation of EU consumer protection rules (Modernisation directive), Committee on the Internal Market and Consumer Protection, 19 July 2018, PE 625.551v01-00. http://www.europarl.europa.eu/sides/getDoc.do?type=COMPARL&mode=XML&language=EN&reference=PE625.551 [https://perma.cc/CQT4-4FG8]

European Parliament and Council (2009) Directive 2009/72/EC of 13 July 2009 Concerning Common Rules for the Internal Market in Electricity, OJ L 211/55

Gal M, Elkin-Koren N (2017) Algorithmic consumers. Harv J Law Technol 30:309

Gerber D (2001) Law and competition in twentieth-century Europe: protecting prometheus. Oxford University Press, Oxford

Howells G (2005) The potential and limits of consumer empowerment by information. J Law Soc 32–33:349–370

Howells G, Twigg-Flessner C, Whilhelmsson T (2018) Rethinking EU consumer law. Routledge, Abingdon

Israeli Antitrust Authority (2014) Opinion 1/14: Prohibition of Excessive Pricing by a Monopolist

Israeli Antitrust Authority (2017) Public Statement 1/17: The Antitrust Director General's Considerations in Enforcing the Prohibition Against Unfairly High Prices

Korobkin RB (2003) Bounded rationality, standard form contracts, and unconscionability. Univ Chicago Law Rev 70:1203

Lianos I (2007) La Transformation du Droit de la Concurrence par le Recours à l'Analyse Économique. Bruylant-Sakkoulas, Brussels-Athens

Micklitz H-W (2012) The expulsion of the concept of protection from the consumer law and the return of social elements in the civil law: a bittersweet polemic. J Consumer Policy 35:283–296

Rueff J (1965) La Cour et l'économie politique. In: Pescatore P (ed) Dix ans de jurisprudence de la Cour de justice des Communautés européennes. Carl Heymans Verlag, Cologne

Sibony A-L (2008) Le juge et le raisonnement économique en droit de la concurrence. LGDJ, Paris

Sibony A-L (2014) Can EU consumer law benefit from behavioural insights? An analysis of the unfair practices directive. Eur Rev Priv Law 22(6):903–942

Sibony A-L (2019) European unfairness and American unconscionability: a letter from a European lawyer to American friends. Eur Rev Contract Law 15(2)

Siciliani P, Riefa C, Gamper H (2019) Consumer theories of harm: an economic approach to consumer law enforcement and policy making. Bloomsbury, London

Trebilcock MJ (1997) The limits of freedom of contract. Harvard University Press, Cambridge

Twigg-Flessner C (2007) No sense of purpose or direction? The modernisation of European consumer law. Eur Rev Contract Law 3:198

Vesterdoft B (2005) Standard of proof in merger cases: reflections in the light of recent case law of the community courts. Eur Compet J, pp 3–33

Weatherill S (2016) Empowerment is not the only fruit. In: Leczykiewicz D, Weatherill S (eds) The images of the consumer in EU law legislation, free movement and competition law. Hart, Oxford

Whitman JQ (2007) Consumerism versus producerism: a study in comparative law. Yale Law J 117:340

Fabrizio Esposito UCLouvain. Postdoctoral Fellow in the ARC PROSEco Project at the Catholic University of Louvain (Louvain-La-Neuve, Belgium). Place Montesquieu, 2 bte L2.07.01 B-1348-Louvain-La-Neuve fabrizio.esposito@eui.eu Fields of Interest: Law and Economics, Legal Reasoning, Internal Market Law, Consumer Law, Competition Law.

Anne-Lise Sibony UCLouvain. Professor of EU law at the Catholic University of Louvain (Louvain-La-Neuve, Belgium). Place Montesquieu, 2 bte L2.07.01 B-1348-Louvain-La-Neuve anne-lise.sibony@uclouvain.be Fields of Interest: Behavioural Analysis of Law, EU law, Internal Market Law, Consumer Law, Competition Law.

Limits to Behavioural Consumer Law and Policy: The Case of EU Alcohol Labelling

Hanna Schebesta and Kai Purnhagen

Abstract Limits of the implementation of findings from behavioural science into law and policy are increasingly recognized in the literature. In this contribution, we analyse the example of alcohol nutrition labelling to show the potential and the limits of how behavioural science can be meaningfully used to inform policy makers. We first explain what we understand to be proxies for the limit of the implementation of behavioural science into policy. Subsequently we illustrate how alcohol nutrition labelling is currently regulated and survey the on-going policy process, including an analysis of the self-regulatory proposals that have been tabled by the alcohol beverages industry. We then survey and apply existing consumer studies. Our research shows that behavioural insights support stronger alcohol nutrition labelling at a general level. However, the different options of labelling are currently understudied and provide an insufficiently sound empirical basis for policy making.

1 Introduction

The use of behavioural research is gaining prominence as a tool to assess policies[1] and, increasingly, also, the law itself.[2] At EU level, this approach is applied with increasing prominence to the area of consumer contract law, in particular unfair commercial practices law[3] and information legislation, which can be summarised as a new field of research of behavioural EU law.[4] Initial applications were largely enthusiastic about the potential of behavioural insights for internal market law,

[1]See e.g. Straßheim and Beck (2019).

[2]Alemanno and Sibony (2015) and Mathis (2015).

[3]Herpen and Purnhagen (2018) and Sibony (2015).

[4]Purnhagen and Schebesta (2019).

H. Schebesta (✉) · K. Purnhagen
Law Group, Wageningen University and Research, Wageningen, The Netherlands
e-mail: Hanna.schebesta@wur.nl; kai.purnhagen@wur.nl

K. Mathis, A. Tor (eds.), *Consumer Law and Economics*, Economic Analysis of Law in European Legal Scholarship 9, https://doi.org/10.1007/978-3-030-49028-7_13

applying the insights largely uncritical to the interpretation and assessment of EU law.[5] With EU behavioural law coming of age, more nuanced and critical appraisal take centre stage in scholarship. Increasingly, scholars look into the question which criteria shall be applied to draw meaningful conclusions from behavioural research for internal market law.[6] This raises the question: What are the limits for the implementation of behavioural analysis into EU law? Our contribution uses the case of alcohol labelling law in the EU to illustrate how the implementation of behavioural science research is both, a welcome science-based approach to justify regulation and a tool which can be used to hide behind science to "legitimise" policy considerations not backed up by the underlying behavioural science (and thereby constituting the limits of implementation of behavioural science research).

In order to do so, this contribution first illustrates the existing literature on the limits of the implementation of behavioural science into law. Second, the special case of alcohol labelling in the EU is introduced and the existing behavioural studies used for their assessment. The case of alcohol labelling is particularly appealing, as it is the only area in EU food information law that is systematically exempted from general food labelling provisions,[7] while behavioural science is conventionally interpreted in a way which does not justify such an exemption. Third, we show how the application of behavioural science has been used to analyse cases of alcohol labelling, sometimes leading to valuable insights and sometimes to justify policy claims not covered by the science in question. Based on this illustration, we will close with a call for more quality in the use of insights from behavioural science in EU consumer law.

2 Limits to the Implementation of Insights from Behavioural Sciences into Law: A Short Literature Review

A strand of literature exists, which rejects the use of behavioural insights into policy or law-making *per se*.[8] We do not deal with this criticism here. Rather, we look into the criticism of those scholars who are in principle open to using insights of behavioural science into law-making, but raise specific, thoughtful concerns that one may engage with to improve the system of behavioural policy making. These criticism can be summarised in four clusters, namely legality, legal validity, scientific validity and social validity of behavioural interventions. Together, they form a

[5] Purnhagen (2014), Purnhagen (2015) and Sibony (2015).

[6] Fabbri and Faure (2018), Purnhagen and Feindt (2015) and Purnhagen (2018).

[7] Purnhagen and Schebesta (2019).

[8] See for a summary Fabbri and Faure (2018), pp. 248–249.

regulatory validity test, which can be applied to identify robust behavioural interventions into legal systems.[9]

2.1 Legality Concerns

The category 'legality concerns' comprises concerns that relate to the compliance of behavioural intervention with legal standards. In this way, most types of behavioural interventions are used as a tool for the executive.[10] It has been argued that they hence have a problem with democratic legitimacy.[11] Depending on the respective legal system, some scholars claim for a formal legal review of the use of behavioural interventions.[12] They have been argued to violate human rights,[13] particularly human dignity,[14] or, in the case of Germany, at least require justification for violation of basic rights granted by the national constitution.[15] Most of these criticism based on legality target public nudging approaches, and hence interventions where the executive makes use of behavioural findings to steer behaviour. These critiques carry an undertone that by using nudges, the executive would eventually circumvent established checks and balances. Interestingly, to our knowledge no-one has ever argued that nudges shall not be subject to legal review. Quite the contrary: Most prominently it has been argued that all governmental action, including nudges, shall be subject to justification and hence to a legality review.[16] Either way, we do not address this criticism as this contribution does not engage primarily with nudging by the executive, but rather with the evaluation of legislative measures in the area of alcohol labelling.

2.2 Legal Validity

Legal validity refers to value or policy commitments in the underlying legal regime that directly or indirectly affect requirements or expectations of which data are to be included and how these data are to be accessed or collected.[17] This particularly applies to situations where behavioural insights are used for assessment of

[9]Purnhagen (2018).

[10]McCrudden and King (2015), p. 123 and Hansen and Jespersen (2013), p. 5.

[11]McCrudden and King (2015), p. 123 and Hansen and Jespersen (2013), p. 5.

[12]Van Aaken (2015) and Purnhagen and Reisch (2016).

[13]Alemanno and Spina (2014), p. 446.

[14]McCrudden and King (2015), pp. 100–104.

[15]Purnhagen and Reisch (2016).

[16]Sunstein (2015).

[17]Purnhagen (2018) p. 290.

legislation. Do the studies and the policy recommendations really take into account the value commitments the law carries? To take an example from food information law for illustration: Suppose data from behavioural science shows that if consumers have a wider information base on the risks and benefits of GMOs they would also be more supportive of GMO introduction to the market.[18] As a consequence, as a policy tool, proper labelling may be a better alternative than an authorization procedure. However, it would make little sense to require labelling of GMOs to replace the authorisation procedure, as in some legal systems the authorisation procedure reflects the constitutional principle of precaution and is the outcome of a well-balanced compromise under WTO law. It would make sense, however, to base the same policy consideration on behavioural science, if this science illustrates that labelling can serve the purposes of the precautionary principle better and is better to deal with the requirements of WTO law. Such concerns of a neglect of legal considerations in behavioural analysis of EU law were particularly voiced where behavioural science was implemented into the review of policy making at the EU level. In particular, this criticism concerned the incorporation of behavioural science into the regulatory impact assessment,[19] the determination of the "vulnerable consumer"[20] and the "average consumer"[21] benchmark in EU consumer law.

2.3 *Scientific Validity*

Scientific validity conventionally distinguishes between internal[22] and external[23] validity. Internal validity refers to whether observed covariations should be interpreted as a causal relationship.[24] In other words, whether the single observed behavioural patterns can be reasonably connected to the influence under investigation. For example, can one really infer from a study where students are misled according to the size of a product that their purchase decision is affected?[25] Is the underlying measurement method, the stimuli used in the right setting and can this really result in the observed behaviour? External validity describes whether internally valid causal relationships can be generalised to different measures, persons, setting and times outside of the experiment.[26] For example, can we extrapolate

[18]Heiman and Zilberman (2011).

[19]Purnhagen and Feindt (2015).

[20]Purnhagen (2018), pp. 283–289, 290–293.

[21]Purnhagen and van Herpen (2017).

[22]Campbell and Stanley (1966).

[23]Calder et al. (1982).

[24]Campbell and Stanley (1966).

[25]Paraphrasing our study on the Mars-case Herpen and Purnhagen (2018).

[26]Calder et al. (1982), pp. 240–244.

findings on misleadingness of student consumers tested on a coffee pack to other products and groups of human beings?

2.4 *Social Validity*

Social validity requires that relevant findings resonate with the values and concerns of affected groups.[27] That means, that the design of the experimental research for policy considerations is not detached from the legal and policy considerations, but rather a co-production process between scientists, policy-makers, regulators and stakeholders.[28] For example, an experiment to determine whether young children require nutrition labelling of alcohol can be conducted in the best scientifically valid manner, but makes little sense when taking into account that in many societies young children are very unlikely to drink alcohol. Likewise, if behavioural interventions are not being accepted by the addressees, social acceptance of such interference is likely to trigger resistance and hence not very promising.

2.5 *Validity and Behavioural Interventions in the Law*

Unfortunately, overgeneralisation, cherry-picking of studies, investigation of a selected number of policy tools, and neglect of societal value commitments as enshrined in the law are a steady companion to policy claims based on scientific studies and in particular behavioural studies.[29] Following this practice, the danger exists that science is used as a shield to hide behind for justifying normative policy decisions. In the subsequent section, we will illustrate how such uses of behavioural sciences can materialise on the example of the EU law on alcohol labelling.

3 Alcohol Labelling in EU Law, Policy and Behavioural Sciences

When it comes to being regulated, the alcoholic beverages sector is, on one hand, subject to an important amount of sector-specific regulation, making alcohol a highly regulated area through *lex specialis*. On the other hand, it was also highly successful in securing exemptions within legislation. Within food regulation, alcohol must be regarded as exceptional. As such, as we will illustrate below, alcoholic beverages are

[27]Purnhagen (2018).
[28]Gibbons et al. (1994).
[29]Zeiler (2010).

widely exempt from food information labelling, and do not need to bear a list of ingredients or a nutrition declaration. A policy discussion on how to regulate alcoholic beverages in the future is ongoing, and we discuss relevant evidence from behavioural law, and how it will shape policy considerations including the impact on future regulation.

3.1 *Alcohol Labelling Law in the EU*

Alcohol labelling enjoys a special treatment in the EU Food Information Regulation ('FIR'). Part of these specific regulations are justified as to the "specific nature of alcoholic beverages,"[30] without indicating further what makes this nature specific. Indeed, most of the special provisions concerning alcoholic beverages in the FIR[31] are linked to the minimum amount of alcohol contained in the beverage (>1,2% by volume).

Another reason for special treatment mentioned in the FIR is more explicitly connected to the intoxicating effect, namely in relation to alcohol beverages and the attraction to the specific vulnerable groups, such as young people. Recital 40 explicitly stipulates that there is "general public concern about alcohol-related harm especially to young and vulnerable consumers". Hence "the Commission, after consultation with stakeholders and the Member States, should consider the need for a definition of beverages such as 'alcopops', which are specifically targeted at young people." This aim was taken up as a regulation in Art. 16 (4) para 2 FIR.

Thus, according to the FIR, the intoxicating effect of alcohol beverages justifies special labelling regimes towards average consumers. However, if alcoholic beverages are designed to attract consumption by young people, the FIR defines this group as a specifically vulnerable group of consumers, which may mandate also more specific regulation.

While alcoholic beverages above 1,2% by volume of alcohol must mention their alcoholic strength by volume,[32] they are exempted from a nutrition declaration and the list of ingredients.[33] They do need to comply with the other mandatory requirements, i.e. the name, allergen labelling, quantity of certain ingredients, date marking, business operator and country of origin, and instructions for use.

On one hand, therefore, the FIR imposes more stringent requirements on food business operators. Art. 9 (1) lit. k FIR requires for all "beverages containing more

[30]Recital 40 FIR.

[31]Such as Art. 9 (1) lit. k, 16 (4), 28, and 41 FIR.

[32]Art. 9 (1) lit. k FIR requires for all "beverages containing more than 1,2% by volume of alcohol" to indicate "the actual alcoholic strength by volume" as a mandatory food information to consumers.

[33]Art. 16 (4) subpara 1 FIR relaxes food information obligations "for beverages containing more than 1,2% by volume of alcohol" in a way that the "list of ingredients or a mandatory nutrition declaration" is not needed.

than 1,2% by volume of alcohol" to indicate "the actual alcoholic strength by volume" as a mandatory food information to consumers.

Alcohol beverages must also comply with allergen labelling, such as sulphur dioxide/sulphites, egg and milk products, glycyrrhizinic acid, ammonium salt etc. These must be added/highlighted in the list of ingredients or, in the absence of such, accompany the name of the beverage. A date of minimum durability only applies for beverages of <10% abv.

On the other hand, Art. 16 (4) subpara 1 FIR relaxes food information obligations for beverages of >1,2% abv in a way that the "list of ingredients or a mandatory nutrition declaration" is not needed. Regarding the nutrition declaration, Article 30 (4) specifies that a voluntary nutrition declaration on alcoholic beverages may be limited to the energy value only.

Deviating from the maximum harmonization approach of the FIR, Art. 41 FIR opens the possibility for Member States to maintain national measures for the *ingredient list*.

At EU level, alcohol is thus exempt from the two most important tools of consumer information that other foods need to provide.

At the same time, alcoholic beverages with 1,2% abv may not make nutrition claims,[34] apart from the alcohol specific ones relating to a reduction in the alcohol or energy content. Additionally, it appears that vitamins or minerals may not be claimed on these beverages: the NHCR lists a "source of [vitamin/mineral]" claim, which is defined as "(a) claim that a food is a source of vitamins and/or minerals, and any claim likely to have the same meaning for the consumer". The nutrition declaration would seem to satisfy this point. Since alcoholic beverages may only make the aforementioned specified claims, they are barred from claiming the presence of vitamins and minerals, including in a nutrition declaration.

Alcohol is subject to a lot of sector-specific exemptions and is a typical case for *lex specialis*. Generally, alcohol beverages are distinguished along the categories of wine, spirits, beer and cider and fruit wines.

Labelling for wine has always been subject to a complementary special regime for the wine sector, originally in the framework of the Wine CMO Regulation.[35] It instituted a legal regime and defined categories of grapevine products. Additionally, wines with PDO and PGI are subject to the specific wine rules in the framework of the EU Quality Schemes Regulation. To date, the 2013 CMO Regulation[36] lays

[34]Article 4(3)b of Regulation (EC) No 1924/2006 of the European Parliament and of the Council of 20 December 2006 on nutrition and health claims made on foods, OJ L 404, 30.12.2006, pp. 9–25.

[35]Originally Council Regulation (EC) No 479/2008 of 29 April 2008 on the common organisation of the market in wine, amending Regulations (EC) No 1493/1999, (EC) No 1782/2003, (EC) No 1290/2005, (EC) No 3/2008 and repealing Regulations (EEC) No 2392/86 and (EC) No 1493/1999 [now repealed].

[36]General CMO-Regulation of 2013, Regulation (EU) No 1308/2013 of the European Parliament and of the Council of 17 December 2013 establishing a common organisation of the markets in agricultural products and repealing Council Regulations (EEC) No 922/72, (EEC) No 234/79, (EC) No 1037/2001 and (EC) No 1234/2007 – OJ L 347, 20.12.2013, p. 672.

down compulsory labelling particulars for the wine sector. The horizontal FIR rules are applicable, unless superseded by a specific rule of the CMO regime. The compulsory particulars include for instance the designation of grapevine category. The EU compositional and production rules for the grapevine sector are very detailed (now in the 2013 CMO Regulation), and therefore the main consumer protection derives from the fact that in order to use the recognized grapevine product categories[37] as name, producers must comply with a tight set of intricate rules. In the case of sparkling wine, aerated sparkling wine, quality sparkling wine or quality aromatic sparkling wine, an indication of the sugar content is compulsory.[38]

Similarly, spirits[39] are subject to stringent definition about the sales denominations, production (e.g. of the ethyl alcohol) and composition. Aromatised wines,[40] next to fixed sales denominations, may be supplemented with particulars that depend on their respective sugar content, i.e. extra-dry is a sugar content of less than 30 g/litre or sweet for a sugar content of 130 g/liter or more. Beer, on the other hand, has so far eschewed any particular EU rules next to the general horizontal regime for alcoholic beverages.

The overview demonstrates that alcohol is a legal regulatory outlier. Paradoxically, in some respects alcoholic beverages are highly regulated, including compositional and process requirements that specific categories of alcoholic drinks have to satisfy. They are also barred from most nutrition claims. At the same time, they are exempt from the main pillars of general food information law, the list of ingredients and the nutrition declaration.

3.2 *Alcohol Labelling Policy Initiatives*

Alcohol food information regulation has been a contentious affair all along in the political process.[41] Exemptions were made, and the study of a 'future inclusion'

[37]The recognized categories of grapevine products (Annex VII 2013 CMO Regulation) are wine, new wine still in fermentation, liqueur wine, sparkling wine, quality/aerated/semi- sparkling wine, grape must (partially fermented, concentrated, rectified), wine from raisined overripe grapes, wine vinegar. Wine, by definition, may be obtained exclusively from the total or partial alcoholic fermentation of fresh grapes.

[38]Now Article 119(1)(g) of 2013 CMO Regulation, ex-Article 59 of Wine CMO Regulation.

[39]Regulation 110/2008 on the definition, description, presentation, labelling and the protection of geographical indications of spirit drinks and repealing Council Regulation (EEC) No 1576/89, Regulation (EC) No 110/2008 of the European Parliament and of the Council on the definition, description, presentation, labelling and protection of geographical indications of spirit drinks—OJ L 39, 13.2.2008, p. 16.

[40]Regulation (EU) No 251/2014 of the European Parliament and of the Council of 26 February 2014 on the definition, description, presentation, labelling and the protection of geographical indications of aromatised wine products and repealing Council Regulation (EEC) No 1601/91 – OJ L 84, 20.3.2014, pp. 14–34.

[41]See González Vaqué (2018), p. 233.

promised in various legislative texts. Also, the FIR of 2011 promises a review of the special treatment of alcohol. Art. 16 (4) subpara 2 FIR mandates the Commission to review this special treatment of alcoholic beverages in the FIR with a view on inter alia determining whether the policy of the non-inclusions of the list of ingredients and the information on nutrition as mandatory requirements "should in the future be covered". The Commission adopted its report 13 March 2017. The report acknowledges that there may be a link between food information labelling and "a more moderate alcohol consumption", but *excludes* this issue, looking exclusively at the consumer information. The Commission concludes that it "has not identified objective grounds that would justify the absence of information on ingredients and nutrition information on alcoholic beverages", but will first consider the self-regulatory proposals by the sector.

On 12 March 2018, Commissioner Andriukaitis met the alcoholic beverages industry, in which the industry proposed a self-regulatory proposal. The self-regulation proposal comes with distinct Annexes of the four predominant alcoholic beverages sectors (spirits, wine, beer and cider and fruit wine), testifying to their individual and often not homogeneous concerns.

The general industry commitment is weak. Although a lot of emphasis is placed on developing online tools, and joint information websites, the industry remains uncommitted to food labelling and wants to keep information off the package.

The spirits sector underlines that "spirits, unlike most other food sectors, are subject to stringent rules on their production and composition - Regulation 110/2008. How spirits are made and what they are made from is therefore legally defined."

In light of these statements it is questionable for the beverages industry what the advantage of self-regulation would be over mandatory labelling obligations. If, for instance, the beer brewers recommend to their members to simply comply with the Regulation, then this is either not a serious commitment, or they would not have an issue with EU regulation.

Overall, the main proposals are different for the sectors. There is a partial commitment in the sector of beer for full voluntary compliance with all food information law. All sectors highlight their commitment to improve off pack labelling, including nutrition information about alcoholic beverages. A specific issue that was highlighted (particularly by the spirits sector) is whether the current 100ml labelling is a suitable way of indicating nutrition information.

Why have alcoholic beverages been exempt from mainstream food information obligations, and should this continue to be the case? It is hard to identify the scientific or consumer-based reasons that led to the alcoholic beverage exemption. Certainly, it was politically difficult[42] to gain consensus for labelling, but this appears to be have resulted from hard industry concerns, rather than scientific or consumer-based reasons.

---

[42]See overview González Vaqué (2018), p. 233.

3.3 *Behavioural Studies on Alcohol Labelling*

Available behavioural studies on alcohol labelling can be clustered into studies which look into first whether consumers want nutrition information about alcoholic beverages and second into what kind of nutrition information on alcoholic beverages will be useful to consumers.

3.3.1 Do Consumers Want Nutrition Information About Alcoholic Beverages?

A GfK study from the Gesellschaft für Konsumforschung (GfK, Consumer Insights Study) of consumers across the EU (n = 9000)[43] showed that an overwhelming 86% would welcome the same nutrition information per 100 ml for alcoholic beverages as for regular foodstuffs. The interest is high on average for all specific food information—ingredients (74%), energy value (71%) and the full nutrition declaration (71%). Across Member States, however, the expressed interest varies very significantly (around 90% in Italy, around 50% in the Netherlands). Due to the specific scope of this study, it is the most pertinent study on the issue identified. Other studies support these findings.[44]

On the particular issue of energy labelling in alcoholic beverages, a systematic literature review conducted by EUFIC[45] found that studies generally show a misconception by consumers of calories in alcohol. The majority of consumers (around 60–70%) was shown to overestimate the caloric content of beer and wine, while a smaller share underestimated the caloric content (roughly 20%). The same literature review found that consumer demand for calorie labelling is strongly supported by studies (ranging between 60 and 80%).

An overwhelming majority of consumers across the EU would welcome nutrition labelling of alcohol.

3.3.2 What Kind of Means of Nutrition Information on Alcoholic Beverages Will be Useful to Consumers?

Behavioural data show that on-pack label information is the predominant mode used by consumers to acquire nutrition information. The Consumer Insights Study concludes that there is a "growing use of digital platforms, combined with traditional information sources".[46] A critical look at the data, however, reveals that for

---

43 GfK Consumer Insights Study, Report for the Brewers of Europe by GfK Belgium (2016).

44 E.g. Thomson et al. (2012), VicHealth (2009) and Kypri et al. (2007).

45 On file with authors.

46 GfK Consumer Insights Study, Report for the Brewers of Europe by GfK Belgium (2016), available at http://www.beerwisdom.eu/downloads/GfK-Consumer-Insights-Study.pdf, p. 4.

nutritional values, 31% of consumers *only* uses traditional methods, with another 44% using both digital and traditional methods. In the mixed method category, on-pack labels remain the most important information source with 71%. In addition, around 60% of consumers indicated that they never or rarely use any of the off-label information sources, with 20% using them occasionally.

This puts the self-regulatory initiative into a dire perspective—it shows a high commitment to off-pack data provision, but—at least in the current state of consumers' information acquisition—this solution does not meet consumer needs for information acquisition.

4 The Limits of the Behavioural Policy Debate: What Kind of Labelling?

If we look at the available evidence from behavioural science and nutrition labelling as the only information requirement on pack in isolation, we put forward that nutrition labelling of alcoholic beverages should occur on pack. This conclusion, however, only rests on a model with two options, namely information yes or information no. It does not give any guidance as to how such information shall be designed. If we divert attention to the "how", an articulation about the regulatory goal such an information shall achieve is warranted. Information as such is never neutral, it always works in a context towards achieving a certain goal. This also accounts for labelling of alcohol. Compared to the majority of other foods, alcohol is special in that it is scientifically clearly linked to negative health consequences (the same would be true for sugar[47]). The effect of alcohol on health is not only a link in terms of caloric value, or other nutrients. The substance alcohol affects health independently, due to its toxic effect. Under current EU legislation, alcohol content must be indicated by % of volume on a product, but this information can be in a different visual field and does not immediately provide an absolute amount. While, therefore, caloric and other standard nutrition particulars are an important variable to show about alcohol, the nutrition declaration does not provide information about the alcoholic content.

The health effects of alcohol are currently entirely neglected in labelling, and the Commission explicitly excludes this topic in their report.[48] This is a notable deficit in the ongoing debate and in the policy proposals. The discussion about the ingredient list and nutrition declaration labelling diverts attention from the question of whether

---

[47]See on the parallels Lustig (2010) and Lustig et al. (2012).

[48]Report from the European Commission to the European Parliament and the Council regarding the mandatory labelling of the list of ingredients and the nutrition declaration of alcoholic beverages, Brussels, 13.3.2017, COM(2017) 58 final, section 1: "While nutrition labelling can play a certain role in the promotion of a more moderate alcohol consumption, the issue of the labelling of the list of ingredients and the nutrition declaration for alcoholic beverages is examined in this report under the perspective of consumer information about the identity and the properties of a food."

the alcohol content should be immediately included in the nutrition declaration. In determining how nutrition labels shall be designed, regard shall be had as to how nutrition labels can contribute to a healthier diet, so-called directive labelling.[49]

We hypothesise that the empirical evidence of the effectiveness of directive labelling is sparse and to our knowledge non-existent for non-directive alcohol labels. However, in our view, it is one of the most pressing issues that needs further study and policy consideration in the future.

4.1 Limited Data Availability on Different Policy Options

A systematic literature review on 46 empirical, English-language, peer-reviewed studies addressing alcohol labelling from a consumer point of view showed two serious limitations in studies addressing alcohol labelling on alcoholic beverages.[50] These are, notably:

(1) **The specifics of intervention measures that were subject to consumer studies are often overlooked and heavily over-generalized**. For instance, a cluster of the earlier—and well quoted—studies on alcohol labelling were done in the US context. Under the US Alcoholic Beverage Labeling Act (ABLA), government warnings on alcoholic beverages address pregnancy risks, ability to drive a car and a short 'may cause health problems'.[51] These are *specific sentences* that group *three distinct risks (alcohol-pregnancy/alcohol-driving/alcohol-health)* that have to be stated in *textual form*. The health warning is non-prominent, and formulated in a 'may' format, thus being semi-directive.

Such generalization can be questioned, for instance, for studies relating only to the 'pregnancy warning' logo. The generalizability is limited due to the specificity of the risk they are indicating, as well as for the design of the intervention measure (simply a logo, as opposed to the US textual warning, for instance, *According to the Surgeon General, women should not drink alcoholic beverages during pregnancy because of the risk of birth defects.*)

Studies on intervention measures, in addition, are often insufficiently clear in their reporting as to what exactly was shown to consumers and lead to drawing conclusions that may be overgeneralizing.

Even if studies are specific in mentioning the intervention measures used, the findings are often abused way beyond a specific kind of intervention measure at issue. In assessing the utility of a consumer study on alcohol labelling, it is therefore

[49] Hodgkins et al. (2012) and Bialkova et al. (2013).

[50] On file with one of the authors.

[51] Alcoholic Beverage Labeling Act (ABLA) of the Anti-Drug Abuse Act of 1988, Pub.L. 100–690, 102 Stat. 4181, enacted November 18, 1988, H.R. 5210.

necessary to carefully consider (a) the design of the intervention measure, (b) the risk addressed, and the (c) directiveness of the message.

(2) **Not all policy options are equally represented in consumer research, and some not at all.** Not the full range of policy options has equal attention, and some policy options are understudied or not studied at all. The literature review showed that around half of the consumer studies have been conducted on health warning messages, and around a third on Standard Drink Units and Standard Drink Guidelines, i.e. very directive or semi-directive options. No studies address the pure non-directive option of including the alcohol content in gram.

The alcohol labelling case study shows that there is limited availability of scientific data matched to different policy options that could be considered by the policy makers. It is therefore paramount for policy makers to examine whether consumer insights on the different policy options under consideration is available at all.

One explanation of the lack of a non-directive pure alcohol gram labelling option in policy discussions is the fact that such intervention measure is not currently studied in consumer studies. One risk is that policy makers' options are limited and influence by studies on what is available, instead of the other way around (policy makers formulating questions to study) as it should be. This strikes us as a plausible hypothesis.

5 Conclusions and the Way Forward

Currently available studies from behavioural and health and safety science do not justify the current exemption of alcohol labelling from the major food labelling requirements in EU law. Quite the contrary, particularly insights from food, health and safety science mandate policy interventions in order to protect consumers. The self-regulatory proposals from industry are unlikely to be a sufficient response to the health and safety requirements, nor do they outbalance the lack of justification of the current exemption from the most important labelling requirements in Union law. However, with respect to what exactly should be done instead in order to communicate to consumers effectively about the risks involved with alcohol consumption there is only limited valid data available. As a default, long known deficiencies about the 'information overload' of consumers in the food chain[52] indicate that a simple application of all provisions of EU food information law on alcoholic beverages may not be fit for the purpose to effectively communicate risks to consumers. However, acquiring data on the effect of policy options is difficult,[53] and those who make

[52]Verbeke (2005).

[53]Purnhagen and van Kleef (2018), p. 126.

policy recommendations based in currently available data from behavioural science base their recommendations of patchy data.

Concluding, an overwhelming evidence from especially health and safety science require intervention into drinking behaviour of European consumers. However, limited data on the effect on policy interventions exists. So, which policy options to choose on which basis?

On one hand, one could meaningfully conclude that some data is better than no data, hence, in light of the requirement to act, rather than having no indication one could at least base one's intervention on the little and patchy data available. However, if this argument is followed, other policy problems may emerge. "(P) atchy data might be misleading if the patterns of omission are unknown, and often data collected for other purposes might carry categories that are not suited to the regulatory purpose at hand."[54] As a consequence, a rigorous application of a regulatory validity test is warranted to justify robust policy advice on how to design alcohol labelling laws.[55]

First legal validity. The exemption in EU labelling law concerns the nutrition label and the list of ingredients. Hence, EU-related studies on whether consumers endorse such an exemption relate to ingredient and nutrition labelling, which directly refers to the legal requirement. However, with regards to how one shall interfere, most alcohol labelling studies concern labelling of health risks and/or risks to specific vulnerable groups such as pregnant women. From the perspective of legal validity, the studies may only carry some normative value to determine if consumer want nutrition and ingredients information. When determining which kind of labelling is required, studies do not refer to nutrition and health labelling, which makes it difficult to connect to the fact that only nutrition and health labelling are exempted. Furthermore, the studies concerning nutrition and ingredients information do not distinguish between the different vulnerability levels and type of alcohol as required by the FIR. For example, alcopops and teenagers are treated in the same category as senior wine drinkers. This also limits the legal validity of the studies, as EU law requires a different yardstick to be applied to alcohol typically consumed by teenagers and other consumers.

With regards to scientific validity, most of the studies investigating different policy tools did not include all of the relevant policy options into their assessment. It is hence impossible to make a final judgment regarding which policy options are the "better" ones, as most have simply not been included in the analysis. The type of interventions are also often confused, comparing textual with pictorial claims (or disregarding the fact that pictorial claims may be the better policy option).

Social validity is a concern throughout all studies, as neither stakeholders were sufficiently engaged in the research design nor was acceptability of the application of respective behavioural findings tested on stakeholders.

---

[54] Purnhagen and Feindt (2015).

[55] See on the requirement to conduct a regulatory validity test Purnhagen (2018).

No robust conclusion can hence be made relying on the available behavioural science. However, relatively robustly one can conclude that consumers want to know more about the nutritional value and the ingredients of the alcohol they consume. A recommendation how such information shall be conveyed cannot be based on behavioural science research so far available. Safety science, however, indicates that such information shall be directed more clearly towards enabling consumers to drink healthier.

References

Alemanno A, Sibony A-L (eds) (2015) Nudge and the Law. Hart, Oxford

Alemanno A, Spina A (2014) Nudging legally: on the checks and balances of behavioral regulation. Int J Const Law 12:429–456

Bialkova S, Grunert K, van Trijp H (2013) Standing out in the crowd: the effect of information clutter on consumer attention for front-of-pack nutrition labels. Food Policy 41:65–74

Calder B, Phillips L, Tybout A (1982) The concept of external validity. J Consum Res 9:240–244

Campbell D, Stanley J (1966) Experimental and quasi-experimental designs for research. Rand McNally

Fabbri H, Faure M (2018) Toward a "constitution" for behavioral policy-making. Int Rev Econ 65 (3):241–270

GfK Consumer Insights Study, Report for the Brewers of Europe by GfK Belgium (2016). Available at http://www.beerwisdom.eu/downloads/GfK-Consumer-Insights-Study.pdf

Gibbons M, Limoges C, Nowotny H, Schwartzman S, Scott P, Trow M (1994) The new production of knowledge: the dynamics of science and research in contemporary societies. Sage

González Vaqué L (2018) Listing ingredients on the labels of alcoholic beverages in the EU: a reality? Eur Food Feed Law Rev 13(3):233–240

Hansen PG, Jespersen AM (2013) Nudge and the manipulation of choice. A framework for the responsible use of the nudge approach to behavioral change in public policy. Eur J Risk Regul 4 (1):3–28

Heiman A, Zilberman D (2011) The effects of framing on consumers' choice of GM foods. AgBioForum 14:171–179

Herpen E, Purnhagen K (2018) Can bonus packs mislead consumers? A demonstration of how behavioural consumer research can inform unfair commercial practices law on the example of the ECJ's mars judgement. J Consum Policy 40(2):217–234

Hodgkins C, Barnett J, Wasowicz-Kirylo G, Stysko-Kunkowska M, Gulcan Y, Kustepeli Y, Akgungor S, Chryssochoidis G, Fernández-Celemin L, Storcksdieck Genannt Bonsmann S, Gibbs M, Raats M (2012) Understanding how consumers categorise nutritional labels: a consumer derived typology for front-of-pack nutrition labelling. Appetite 59(3):806–817

Kypri K, Langley JD, Saunders JB, Cashell-Smith ML (2007) Assessment may conceal therapeutic benefit: findings from a randomized controlled trial for hazardous drinking. Addiction 102:62–70

Lustig H, Schmidt LH, Brindis CD (2012) The toxic truth about sugar. Nature 482:27–29

Lustig RHJ (2010) Fructose: metabolic, hedonic, and societal parallels with ethanol. Am Diet Assoc 110:1307–1321

Mathis K (ed) (2015) European perspectives on behavioural law and economics. Springer Science, New York et al

McCrudden C, King J (2015) The dark side of nudging: the ethics, political economy, and law of libertarian paternalism. Michigan Law, Public Law and Legal Theory Research Paper Series, Paper No. 485, November 2015. http://ssrn.com/abstract=2685832. Accessed 27 July 2017, pp 189–200

Purnhagen K (2014) The behavioural law and economics of the precautionary principle in the EU and its impact on internal market regulation. J Consum Policy 37(3):453–464

Purnhagen K (2015) Why do we need responsive regulation and behavioural research in EU internal market law? In: Mathis K (ed) European perspectives on behavioural law and economics. Springer Science, New York et al, pp 51–69

Purnhagen K (2018) Regulatory validity. In: Micklitz H-W, Sibony A-L, Esposito F (eds) Research methods in consumer law. Edward Elgar, Cheltenham, pp 276–295

Purnhagen K, Feindt P (2015) Better regulatory impact assessment: making behavioural insights work for the commission's new better regulation strategy. Eur J Risk Regul 6(3):361–368

Purnhagen K, Reisch L (2016) "Nudging Germany"? Herausforderungen für eine verhaltensbasierte Regulierung in Deutschland. Zeitschrift für Europäisches Privatrecht, 529–655

Purnhagen K, Schebesta H (2019) Food Labelling for Consumers – EU Law, Regulation and Policy Options. Department for Citizens' Rights and Constitutional General for Internal Policies of the Union PE 608.871 - April 2019, available at http://www.europarl.europa.eu/RegData/etudes/STUD/2019/608871/IPOL_STU(2019)608871_EN.pdf

Purnhagen KP, van Herpen E (2017) Can Bonus Packs Mislead Consumers? A demonstration of how behavioural consumer research can inform unfair commercial practices law on the example of the ECJ's Mars Judgement. J Consum Policy 40(2):217–234

Purnhagen K, van Kleef E (2018) Commanding to "Nudge" via the proportionality principle? - a case study on diets in EU food law. In: Bremmers H, Purnhagen K (eds) Regulating and managing food safety in the EU. Springer Science, New York et al, pp 151–168

Report from the European Commission to the European Parliament and the Council regarding the mandatory labelling of the list of ingredients and the nutrition declaration of alcoholic beverages, Brussels, 13.3.2017, COM(2017) 58 final

Sibony A-L (2015) Can EU consumer law benefit from behavioural insights? In: Mathis K (ed) European perspectives on behavioural law and economics. Springer Science, New York et al, pp 71–106

Straßheim H, Beck S (eds) (2019) Handbook of behavioural change and public policy. Edward Elgar, Cheltenham

Sunstein C (2015) The ethics of nudging. Yale J Regul 32(2):413–450

Thomson LM, Vandenberg B, Fitzgerald JL (2012) An exploratory study of drinkers views of health information and warning labels on alcohol containers. Drug Alcohol Rev 31(2):240–247

Van Aaken A (2015) Judge the nudge: in search of legal limits of paternalistic nudging in the EU. In: Alemanno A, Sibony AL (eds) Nudging and the law: what can EU law learn from the behavioral sciences? Hart, Oxford, pp 83–112

Verbeke W (2005) Agriculture and the food industry in the information age. Eur Rev Agric Econ 32 (3):347–368

VicHealth (2009), Alcohol health information labels. Available at https://www.vichealth.vic.gov.au/-/media/ProgramsandProjects/ReducingAlcoholMisuse/Attachments/Background-Paper-Labels_FINAL.pdf

Zeiler K (2010) Cautions on the use of economic experiments in law. J Inst Theor Econ 166:178–193

Hanna Schebesta Associate Professor of Law at the Wageningen University & Research. P.O. Box 8130, 6700 EW Wageningen, Fields of Interest: EU Law, Food and Agricultural Law, Public Procurement Law.

Kai Purnhagen Associate Professor of Law at the Wageningen University & Research. P.O. Box 8130, 6700 EW Wageningen. Fields of Interest: EU Law, International Economic Law, Law and Behavioural Science, Risk Regulation (incl. Food Law), Comparative Law.

Environmental Protection by Means of Consumer Law? Sustainability and Civil Law: The Example of Climate Protection

Felix Ekardt and Jutta Wieding

Abstract This chapter intends to show the Law & Economics (or Law & Governance) perspective on the question of whether consumer law can be regarded as a core policy instrument for pursuing ecological concerns. Consumer law regulations for more environmental protection refer to mandatory disclosure of product information, but also to further approaches such as warranty periods and liability claims. The discussion on environmental protection through consumer law is part of a broader discussion on "environmental protection through private law". It is necessary to precisely distinguish between different environmental problems for a discussion on environmental protection through consumer law (and also generally through civil law). Immediate health hazards are more accessible to consumer legislation than quantity problems such as climate change, dwindling biodiversity or disturbed nitrogen and phosphorus cycles. There, quantity governance proves to be a far more effective instrument and also more compatible with the liberal democratic separation of powers. Consumer law can only play a complementary role. The basis for all these assessments consists in triangulated basic concepts of behavioral science (also, but not only) on environmental issues. The issues analysed were also the subject of two three-year projects each for the German Federal Government (one on the further development of climate protection law, another one on the social transformation of energy systems) and a study for the German Federal Parliament (on environmental protection through general civil law and in particular company law).

1 Problem Outline

Law & Economics is known to constitute an analysis of legal topics using economic approaches. This regards both the legal interpretation and the governance assessment of the effectiveness of a specific policy instrument, i.e. the determination or

F. Ekardt · J. Wieding (✉)
Research Unit Sustainability and Climate Policy, Leipzig, Germany
e-mail: felix.ekardt@uni-rostock.de

K. Mathis, A. Tor (eds.), *Consumer Law and Economics*, Economic Analysis of Law in European Legal Scholarship 9, https://doi.org/10.1007/978-3-030-49028-7_14

assessment of the steering effect of certain legal regulations. This chapter will direct such a (governance) perspective to asking whether consumer law can be regarded as a key legal instrument for regulating ecological concerns. It is not focussed on describing the details of individual legal systems, but rather on reviewing possible governance options with regard to their effectiveness.

Consumer legislation for more environmental protection refers, for example, to approaches such as mandatory disclosure of product information, which play a role in some contributions in this volume. Other areas include warranty law and liability regulations. The question of whether a standard for "sustainability" or "climate friendliness" can be established under consumer law as an enforceable requirement for products will be discussed in particular detail here. Another look will be taken at tenant protection regulations (which are more in line with consumer law in the broader sense) and the tenant-owner dilemma. Within this scope, the present contribution will pursue several topics and hypotheses. Climate protection will serve as an example here, while the possible peculiarities of other environmental problems will also be discussed. It has been repeatedly argued that climate change is a top-ranking existential and economic problem for humanity. This is underlined by the fact that global warming threatens to increase the severity and the frequency of food and water scarcity, major natural disasters, huge migratory movements, wars and civil wars.

In the debate on governance instruments, it is often forgotten that the effectiveness of governance instruments can only be measured against a specific objective.[1] A few introductory remarks are therefore required on the global target framework for climate protection before the contribution explains the methodology in more detail and then discusses the instruments for consumer protection mentioned. More detailed deliberations on this have been made elsewhere.[2] However, our first remarks have to take a look at the target against which we assess instruments in the following. The international Paris Climate Agreement (PA) may be disappointing in details (due to the voluntary character of state obligations etc.)—but at the same time, the agreement is very ambitious in terms of its overall objective. It requires that a balance of emissions and sinks is reached by the end of the twenty-first century at the latest (Art. 4 para. 1 PA) and to keep—which is even more ambitious—global warming well below 2 degrees Celsius with pursuing efforts for 1.5 degrees (Art. 2 para. 1 PA). Art. 2 PA in particular is clearly legally binding, since, according to Art. 3 PA, the norm is the binding basis for the efforts of the states. But what is meant by "well below" 2 degrees? The wording suggests about 1.7 or 1.8 degrees as temperature limit, as it has to be significantly—"well"—below 2, but more than 1.5 degrees. "Pursuing efforts" towards 1.5 degrees does not mean that this objective can be easily dismissed legally. Rather, actual measures have to be taken, which try to reduce more emission than necessary to stay with 1.7 or 1.8 degrees. The wording does not clarify the scope of these measures. Its evolution,

[1] On the following see in detail Ekardt et al. (2018), Ekardt (2019a) and Ekardt et al. (2015).

[2] Ekardt (2016a).

meaning the negotiation process leading to the PA, however suggests that 1.5 degrees are actually to be achieved, unless this is already impossible. We have seen in earlier contributions by us that this interpretation is supported by human rights. 1.5 degrees requires global zero emissions in all sectors in roundabout two decades. This is therefore the binding target for all debates about climate policy instruments.

2 Methodology of Legal Impact Research: Behavioural Research, Behavioural Economics and Governance Problems

This contribution links the debate on consumer law with the debate on environmental law. So far, both debates have mostly existed side by side. The issues analysed below were the subject of two projects by the German government lasting three-years each (one on the further development of climate protection law, the other on the social transformation of energy systems) and a study by the German parliament, the Bundestag (on environmental protection through civil law and in particular company law).

The basis for all the assessments in the following is (in addition to the legal interpretation) a multi-method qualitative governance examination. It combines the methods and results of various disciplines such as economics, law, political science, sociology, ethnology, cultural studies, psychology and socio-biology in order to investigate behaviour and the effectiveness of governance instruments. The combined, respectively triangulating, approach to analyse human behavioural motives provides an analysis of the causes of non-sustainability respectively the conditions for a transformation towards sustainability. This can provide the basis for identifying concrete political and legal instruments to reach the respectively supposed targets. For the purpose of this chapter an overview of this methodology in all brevity:[3]

- Human behaviour patterns and especially behavioural motives can be analysed by a multi-method approach. Surveys and experiments, as economists like to conduct, can contribute to this assessment (e.g. to price elasticities among the addressees), however, all of these have their limits described in detail in other publications. And in particular it is not enough to assume that every actor is purely selfish and constantly consciously-calculating as the economic mainstream does with game theory. In this respect, the multi-method approach to behavioural research must not purely rely on experiments and surveys, but combines those approaches with participant observation, sociobiological analysis, self-observation and further methods. This is the indispensable basis to estimate the effectiveness of governance instruments, particularly in the case (which is typical

[3]On details see Ekardt (2019a).

for sustainability issues), that instruments are developed, which do not yet exist—or under different circumstances—in real life. It follows that the behaviour of those addressed by the governance has to be anticipated by means of findings about their motivation. It has been shown elsewhere[4] that politicians, citizens, entrepreneurs and consumers (both individually and as structures) block each other in vicious circles. For all those involved, a lack of knowledge often appears to be a minor problem on the road to sustainability. In particular, factors such as established conceptions of normality, fundamental human emotions (convenience, lack of spatio-temporal distance orientation, denial, lack of thinking in complex causalities, etc.), self-interested calculations—in the case of companies, but also investors currently aiming at short-term profit in the basic trend—, outdated values, path dependencies and problems of collective goods make it unlikely that more sustainability will occur of its own accord.[5] Any policy or legislation must also be constructed taking these motivational factors into account—and the fact that adequate legislation has not yet been put in place is again attributable to these factors. Because not only citizenship, companies and interest groups, but also politics is (obviously) made by people whose behaviour is subject to the above-mentioned impulses. Incentivising voluntary change in companies and citizenship might principally be conceivable due to the interdependence of all actors (which almost always makes social change possible only in the interplay of different stakeholders), however, without binding political and legal measures a decisive link is missing.

- The behavioural motives regarding (non-)sustainability that can be found, form a basis for making certain expected governance problems plausible to a high degree.[6] Looking at governance problems is crucial for the examination of instruments for effectiveness on the basis of the given targets (and strategies) for sustainability. This applies not only to hypothetical governance options, but also to those instruments that are already in place, because it is often difficult even in those cases to answer which social developments can really be attributed precisely to the governance instrument to be examined. With regard to sustainability issues, these are particularly rebound effects (including welfare effects), shifting effects to another region, another sector or another environmental strain, problems of depicting, lacking ambition of targets and enforcement deficits. The existence of just those governance problems cannot be simply detected in reality, because we are dealing with governance constellations, which have never existed before (e.g. with a complete decarbonisation within a few years). Therefore, behavioural research is a necessary basis. At the same time, other empirical insights besides behavioural research are also important. The fact, that

[4]On details see Ekardt (2019a), Ekardt (2016a).

[5]On behavioural motives see Ekardt (2019a), Milinski and Marotzke (2015), Liedtke (2011), pp. 37 et seq.; Kahneman (2011), Akerlof and Shiller (2009), pp. XI, 21 and *passim*; Steinberg (2013) and Dean (2013).

[6]Ekardt et al. (2018), Ekardt (2019a), Hennig (2017) and von Bredow (2013).

macroeconomically e.g. greenhouse gas emissions can be shifted, can actually be measured in parts (however, with great difficulties), by determining the greenhouse-gas intensity of products based on technical data, and then combining them with statistical data on imports and exports.[7] Regarding the rebound effect, this is admittedly more difficult, because the causality between various single aspects is hard to pin down.[8] Nevertheless, with regard to existing or alternative policy instruments, also text content, implementation studies and possible comparisons are useful, since supplementary factors such as the obvious characteristics of the instruments and other scientific, technical and economic conditions contribute to identifying certain instruments to likely be effective or ineffective.

- In any case, there is much to suggest that the multi-methodological governance analysis outlined in this way should be carried out qualitatively and that supposedly exact quantifications should be used more cautiously than has been the case up to now.[9] This is because the behavioural motives alone and the governance problems caused by disregarding them cannot be quantified comprehensively and precisely, but rather only selectively. Therefore, it is also not possible to use them mathematically, or it can only be calculated by accepting the problem that a large number of assumptions are made that might not be correct. In doing so, even meaningful probabilities for the occurrence of certain factors cannot be mathematically determined, because these probabilities are generally not known; however, this then thwarts calculations. The same goes for other natural scientific, technical and economic findings. Each case is further complicated by unclear causal relationships between various factors and, especially in sustainability issues, the ultimately global framework of reference. Therefore, it would not be enough to pay attention to external factors such as political majorities or characteristics of institutions[10]—which are important, but which in turn are an expression of the motivational situations mentioned. In any case, only optimally designed instruments or instruments that are strongly deficient can be compared respectively—the popular exercise of evaluating an idealised instrument against a misconstrued alternative in practice gets us nowhere. In contrast, the fixation on numbers of the empirical paradigm encounters various limitations. Because, without exhausting space in this chapter on the details: Not only is behaviour not countable. Also, facts of biodiversity, ecological assessment and scenarios are largely not countable either.[11] It is even less feasible[12] to substitute a normative

---

[7] Peters et al. (2011).

[8] On the discussion Santarius (2015).

[9] Ekardt (2019a, b).

[10] On these aspects Abson et al. (2017), Droste-Frank (2015), Newig et al. (2015), Juerges and Newig (2015), Klein (2014), Klinsky et al. (2012), Herrmann-Pillath (2015, 2016).

[11] On the latter Dieckhoff (2015), Ekardt et al. (2018); on the first Ekardt and Hennig (2015).

[12] More detailed Ekardt (2018).

justification of sustainability with an alleged cost-benefit analysis,[13] which quantifies everything, meaning to make it countable.

All in all, the acquisition of knowledge in sustainability questions remains bound to be transdisciplinary due to the big challenges the subject matter in itself presents. Transdisciplinary means in this context to start thinking from the research questions at hand and not along dogmatic boundaries of a discipline, or even a school. Moreover, there is a need to work with a great number of approaches and arguments. Citable literature exists for almost all thinkable hypotheses, especially in behavioural research, while the respective fields of research often show certain tendencies to self-evidence, secured by notoriously leaving aside all other disciplines, schools and findings.[14] Seen in this light, there is no way to justify that different behavioural sciences largely ignore each other. Therefore, reservations of most sociologists against socio-biologists, neurologists and economists urgently need to be re-evaluated—and vice versa. Comparing the findings of different disciplines, triangulating methods and thus assessing them critically, can result in interesting findings. It might be accurate that this could cause an overload to the individual scientist—especially since sustainability issues suggest to question otherwise common starting points in natural sciences, like scenarios with their thousands of underlying assumptions.

3 Which Environmental Problems Are Amenable to Civil Law Regulation?

It is imperative for a discussion on environmental protection through consumer law (and also generally through civil law) to distinguish precisely between different environmental problems. Immediate health hazards may be far more likely to be the subject of consumer legislation than climate change, biodiversity loss or disrupted nitrogen and phosphorus cycles. However, a consumer law approach runs the risk of repeating problems of command-and-control law. In order to understand this, the nature of environmental problems needs to be described in more detail.[15]

The effect of the existing domestic and transnational sustainability instruments has been limited so far. As seen, sustainability governance and (also) energy and climate protection law typically work with specifications for individual products, facilities or activities, such as cars, buildings or at any rate individual areas of life, which are determined and possibly sanctioned in the event of non-compliance. Modern resource and sink problems, however, are ultimately quantity problems.

---

[13]Critical Ekardt (2019b).

[14]On the problem especially of the human inclination of simplification, even in scientific circles Ekardt (2017).

[15]On civil law and sustainability see in general Caterini (2018), Iftime (2014) and Ekardt (2016b).

This means: as a general rule, environmental problems are less relevant to individual exposures than to the total quantity of exposures or a specific total extraction of resources. This is particularly evident in the case of climate change, and it is also true in the case of the finite nature of natural resources. Other examples are biodiversity loss, pollutants, radiation or noise, in all of which the total amount of intervention is of key importance—in addition to the local pollution that may be relevant there (unlike in the case of the climate).

Especially local hotspots are still a well-suited topic for partial command-and-control regulation that addresses individual sites, actions and products. On the other hand, the quantitative nature of problems, if largely ignored as in previous practice and discourses, leads to some governance problems such as the ones mentioned above (especially rebound effects and shifting effects, as we will see in more detail in the following). Those problems cannot be solved by instruments that are oriented towards individual products, individual plants or also towards individual subject areas or limited geographical areas, which is the case especially for command-and-control law. It is important that the same problems also exist with voluntary activities by companies, i.e. self-regulation, and ultimately with voluntary activities by consumers.[16]

These experiences so far suggest that consumer protection law—which naturally also addresses individual products and actions—also reaches its limits when it comes to environmental protection. This will be further examined in the following. Most of the time, climate protection will serve as an example.

4 Standardising Sustainability and Climate Friendliness in Civil Law: Learning from Company Law

A concrete consumer protection approach to climate protection could lie in the law on deficiency warranties. For example, one could—either by interpreting the law or by changing the law—think of a lack of climate friendliness as a material defect of products. If climate policy has yet changed little of our per capita ecological footprint in Western countries (and emerging markets): Why not try a new climate policy approach in consumer law? The discussion on environmental protection through consumer law is part of a broader discussion on "environmental protection through civil law" at this aspect in particular. This discussion (up to and including company law or even climate liability suits against transnational fossil corporations) deserves a critical examination, because of the many years of experience with calling for ever new instruments of environmental protection which, according to previous experience, might be even less effective than the "classical" command-and-control approaches (if those were only used correctly). Establishing sustainability itself as

[16] Hennig (2017), Ekardt (2019a), von Bredow (2013), mostly overlooked in the current debate, e.g. by Bernauer and Schaffer (2010) and Biermann et al. (2009).

a benchmark is not only considered in consumer law, but also, for example, in company law. In any case, a sustainability approach in this area of law is based on changing the rules between different private law subjects. In the following, we will consider how effective such an approach can be.[17]

The attempt to establish climate friendliness—or even sustainability as a whole—as a material benchmark anchored in consumer protection law is courageous already against the background of the very ambitious target. In addition, it is very difficult to issue the desired standard with the necessary individual concreteness—or more precisely, the concreteness related to the respective product. It is a common criticism that the term sustainability is frequently filled with a rather arbitrary content. Instead of permanently and globally tenable ways of living and working, sustainability is often only a matter of trivial demands such as weighing up different things in life. However, this is not exclusively due to the unfavourable motivation of many stakeholders (see above), but also due to the fact that sustainability needs to be concretised to a high degree. Sustainability, if understood as long-term and globally durable ways of living and economic activity, is still easier to grasp than e.g. the completely open concept of the common good. However, at least at the moment (and this is what is at stake in civil or consumer protection law) when an individual product is to be evaluated, the lack of conceptual concretisation becomes apparent. Where exactly is the line between allowed and forbidden behaviour? It is precisely the task of the law to clearly determine this.

This applies not only to sustainability as a whole, but also and especially to climate friendliness. Even if it may be possible to imagine that all products could be expected to produce and use zero emissions in two decades (based on Art. 2 para. 1 PA), what does this imply in the short run? What does that mean, for example, for the products of a car company—which intermediate goals apply? How should these be distributed among different car types? In what order must different sectors such as electricity, heat, transport, agriculture and plastics—which encounter very different difficulties—be decarbonised? Identical questions also arise for every other type of company and product, such as airlines and the trips they offer. Are airlines simply not allowed any longer? If they are, how many flights can there still be? Are there any transitional periods, and if so, which ones? Should meat consumption be prohibited as a whole; or should the amounts of meat produced be limited? Should not the consumption of animal products be strictly prohibited, and not only the consumption of meat, because land use always produces emissions even if the mineral fertiliser is not used and even minor climate changes endanger human lives? In other words, how many emissions do we believe we can offset through improved land use and wetland management and thus accept without worries? And how can we deal with the complex interrelations of various sustainability problems such as climate, energy, biodiversity, water and soil protection? How should we set the priorities for difficult balancing issues?

[17] See also Ekardt (2016b).

If general sustainability or climate-friendliness clauses were to be integrated into consumer protection law (or generally into civil law, like company law), all of this would in future have to be concretised by a civil court on the occasion of a single case, a single product or a single company. And it is not clear how this could be achieved. Another continuous problem is the complete transparency of complex production chains, the achievement of which will often not be possible in individual cases. It is not possible to avoid either the problem of actual concretisation or the associated problem of production chains by merely demanding to not cause harm, e.g. under a slogan like "no externalisation of social costs". For as long as environmental impacts occur at all, damage always occurs somewhere; they are certainly (strongly) minimisable, but the manner in which the action should take place requires concrete decisions.

The problems described become even greater if one wanted to make "the common good" in general or very abstractly articulated social concerns such as "the fair distribution of income" and "equality of educational and employment opportunities" a standard of civil law beyond a sustainability that focuses on questions relating to the future and globality, i.e. above all on resource issues.[18] The core content expected of companies there is then all the more unclear without detailed concretisation, because very different concepts of social distribution are conceivable, as is also common in the legal debate on the welfare state and the philosophical debate on egalitarianism.[19]

Moreover, the yardstick for effective policy instruments is not to just randomly improve the situation—but rather to achieve the target line from Art. 2 para. 1 PA. It is not enough—for example—to save small amounts of greenhouse gases, optimise a few production processes, etc. in climate protection. It is necessary to cut down the emissions to zero within two decades.[20] In addition, the question of the long-term relationship between sustainability and the growth paradigm is rather camouflaged by unspecific general-phrase-like civil law norms. In general, it is probably important for the sustainability discourse (even if future technical innovations can of course never be definitively foreseen) not to look solely at solutions through new technologies, but (especially in the industrialised countries) also to consider frugality with regard to various actions common today. However, this can hardly be meaningfully translated into a standard for an individual product, so that not only the question of the individual company, but also of a sustainable economy, which will possibly have to manage without growth, should be posed as a whole.[21]

[18]Attempting to do just that Felber (2012), passim; Hoffmann and Hofmann (2015), pp. 6 et seq.

[19]See Lowitzsch et al. (2015), pp. 13 et seq.; Ekardt (2016a), § 4 F. III.

[20]Using data from the IPCC (2007, 2014)—closer elaborated in Ekardt et al. (2018) opposing the purely technical and growth-oriented perspective of e.g. Stern (2009).

[21]See Paech (2012), Higgins (2015), Jackson (2009), Nørgård and Xue (2016), Ekardt (2016a), § 1 B. V. There are numerous examples of multinational companies that already operate ecologically according to their self-perception. Sukhdev (2013), *passim* analyses companies that produce cotton more ecologically, global coffee chains that sell organic coffee, and long-distance tour operators that care about the social and ecological situation in a holiday destination, sports-shoe

When considering existing regulations in consumer protection law, one must therefore take into account, among other things, that companies within the EU, but often also beyond it, enjoy freedom of movement and can thus react to certain regulations. Regulations that are perceived as massively disadvantageous by companies are thus confronted with potential shifting effects as they might just relocate their production or service activities elsewhere. Relocation here does not only mean moving away and shifting problems to other sectors, but also the question of where new investments arise. Also rebound effects cannot be sensibly avoided with regulations based on individual products.

In addition to all these concerns about the ecological effectiveness of consumer protection law as an instrument, there is a constitutional problem. Sustainability regulations under civil law and thus also under consumer protection law are, if they are supposed to preserve the regulatory system of civil law with its many judicial concretisations, subject to greater concerns from the perspective of democracy and separation of powers. After all, a liberal-democratic law represents the legislative balancing of a multitude of affected spheres of freedom. There would therefore be a danger that a focus on civil law would pass a lot of power from the parliaments to the courts of instance.

This constitutional reference is certainly not to be understood as meaning that sustainability is at the discretion of the legislature.[22] Rather, the guarantees of the elementary preconditions of freedom such as life, health, minimum subsistence in the form of food, water, security, etc. call for fundamental sustainability in the sense of long-term and global preservation of the natural foundations of life. However, there is a political scope for balancing due to the collision of these guarantees with the freedom rights of companies and consumers living here and now. Exactly this complex weighing, however, can only be done by freedom-friendly institutions (specifically by a democracy based on checks and balances) and not primarily by a civil court or an individual company. The question of what exactly is owed to the whole of society and the world in terms of, e.g., climate protection, cannot be reduced to the individual or the individual company thereby making it possible to say exactly which types of entrepreneurial actions, purchases or investments are still permissible and which are not.

---

manufacturers and global cosmetics chains that produce their products with less resources, etc. But both long-distance travel and fashionable footwear for all kinds of sports and cosmetics are examples of products that nobody seemed to need some time ago. Twenty years ago, nobody would have thought that a coffee machine producing one standard coffee would not be sufficient in the office, but that instead a multitude of specialities, aromas and foams would be needed. In a nutshell, all these products can be regarded as the results of an attempt to enable sales and economic growth in a rather saturated western world—by the way without guaranteeing increasing happiness. Therefore, it will not work as a sustainability strategy to just make some additional products greener: Long-distance flights, which would not have been undertaken in the past, do not benefit the environment by making aircraft more energy-efficient.

[22]On the following e.g. Ekardt (2016a), §§ 4, 5 taking the example of the human-rights discourse in Germany, EU law and especially in international law; generally, e.g. Unnerstall (1999) and Jonas (1979).

In the sense of "better than nothing", a product standard that specifies zero emissions from a deadline in two decades would certainly be worth considering. It could also be considered to apply the German environmental standards throughout the entire production chain, including processes abroad, as a product requirement. Due to the high level of prosperity, the ecological footprint per capita in Europe is greater than in developing or emerging countries; nevertheless, the individual requirements for products and plants are often higher in Europe. The latter, however, can essentially only improve the direct defence against dangers for the consumer, not climate protection. In general, product-related climate friendliness or sustainability clauses resemble in its effect somewhat poorly designed versions of better levy or emissions trading systems. Ultimately, they are not a civil law regulation, but a disguised environmental law (command-and-control) regulation. Also, they operate without the trade component that makes e.g. certificate markets (and indirectly emissions systems) relatively cost-efficient. We will therefore return to this point at the end of this contribution.

5 Causality: Learning from Climate Litigation Against Corporations

Claims under consumer law regarding environmental protection could, however, also be approached differently, namely by establishing a liability claim for a lack of climate friendliness—be it under warranty law or under tort law. However, the classic problem of civil environmental law would arise here which is the issue of causality. This question is already difficult in classical precautionary constellations—i.e. when health damage occurs that has occurred in the long term or multicausal (or under uncertainty). Nevertheless, liability issues in climate protection[23] are currently the subject of much debate, albeit somewhat outside consumer protection law.

The 5th Civil Senate of the Higher Regional Court (OLG) Hamm in Germany has recently delivered an interesting decision in the civil law dispute between the Peruvian farmer Saúl Lliuya and RWE AG.[24] The farmer demands that a fundamental obligation to compensate the energy company for foreseeable climate change consequential damage caused by a melting glacier in his home country be established in accordance with § 1004 of the German Civil Code (BGB). The background to this is that global warming—particularly caused by the use of fossil fuels for electricity, heat, fuel, plastics and fertilisers—can have the existential consequences described in the introduction, such as natural disasters. Attempts to translate all this not only into commitments to political action, but also into

[23]See in general Verheyen (2006), UNEP (2017), Boom et al. (2017).

[24]File no. 5 U 15/17 OLG Hamm; see in detail Ekardt (2017).

compensation obligations on the part of major emitters such as coal companies have therefore been going on for some time.

To the surprise of many, the OLG Hamm stated in a hearing in November 2017 that it considered the claim for compensation under § 1004 BGB to be conclusive. With its main request, the plaintiff demands the statement that the energy company RWE is obligated to proportionally refund it expenditures for the installed protective measures in favour of its property. Proportionately, because statistically it is possible to allocate about 0.47% of global greenhouse gas emissions to RWE. According to the decision of the OLG Hamm, climate science expert opinions are to be used to obtain evidence on several aspects. The plaintiff's house property below a glacier lagoon may be seriously threatened by flooding and/or a mudslide, because the size and the water volume of the lagoon have increased considerably. The reason for this most likely lies with the scientific phenomenon of a human-induced climate change.

However, it remains to be clarified whether it can be said that, as a result of the rise in local temperatures, glacier melting and lagoon growth will increase to such an extent that damage to farmers is imminent—and whether a measurable and calculable proportion of this can be attributed to RWE.

The controversy over all this has a foreseeable global significance. Finally, climate change is attributed to the multitude of possible consequences described above. At the same time, it is possible to identify at least some major emitters that account for a tangible percentage of global greenhouse gas emissions. If the plaintiff were to succeed, the lawsuit would therefore be likely to give a strong boost to global climate protection, which has so far been rather slow. It is difficult to predict whether the OLG Hamm will actually uphold the complaint and whether this will then also be upheld before the Federal Court of Justice and possibly—in the case of a constitutional complaint by RWE—before the Federal Constitutional Court.

Irrespective of the current great excitement surrounding this proceeding, it is actually easy to make two observations. Firstly, climate change is not abstract, but has very concrete and fatal consequences, for which people will have to answer in one way or another—and this should obviously not be the victims, but the injuring parties. Secondly, the OLG's statement is clearly correct that § 1004 BGB also provides for liability for legal actions, for example for the authorised operation of lignite-fired power plants by RWE. The approval under emission control law and the (mandatory) participation in EU emissions trading do not mean that the company can be exempted from the remaining consequences of its actions. This is expressly stated in § 14 of the German Federal emission Control Act. Moreover, for a long time while RWE was releasing emissions, there was no emissions trading at all; and carbon dioxide remains in the atmosphere for decades and contributes to climate change.

In the proceedings before the OLG Hamm and beyond, two points will still have to be extensively debated. Firstly, the court suggests that compensation for impairments due to climate models is conceivable. But the concrete attribution of a single consequence of damage to global climate change is only possible through complex models, which depend not only on a large number of comprehensively proven facts but also on assumptions. If liability claims are justified on this basis, this would trigger a breach of system in civil law (and possibly also in criminal law). A second point of interest for the procedure can, on the other hand, be clarified relatively easily. One could argue that in reality it is not only the companies that produce electricity, heat, fuel, fertilizer and plastics that are responsible. Rather, this always includes customers—and politicians—who allow the whole thing by law. This reference is important and unreservedly correct. But if companies like RWE were condemned, they would of course try to pass the costs on to their customers. Consumers are in the boat anyway. And even a discussion as to whether state liability would not be more appropriate than corporate liability, if politicians have not yet decided to fight climate change, would only make limited sense. After all, state liability claims would also have to affect the entire population—through higher tax burdens.

However, the problem of causality and model-like projections described above remains. Turning from corporate liability to consumer protection, the problem becomes even greater, because it is hardly possible to explain the relevance of a single product for the global climate. Apart from that, consumer protection law is constituted by a disadvantage for the respective consumers themselves—which would be difficult to explain in this case.

6 Warranty Periods and Planned Obsolescence

If new product standards or liability claims are made with regard to climate protection, one could instead think of extended warranty periods for defects.[25] Unlike the approaches we have just discussed, no detailed specifications are needed for such an instrument. Rather, the aim is simply to make products more durable and easier to repair. This is not viable for many products, such as food, and for some other products, such as cars, this aspect is already applied, simply because they are so expensive. However, it is a relevant aspect in the case of various household and electronic appliances. Despite all climate problems or scarcity of resources, in everyday life, easily addressable resource conservation potentials are readily given away. Laptops, stereos and mobile phones, for example, are breaking down faster and faster, and repairs are often hardly possible. This ever faster "product throughput" not only consumes scarce raw materials and generates unnecessary greenhouse gas emissions, but also the time and financial budgets of consumers are being massively strained. The whole thing is by no means a kind of regrettable oversight: it is called "planned obsolescence" when companies increasingly specifically design short-lived products in order to secure sales and growth through regular new purchases. For reasons of economic growth, some politicians even welcome this trend, which has been under discussion for around 150 years.

Though many consumers are happy when laptops or electrical appliances are becoming cheaper and cheaper at media discount stores or on the internet. But if

[25]On warranty periods in general see Hosseini-Motlagh et al. (2018), Huang et al. (2017), Mai et al. (2017), Blischke and Murthy (1992).

you have to replace them all the time and also have trouble with unwilling repairers who would rather sell than repair, we face the question of better solutions. Especially because the customer is usually in the hands of the seller, as long as sellers do not bear the burden of proof completely. In addition, disinterested judges and lawyers often force a settlement. With regard to the litigation costs, it is easier to throw away the laptop straight away. The resource disaster is further exacerbated by the fact that the discarded products are often not even recycled. Firstly, it is not in the strong interest of companies to do so. Secondly, recycling is often technically more difficult than expected. The collection of end-of-life products is still difficult, as is the recovery of resources from mixed products. In general, recycling remains the “second best” ecological option over long-lasting products—and sometimes even over abstaining.

Better for consumers and resource conservation alike would be products which last longer and which are also easy to repair and can be easily retrofitted for increasing technical requirements (laptops, mobile phones). Politicians have so far failed to steer entrepreneurial creativity in this direction. Despite all statements to the contrary, the naive belief prevails that economic growth is good for everyone—if necessary, generated through constantly broken and newly purchased products. But what would speak against a world in which companies sell fewer products, which are more expensive, more durable, easier to retrofit and repair—and therefore often consume significantly less resources?

For example, five instead of two years as a warranty period seem at first glance to be a good approach to promote more durable and retrofittable products. Simpler court procedures would also be helpful, by the way for other areas of life as well. Arbitration tribunals without correspondence with immediate verbal verdicts on small everyday conflicts, for example about a broken laptop, could build up pressure to ensure that repairable devices are actually repaired by unwilling sellers. Warranty periods are, of course, only effective if the burden of proof lies with the seller. However, it is difficult to determine at the level of the individual product whether a more efficient new product or an inefficient but long-used old product has the smaller ecological footprint. The starting point for warranty periods is therefore confronted with the problem that sustainability can only be meaningfully discussed to a limited extent for individual cases.

7 Mandatory Disclosure, Overestimation of Knowledge and the Interaction Between Different Instruments

Another approach to climate protection from consumer protection law could also be considered: extended mandatory disclosure of product information to make it easier for consumers to behave in a climate-friendly manner.[26]

If there are complaints about a lack of e.g. climate protection, the most common statement is that many people have not yet fully understood the extent of the climate

[26]See on mandatory disclosure Dahm et al. (2018), Bertomeu and Magee (2015) and Huang (2008).

catastrophe. Consequently, more education is needed.[27] But, is this really the main message to all those who want to understand and change their behaviour? Knowledge as the sole or at least primary key to a better world? The fact that knowledge is easy to grasp in surveys and experiments, as well as values or self-interest calculations, increases the expectable enthusiasm for these factors among researchers, especially among sustainability researchers.[28] But are these factors really so important? Let us begin with knowledge.

There is no doubt that different people—also in different countries and different social groups—know different things about climate change. There are even some things that no one knows at all, and even some that no human being will probably ever know in the future either. Science faces complex uncertainties, especially when it comes to sustainability issues. Climate change and the huge diversity of ecosystems are examples of this, as are traditional environmental protection issues such as the cumulative and long-term effects of air pollutants.[29] Accordingly, the exact (!) life-cycle assessment of each individual product purchased is too complex even for experts. Complex company interdependencies and supplier relationships make all this even more difficult. The fact that we do not know everything can also be found out through surveys.[30] But how relevant is revealing all the details of sustainability impacts and the consequences of each action in order to explain and overcome the lack of sustainability action by individuals and entire societies?

We can start with an obvious initial observation: you can know everything about the dangers of smoking and still smoke. However, this striking phenomenon does not only exist in smoking. So far, we seem to have been quite successful in ignoring the fact that our resource—and greenhouse gas—intensive lifestyle is putting the lives and health of many people in other parts of the world and future generations at risk. Not to mention the threatening existential, military and economic disadvantages for ourselves. Yet there is no lack of discourses, theories, technical ideas, beautiful conferences, exciting television programmes and articulated goodwill, just as there is no lack of ministries and institutions that deal with sustainability.

The first aspect that often puts all this factual knowledge on the spot is that factual knowledge does not provide a normative yardstick as to whether we should act or not. The fact that there is climate change does not in itself imply that it must necessarily be prevented by us, especially if we then would have to put other concerns such as economic growth or freedom of consumption on the back burner. Appropriate values are needed for this. Or at least selfish preferences that tell someone what they want for themselves or for a group of people they like. Or feelings like pity.

In addition, the relevance of knowledge is subject to further limitations. It is an everyday observation that the degree of interest in a matter determines whether one

---

[27] Instead of many Russell-Smith et al. (2015), Fazey et al. (2018); partly also Schellnhuber (2015).

[28] See e.g. Lang et al. (2014) and Fazey et al. (2018).

[29] Ekardt (2019a).

[30] Kuckartz (2014), Welzer (2008) and Ekardt (2001).

appropriates something, remembers information and even actively obtains information. Furthermore, in view of government information campaigns on environmental protection, extensive sustainability education and comprehensive information and consulting services, ignorance cannot be that great, at least not in the industrialised countries. The limited relevance of knowledge, for example, for purchasing decisions as well as for the actions of politicians can be extensively shown experimentally.[31] The common explanation for this (in economics, psychology, etc.) is that knowledge is always perceived only in parts, simplified and often distorted.[32] However, this leads us to factors other than knowledge.

Just how little can be achieved through knowledge alone can be seen from the fact that it is the ecologically particularly well-informed who are statistically the larger resource consumers—with increasing prosperity and higher education, factors such as air travel, car travel, apartment size and heating consumption or ownership of consumer electronics are increasing. The Green voters, for example, who are statistically relatively well off in terms of prosperity and education, fly the most on average, although they are also the most critical of flying; the proverbial retiree without a great deal of environmental knowledge often has a better record, especially because important markers such as cars, flights, meat consumption and heating are less relevant to them.[33] Various everyday observations e.g. by the lead author in the approximately 60 annual discussions following his sustainability lectures—and an evaluation of internet forums like in the ZEIT[34] and on Facebook with regard to young sustainability activists[35]—have also shown that there is a large number of highly educated people, often equipped with sound ecological values, who nevertheless have no intention of addressing some "big" chunks of their footprint such as meat consumption and flights. Moreover, the approximate sustainability effect of many behavioural traits is quite obvious. Many people, also politicians, are well aware of this. Furthermore, the scientific uncertainty in ecological questions usually refers only to the extent of a certain development, but not to the existence in principle, for example of climate change. At least approximately adequate measures could therefore be taken.

All this does not mean that knowledge is totally irrelevant. Nevertheless, there is much to suggest that a knowledge problem only becomes a problem because most protagonists perhaps meet sustainability with verbal agreement, but ultimately with inner reserve. However, the debate on mandatory disclosure (and the underlying debate on informational tools) should not stop at the—true—realisation that people are far less knowledge-driven than some might think. This is because knowledge revealed through mandatory disclosure may well interact with other motivational

---

[31] Klöhn (2006).

[32] Piaget (1972), Berger and Luckmann (1966) and Axelrod (1973).

[33] Wuppertal Institute (2008) and Ekardt (2019a).

[34] Ekardt (2018).

[35] Ekardt (2019a), Ch. 1.7.

factors such as self-interest, values, feelings, path dependencies and notions of normality.[36] Likewise, it can be said at the instrument level that information can play an important role to complement economic instruments that make fossil fuels more expensive, for example. In this respect, information obligations—based on civil and public law—are fundamentally helpful. They are just not suitable as the main instrument for sustainability.

8 Tenancy Law and the Investor-User Dilemma

As an example of the possibility of consumer law regulations in the more literal sense of the term, one can discuss tenancy law in climate protection issues. In view of the fact that the vast majority of people in countries such as Germany live in apartment buildings, this dilemma arises in the following situation: investment costs are initially incurred for climate protection measures in buildings; the landlord will, however, have to bear these costs in the near future, while the tenant is more likely to benefit from energy efficiency measures due to lower operating costs. With renewable energy measures, on the other hand, even the tenant may have only minor short or medium-term financial advantages, so that neither the landlord nor the tenant may be interested in such measures; however, from a long-term perspective, the tenant has advantages insofar as he or she does not rely on rising oil and gas prices. Landlords could also see this as a longer-term advantage for them, especially as it makes their real estate more valuable (and, of course, every climate protection measure is helpful in the long run, at least for society or even for humanity as a whole). In practice however, building refurbishment is stagnating at the moment. This is because a landlord refurbishing a building takes a financial risk which, in the case of energy efficiency, brings immediate advantages for the tenant (but which may also be offset by a higher net rent; see below)—but which has uncertain consequences for the landlord. Tenancy law in Germany allows for investments in energy efficiency (but not in renewable energies under certain circumstances) to be allocated to the tenant for an unlimited period of time, with a percentage of the investment sum per year. However, this additional charge (a) only leads to long-term amortisation and (b) is also limited by the level of the rent index. Often (c) a rent increase is also simply prevented by the fact that a corresponding rent cannot be obtained on the market. This will (d) be radicalised from the point of view of demographic change, which will increasingly devalue real estate, from all perspectives (although this last aspect is generally not seen at all in the debate).

On the other hand, a pricing instrument for fossil fuels would probably change the situation significantly. Renovations would then be essential for tenants because of

[36] Ekardt (2019a).

the high energy costs, so a renovated, more expensive apartment would be easier to let. Nevertheless, there may still be a need for the landlord to be able to quickly deduct refurbishment costs and to have legal certainty about passing on those costs to the tenant. Although it is well known that when a realistic anthropology is laid down as a basis, it is quite obvious that people act predominantly selfishly and, last but not least, seek economic advantages, this is also overshadowed by other factors such as conceptions of normality and feelings.

There are some bullet points to be made which are specifically of interest regarding the investor-tenant dilemma,[37] e.g.: short-term lower profits are often perceived more interesting than longer-term higher profits; saving is often found not to be very attractive; "positive revenues" are more interesting than cost avoidance; estimations of probabilities regarding certain future events are frequently skewed and so on. These realisations lead to certain conclusions also regarding climate policy for buildings. It might thus be well-advised to not only consider the climate policy costs and benefits of building refurbishments—but also to make sure that the benefits of such measures are obvious and relatively immediate to the respective parties concerned. For the refurbishment of buildings to improve energy efficiency, this is relevant because many might find it subjectively only "profitable in the long run". Another likely adverse factor are the just now again mentioned "general" human sensitivities, such as a certain tendency to convenience and habits: even if the landlord would not face costs for themselves or even generate revenues in the medium term by making energetic improvements, they might ask themselves e.g. why they should even bother instead of just sticking with fossil fuels for heating. This tendency is reinforced as climate protection poses a fundamental problem also on an emotional level—because people have a hard time to empathise with humans being harmed far away or in the more distant future. Pricing instruments with a long-term effect could in contrast help long-term planning and support overcoming short-term thinking. The pricing always remains key. For example, these laws do not prevent residents in an old building retrofitted with insulation from constantly ventilating through open windows due to the deteriorated air supply instead of installing professional ventilation—the climate protection effect of the insulation can thus be minimised or even counteracted. Economic instruments could prevent this, as does the fact that the saved energy costs are simply flown to Thailand (shifting effects and rebound effects).

We have seen however that exactly those problem cannot be solved in civil law. In the end, the bigger drive in climate policy will simply depend on an appropriate pricing. The conclusion regarding consumer law is therefore the same as for the approaches discussed before.

---

[37]On the following Ekardt (2019a).

9 Conclusion: Economic Instruments: Only to be Complemented by Consumer Law (and Civil Law in General), as Well as by Command-and-Control Law

We have seen: Regulation in consumer law necessarily targets individual cases. This leads to similar problems as those already established in the debate about command-and-control law with regard to environmental protection. Regulations for individual products, activities or plants might play a big supplementary role, especially with regard to so called hot spot problems. At its core, it is however necessary to understand sustainability as quantity problem and to address it as such.[38] Economic instruments drastically minimise questions of the actual implementation and liability questions as well as the absolutism of a complete prohibition of impairment. Instead, they leave essential choices to the individual—all within the boundaries of allowed quantities respectively levy rates. They do so, based on a fundamental decision of democratic parliaments on increasing prices respectively reducing quantities. Economic instruments also help a gradual transition towards more sustainability.[39]

Economic instruments promise to effectively solve certain governance problems such as rebound effects, spatial and sectoral shifting effects, enforcement problems and depicting problems, which can hardly be effectively solved otherwise.[40] This is especially true in the example of climate change and the pricing of fossil fuels with the goal to remove them completely from the market. Both a cap in trading allowances and sufficiently high tax rates avoid the rebound effect that is always then imminent when regulatory measures are taken against individual products or investments. This is because the mechanism of quantity control—directly or indirectly via prices—and its immanent focus on absolute consumption reductions prevent increased actions or generally greater prosperity as a result to ecologically improved actions. Likewise, cap and trade schemes and levies can prevent shifting effects if they are used across a wide geographical area and in all sectors. Shifting effects will no longer exist: after all, all areas and sectors are covered (at least if border adjustments are implemented).

Economic instruments motivationally appeal first to the self-interest of citizens and companies by setting a price incentive, directly or indirectly via quantity restrictions.[41] They also eliminate the problem of public goods, which is typical for environmental problems, by urging everyone to act, not just individuals, given

[38] See more detailed Hennig (2017), Ekardt (2019a), Ekardt et al. (2018) and von Bredow (2013).

[39] See generally on the debate Milne (2014), Joseph (2014), Acworth et al. (2017), Garske (2013), Franks et al. (2015), Klinsky et al. (2012), Ekardt (2019a), Ismer (2014) and Ekardt (2019b).

[40] In detail on the following Ekardt (2019a), Hennig (2017), Ekardt et al. (2018).

[41] On the following Ekardt (2019a), Hennig (2017), Ekardt et al. (2018) and von Bredow (2013).

that they are established on a broad sectoral and geographical scale. However, other factors are also addressed which the narrow homo-oeconomicus model does not take into account. For example, new conceptions of normality are triggered (as well as new values); the image of free consumption of nature will gradually be replaced by a more careful use of scarce environmental resources. And this is absolutely necessary to achieve social change. Thus, economic instruments are not automatically based on homo oeconomicus, therefore its affirmation or criticism does not automatically affect the use of economic instruments. All this does not rule out the need for additional instruments, e.g. informational measures. Therefore, the idea that economic instruments do not influence the given situation of companies, consumers and so on does not apply. Worries about price elasticity which are articulated over and over are also inappropriate. Firstly, practical experience with environmental economic instruments refers solely to very moderate price effects, and not to the much higher prices, which would be necessary to achieve the objectives of the Paris Agreement, for example. Secondly, the notion of a cap-and-trade approach (unlike levies) is overseen by the debate on price elasticity. This is because a cap as such is inevitably achieved if it is properly executed.

Also, economic instruments address technological change and behavioural change simultaneously and leave all choices of detail to the individual. For example, if the necessary reduction targets were translated into a cap-and-trade system that would gradually phase out fossil fuels from the market completely within two decades (according to Art. 2 para. 1 Paris Agreement), greenhouse gas emissions would be strictly limited, creating an incentive for more renewable energies, efficiency and, if necessary, frugality. Because if technology alone is simply not enough to achieve the cap, such an approach also triggers frugality, since the cap as such is strictly binding. In principle, however, something similar can also be said about pricing, e.g. by means of levies, even if it does not provide for the same reliability, because the price and thus only indirectly a cap is determined there. Nevertheless, the antagonism of economic instruments and post-growth approaches that seems obvious from the point of view of both friends and critics of such instruments does not exist.

The bottom line is, there are no concerns against the conformity even of incisive economic instruments with human rights e.g. in light of the freedom of competition and the freedom of property, if the human-rights guarantees in favour of climate protection are considered.[42] This would be different, if intending to create similar effects with the detailed regulations of consumer law or command-and-control law. This is hardly possible, as seen. Furthermore, such a detailed approach would possibly also be disproportionate, because it would imply a much bigger infringement of freedoms than framework-based economic instruments would.

[42] See in detail Ekardt et al. (2018) and Ekardt (2019a).

References

Abson D, Fischer J, Leventon J et al (2017) Leverage points for sustainability transformation. Ambio 46:30–39. https://doi.org/10.1007/s13280-016-0800-y

Acworth W, Ackva J, Burtraw D, Edenhofer O, Fuss S, Flachsland C, Montes de Oca M (2017) Emissions trading and the role of a long run carbon price signal: achieving cost effective emission reductions under an emissions trading system. International Carbon Action Partnership, Berlin

Akerlof GA, Shiller RJ (2009) Animal spirits. How human psychology drives the economy, and why it matters for global capitalism. Princeton University Press, Princeton

Axelrod R (1973) Schema theory. An information processing model of perception and cognition. Am Polit Sci Rev 67:1248 et seq.

Berger P, Luckmann T (1966) The social construction of reality. Open Road Media London

Bernauer T, Schaffer L (2010) Climate Change Goverance, CIS Working Paper No. 60, Zürich

Bertomeu J, Magee RP (2015) Mandatory disclosure and asymmetry in financial reporting. J Account Econ 59(2):284–299

Biermann F et al (2009) Earth System Governance. Science and Implementation Plan of the Earth System Governance Project. IHDP-Report No. 20, Bonn

Blischke WR, Murthy DNP (1992) Product warranty management – I: a taxonomy for warranty policies. Eur J Oper Res 62(2):127–148

Boom K, Richards JA, Leonard S (2017) Climate justice. The international momentum towards climate litigation. Heinrich Böll Stiftung, Berlin

Caterini E (2018) Sustainability and civil law. Ital Law J 4(2):289–314

Dahm M, González P, Porteiro N (2018) The enforcement of mandatory disclosure rules. J Public Econ 167:21–32

Dean J (2013) Making habits, breaking habits. How to make changes that stick. OneWorld Publications, London

Dieckhoff C (2015) Modellierte Zukunft. Energieszenarien in der wissenschaftlichen Politikberatung In: Dieckhoff C, Leuschner A (eds) Die Energiewende und ihre Modelle. Was uns Energieszenarien sagen können – und was nicht, Bielefeld

Droste-Frank B et al (2015) Improving energy decisions. Towards better scientific policy advice for a safe and secure future energy system. Springer, Heidelberg

Ekardt F (2001) Steuerungsdefizite im Umweltrecht: Ursachen unter besonderer Berücksichtigung des Naturschutzrechts und der Grundrechte. Zugleich zur Relevanz religiösen Säkularisats im öffentlichen Recht, Sinzheim

Ekardt F (2016a) Theorie der Nachhaltigkeit. Ethische, rechtliche, politische und transformative Zugänge – am Beispiel von Klimawandel, Ressourcenknappheit und Welthandel. 3rd ed (= 2nd ed. of the revised version). Nomos, Baden-Baden

Ekardt F (2016b) Umweltschutz und Zivilrecht: Nachhaltigkeit durch Kapitalgesellschaftsrecht?, ZUR 463 et seq

Ekardt F (2017) Klimahaftung: Wie ein peruanischer Bauer das Recht verändern könnte. Legal Tribune/Spiegel Online 1(12):2017

Ekardt F (2019a) Sustainability – transformation, governance, ethics, law. Springer, Dordrecht

Ekardt F (2019b) Economic evaluation, cost-benefit analysis, economic ethics. A critique with regard to climate economics - about figures in the sustainability discourse. Springer, Dordrecht

Ekardt F, Hennig B (2015) Ökonomische Instrumente und Bewertungen von Biodiversität. Lehren für den Naturschutz aus dem Klimaschutz? Metropolis, Marburg

Ekardt F, Wieding J, Henkel M (2015) Climate Justice 2015. BUNDposition, BUND, Berlin

Ekardt F, Wieding J, Zorn A (2018) Paris agreement, precautionary principle and human rights: zero emissions in two decades? Sustainability 2812 et seq

Fazey I et al (2018) Ten essentials for action-oriented and second order energy transitions, transformations and climate change research. Energy Res Soc Sci 40:54 et seq

Felber C (2012) Die Gemeinwohl-Ökonomie. Das Wirtschaftsmodell der Zukunft. Wien

Franks M, Edenhofer O, Lessmann K (2015) Why finance ministers favor carbon taxes, even if they do not take climate change into account. Environ Resour Econ 1 et seq

Garske B (2013) Joint Implementation. Ökonomische Klimaschutzinstrumente und Technologiediffusion in Transformationsstaaten. Metropolis, Marburg

Hennig B (2017) Nachhaltige Landnutzung und Bioenergie. Ambivalenzen, Governance, Rechtsfragen. Metropolis, Marburg

Herrmann-Pillath C (2015) Energy, growth and evolution. Towards a naturalistic ontology of economics. Ecol Econ 119:432 et seq

Herrmann-Pillath C (2016) Constitutive explanations as methodological framework for integrating thermodynamics and economics. Entropy 18:18 et seq

Higgins KL (2015) Applying the brakes: factors that limit growth. In: Higgins KL (ed) Economic growth and sustainability. Academic Press, San Diego, pp 73–93

Hoffmann J, Hofmann G (2015) Rahmenbedingungen für nachhaltigen Wettbewerb in Deutschland, der EU und der WTO. In: Friedrich-Ebert-Stiftung (ed) Nachhaltigkeit im Wettbewerb verankern. WISO Diskurs, Bonn, p 6 et seq

Hosseini-Motlagh S-M, Nematollahi M, Nouri M (2018) Coordination of green quality and green warranty decisions in a two-echelon competitive supply chain with substitutable products. J Cleaner Prod 196:961–984

Huang H (2008) Risk aversion, mandatory disclosure and the concealment of information. Econ Lett 99(1):2–9

Huang Y-S, Huang C-D, Ho J-W (2017) A customized two-dimensional extended warranty with preventive maintenance. Eur J Oper Res 257(3):971–978

Iftime E (2014) Liability for Damage Caused by Dangerous Situations and Activities to the Environment. LUMEN 2014 – From Theory to Inquiry in Social Sciences, Iasi, Romania, 10–12 April 2014 149:417–23

IPCC (2007) Climate Change 2007, Fourth Assessment Report. Cambridge

IPCC (2014) Climate Change 2014, Fifth Assessment Report. Cambridge

Ismer R (2014) Klimaschutz als Rechtsproblem. Steuerung durch Preisinstrumente vor dem Hintergrund einer parallelen Evolution von Klimaschutzregimes verschiedener Staaten. Tübingen

Jackson T (2009) Prosperity without growth. Earthscan, London

Jonas H (1979) Das Prinzip Verantwortung. Frankfurt a.M

Joseph S-A (2014) Environmental taxes – definitional analysis: behavioural change or revenue raising. In: Kreiser L et al (eds) Environmental taxation and green fiscal reform. Theory and impact. Edward Elgar, Cheltenham, p 187 et seq

Juerges N, Newig J (2015) What role for frames in scalar conflicts? Land Use Policy 49:426–434

Kahneman D (2011) Thinking – fast and slow. Farrar, Straus and Giroux, New York

Klein N (2014) This changes everything. Capitalism versus the climate. Simon & Shuster, New York

Klinsky S, Mehling M, Tuerk A (2012) Beyond Déjà Vu. Opportunities for policy learning from emissions trading in developed countries. Carbon Clim Law Rev 4:291 et seq

Klöhn L (2006) Kapitalmarkt, Spekulation und Behavioral Finance. Berlin

Kuckartz U (2014) Mixed methods. Springer, Wiesbaden

Lang D, Rode H, von Wehrden H (2014) Methoden und Methodologie in den Nachhaltigkeitswissenschaften. In: Heinrichs H, Michelsen G (eds) Nachhaltigkeitswissenschaften. Heidelberg, p 115 et seq

Liedtke M (2011) Der Mensch zwischen Gefühl und Verstand – Grenzen und Chancen des rationalen (und nachhaltigen) Verhaltens. In: Korczak D (ed) Die emotionale Seite der Nachhaltigkeit. Kröning, p 37 et seq

Lowitzsch J, Roggemann H, Suarsana D (2015) Rechtliche Verankerung eines eigentumsrechtlich ausgestalteten Externalisierungsverbots. In: Friedrich-Ebert-Stiftung (ed): Nachhaltigkeit im Wettbewerb verankern. WISO Diskurs, Bonn, p 13 et seq

Mai DT, Liu T, Morris MDS, Sun S (2017) Quality coordination with extended warranty for store-brand products. Eur J Oper Res 256(2):524–532

Milinski M, Marotzke J (2015) Das Klimaspiel. Warum scheitern Klimaverhandlungen? In: Marotzke J, Stratmann M (eds) Die Zukunft des Klimas. Neue Erkenntnisse, neue Herausforderungen. München p 93 et seq

Milne J (2014) Environmental taxes and fees – wrestling with theory. In: Kreiser L et al (eds) Environmental taxation and green fiscal reform. Theory and impact. Edward Elgar, Cheltenham p 5 et seq

Newig J et al (2015) Exploring governance learning. Environ Sci Policy 55:353 et seq

Nørgård J, Xue J (2016) Between green growth and degrowth: decoupling, rebound effects and the politics for long-term sustainability. In: Santarius T, Walnum HJ, Aall C (eds) Rethinking climate and energy policies: new perspectives on the rebound phenomenon. Springer, Cham, pp 267–284

Paech N (2012) Liberation from Excess. Oekom, München

Peters G, Minx J, Weber C, Edenhofer O (2011) Growth in emission transfers via international trade from 1990 to 2008. PNAS 108:8903 et seq

Piaget J (1972) Die Psychologie des Kindes. Olten

Russell-Smith J, Costanza R et al (2015) Moving beyond evidence-free environmental policy. Front Ecol Environ 13:441 et seq.

Santarius T (2015) Der Rebound-Effekt. Ökonomische, psychische und soziale Herausforderungen für die Entkopplung von Wirtschaftswachstum und Energieverbrauch. Marburg

Schellnhuber HJ (2015) Selbstverbrennung. Die fatale Dreiecksbeziehung zwischen Klima, Mensch und Kohlenstoff. München

Steinberg R (2013) Die Repräsentation des Volkes. Menschenbild und demokratisches Regierungssystem. Baden-Baden

Stern N (2009) A blueprint for a safer planet: how to manage climate change and create a new era of progress and prosperity. Cambridge University Press Cambridge

Sukhdev P (2013) Corporation 2020. Warum wir Wirtschaft neu denken müssen, oekom München

UNEP (2017) The status of climate change litigations – a global review. UNEP, Nairobi

Unnerstall H (1999) Rechte zukünftiger Generationen. Würzburg

Verheyen R (2006) Climate change damage and international law: prevention duties and state responsibility. Martinus Nijhoff Publishers, Leiden

Von Bredow H (2013) Energieeffizienz als Rechts- und Steuerungsproblem. Unter besonderer Berücksichtigung der erneuerbaren Energien. Marburg

Welzer H (2008) Klimakriege. Wofür im 21. Jahrhundert getötet wird. Frankfurt a.M

Wuppertal Institute (2008) Zukunftsfähiges Deutschland in einer globalisierten Welt. Frankfurt a.M

Felix Ekardt Leipzig. Director of Research Unit Sustainability and Climate Policy Leipzig, Berlin and Professor of Public Law and Legal Philosophy at the Universities of Rostock, Erfurt and Halle. Könneritzstrasse 41, D-04229 Leipzig. Tel. +49 (0)341 4927 78 66; Fax +49 (0)341 2465 98 76. felix.ekardt@uni-rostock.de. Fields of Interest: Governance of Sustainability, International Climate Law, European and International Agricultural Policy.

Jutta Wieding Dresden. PhD candidate at Research Unit Sustainability and Climate Policy Leipzig, Berlin and at the University of Erfurt, scholarship by Heinrich Böll Foundation. Könneritzstrasse 41, D-04229 Leipzig. Tel. +49 (0)177 415 88 34; Fax +49 (0)341 2465 98 76. jutta.wieding@posteo.de. Fields of Interest: Governance of Sustainability, International Climate Law, European and International Agricultural Policy.

Index

K. Mathis, A. Tor (eds.), *Consumer Law and Economics*, Economic Analysis of Law in European Legal Scholarship 9, https://doi.org/10.1007/978-3-030-49028-7

D

E

F

G

H

I

K